The 2010/2011
Comprehensive Vintage Motorcycle Price Guide

Antique, classic, and special interest motorcycles

Model years 1901 through 1995

Data compiled by the
Vintage Japanese and European Motorcycle Club

Whitehorse Press
Center Conway, New Hampshire

Whitehorse Press books are also available at discounts in bulk quantity for sales and promotional use. For details about special sales or for a catalog of Whitehorse Press motorcycling books, write to the publisher:

Whitehorse Press
107 East Conway Road
Center Conway, New Hampshire 03813
Phone: 603-356-6556 or 800-531-1133
E-mail: CustomerService@WhitehorsePress.com
Internet: www.WhitehorsePress.com

ISBN: 978-1-884313-85-1

5 4 3 2 1

Printed in the United States

CONTENTS

THE PRICE MART SHOWROOM

What Do the "Experts" See with Prices for 2010?

For the fourth year in a row, here it is! We present to you the fourth annual, the 2010/2011 edition of the *Comprehensive Vintage Motorcycle Price Guide* (CVMPG). Through hundreds of hours of research and data entry, formed by the opinions of dozens of dealers, auctioneers, collectors, and experts in the vintage field, we believe this is the most accurate price guide written for vintage motorcycles. It also contains more data than any other, as all major marques (and many lesser known marques) are included with data through 1995. Each year, the guide will expand to add another year (next year, we will go through 1996) so as to be consistent with the VJEMC's policy of including all motorcycles 15 years old and older in the "vintage" category. It is also our intent to add additional marques each year. This year, we have added listings for nine new marques, with more to come. To help determine rarity and value, we will continue to add manufacturing quantities for each model as we obtain new information. These numbers, when available, are found in parentheses right after the model and year. Additionally, it is our goal to add the very early years of some of the marques that go unreported in other publications. This year, an example includes the early years of Royal Enfield. The CVMPG will continue to grow and evolve, and we appreciate your comments and input! Please e-mail us at info@vinjapeuromcclub.org with any ideas you may have to improve the price guide.

Additionally, we have collected data for at least 50 other marques, but information for the years and models is scattered, so we have not published them yet. We suggest that if you need help finding information for a bike not listed, e-mail us at info@vinjapeuromcclub.org, and we will try to put you in contact with an expert for that marque.

As we have gone through the task of evaluating thousands of prices, remember, that this is a *guide;* these prices are not etched in stone. Rarity, demand, and condition are all factors that drive prices. These prices have been determined through research using other pricing sources, dealer sales, auctions, private sales, eBay sales, and experts from each marque. With this in mind, we have seen the following trends emerge in the last 12 months:

1. There seems to be continued demand for Ariel models in top conditions. This may be a good place to invest your vintage motorcycle money at this time.

2. Early BMW models continue to hold their value or even creep upward. We anticipate that more high-quality machines may come out of the woodwork in the ensuing months. There seems to be a demand, and it is rare that we see a major sale with more than a handful of early BMWs, so when they do become available, the prices are strong.

3. BSA motorcycles continue to be a great investment. There is a lot of demand and the majority that are available seem to sell well at every major auction or sale.

4. If you are a scooter enthusiast, this might be a great time for you to take advantage of the vintage scooter market. Many nice Cushmans, Vespas, and Mustangs are com-

ing across the sale lists right now and are drawing good money. For a long time, these small two-wheelers were "pooh-poohed" by motorcycle collectors and investors. Now, with the popularity of new models all over the streets, there seems to be acceptance, and even an increased interest in these little machines.

5. Well preserved or restored Ducatis are in high demand right now, and perhaps that is because it is rare to see many of them in a major sale. Those that are available get snapped up quickly. You may wish to do the same!

6. Could this be the year that Harley-Davidson prices make a comeback? We are cautious but intrigued about the prospects for these bikes. Many tend to go up for sale at each auction we attend, but in the past, fewer than half have actually sold. Recently, there seems to be an upward trend for prices, especially for early, well restored or original models, and especially those of the 1940s and earlier. Some of these models may even be undervalued. A few prices have also crept up on later models. Unlike some of the major declines in recent years, prices for more of the Harley models have held steady, which is interesting considering the recent economy in the USA and around the world.

7. Perhaps the Japanese market could be a reflection of the Harley market right now, which seems very odd to say. Early models and rarer models continue to draw good money, and we notice a continued increase in some of the small-displacement models and off-road models that are well-preserved or restored. However, we have also noticed that at recent sales, there have been fewer Japanese bikes

available as a whole, especially those in top quality. Perhaps people are holding on to them in anticipation of a big boost when the economy recovers? While we still feel a majority of them are undervalued, we predict that the market will remain constant here, with slight increases, depending on the marque, rarity, demand, and model.

8. Last year we noted that Indian motorcycles could be the "sleeping giant." This seems to have played itself out in the fact that good models have continued to increase at all major sales attended this year. We predict that this trend will continue. We think that some of the interest in Harley and Indian this year has been caused by the interest and promotion of other lesser-known American motorcycles that have come up for sale. At one point, there were more than 220 motorcycle manufacturers in the USA in the first half of the 20th century. While few survived, some of these rarer marques are garnering historical interest and some are even popping up at sales. Prices for some of these marques, though, are all over the board, as there has not truly been a public market for them to date, so we are watching these trends before adding some of these models into the CVMPG.

9. On a specific Japanese marque, watch out for Kawasaki triples, in the 250, 350, 400, 500, and 750cc displacements. Some of the smaller displacements seem to have been undervalued and have been selling for double the book price in some cases, while the 500 and 750 models have also done well, even in lower conditions. With parts like original mufflers, carb rubbers, and other items

almost impossible to find for many of these motorcycles, demand is high, and so are prices.

10. We are wondering if this might be the year for an increase in Moto Guzzi interest. At least here in the USA they are treated almost like someone's unwanted stepbrother. Not many are seen for sale, and not many excellent examples are seen when one does come up for bid. Most of them tend to be later models, too. This leads us to think that good, older models might be ready for a spike.

11. There is still a solid demand for Norton motorcycles, and we see this trend continuing. Prices have gone up on selected models, and members of the VJEMC have reported that it is hard to find the exact bike they want if looking for an old Norton. Many have said they would pay a premium if the right bike was available. This leads us to believe that Nortons are a good place to invest your money.

12. Could Triumph be on the comeback after several consecutive years of plummeting prices? We cautiously say this might be the case. Though there have not been many periods of increasing prices for Triumph, the decline seems to have leveled off, and there is a demand for nice Condition 1 or Condition 2 motorcycles that are reasonably priced. There is also a solid demand for earlier models, which seems to be a general trend for all marques. If a good 1940s or earlier model of just about any marque comes up for sale, it seems to command solid prices. Some people have recently commented that these early Triumphs could be likened to works of art, and this is a valid statement for many motorcycles of that era.

13. On the whole, we have the impression that the market is slightly better than flat right now. Creeping upward slowly, with a few spikes in selected marques, but in general, holding steady. With the economy also in a state of flux, perhaps this is a good indication of things to come in the vintage motorcycle market. Especially in the last 10 to 20 years, an investment in a vintage vehicle that is well-kept or maintained certainly has not lost money. We feel that the greatest excitement in the market is yet to come, though it may be a few years away yet.

VJEMC Recommended Dealer List on the Web

To make it easier for vintage motorcycle enthusiasts to find quality products and services for use with their vintage rides, the VJEMC has created a Recommended Dealer List on the club website. If you know a vintage motorcycle-related dealer who has gone beyond the call of duty and whom you would like to see added to this list, contact us by e-mail at info@vinjapeuromcclub.org so we can send them a dealer interview form and have them join us. These dealers offer discounts on parts and service to VJEMC members and have been recommended to us by YOU for their honesty, integrity, quality of service, and quality of products.

We encourage you to check out the Recommended Dealer List at www.vinjapeuromcclub.org. Remember to tell these dealers that you found out about them through the VJEMC!

Can you help us to upgrade and improve the Comprehensive Vintage Motorcycle Pricing Guide?

Become a member of our Pricing Network!

The VJEMC is always looking to add dealers, auction services, and experts in each marque to the network of businesses and individuals who contribute their data from sales of motorcycles to us each year as we update and improve this publication each year. Qualifications to become a part of this network are your interest in learning how to fairly grade motorcycles in an unbiased way, as well as being able to send us a list of motorcycles that you have sold or have seen sold in the last calendar year.

We also are looking for experts who deal in some of the lesser known marques who can help us gather model information, displacements, and manufacturing quantities so as to improve the CVMPG with more factual data each year and make it more useful. If you are an expert in Adler, Douglas, Cyclone, Zundapp, or anything in between, we'd love to have you join us and will be certain to recognize you in next year's issue.

If you would like to join us, please contact the VJEMC at 877-853-6210, or e-mail us at info@vinjapeuromcclub.org.

Thank you!

HOW TO GRADE AND EVALUATE A MOTORCYCLE

The VJEMC and the *Comprehensive Vintage Motorcycle Price Guide* use a six-level grading scale to determine the value of a vintage motorcycle. By using this scale, you should be able to make a reasonably accurate assessment of the condition and value of any motorcycle in your collection or for sale. We recommend that you consult with experts in the field if questions arise, and recommend certification by such firms as the Vintage Motorcycle Certification Service (VMCS) for major purchases in order to be assured that the bike you are purchasing meets these criteria. The VMCS can be found at major vintage events where the VJEMC is present, such as Vintage Days at Mid-Ohio, the Barber Vintage Festival, most major auctions, and the International Vintage Motorcycle Show and Swap Meet held each year in Wisconsin. The VMCS can be reached at 877-853-6210.

Condition 1 – PERFECT/NEW
New, unused motorcycles or perfect restorations. It should be noted that there are almost no Condition 1 motorcycles on the road. These are bikes that would have just left the showroom floor, or have been restored to showroom condition with proper factory specifications. Everything runs and operates perfectly. These bikes are rarely ridden, and often will be show winners. Many people save these bikes in climate-controlled rooms or museums as investment pieces or works of art. Note that in relationship to this price guide, there are often differences in prices between a

Condition 1 original bike, and a Condition 1 restored bike, related to the demand and rarity. This is a factor that must be taken into consideration when purchasing a Condition 1 motorcycle.

Condition 2 – EXCELLENT

Without close examination, many Condition 2 motorcycles may appear as Condition 1. It may be a bike that is ridden, but usually for limited miles. It may be a well-restored bike, or a well-preserved original. There is almost no wear, or very minimal wear, on these motorcycles.

Condition 3 – VERY GOOD

Most bikes that are seen on the road are in Condition 3 or Condition 4. They are operable original bikes, or perhaps older restorations that have some wear. It may look good as you gaze at it in a parking lot, but as you get closer, you may see paint nicks or light fading; wear on the plastic, rubber, or leather parts; or light dulling of the chrome. All components of the bike are in working order.

Condition 4 – GOOD

This is a basic, usable motorcycle. This can be an original, well-used model, or a restoration that has been ridden and has begun to deteriorate. This bike may need some minor work, but most of the systems should function. Even from a distance, it is obvious that there are chips and fading in the paint, small dents, rust, poor chrome, or other areas of the motorcycle that need attention. Again, it is important to note that most motorcycles on the road would grade out as Condition 3 or Condition 4.

Condition 5 – FAIR

This is a motorcycle that needs close to a full restoration. It may or may not be running, but is in better shape than a Condition 6 motorcycle. These bikes usually have all of the original parts, or the parts may be available from the owners if they have modified the bike and have not discarded the original equipment. It has rust, faded or scratched paint, pitted or dull chrome, but not throughout the entire bike. This is a bike that would be considered as a good base for a restoration and would not present the restorer with a huge chore to find parts and supplies.

Condition 6 – POOR

These bikes are not running. They may be missing parts, may have been wrecked, and are in poor shape throughout, with faded and scratched paint, lots of rust, badly pitted or rusted chrome, tears in seats, cracked plastic and leather, worn or torn rubber pieces, and other problems. These bikes are usually good for parts to be used on other restorations, but can also be in the form of a complete bike in bad shape.

What to Look for When Inspecting a Bike for Condition

Helpful hints

- Cracked or worn footpeg rubbers/grips
- Torn seat covers, bad seat foam
- Holes in the mufflers/rusted mufflers. Run your hand underneath them, behind them and see what's there
- Paint fade, paint chips, paint bubbling, poor repainting
- Chrome pitting or peeling, rust in all areas
- Leaks of oil, forks, brake fluid, master cylinder, caliper, head gaskets, exhaust leaks
- Excessive play in levers, brakes, clutch, throttle
- Electrical: Is there a lot of electrical tape? Are there a lot of spliced wires? Exposed wires? Hanging wires? Do the electrics work?
- Decal and badge chipping and wear, bent badges
- Tire condition (cracks, wear, hole plugs)
- Bent wheels, bent forks, rusted or poorly maintained chains
- Look under the seat and side covers! Is the battery full of corrosion? Is there rust? Is there a lot of dirt and grime?
- How does the wiring look? Examine areas hidden to the eye!
- Pull the spark plugs. Plug condition can tell a lot.

PRICE GUIDE

Notes:

- Prices that have gone up in the last year are in BOLD, while prices that have gone down have a minus sign (–) in front of them
- Where available, we have included production quantity in parentheses after some model names; see for example, early Harley-Davidson
- To save space in the listings, we have substituted the letter "K" for thousands, and "MM" for millions, in prices 100,000 and higher. Thus 240,000 is abbreviated 240K; 1,000,000 is abbreviated 1MM.
- All prices are in U.S. dollars
- As this book goes to press, the exchange rates for certain currencies are as follows:

TO CONVERT A PRICE

From	To	Multiply by
US dollars	British pounds	.616
US dollars	Euros	.707
US dollars	Canadian dollars	1.057
US dollars	Australian dollars	1.106
US dollars	Mexican pesos	12.86
British pounds	US dollars	1.624
Euros	US dollars	1.415
Canadian dollars	US dollars	.946
Australian dollars	US dollars	.904
Mexican pesos	US dollars	.0778

	6	5	4	3	2	1
ACE						
1920						
Ace Four (78-cid, inline 4-cyl.).	13,000	20,000	29,000	39,000	52,000	65,000
1921						
Ace Four (78-cid, inline 4-cyl.).	13,000	20,000	29,000	39,000	52,000	65,000
1922						
Ace Four (78-cid, inline 4-cyl.).	13,000	20,000	29,000	39,000	52,000	65,000
1923						
Ace Four (78-cid, inline 4-cyl.).	13,000	20,000	29,000	39,000	52,000	65,000
Sporting Solo (78-cid, inline 4-cyl, alloy pistons)	13,000	20,000	30,000	40,000	54,000	67,000
1924						
Ace Four (78-cid, inline 4-cyl.).	13,000	20,000	29,000	39,000	52,000	65,000
Sporting Solo (78-cid, inline 4-cyl, alloy pistons)	13,000	20,000	30,000	40,000	54,000	67,000
1926						
Ace Four (78-cid, inline 4-cyl.).	13,000	20,000	29,000	39,000	52,000	65,000
Sporting Solo (78 cid, inline 4-cyl, alloy pistons)	13,000	20,000	30,000	40,000	54,000	67,000
1927						
Ace Four (78-cid, inline 4-cyl.).	14,000	20,000	31,000	41,000	54,000	68,000
Sporting Solo (78-cid, inline 4-cyl, alloy pistons)	14,000	21,000	31,000	41,000	55,000	69,000
AJS						
1923						
350	7,000	11,000	14,000	17,000	20,000	23,000
1927						
V-Twin.	6,000	10,000	13,000	16,000	19,000	22,000
Big Port H6	3,500	6,000	8,000	10,000	14,000	18,000
1930						
R12	1,800	3,600	5,400	8,000	12,000	16,000
1931						
V-Twin.	1,500	3,000	4,500	7,000	10,000	13,000
1935						
Model 22	1,800	3,600	5,400	8,000	12,000	16,000
1939						
Dual Port (350cc single).	3,500	70,000	10,000	14,500	17,500	20,500
1942						
16M Military (350cc single)	2,000	2,500	3,500	4,600	6,800	8,000
18 (500cc single)	2,000	2,600	3,600	4,700	7,000	8,500
1943						
16M Military (350cc single)	2,000	2,500	3,500	4,600	6,800	8,000
18 (500cc single)	2,000	2,600	3,600	4,700	7,000	8,500
1944						
16M Military (350cc single)	2,000	2,500	3,500	4,600	6,800	8,000
18 (500cc single)	2,000	2,600	3,600	4,700	7,000	8,500
1945						
18 (500cc single)	1,500	2,300	3,400	4,500	6,000	7,500
1946						
16M (350cc single)	1,400	2,100	3,200	4,200	5,600	7,000
16MC (350cc single)	1,400	2,100	3,200	4,200	5,600	7,000
18 (500cc single)	1,500	2,300	3,400	4,500	6,000	7,500
1947						
16M (350cc single)	1,400	2,100	3,200	4,200	5,600	7,000
16MC (350cc single)	1,400	2,100	3,200	4,200	5,600	7,000
18 (500cc single)	1,500	2,300	3,400	4,500	6,000	7,500
18C (500cc single)	1,500	2,300	3,500	4,600	6,200	7,700
1948						
7R Racer (350cc single).	5,000	7,500	11,300	15,000	20,000	25,000

	6	5	4	3	2	1
16M (350cc single)	1,400	2,100	3,200	4,200	5,600	7,000
16MC (350cc single)	1,500	2,200	3,300	4,400	5,900	7,400
18 (500cc single)	1,300	2,000	2,900	3,900	5,200	6,500
18C (500cc single)	1,400	2,200	3,200	4,300	5,800	7,200
1949						
7R Racer (350cc single).	5,000	7,500	11,300	15,000	20,000	25,000
16M (350cc single)	1,400	2,100	3,200	4,200	5,600	7,000
16MC (350cc single)	1,500	2,200	3,300	4,400	5,900	7,400
16MS (350cc single)	1,400	2,100	3,200	4,200	5,600	7,000
18 (500cc single)	1,300	2,000	2,900	4,500	6,000	7,200
18C (500cc single)	1,400	2,200	3,200	4,300	5,800	7,200
20 (500cc twin)	1,200	1,900	2,800	3,700	5,000	6,200
20CSR (500cc twin).	1,400	2,100	3,200	4,200	5,600	7,000
1950						
7R Racer (350cc single).	5,000	7,500	11,300	15,000	20,000	25,000
16M (350cc single)	1,400	2,100	3,200	4,200	5,600	7,000
16MC (350cc single)	1,500	2,200	3,300	4,400	5,900	7,400
16MCS (350cc single).	1,400	2,100	3,100	4,100	5,500	6,900
16MS (350cc single)	1,400	2,100	3,200	4,200	5,600	7,000
18 (500cc single)	1,300	2,000	2,900	3,900	5,200	6,500
18C (500cc single)	1,400	2,200	3,200	4,300	5,800	7,200
18CS (500cc single).	1,400	2,200	3,200	4,300	5,800	7,200
18S (500cc single)	1,200	1,900	2,800	3,700	5,000	6,200
20 (500cc twin)	1,200	1,900	2,800	3,700	5,000	6,200
20CSR (500cc twin).	1,400	2,100	3,200	4,200	5,600	7,000
1951						
7R Racer (350cc single).	5,000	7,500	11,300	15,000	20,000	25,000
16M (350cc single)	1,400	2,100	3,200	4,200	5,600	7,000
16MC (350cc single)	1,500	2,200	3,300	4,400	5,900	7,400
16MCS (350cc single).	1,400	2,100	3,100	4,100	5,500	6,900
16MS (350cc single)	1,400	2,100	3,200	4,200	5,600	7,000
18 (500cc single)	1,300	2,000	2,900	3,900	5,200	6,500
18C (500cc single)	1,400	2,200	3,200	4,300	5,800	7,200
18CS (500cc single)	1,400	2,200	3,200	4,300	5,800	7,200
18S (500cc single)	1,200	1,900	2,800	3,700	5,000	6,200
20 (500cc twin)	1,200	1,900	2,800	3,700	5,000	6,200
20CSR (500cc twin).	1,400	2,100	3,200	4,200	5,600	7,000
1952						
7R Racer (350cc single).	5,000	7,500	11,300	15,000	20,000	25,000
16M (350cc single)	1,400	2,100	3,200	4,200	5,600	7,000
16MC (350cc single)	1,500	2,200	3,300	4,400	5,900	7,400
16MCS (350cc single).	1,400	2,100	3,100	4,100	5,500	6,900
16MS (350cc single)	1,400	2,100	3,200	4,200	5,600	7,000
18 (500cc single)	1,300	2,000	2,900	3,900	5,200	6,500
18C (500cc single)	1,400	2,200	3,200	4,300	5,800	7,200
18CS (500cc single).	1,400	2,200	3,200	4,300	5,800	7,200
18S (500cc single)	1,300	2,000	2,900	3,900	5,200	6,500
20 (500cc twin)	1,200	1,900	2,800	3,700	5,000	6,200
20CSR (500cc twin).	1,400	2,100	3,200	4,200	5,600	7,000
1953						
7R Racer (350cc single).	5,600	8,400	12,600	16,800	22,400	28,000
16M (350cc single)	1,400	2,100	3,200	4,200	5,600	7,000
16MC (350cc single)	1,500	2,200	3,300	4,400	5,900	7,400
16MCS (350cc single).	1,400	2,100	3,100	4,100	5,500	6,900
16MS (350cc single)	1,400	2,100	3,200	4,200	5,600	7,000
18 (500cc single)	1,300	2,000	2,900	3,900	5,200	6,500
18C (500cc single)	1,400	2,200	3,200	4,300	5,800	7,200
18CS (500cc single)	1,400	2,200	3,200	4,300	5,800	7,200
18S (500cc single)	1,300	2,000	2,900	3,900	5,200	6,500

	6	5	4	3	2	1
20 (500cc twin)	1,200	1,900	2,800	3,700	5,000	6,200
20CSR (500cc twin)	1,400	2,100	3,200	4,200	5,600	7,000
1954						
7R Racer (350cc single)	6,000	9,000	13,500	18,000	24,000	30,000
16M (350cc single)	1,400	2,100	3,200	4,200	5,600	7,000
16MC (350cc single)	1,500	2,200	3,300	4,400	5,900	7,400
16MCS (350cc single)	1,400	2,100	3,100	4,100	5,500	6,900
16MS (350cc single)	1,400	2,100	3,200	4,200	5,600	7,000
18 (500cc single)	1,300	2,000	2,900	3,900	5,200	6,500
18C (500cc single)	1,400	2,200	3,200	4,300	5,800	7,200
18CS (500cc single)	1,400	2,200	3,200	4,300	5,800	7,200
18S (500cc single)	1,300	2,000	2,900	3,900	5,200	6,500
20 (500cc twin)	1,200	1,900	2,800	3,700	5,000	6,200
20CSR (500cc twin)	1,400	2,100	3,200	4,200	5,600	7,000
20B (545cc twin)	1,300	2,000	3,000	4,000	5,400	6,700
1955						
7R Racer (350cc single)	6,000	9,000	13,500	18,000	24,000	30,000
16M (350cc single)	1,400	2,100	3,200	4,200	5,600	7,000
16MC (350cc single)	1,500	2,200	3,300	4,400	5,900	7,400
16MCS (350cc single)	1,400	2,100	3,200	4,200	5,600	7,000
16MS (350cc single)	1,400	2,100	3,200	4,300	5,700	7,100
18 (500cc single)	1,300	2,000	3,000	4,000	5,400	6,700
18C (500cc single)	1,400	2,200	3,200	4,300	5,800	7,200
18CS (500cc single)	1,400	2,200	3,200	4,300	5,800	7,200
18S (500cc single)	1,300	2,500	4,000	6,000	7,000	8,000
20 (500cc twin)	1,200	1,900	2,800	3,700	5,000	6,200
20CSR (500cc twin)	1,400	2,100	3,200	4,200	5,600	7,000
20B (545cc twin)	1,300	2,000	3,000	4,000	5,400	6,700
1956						
7R Racer (350cc single)	6,000	9,000	13,500	18,000	24,000	30,000
16MCS (350cc single)	1,400	2,100	3,200	4,200	5,600	7,000
16MS (350cc single)	1,400	2,200	3,200	4,300	5,800	7,200
18CS (500cc single)	1,400	2,200	3,200	4,300	5,800	7,200
18S (500cc single)	1,300	2,000	3,000	4,000	5,300	6,600
20 (500cc twin)	1,200	1,900	2,800	3,700	5,000	6,200
20CSR (500cc twin)	1,400	2,100	3,200	4,200	5,600	7,000
30 (600cc twin)	1,300	1,900	2,800	3,800	5,000	6,300
30CSR (600cc twin)	1,400	2,100	3,200	4,200	5,600	7,000
1957						
7R Racer (350cc single)	6,000	9,000	13,500	18,000	24,000	30,000
16MCS (350cc single)	1,400	2,200	3,200	4,300	5,800	7,200
18CS (500cc single)	1,400	2,200	3,200	4,300	5,800	7,200
18S (500cc single)	1,300	2,000	3,000	4,000	5,300	6,600
20 (500cc twin)	1,200	1,900	2,800	3,700	5,000	6,200
20CSR (500cc twin)	1,400	2,100	3,200	4,200	5,600	7,000
30 (600cc twin)	1,300	1,900	2,800	3,800	5,000	6,300
30CSR (600cc twin)	1,400	2,100	3,200	4,200	5,600	7,000
1958						
14 (250cc single)	800	1,200	1,800	2,400	3,200	4,000
7R Racer (350cc single)	6,000	9,000	13,500	18,000	24,000	30,000
16MCS (350cc single)	1,400	2,200	3,200	4,300	5,800	7,200
18CS (500cc single)	1,400	2,200	3,200	4,300	5,800	7,200
18S (500cc single)	1,300	2,000	3,000	4,000	5,300	6,600
20 Deluxe (500cc twin)	1,200	1,900	2,800	3,700	5,000	6,200
20 (500cc twin)	1,200	1,900	2,800	3,700	5,000	6,200
20CSR (500cc twin)	1,400	2,100	3,200	4,200	5,600	7,000
30 (600cc twin)	1,300	1,900	2,800	3,800	5,000	6,300
30CSR (600cc twin)	1,400	2,100	3,200	4,200	5,600	7,000

	6	5	4	3	2	1
1959						
14 (250cc single)	700	1,100	1,600	2,100	2,800	3,500
14CS (250cc single)	800	1,200	1,800	2,300	3,100	3,900
7R Racer (350cc single)	6,000	9,000	13,500	18,000	24,000	30,000
16 (350cc single)	1,100	1,600	2,400	3,200	4,300	5,400
16C (350cc single)	1,300	2,000	3,000	4,000	5,400	6,700
16CS (350cc single)	1,300	2,000	3,000	4,000	5,400	6,700
18CS (500cc single)	1,400	2,200	3,200	4,300	5,800	7,200
18S (500cc single)	1,300	2,000	3,000	4,000	5,300	6,600
20 Deluxe (500cc twin)	1,200	1,900	2,800	3,700	5,000	6,200
20 (500cc twin)	1,200	1,900	2,800	3,700	5,000	6,200
20CSR (500cc twin)	1,400	2,100	3,200	4,200	5,600	7,000
31 Deluxe (650cc twin)	1,200	1,800	2,700	3,600	4,800	6,000
31 (650cc twin)	1,200	1,800	2,700	3,500	4,700	5,900
31CSR (650cc twin)	1,400	2,100	3,200	4,200	5,600	7,000
1960						
14 (250cc single)	700	1,000	1,500	2,000	2,600	3,300
14CS (250cc single)	700	1,100	1,700	2,200	3,000	3,700
7R Racer (350cc single)	6,000	9,000	13,500	18,000	24,000	30,000
8 (350cc single)	900	1,300	2,000	2,600	3,500	4,400
16 (350cc single)	1,100	1,600	2,400	3,200	4,300	5,400
16C (350cc single)	1,300	2,000	3,000	4,000	5,400	6,700
18CS (500cc single)	1,300	2,000	3,000	4,000	5,400	6,700
18S (500cc single)	1,400	2,200	3,200	4,300	5,800	7,200
20 (500cc twin)	1,200	1,900	2,800	3,700	5,000	6,200
20CSR (500cc twin)	1,400	2,100	3,200	4,200	5,600	7,000
31 Deluxe (650cc twin)	1,200	1,800	2,700	3,600	4,800	6,000
31 (650cc twin)	1,200	1,800	2,700	3,500	4,700	5,900
31CSR (650cc twin)	1,400	2,100	3,200	4,200	5,600	7,000
1961						
14 (250cc single)	700	1,000	1,500	2,000	2,600	3,300
14CS (250cc single)	700	1,100	1,700	2,200	3,000	3,700
14S (250cc single)	800	1,200	1,800	2,300	3,100	3,900
7R Racer (350cc single)	6,000	9,000	13,500	18,000	24,000	30,000
8 (350cc single)	900	1,300	2,000	2,600	3,500	4,400
16 (350cc single)	1,100	1,600	2,400	3,200	4,300	5,400
16C (350cc single)	1,400	2,100	3,100	4,100	5,500	6,900
18CS (500cc single)	1,500	2,200	3,300	4,400	5,800	7,300
18S (500cc single)	1,300	1,900	2,900	3,800	5,100	6,400
20 (500cc twin)	1,200	1,900	2,800	3,700	5,000	6,200
20CSR (500cc twin)	1,400	2,100	3,200	4,200	5,600	7,000
31 Deluxe (650cc twin)	1,200	1,800	2,700	3,600	4,800	6,000
31 (650cc twin)	1,200	1,800	2,700	3,500	4,700	5,900
31CSR (650cc twin)	2,000	4,000	6,000	8,000	10,000	12,000
1962						
14 (250cc single)	700	1,000	1,500	2,000	2,600	3,300
14CS (250cc single)	700	1,100	1,700	2,200	3,000	3,700
14CSR (250cc single)	800	1,300	1,900	2,500	3,400	4,200
14S (250cc single)	800	1,200	1,800	2,300	3,100	3,900
7R Racer (350cc single)	6,000	9,000	13,500	18,000	24,000	30,000
8 (350cc single)	900	1,300	2,000	2,600	3,500	4,400
16 (350cc single)	1,000	1,600	2,300	3,100	4,200	5,200
16C (350cc single)	1,400	2,100	3,100	4,100	5,500	6,900
16S (350cc single)	1,000	1,600	2,300	3,100	4,200	5,200
18CS (500cc single)	1,500	2,200	3,300	4,400	5,800	7,300
18S (500cc single)	1,200	1,900	2,800	3,700	5,000	6,200
31 (650cc twin)	1,200	1,800	2,700	3,500	4,700	5,900
31CSR (650cc twin)	1,400	2,100	3,200	4,200	5,600	7,000

	6	5	4	3	2	1
1963						
14 (250cc single)	700	1,000	1,500	2,000	2,600	3,300
14CSR (250cc single)	800	1,300	1,900	2,500	3,400	4,200
7R Racer (350cc single)	6,000	9,000	13,500	18,000	24,000	30,000
16 (350cc single)	1,000	1,600	2,300	3,100	4,200	5,200
16C (350cc single)	1,300	2,000	3,000	4,000	5,400	6,700
18CS (500cc single)	1,500	2,200	3,300	4,400	5,800	7,300
18S (500cc single)	1,200	1,800	2,700	3,600	4,800	6,000
31 (650cc twin)	1,200	1,800	2,700	3,500	4,700	5,900
31CSR (650cc twin)	1,400	2,100	3,200	4,200	5,600	7,000
1964						
14CSR (250cc single)	800	1,300	1,900	2,500	3,400	4,200
16 (350cc single)	1,000	1,600	2,300	3,100	4,200	5,200
16C (350cc single)	1,300	2,000	3,000	4,000	5,400	6,700
18CS (500cc single)	1,400	2,100	3,200	4,300	5,700	7,100
18S (500cc single)	1,200	1,800	2,700	3,600	4,800	6,000
31 (650cc twin)	1,200	1,800	2,700	3,500	4,700	5,900
31CSR (650cc twin)	1,400	2,100	3,200	4,200	5,600	7,000
33 (750cc twin)	1,100	1,700	2,500	3,300	4,400	5,500
33CSR (750cc twin)	1,400	2,100	3,200	4,200	5,600	7,000
1965						
14CSR (250cc single)	800	1,300	1,900	2,500	3,400	4,200
16 (350cc single)	1,000	1,600	2,300	3,100	4,200	5,200
18CS (500cc single)	1,400	2,100	3,200	4,300	5,700	7,100
18S (500cc single)	1,200	1,800	2,700	3,500	4,700	5,900
31 (650cc twin)	1,200	1,800	2,700	3,500	4,700	5,900
31CSR (650cc twin)	1,400	2,100	3,200	4,200	5,600	7,000
33 (750cc twin)	1,100	1,700	2,500	3,300	4,400	5,500
33CSR (750cc twin)	1,300	2,000	2,900	3,900	5,200	6,500
1966						
14CSR (250cc single)	800	1,300	1,900	2,500	3,400	4,200
16 (350cc single)	1,000	1,600	2,300	3,100	4,200	5,200
18S (500cc single)	1,100	1,700	2,500	3,300	4,400	5,500
31 (650cc twin)	1,200	1,800	2,700	3,500	4,700	5,900
31CSR (650cc twin)	1,400	2,100	3,200	4,200	5,600	7,000
33 (750cc twin)	1,100	1,700	2,500	3,300	4,400	5,500
33CSR (750cc twin)	1,300	2,000	2,900	3,900	5,200	6,500
1967						
33 (750cc twin)	1,100	1,700	2,500	3,300	4,400	5,500
33CSR (750cc twin)	1,300	2,000	2,900	3,900	5,200	6,500
1968						
37A Trials (250cc single)	1,000	1,500	2,300	3,000	4,000	5,000
33 (750cc twin)	1,100	1,700	2,500	3,300	4,400	5,500
33CSR (750cc twin)	1,300	2,000	2,900	3,900	5,200	6,500
1969						
37A Trials (250cc single)	1,000	1,500	2,300	3,000	4,000	5,000
33 (750cc twin)	1,100	1,700	2,500	3,300	4,400	5,500
33CSR (750cc twin)	1,300	2,000	2,900	3,900	5,200	6,500
1970						
Y40 Stormer (250cc single)	600	900	1,400	1,800	2,400	3,000
Y50 Stormer (370cc single)	700	1,000	1,500	2,000	2,700	3,300
1971						
Y41 Stormer	500	700	1,200	2,000	2,700	3,300
Y51 Stormer	600	800	1,300	2,200	3,000	3,600
APRILIA						
1988						
TRX 312	100	300	600	900	1,200	1,500
1989						
Climber 300	100	300	700	1,000	1,300	1,600

	6	5	4	3	2	1
1990						
Climber 300	100	300	700	1,100	1,300	1,600
1991						
Climber 300	100	200	400	900	1,300	1,600
1992						
Climber 280R	100	200	500	1,000	1,400	1,800
1993						
Climber 280R	100	200	500	1,000	1,400	1,800
1994						
Climber 280R	100	200	500	1,000	1,500	1,900
ARIEL						
1920						
Solo (498cc single)	1,200	1,800	2,700	3,600	4,800	6,000
Solo (586cc single)	1,400	2,000	3,000	4,100	5,400	6,700
Solo/SC (670cc V-twin)	3,000	4,500	6,800	9,000	12,000	15,000
Solo/SC (795cc V-twin)	3,000	4,500	6,800	9,000	12,000	15,000
1921						
Solo (498cc single)	1,200	1,800	2,700	3,600	4,800	6,000
Solo (586cc single)	1,500	2,300	3,400	4,500	6,000	7,500
Solo/SC (670cc V-twin)	3,000	4,500	6,800	9,000	12,000	15,000
Solo/SC (795cc V-twin)	3,000	4,500	6,800	9,000	12,000	15,000
1922						
Solo (498cc single)	1,200	1,800	2,700	3,600	4,800	6,000
Solo (665cc single)	1,500	2,300	3,400	4,500	6,000	7,500
Solo/SC (795cc V-twin)	2,800	4,200	6,300	8,400	11,200	14,000
Solo/SC (993cc V-twin)	3,600	5,400	8,100	10,800	14,400	18,000
1923						
Solo (249cc single)	1,100	1,700	2,500	3,300	4,400	5,500
Solo (498cc single)	1,200	1,800	2,700	3,600	4,800	6,000
Solo (665cc single)	1,500	2,300	3,400	4,500	6,000	7,500
Solo/SC (795cc V-twin)	2,800	4,200	6,300	8,400	11,200	14,000
Solo/SC (993cc V-twin)	3,600	5,400	8,100	10,800	14,400	18,000
1924						
Solo (249cc single)	1,100	1,700	2,500	3,300	4,400	5,500
Solo 1 (498cc single)	1,200	1,800	2,700	3,600	4,800	6,000
Solo 2 (498cc single)	1,200	1,800	2,700	3,600	4,800	6,000
Solo 3 (498cc single)	1,200	1,800	2,700	3,600	4,800	6,000
Solo/SC (993cc V-twin)	3,600	5,400	8,100	10,800	14,400	18,000
1925						
Solo (249cc single)	1,100	1,700	2,500	3,300	4,400	5,500
Sports (498cc single)	1,500	2,300	3,400	4,500	6,000	7,500
1926						
Sports C (500cc single)	1,200	1,800	2,700	3,600	4,800	6,000
Touring D (500cc single)	1,200	1,800	2,700	3,600	4,800	6,000
Sports A (557cc single)	1,600	2,400	3,600	4,800	6,400	8,000
Touring B (557cc single)	1,600	2,400	3,600	4,800	6,400	8,000
1927						
Sports C (500cc single)	1,200	1,800	4,000	6,000	8,000	10,000
Sports E (500cc single)	1,200	1,800	4,000	6,000	8,000	10,000
Touring D (500cc single)	1,200	1,800	4,000	6,000	8,000	10,000
Sports A (557cc single)	1,600	2,400	4,000	6,000	8,000	10,000
Touring B (557cc single)	1,600	2,400	4,000	6,000	8,000	10,000
1928						
Sports C (500cc single)	1,200	1,800	2,700	3,600	4,800	6,000
Sports E (500cc single)	1,200	1,800	2,700	3,600	4,800	6,000
Touring D (500cc single)	1,200	1,800	2,700	3,600	4,800	6,000
Sports A (557cc single)	1,600	2,400	3,600	4,800	6,400	8,000
Touring B (557cc single)	1,600	2,400	3,600	4,800	6,400	8,000

	6	5	4	3	2	1
1929						
LB Colt (250cc single)	1,300	2,000	3,500	4,400	5,700	7,000
LF Colt (250cc single)	1,300	2,000	3,500	4,400	5,700	7,000
Deluxe F (500cc single)	1,500	2,300	3,400	4,500	6,000	7,500
Model E (500cc single)	1,500	2,300	3,400	4,500	6,000	7,500
Deluxe B (557cc single)	1,600	2,400	3,600	4,800	6,400	8,000
Model A (557cc single)	1,600	2,400	3,600	4,800	6,400	8,000
1930						
LB Colt (250cc single)	1,300	2,000	2,900	3,900	5,200	6,500
LF Colt (250cc single)	1,300	2,000	2,900	3,900	5,200	6,500
LG Colt (250cc single)	1,300	2,000	2,900	3,900	5,200	6,500
Deluxe F (500cc single)	1,500	2,300	3,400	4,500	6,000	7,500
Model E (500cc single)	1,500	2,300	3,400	4,500	6,000	7,500
Model G (500cc single)	1,500	2,300	3,400	4,500	6,000	7,500
Deluxe B (557cc single)	1,600	2,400	3,600	4,800	6,400	8,000
Model A (557cc single)	1,600	2,400	3,600	4,800	6,400	8,000
1931						
LB31 (250cc single)	1,200	1,800	2,700	3,600	4,800	6,000
L1F31 (250cc single)	1,200	1,800	2,700	3,600	4,800	6,000
L2F31 (250cc single)	1,200	1,800	2,700	3,600	4,800	6,000
MF (250cc single)	1,200	1,800	2,700	3,600	4,800	6,000
VF (500cc single)	1,200	1,800	2,700	3,600	4,800	6,000
SF31 (500cc single)	1,200	1,800	2,700	3,600	4,800	6,000
SG31 (500cc single)	1,200	1,800	2,700	3,600	4,800	6,000
4F Square Flour (500cc four)	3,000	4,500	6,750	9,000	12,000	15,000
VG31 (500cc single)	1,100	1,700	2,500	3,300	4,400	5,500
SB31 (557cc single)	1,400	2,100	3,150	4,200	5,600	7,000
VB (557cc single)	1,400	2,100	3,150	4,200	5,600	7,000
1932						
LB32 (249cc single)	1,100	1,700	2,500	3,300	4,400	5,500
LF32 (249cc single)	1,100	1,700	2,500	3,300	4,400	5,500
MB32 (348cc single)	1,200	1,700	2,600	3,500	4,600	5,800
MF32 (348cc single)	1,200	1,700	2,600	3,500	4,600	5,800
MH32 (348cc single)	1,200	1,700	2,600	3,500	4,600	5,800
VG32 (499cc single)	1,200	1,800	2,700	3,600	4,800	6,000
SG32 (499cc single)	1,200	1,800	2,700	3,600	4,800	6,000
VH32 RH (499cc single)	1,700	2,600	3,900	5,100	6,800	8,500
VB32 (557cc single)	1,200	1,900	2,800	3,700	5,000	6,200
SB32 (557cc single)	1,200	1,900	2,800	3,700	5,000	6,200
4F/6 Square Four (601cc four)	5,000	10,000	20,000	30,000	40,000	50,000
1933						
LH (248cc single)	1,100	1,700	2,500	3,300	4,400	5,500
NF (346cc single)	1,200	1,800	2,700	3,600	4,800	6,000
NH (346cc single)	1,200	1,800	2,700	3,600	4,800	6,000
VF (499cc single)	1,400	2,100	3,200	4,200	5,600	7,000
VH (499cc single)	1,700	2,600	3,800	5,100	6,800	8,500
VA (557cc single)	1,200	1,900	2,800	3,700	5,000	6,200
VB Deluxe (557cc single)	1,300	2,000	**3,500**	**5,000**	**7,000**	**9,000**
4F/6 Square Four (601cc four)	5,000	10,000	20,000	30,000	40,000	50,000
1934						
LF (248cc single)	900	1,400	2,100	2,800	3,800	4,700
LH/RH Sport (248cc single)	1,000	1,600	2,300	3,100	4,200	5,200
NF (346cc single)	1,200	1,700	2,600	3,500	4,600	5,800
NH/RH Sport (346cc single)	1,300	2,000	3,000	4,000	5,300	6,600
VF (499cc single)	1,400	2,200	3,200	4,300	5,800	7,200
VH/RH Sport (499cc single)	1,700	2,600	3,800	5,100	6,800	8,500
VA (557cc single)	1,200	1,900	2,800	3,700	5,000	6,200
VB Deluxe (557cc single)	1,300	2,000	**3,500**	**5,000**	**7,000**	**9,000**
4F/6 Square Four (601cc four)	5,000	10,000	20,000	30,000	40,000	50,000

	6	5	4	3	2	1
1935						
LF (248cc single)	900	1,400	2,100	2,800	3,800	4,700
LH/RH Sport (248cc single)	1,000	1,600	2,300	3,100	4,200	5,200
NF (346cc single)	1,200	1,700	2,600	3,500	4,600	5,800
NH/RH Sport (346cc single)	1,300	2,000	3,000	4,000	5,300	6,600
VF (499cc single)	1,400	2,100	3,200	4,200	5,600	7,000
VG Deluxe (499cc single)	1,400	2,100	3,200	4,200	5,600	7,000
VH/RH Sport (499cc single)	1,700	2,600	3,800	5,100	6,800	8,500
VA (557cc single)	1,200	1,900	2,800	3,700	5,000	6,200
VB Deluxe (557cc single)	1,300	2,000	**3,500**	**5,000**	**7,000**	**9,000**
4F/6 Square Four (601cc four)	2,500	5,000	10,000	15,000	20,000	25,000
1936						
LG Deluxe (248cc single)	900	1,400	2,100	2,800	3,800	4,700
LH/RH Sport (248cc single)	1,000	1,600	2,300	3,100	4,200	5,200
NG Deluxe (346cc single)	1,200	1,700	2,600	3,500	4,600	5,800
NH/RH Sport (346cc single)	1,300	2,000	3,000	4,000	5,300	6,600
VG Deluxe (499cc single)	1,400	2,100	3,200	4,200	5,600	7,000
VH/RH Sport (499cc single)	1,700	2,600	3,800	5,100	6,800	8,500
VB Deluxe (557cc single)	1,300	2,000	**3,500**	**5,000**	**7,000**	**9,000**
4F/6 Square Four (601cc four)	3,400	5,100	7,700	10,200	13,600	17,000
4G Square Four (1,000cc four)	2,500	5,000	10,000	15,000	20,000	25,000
1937						
LG Deluxe (248cc single)	900	1,400	2,100	2,800	3,800	4,700
LH/RH Sport (248cc single)	1,000	1,600	2,300	3,100	4,200	5,200
NG Deluxe (346cc single)	1,200	1,700	2,600	3,500	4,600	5,800
NH/RH Sport (346cc single)	1,300	2,000	3,000	4,000	5,300	6,600
VG Deluxe (499cc single)	1,400	2,100	3,200	4,200	5,600	7,000
VH/RH (499cc single)	1,700	2,600	3,800	5,100	6,800	8,500
VB Deluxe (598cc single)	1,300	2,000	**3,500**	**5,000**	**7,000**	**9,000**
4F/6 Square Four (601cc four)	3,400	5,100	7,700	10,200	13,600	17,000
4G Square Four (1,000cc four)	2,500	5,000	10,000	15,000	20,000	25,000
1938						
LG Deluxe (248cc single)	900	1,400	2,100	2,800	3,800	4,700
LH/RH (248cc single)	1,000	1,500	2,300	3,000	4,000	5,000
NG Deluxe (346cc single)	1,200	1,800	2,700	3,500	4,700	5,900
NH/RH (346cc single)	1,300	2,000	2,900	3,900	5,200	6,500
VG Deluxe (499cc single)	1,400	2,100	3,200	4,200	5,600	7,000
VH/RH (499cc single)	1,700	2,600	3,800	5,100	6,800	8,500
VB Deluxe (598cc single)	1,400	2,100	**3,500**	**5,000**	**7,000**	**9,000**
4F Square Four (600cc four)	3,800	6,000	11,000	14,000	18,000	22,000
4G Square Four (995cc four)	2,500	5,000	10,000	15,000	20,000	25,000
4H Square Four (995cc four)	2,500	5,000	10,000	15,000	20,000	25,000
1939						
OG Deluxe (248cc single)	900	1,400	2,000	2,700	3,600	4,500
OH/RH (248cc single)	1,000	1,500	2,300	3,000	4,000	5,000
NG Deluxe (346cc single)	1,200	1,800	2,700	3,500	4,700	5,900
NH/RH (346cc single)	1,300	2,000	2,900	3,900	5,200	6,500
VG Deluxe (499cc single)	1,400	2,100	3,200	4,200	5,600	7,000
VH/RH (499cc single)	1,700	2,600	3,800	5,100	6,800	8,500
VB Deluxe (598cc single)	1,400	2,100	**3,500**	**5,000**	**7,000**	**9,000**
4F Square Four (600cc four)	3,800	6,000	9,000	12,000	16,000	20,000
4G Square Four (995cc four)	2,500	5,000	10,000	15,000	20,000	25,000
4H Square Four (995cc four)	2,500	5,000	10,000	15,000	20,000	25,000
1940						
OG Deluxe (248cc single)	900	1,400	2,000	2,700	3,600	4,500
OH/RH (248cc single)	1,000	1,500	2,300	3,000	4,000	5,000
NG Deluxe (346cc single)	1,200	1,800	2,700	3,500	4,700	5,900
NH/RH (346cc single)	1,300	2,000	2,900	3,900	5,200	6,500
VG Deluxe (500cc single)	1,400	2,100	3,200	4,200	5,600	7,000

	6	5	4	3	2	1
VH/RH (500cc single).	1,700	2,600	3,800	5,100	6,800	8,500
VA Deluxe (598cc single)	1,400	2,100	3,200	4,200	5,600	7,000
VB Deluxe (598cc single)	1,400	2,200	**3,500**	**5,000**	**7,000**	**9,000**
4F Square Four (600cc four)	3,800	5,700	8,600	11,400	15,200	19,000
4G Square Four (995cc four)	2,500	5,000	10,000	15,000	20,000	25,000
4H Square Four (995cc four)	2,500	5,000	10,000	15,000	20,000	25,000
1941-1945 (military production)						
Model W/NG (346cc single)	1,300	2,000	2,900	3,900	5,200	6,500
1946						
NG Deluxe (346cc single)	1,300	2,000	2,900	3,900	5,200	6,500
NH (346cc single)	1,300	2,000	2,900	3,900	5,200	6,500
VG Deluxe (500cc single)	1,200	1,800	2,700	3,600	4,800	6,000
VH (500cc single)	1,600	2,400	3,600	4,800	6,400	8,000
VB Deluxe (598cc single)	1,300	2,000	**3,500**	**5,000**	**7,000**	**9,000**
4G Square Four (995cc four)	2,500	5,000	10,000	15,000	20,000	25,000
1947						
NG (347cc single)	1,300	2,000	2,900	3,900	5,200	6,500
NH (347cc single)	1,300	2,000	2,900	3,900	5,200	6,500
VG (497cc single)	1,200	1,800	2,700	3,600	4,800	6,000
VH (497cc single)	1,600	2,400	3,600	4,800	6,400	8,000
VB (598cc single)	1,300	2,000	**3,500**	**5,000**	**7,000**	**9,000**
4G Square Four (997cc four)	2,500	5,000	10,000	15,000	20,000	25,000
1948						
NG (347cc single)	1,300	2,000	2,900	3,900	5,200	6,500
NH (347cc single)	1,300	2,000	2,900	3,900	5,200	6,500
VH (497cc single)	1,600	2,400	3,600	4,800	6,400	8,000
KG Deluxe (498cc twin)	1,400	2,200	3,200	4,300	5,800	7,200
KH (498cc twin)	1,800	2,800	4,100	5,500	7,400	9,200
VB (598cc single)	1,300	2,000	**3,500**	**5,000**	**7,000**	**9,000**
4G Mk. 1 Square Four (997cc four)	2,500	5,000	10,000	15,000	20,000	25,000
1949						
NG (347cc single)	1,300	2,000	2,900	3,900	5,200	6,500
NH (347cc single)	1,300	2,000	2,900	3,900	5,200	6,500
VG (497cc single)	1,200	1,800	2,700	3,600	4,800	6,000
VH (497cc single)	1,600	2,400	3,600	4,800	6,400	8,000
KH (498cc twin)	1,800	2,800	4,100	5,500	7,400	9,200
VB (598cc single)	1,300	2,000	**3,500**	**5,000**	**7,000**	**9,000**
4G Mk. 1 Square Four (997cc four)	3,000	4,500	7,000	10,000	13,000	16,000
1950						
NH (347cc single)	1,300	2,000	2,900	3,900	5,200	6,500
VCH (497cc single)	1,500	2,200	3,300	4,400	5,900	7,400
VG (497cc single)	1,200	1,800	2,700	3,600	4,800	6,000
VH (497cc single)	1,600	2,400	3,600	4,800	6,400	8,000
KG Deluxe (498cc twin)	1,400	2,200	3,200	4,300	5,800	7,200
KH (498cc twin)	1,900	2,900	4,300	5,700	7,600	9,500
VB (598cc single)	1,300	2,000	**3,500**	**5,000**	**7,000**	**9,000**
4G Mk. 1 Square Four (997cc four)	3,000	4,500	7,000	10,000	13,000	16,000
1951						
NH (347cc single)	1,300	2,000	2,900	3,900	5,200	6,500
VCH (497cc single)	1,600	2,400	3,600	4,800	6,400	8,000
VH (497cc single)	1,600	2,400	3,600	4,800	6,400	8,000
KG Deluxe (498cc twin)	1,400	2,200	3,200	4,300	5,800	7,200
KH (498cc twin)	1,800	2,700	4,100	5,400	7,200	9,000
VB (598cc single)	1,300	2,000	**3,500**	**5,000**	**7,000**	**9,000**
4G Mk. 1 Square Four (997cc four)	3,000	4,500	7,000	10,000	13,000	16,000
1952						
NH (347cc single)	1,300	2,000	2,900	3,900	5,200	6,500
VCH (497cc single)	1,600	2,400	3,600	4,800	6,400	8,000
VH (497cc single)	1,600	2,400	3,600	4,800	6,400	8,000

	6	5	4	3	2	1
VHA (497cc single)	2,000	3,000	4,500	6,000	8,000	10,000
KH (498cc twin)	1,600	2,400	3,600	4,800	6,400	8,000
VB (598cc single)	1,300	2,000	**3,500**	**5,000**	**7,000**	**9,000**
4G Mk. 1 Square Four (997cc four)	2,400	3,600	5,400	7,200	9,600	12,000
4G Mk. 2 Square Four (997cc four)	5,000	7,500	10,000	15,000	20,000	25,000
1953						
LH (197cc single)	1,000	1,500	2,300	3,000	4,000	5,000
NH (347cc single)	1,300	2,000	2,900	3,900	5,200	6,500
HT5 Trials (497cc single)	1,200	1,800	2,700	3,600	4,800	6,000
VH (497cc single)	1,600	2,400	3,600	4,800	6,400	8,000
KH (498cc twin)	1,600	2,400	3,600	4,800	6,400	8,000
VHA (500cc single)	2,000	3,000	4,500	6,000	8,000	10,000
KHA (500cc single)	2,000	3,000	4,500	6,000	8,000	10,000
VB (598cc single)	1,300	2,000	**3,500**	**5,000**	**7,000**	**9,000**
4G Mk. 1 Square Four (997cc four)	2,400	3,600	5,400	7,200	9,600	12,000
4G Mk. 2 Square Four (997cc four)	5,000	7,500	10,000	15,000	20,000	25,000
1954						
LH (197cc single)	1,000	1,500	2,300	3,000	4,000	5,000
NH (347cc single)	1,300	2,000	2,900	3,900	5,200	6,500
HS Scrambler (497cc single)	1,200	1,800	2,700	3,600	4,800	6,000
HT5 Trials (497cc single)	1,200	1,800	2,700	3,600	4,800	6,000
VH (497cc single)	1,600	2,400	3,600	4,800	6,400	8,000
KH (498cc twin)	1,700	2,600	3,800	5,100	6,800	8,500
VB (598cc single)	1,300	2,000	**3,500**	**5,000**	**7,000**	**9,000**
FH (650cc twin)	1,300	2,000	2,900	3,900	5,200	6,500
4G Mk. 2 Square Four (997cc four)	5,000	7,500	10,000	15,000	20,000	25,000
1955						
LH (197cc single)	1,000	1,500	2,300	3,000	4,000	5,000
LM (197cc single)	1,100	1,700	2,500	3,300	4,400	5,500
NH (347cc single)	1,300	2,000	2,900	3,900	5,200	6,500
HS Scrambler (497cc single)	1,200	1,800	2,700	3,600	4,800	6,000
HT5 Trials (497cc single)	1,200	1,800	2,700	3,600	4,800	6,000
VH (497cc single)	1,600	2,400	3,600	4,800	6,400	8,000
KH (498cc twin)	1,700	2,600	3,800	5,100	6,800	8,500
VB (598cc single)	1,300	2,000	**3,500**	**5,000**	**7,000**	**9,000**
FH (650cc twin)	1,300	2,000	2,900	3,900	5,200	6,500
4G Mk. 2 Square Four (997cc four)	5,000	7,500	10,000	15,000	20,000	25,000
1956						
LH (197cc single)	1,000	1,500	2,300	3,000	4,000	5,000
LM (197cc single)	1,100	1,700	2,500	3,300	4,400	5,500
HT3 Trials (347cc single)	1,600	2,400	3,600	4,800	6,400	8,000
NH (347cc single)	1,300	2,000	2,900	3,900	5,200	6,500
HS Mk.3 (497cc single)	2,000	3,000	4,500	6,000	8,000	10,000
HT5 Trials (497cc single)	1,200	1,800	2,700	3,600	4,800	6,000
VH (497cc single)	1,600	2,400	3,600	4,800	6,400	8,000
KH (498cc twin)	1,700	2,600	3,800	5,100	6,800	8,500
VB (598cc single)	1,300	2,000	**3,500**	**5,000**	**7,000**	**9,000**
FH (650cc twin)	1,300	2,000	2,900	3,900	5,200	6,500
Cyclone (650cc twin)	1,400	2,100	3,200	4,200	5,600	7,000
4G Mk. 2 Square Four (997cc four)	4,000	6,000	10,000	15,000	20,000	25,000
1957						
LH (197cc single)	1,000	1,500	2,300	3,000	4,000	5,000
HT3 Trials (347cc single)	1,600	2,400	3,600	4,800	6,400	8,000
NH (347cc single)	1,300	2,000	2,900	3,900	5,200	6,500
HS Mk.3 (497cc single)	2,000	3,000	4,500	6,000	8,000	10,000
HT5 Trials (497cc single)	1,200	1,800	2,700	3,600	4,800	6,000
VH (497cc single)	1,600	2,400	3,600	4,800	6,400	8,000
KH (498cc twin)	1,700	2,600	3,800	5,100	6,800	8,500
VB (598cc single)	1,300	2,000	**3,500**	**5,000**	**7,000**	**9,000**

	6	5	4	3	2	1
FH (650cc twin)	1,300	2,000	2,900	3,900	5,200	6,500
Cyclone (650cc twin)	1,400	2,100	3,200	4,200	5,600	7,000
4G Mk. 2 Square Four (997cc four)	3,800	5,700	8,600	12,000	16,000	20,000
1958						
LH (197cc single)	1,000	1,500	2,300	3,000	4,000	5,000
Leader (247cc twin)	**1,000**	**1,500**	**2,500**	**4,000**	**5,500**	**7,000**
HT3 Trials (347cc single)	1,600	2,400	3,600	4,800	6,400	8,000
NH (347cc single)	1,300	2,000	2,900	3,900	5,200	6,500
HS Mk.3 (497cc single)	2,000	3,000	4,500	6,000	8,000	10,000
HT5 Trials (497cc single)	1,200	1,800	2,700	3,600	4,800	6,000
VH (497cc single)	1,600	2,400	3,600	4,800	6,400	8,000
VB (598cc single)	1,300	2,000	**3,500**	**5,000**	**7,000**	**9,000**
FH (650cc twin)	1,300	2,000	2,900	3,900	5,200	6,500
Cyclone (650cc twin)	1,400	2,100	3,200	4,200	5,600	7,000
4G Mk. 2 Square Four (997cc four)	3,800	5,700	8,600	12,000	16,000	20,000
1959						
Arrow (247cc twin)	800	1,200	1,800	2,300	3,100	3,900
Leader (247cc twin)	**1,000**	**1,500**	**2,500**	**4,000**	**5,500**	**7,000**
1960						
Arrow (247cc twin)	800	2,000	3,000	4,000	5,000	6,000
Arrow Sport (247cc twin)	800	1,200	1,800	2,400	3,200	4,000
Leader (247cc twin)	**1,000**	**1,500**	**2,500**	**4,000**	**5,500**	**7,000**
1961						
Fieldmaster	2,000	5,000	8,000	10,000	12,000	14,000
1963						
Pixie (49cc single)	400	600	1,000	1,300	1,700	2,100
Arrow (197cc twin)	800	1,200	1,800	2,300	3,100	3,900
Arrow (247cc twin)	800	1,200	1,900	2,500	3,300	4,100
Arrow Sport (247cc twin)	900	1,300	1,900	2,600	3,400	4,300
Leader (247cc twin)	**1,000**	**1,500**	**2,500**	**4,000**	**5,500**	**7,000**
ATK						
1985						
560	100	200	300	400	500	700
1986						
560	100	200	300	400	500	700
1987						
560	100	200	300	400	500	700
1988						
200	100	200	300	400	500	700
250	100	200	300	400	500	700
406	100	200	300	400	500	700
604	100	200	300	500	700	900
1989						
250	100	200	300	400	500	700
406	100	200	300	400	500	700
604	100	200	300	500	700	900
604 ES	100	200	300	600	900	1,200
1990						
250	100	200	300	500	800	1,100
406	100	200	300	400	600	900
604 Electric Start	100	200	300	600	900	1,200
604 Kick Start	100	200	300	600	800	1,000
1991						
250 CC	100	200	300	700	1,000	1,300
250 MX	100	200	300	500	700	900
350 Electric Start	100	200	400	800	1,200	1,600
350 ES CC	100	200	500	1,000	1,500	2,000
350 ES MX	100	200	300	600	900	1,200
350 MX	100	200	300	500	800	1,100

	6	5	4	3	2	1
350 STD.	100	200	400	700	1,000	1,300
406 CC	100	200	400	700	1,000	1,300
406 MX	100	200	300	500	700	900
604 ES	100	200	400	900	1,300	1,700
604 ES CC	100	200	500	1,000	1,500	2,000
604 ES MX	100	200	300	700	1,000	1,300
604 MX	100	200	300	600	900	1,200
604 STD.	100	200	400	800	1,100	1,400
1992						
250 CC	100	200	400	700	1,000	1,300
250 MX	100	200	300	500	700	900
350 ES	100	200	500	900	1,300	1,700
350 ES CC	100	200	600	1,100	1,600	2,100
350 ES CC EFI	100	200	600	1,100	1,700	2,300
350 ES EFI	100	200	500	1,000	1,500	2,000
350 ES MX	100	200	400	700	1,000	1,300
350 ES MX EFI	100	200	400	800	1,100	1,400
350 MX	100	200	300	600	900	1,200
350 MX EFI	100	200	300	700	1,000	1,300
350 STD.	100	200	400	800	1,100	1,400
350 STD EFI	100	200	500	900	1,300	1,700
406 CC	100	200	400	700	1,000	1,300
406 MX	100	200	300	500	700	900
604 ES	100	200	500	900	1,400	1,900
604 ES CC	100	200	600	1,100	1,700	2,300
604 ES CC EFI	100	200	600	1,100	1,600	2,100
604 ES EFI	100	200	500	1,000	1,500	2,000
604 ES MX	100	200	400	800	1,100	1,400
604 ES MX EFI	100	200	400	800	1,200	1,600
604 MX	100	200	300	600	900	1,200
604 MX EFI	100	200	400	700	1,000	1,300
604 STD.	100	200	400	800	1,200	1,600
604 STD EFI	100	200	500	900	1,400	1,900
1993						
250 CC	100	200	400	800	1,100	1,400
250 MX	100	200	300	500	800	1,100
350 ES	100	200	500	1,000	1,500	2,000
350 ES CC	100	200	600	1,100	1,700	2,300
350 ES CC EFI	100	200	600	1,200	1,800	2,400
350 ES EFI	100	200	600	1,100	1,700	2,300
350 ES MX	100	200	400	800	1,100	1,400
350 ES MX EFI	100	200	400	800	1,100	1,400
350 MX	100	200	300	700	900	1,100
350 MX EFI	100	200	400	800	1,100	1,400
350 STD.	100	200	400	900	1,300	1,700
350 STD EFI	100	200	500	1,000	1,500	2,000
406 CC	100	200	400	800	1,100	1,400
406 MX	100	200	300	500	800	1,100
605 ES	100	200	600	1,100	1,600	2,100
605 ES CC	100	200	600	1,200	1,800	2,400
605 ES CC EFI	100	200	700	1,300	2,000	2,700
605 ES EFI	100	200	600	1,200	1,800	2,400
605 ES MX	100	200	400	800	1,200	1,600
605 ES MX EFI	100	200	500	900	1,300	1,700
605 MX	100	200	400	700	1,000	1,300
605 MX EFI	100	200	400	800	1,200	1,600
605 STD.	100	200	500	900	1,300	1,700
605 STD EFI	100	200	600	1,100	1,600	2,100

	6	5	4	3	2	1
1994						
250 CC	100	200	400	800	1,200	1,600
350 CC	100	200	500	1,000	1,500	2,000
350 DS	100	200	600	1,100	1,700	2,300
350 ES CC	100	200	600	1,100	1,700	2,300
350 ES DS	100	200	700	1,300	1,900	2,500
406 CC	100	200	400	900	1,200	1,500
605 CC	100	200	600	1,100	1,600	2,100
605 DS	100	200	600	1,300	1,800	2,300
605 ES CC	100	200	600	1,300	1,900	2,500
605 ES DS	100	300	700	1,400	2,100	2,800
BENELLI						
1960						
Trail Sport (48cc)	300	500	700	1,600	3,400	5,500
Touring OHV (125cc)	300	500	800	1,700	3,800	5,600
Sprite OHV (200cc)	300	500	900	1,900	4,000	6,000
1961						
Trail Sport (48cc)	300	500	700	1,600	3,400	5,500
Touring OHV (125cc)	300	500	800	1,700	3,800	5,600
Sprite OHV (200cc)	300	500	900	1,900	4,000	6,000
1962						
Trail Sport (48cc)	300	500	700	1,600	3,400	5,500
Touring OHV (125cc)	300	500	800	1,700	3,800	5,600
Sprite OHV (200cc)	300	500	900	1,900	4,000	6,000
Sprite OHV (250cc)	300	500	900	2,100	4,500	6,500
1963						
Trail Sport (48cc)	300	500	700	1,600	3,200	4,800
Touring OHV (125cc)	300	500	800	1,700	3,600	5,400
Sprite OHV (200cc)	300	500	900	1,900	3,800	5,500
Sprite OHV (250cc)	400	600	900	2,100	4,300	6,500
1964						
Trail Sport (48cc)	300	500	700	1,600	3,200	4,800
Touring OHV (125cc)	300	500	800	1,700	3,600	5,400
Sprite OHV (200cc)	300	500	900	1,900	3,800	5,500
Sprite OHV (250cc)	400	600	900	2,100	4,300	6,500
1965						
Trail Sport (48cc)	300	500	700	1,500	3,000	4,500
Touring OHV (125cc)	300	500	800	1,600	3,200	4,800
Sprite OHV (200cc)	300	500	900	1,800	3,400	5,000
Sprite OHV (250cc)	400	600	900	2,000	3,700	5,400
1966						
Trail (50cc)	200	400	600	1,100	2,300	3,500
Fireball (50cc)	200	400	600	1,100	2,400	3,700
Cobra (125cc)	300	500	800	1,500	2,700	3,900
Cobra Scrambler (125cc)	300	500	900	1,600	3,100	4,600
Sprite (125cc)	200	400	600	1,200	2,500	3,800
Sprite (200cc)	200	400	700	1,300	2,700	4,000
Barracuda (250cc)	500	1,000	1,500	3,000	4,500	6,000
1967						
Automatic (50cc)	200	300	500	900	1,900	2,900
Fireball (50cc)	200	400	600	1,100	2,400	3,700
Mini Bike (50cc)	100	200	400	800	1,300	1,800
Trail (50cc)	200	400	600	1,100	2,300	3,500
Mini Sprite (100cc)	200	300	600	900	1,600	2,300
Cobra (125cc)	300	500	800	1,500	2,700	3,900
Cobra California (125cc)	300	500	900	1,600	2,800	4,000
Cobra Scrambler (125cc)	300	500	900	1,700	3,000	4,300
Sprite (125cc)	200	400	600	1,200	2,500	3,800
Sprite (200cc)	200	400	700	1,300	2,700	4,100

	6	5	4	3	2	1
Barracuda (250cc)	500	1,000	1,500	3,000	4,500	6,000
Barracuda California (250cc)	500	1,000	1,500	3,000	4,500	6,000
1968						
Buzzer (50cc)	200	400	600	1,000	1,900	2,800
Dynamo Compact (50cc)	200	400	500	900	1,800	2,700
Fireball Trail (50cc)	200	400	500	900	1,800	2,700
Mini Sprite (100cc)	200	300	600	900	1,500	2,100
Cobra Scrambler (125cc)	300	500	900	1,600	2,800	4,000
Sprite 4 Speed (125cc)	200	400	500	900	2,200	3,500
Sprite 5 Speed (125cc)	200	400	600	1,100	2,300	3,500
Sprite (200cc)	300	500	700	1,200	2,400	3,600
Barracuda (250cc)	500	1,000	1,500	3,000	4,500	6,000
Barracuda 5 Speed (250cc)	500	1,000	1,500	3,000	4,500	6,000
Scorcher (360cc)	300	500	800	1,400	2,600	3,800
Tornado (650cc twin)	500	700	1,200	2,800	4,500	6,200
1969						
Buzzer (50cc)	200	400	600	1,000	1,900	2,800
Dynamo (50cc)	200	400	500	900	1,800	2,700
Dynamo Scrambler (50cc)	300	500	800	1,100	2,000	3,000
Fireball (50cc)	200	400	500	900	1,800	2,700
Hornet (50cc)	200	400	500	900	1,800	2,700
Maverick (50cc)	200	400	500	900	1,800	2,700
Cobra California (125cc)	400	600	700	1,100	2,100	3,100
Cobra Scrambler (125cc)	300	500	900	1,600	2,800	4,000
El Diablo 4 Speed (125cc)	200	400	600	1,100	2,300	3,500
El Diablo California (125cc)	200	400	600	1,100	2,300	3,500
Sprite 4 Speed (125cc)	200	400	500	900	2,200	3,500
Sprite 5 Speed (125cc)	200	400	600	1,100	2,300	3,500
Sprite California (125cc)	200	400	500	900	2,200	3,500
El Diablo 4 Speed (200cc)	300	500	700	1,100	2,400	3,700
Sprite (200cc)	300	500	700	1,200	2,400	3,600
Sprite California (200cc)	200	400	500	900	2,200	3,500
Barracuda 4 Speed (250cc)	500	1,000	1,500	3,000	4,500	6,000
Barracuda 5 Speed (250cc)	500	1,000	1,500	3,000	4,500	6,000
Barracuda California 4 Speed (250cc)	500	1,000	1,500	3,000	4,500	6,000
Barracuda California 5 Speed (250cc)	500	700	1,000	1,800	3,500	5,200
El Diablo 4 Speed (250cc)	300	500	700	1,200	2,500	3,800
El Diablo 5 Speed (250cc)	400	600	700	1,200	2,600	4,000
Tornado (650cc twin)	500	700	1,200	2,800	4,500	6,200
1970						
Buzzer-Hornet (60cc)	200	400	600	1,000	1,900	2,800
Cougar (60cc)	200	400	600	1,000	1,900	2,800
Dynamo Compact (65cc)	300	500	700	1,000	2,000	3,000
Dynamo Scrambler (65cc)	300	500	700	1,000	2,000	3,000
Dynamo Woodsbike (65cc)	300	500	700	1,000	2,000	3,000
Cobra Scrambler (125cc)	300	500	700	1,000	2,100	3,200
Sprite 5 Speed (125cc)	200	400	600	1,100	2,300	3,500
Volcano (180cc)	300	500	700	1,100	2,100	3,100
Sprite El Diablo (200cc)	300	500	700	1,200	2,400	3,600
Barracuda Supersport (250cc)	500	1,000	1,500	3,000	4,500	6,000
Tornado (650cc twin)	500	700	1,200	2,800	4,500	6,200
1971						
Buzzer-Hornet (60cc)	200	400	600	1,000	1,900	2,800
Cougar (60cc)	200	400	600	1,000	1,900	2,800
Dynamo Compact (65cc)	300	500	700	1,000	2,000	3,000
Dynamo Scrambler (65cc)	300	500	700	1,000	2,000	3,000
Dynamo Woodsbike (65cc)	300	500	700	1,000	2,000	3,000
Hurricane (65cc)	300	500	700	1,000	2,000	3,000

	6	5	4	3	2	1
Sprite 5 Speed (125cc)	300	500	600	1,100	2,300	3,500
Motocross (175cc).	300	500	700	1,000	2,000	3,000
Motocross (180cc).	300	500	700	1,100	2,100	3,100
Volcano (180cc).	300	500	700	1,100	2,100	3,100
Barracuda Supersport (250cc)	500	1,000	1,500	3,000	4,500	6,000
Tornado (650cc twin)	500	700	1,200	2,800	4,500	6,200
1972						
Buzzer (65cc)	200	400	600	900	1,900	2,900
Buzzér Jr (65cc).	300	500	700	1,000	2,000	3,000
Cougar (65cc).	200	400	600	900	1,900	2,900
Dynamo Compact (65cc)	200	400	600	900	1,900	2,900
Dynamo Trail (65cc).	200	400	600	900	1,900	2,900
Dynamo Woodsbike (65cc)	200	400	600	900	1,900	2,900
Hornet (65cc)	200	400	600	900	1,900	2,900
Hurricane (65cc).	200	400	600	900	1,900	2,900
Banshee (90cc)	300	500	700	1,000	2,100	3,200
Mini Enduro (90cc).	300	500	700	1,000	2,100	3,200
Panther (125cc)	300	500	700	1,100	2,100	3,100
Road Trail (125cc)	300	500	700	1,000	2,100	3,200
Enduro (175cc)	300	500	700	1,000	2,100	3,200
Volcano (180cc).	300	500	700	1,100	2,100	3,100
Twin Super Sport (250cc)	400	600	800	1,100	2,300	3,500
Tornado (650cc twin)	500	700	1,200	2,800	4,500	6,200
1973						
Buzzer (65cc)	200	400	600	900	1,900	2,900
Compact Chopper (65cc)	300	500	700	1,100	2,100	3,100
Dynamo Compact (65cc)	200	400	600	900	1,900	2,900
Dynamo Sidehack (65cc)	200	400	600	900	1,900	2,900
Dynamo Trail (65cc).	200	400	600	900	1,900	2,900
Dynamo Woodsbike (65cc)	200	400	600	900	1,900	2,900
Hornet (65cc)	200	400	600	900	1,900	2,900
Hurricane (65cc).	200	400	600	900	1,900	2,900
Mini Enduro (65cc)	200	400	600	900	1,900	2,900
Banshee (90cc)	300	500	700	1,000	2,100	3,200
Panther (125cc)	300	500	700	1,100	2,100	3,100
Enduro (175cc)	300	500	700	1,100	2,100	3,100
Volcano (180cc).	300	500	700	1,100	2,100	3,100
Phantom (250cc twin)	300	500	700	1,100	2,100	3,100
Supersport (250cc)	400	600	800	1,200	2,300	3,500
Tornado (650cc twin)	600	800	1,200	2,800	4,500	6,200
1974						
Dynamo Compact (65cc)	200	300	500	900	1,900	2,900
Dynamo Trail (65cc).	200	300	500	900	1,900	2,900
Dynamo Woodsbike (65cc)	200	300	500	900	1,900	2,900
Mini Enduro (65cc)	200	300	500	900	1,900	2,900
Banshee (90cc)	200	400	600	900	1,900	2,900
Panther (125cc)	200	400	600	1,000	2,100	3,200
Enduro (175cc)	200	400	600	900	1,900	2,900
Volcano (180cc).	200	400	600	900	1,900	2,900
Phantom (250cc twin)	200	400	600	1,000	2,100	3,200
Supersport (250cc)	400	600	800	1,200	2,300	3,500
Quattro 4 Cylinder (500cc)	1,000	1,600	2,500	3,000	5,000	7,000
Tornado (650cc twin)	500	700	1,100	2,100	4,000	5,900
SEI 6 Cylinder (750cc)	900	1,300	2,600	5,000	8,000	10,000
1975						
Dynamo Compact (65cc)	200	300	500	900	1,900	2,900
Dynamo Trail (65cc).	200	300	500	900	1,900	2,900
Dynamo Woodsbike (65cc)	200	300	500	900	1,900	2,900
Mini Enduro (65cc)	200	300	500	900	1,900	2,900

	6	5	4	3	2	1
Banshee (90cc)	200	400	600	900	1,900	2,900
Enduro (175cc)	200	400	600	900	1,900	2,900
Volcano (180cc)	200	400	600	900	1,900	2,900
Phantom (250cc twin)	200	400	600	1,000	2,100	3,200
Quattro 4 Cylinder (500cc)	800	1,200	2,000	3,000	5,000	7,000
Tornado (650cc twin)	300	500	900	1,800	3,500	5,200
SEI 6 Cylinder (750cc)	900	1,300	2,600	5,000	8,000	10,000
1976						
Dynamo Trail (65cc)	200	300	500	900	1,900	2,900
Dynamo Woodsbike (65cc)	200	300	500	900	1,900	2,900
Mini Enduro (65cc)	200	300	500	900	1,900	2,900
Banshee (90cc)	200	400	600	900	1,900	2,900
Panther (125cc)	200	400	600	1,000	2,100	3,200
Enduro (175cc)	200	400	600	900	1,900	2,900
Phantom (250cc twin)	200	400	600	1,000	2,100	3,200
Quattro 4 Cylinder (500cc)	800	1,200	2,000	3,000	5,000	7,000
Tornado (650cc twin)	300	500	900	1,800	3,500	5,200
SEI 6 Cylinder (750cc)	900	1,300	2,600	5,000	8,000	10,000
1977						
Dynamo Trail (65cc)	200	300	500	900	1,900	2,900
Dynamo Woodsbike (65cc)	200	300	500	900	1,900	2,900
Mini Enduro (65cc)	200	300	500	900	1,900	2,900
Enduro (175cc)	200	400	600	900	1,900	2,900
Phantom (250cc twin)	200	400	600	1,000	2,100	3,200
Quattro 4 Cylinder (500cc)	700	1,000	2,000	3,000	5,000	7,000
Tornado (650cc twin)	300	500	900	1,800	3,500	5,200
SEI 6 Cylinder (750cc)	900	1,300	2,600	5,000	8,000	10,000
1978						
Dynamo Woodsbike (65cc)	200	300	500	900	1,900	2,900
Phantom (250cc twin)	200	400	600	1,000	2,100	3,200
Quattro 4 Cylinder (500cc)	700	1,000	2,000	3,000	5,000	7,000
Tornado (650cc twin)	300	500	900	1,800	3,500	5,200
SEI 6 Cylinder (750cc)	900	1,300	2,600	5,000	8,000	10,000
1979						
Dynamo Woodsbike (65cc)	200	300	500	900	1,900	2,900
Phantom (250cc twin)	200	400	600	1,000	2,100	3,200
Quattro 4 Cylinder (500cc)	900	1,500	3,000	5,000	7,000	9,000
Tornado (650cc twin)	300	500	900	1,800	3,500	5,200
SEI 6 Cylinder (750cc)	900	1,300	2,600	5,000	8,000	10,000
1980						
Quattro 4 Cylinder (250cc)	300	500	900	1,600	3,200	4,800
Quattro 4 Cylinder (500cc)	700	1,000	2,000	3,000	5,000	7,000
SEI 6 Cylinder (750cc)	900	1,300	2,600	5,000	8,000	10,000
1981						
C2 Long St (50cc single)	200	300	500	900	1,900	2,900
250/4 (250cc four)	500	900	1,800	3,500	5,200	2,700
Quattro 4 Cylinder (500cc)	700	1,000	2,000	3,000	5,000	7,000
SEI 6 Cylinder (750cc)	900	1,300	2,600	5,000	8,000	10,000
1982						
SEI 6 Cylinder (750cc)	900	1,300	2,600	5,000	8,000	10,000
1983						
SEI 6 Cylinder (750cc)	900	1,300	2,600	5,000	8,000	10,000
1984						
SEI 6 Cylinder (750cc)	900	1,300	2,600	5,000	8,000	10,000
1985						
G2 (50cc single)	200	300	500	900	1,900	2,900

	6	5	4	3	2	1
BETA						
TR32 Trials	100	200	400	600	1,000	1,500
1986						
TR32 Trials	100	200	400	600	1,000	1,500
TR33 Trials	100	200	400	600	1,000	1,500
Trekking 230	100	200	500	700	1,200	1,800
1987						
TR33 Trials	100	200	400	600	1,000	1,500
TR34 Trials	100	200	400	600	1,000	1,500
TR50 Trials	100	200	400	600	1,000	1,500
Trekking 230	100	200	400	600	1,000	1,500
1988						
TR34 Trials	100	200	400	600	1,000	1,500
Trekking	100	200	400	600	1,100	1,600
1989						
Mini Trail 50	100	200	300	600	1,000	1,400
Alp 240	100	300	600	900	1,500	2,100
TR 34 Campionato	100	200	300	600	1,000	1,400
TR 34 Replica	100	200	500	700	1,200	1,700
1990						
Alp	100	300	500	800	1,200	1,600
TR34C 125	100	300	600	900	1,500	2,100
TR34C 240	100	300	600	900	1,500	2,100
TR34C 260	200	500	800	1,200	1,800	2,400
1991						
TR35 50	100	200	300	600	1,000	1,400
TR35 125	100	300	600	900	1,500	2,100
TR35 240	100	300	600	900	1,500	2,100
TR35 260	300	500	1,000	1,400	2,000	2,600
Trial Mini	100	200	300	600	1,000	1,400
Trial-Alp 260	300	500	1,000	1,400	2,000	2,600
Zero 240	100	300	600	900	1,500	2,100
Zero 260	300	500	1,000	1,400	2,000	2,600
1992						
Trial Mini	100	200	300	600	1,000	1,400
Alp 240	100	300	600	900	1,500	2,100
Supertrial 240	100	300	700	1,200	1,800	2,400
Synt 260	300	500	1,000	1,400	2,000	2,600
Zero 260	300	500	1,000	1,400	2,000	2,600
1993						
Alp 240	100	300	600	900	1,500	2,100
Supertrial 240	100	300	700	1,200	1,800	2,400
Gara 260	300	500	1,000	1,400	2,000	2,600
Synt 260	100	300	600	900	1,500	2,100
1994						
Alp 50	100	200	300	600	1,000	1,400
MX 50R	100	200	300	600	1,000	1,400
RK 6 50	100	200	300	600	1,000	1,400
Super Trial 50	100	200	300	600	1,000	1,400
Trial Mini 50	100	200	300	600	1,000	1,400
Trial Mini Auto 50	100	200	300	600	1,000	1,400
Zero 50	100	200	300	600	1,000	1,400
Synt 125	100	200	500	700	1,200	1,700
Alp 240	100	300	600	900	1,500	2,100
Super Trial 240	100	200	700	1,200	1,800	2,400
Techno 250	300	500	1,000	1,400	2,000	2,600
Synt 260	100	300	600	900	1,500	2,100

	6	5	4	3	2	1
BIMOTA						
1983						
HB2	150	250	400	700	1,100	1,500
KB2	100	200	300	650	1,000	1,300
KB2/TT	150	250	400	700	1,100	1,500
KB3	100	200	400	700	1,100	1,500
SB3	100	200	300	600	900	1,200
1984						
HB2	100	200	400	900	1,300	1,700
KB2	100	200	400	800	1,300	1,900
KB3	100	200	400	900	1,300	1,700
SB3	100	200	400	700	1,100	1,500
SB4	100	200	400	900	1,300	1,700
1985						
HB3	100	200	600	1,200	1,700	2,200
KB2	100	200	500	1,100	1,600	2,100
KB3	100	200	600	1,200	1,700	2,200
SB4	100	200	600	1,200	1,700	2,200
SB5	100	200	600	1,300	2,000	2,700
1986						
DB1	100	200	600	1,300	1,900	2,500
1987						
DB1	100	300	700	1,500	2,200	2,900
1988						
DB1	200	300	900	1,900	2,800	3,600
YB4	200	400	1,200	2,500	3,700	4,900
YB6	200	400	1,100	2,300	3,400	4,500
1989						
DB1-F1B	200	400	1,000	2,200	3,200	4,200
DB1-SR750	400	600	1,700	3,500	5,300	7,100
YB4-EL750	300	600	1,600	3,200	4,800	6,400
YB5	200	400	1,000	2,100	3,200	4,300
YB6	300	500	1,300	2,700	4,000	5,300
1990						
DB1	200	400	1,200	2,500	3,800	5,100
DB1-SR	400	800	2,200	4,400	6,600	8,800
YB4	400	700	1,800	3,700	5,500	7,300
YB4-ELR	700	1,200	3,300	6,800	10,000	13,000
YB5	200	400	1,200	2,500	3,700	4,900
YB6	300	600	1,500	3,100	4,600	6,100
1991						
Bellaria	500	800	2,100	4,400	6,600	8,800
Dieci	800	1,200	2,500	6,000	8,000	10,000
Tesi 1D 851	800	1,200	3,300	6,800	10,000	13,000
Tesi 1D 906	900	1,300	3,700	7,700	11,500	15,500
Tuatara EL	700	1,000	2,900	5,900	8,900	12,000
YB4-EL	600	900	2,600	5,300	7,800	10,000
YB4-EXUP	500	800	2,200	4,500	6,700	8,900
YB5	300	600	1,700	3,500	5,200	6,900
1992						
Dieci	800	1,200	2,500	6,000	8,000	10,000
Tesi 1D 906 IE	900	1,300	3,700	7,700	11,500	15,500
YB8	500	800	2,000	4,200	6,300	8,400
1993						
DB2	400	700	1,700	3,600	5,400	7,200
Dieci	800	1,200	2,500	6,000	8,000	10,000
Tesi 1D 906 IE	1,000	1,400	4,000	8,200	12,000	16,000
YB8	500	800	2,200	4,500	6,800	9,000

	6	5	4	3	2	1
BMW						
1923						
R32 (494cc twin)	5,000	10,000	15,000	20,000	26,000	32,000
1924						
R32 (494cc twin)	5,000	10,000	15,000	20,000	26,000	32,000
1925						
R32 (494cc twin)	5,000	10,000	15,000	20,000	26,000	32,000
R37 (494cc twin)	5,000	10,000	15,000	20,000	26,000	32,000
R39 (247cc single)	1,400	2,100	3,100	4,100	5,500	6,900
1926						
R32 (494cc twin) (3,090-4 yrs)	5,000	10,000	15,000	20,000	26,000	32,000
R37 (494cc twin) (152-2 yrs)	5,000	10,000	15,000	20,000	26,000	32,000
R39 (247cc single)	1,400	2,100	3,100	4,100	5,500	6,900
R42 (494cc twin)	5,000	10,000	15,000	20,000	26,000	32,000
1927						
R39 (247cc single) (855-3 yrs)	1,400	2,100	3,100	4,100	5,500	6,900
R42 (494cc twin)	5,000	10,000	15,000	20,000	26,000	32,000
R47 (494cc twin)	5,000	10,000	15,000	20,000	26,000	32,000
1928						
R42 (494cc twin) (6,502-3 yrs)	5,000	10,000	15,000	20,000	26,000	32,000
R47 (494cc twin) (1,720-2 yrs)	5,000	10,000	15,000	20,000	26,000	32,000
R52 (486cc twin)	5,000	10,000	20,000	30,000	40,000	50,000
R57 (494cc twin)	5,000	10,000	18,000	25,000	30,000	36,000
R62 (745cc twin)	4,000	7,000	11,000	14,000	18,000	25,000
R63 (735cc twin)	4,000	6,000	9,000	11,000	14,000	18,000
1929						
R11 (745cc twin)	4,000	6,000	9,000	11,000	14,000	18,000
R16 (736cc twin)	4,000	6,000	9,000	11,000	14,000	18,000
R52 (486cc twin) (4,377-2 yrs)	2,600	3,900	5,900	7,800	11,000	13,000
R57 (494cc twin)	5,000	10,000	15,000	20,000	26,000	32,000
R62 (745cc twin) (4,355-2yrs)	4,000	7,000	11,000	14,000	18,000	25,000
R63 (735cc twin) (794-2 yrs)	4,000	6,000	9,000	11,000	14,000	18,000
1930						
R11 (745cc twin)	4,000	6,000	9,000	11,000	14,000	18,000
R16 (736cc twin)	4,000	6,000	9,000	11,000	14,000	18,000
R57 (494cc twin) (1,005-3 yrs)	5,000	10,000	15,000	20,000	26,000	32,000
1931						
R2 (198cc single) (4,161)	1,400	**2,500**	**4,000**	**6,000**	**7,500**	**9,000**
R11 (745cc twin)	4,000	6,000	9,000	11,000	14,000	18,000
1932						
R2 (198cc single) (1,850)	1,400	**2,500**	**4,000**	**6,000**	**7,500**	**9,000**
R4 (398cc single) (1,101)	2,600	3,900	5,900	7,800	10,000	13,000
R11 (745cc twin)	4,000	6,000	9,000	11,000	14,000	18,000
R16 (736cc twin)	4,000	6,000	9,000	11,000	14,000	18,000
1933						
R2 (198cc single) (2,000)	1,400	**2,500**	**4,000**	**6,000**	**7,500**	**9,000**
R4 (398cc single) (1,737)	2,600	3,900	5,900	7,800	10,000	13,000
R11 (745cc twin)	4,000	6,000	9,000	11,000	14,000	18,000
R16 (736cc twin)	4,000	6,000	9,000	11,000	14,000	18,000
1934						
R2 (198cc single) (2,077)	1,400	**2,500**	**4,000**	**6,000**	**7,500**	**9,000**
R4 (398cc single) (3,671)	2,600	3,900	5,900	7,800	11,000	13,000
R11 (745cc twin) (7,500-6 yrs)	4,000	6,000	9,000	11,000	14,000	18,000
R16 (736cc twin) (1,006-5 yrs)	4,000	6,000	9,000	11,000	14,000	18,000
1935						
R2 (198cc single) (2,700)	1,400	**2,500**	**4,000**	**6,000**	**7,500**	**9,000**
R4 (398cc single) (3,651)	2,600	3,900	5,900	7,800	11,000	13,000
R12 (745cc twin)	4,000	6,000	9,000	11,000	14,000	18,000
R17 (735cc twin)	4,000	6,000	**10,000**	**12,000**	**15,000**	**20,000**

	6	5	4	3	2	1
1936						
R2 (198cc single) (2,500)	1,400	**2,500**	**4,000**	**6,000**	**7,500**	**9,000**
R3 (305cc single) (740)	2,600	3,900	5,900	7,800	11,000	13,000
R4 (398cc single) (5,033)	2,600	3,900	5,900	7,800	11,000	13,000
R12 (745cc twin)	4,000	6,000	9,000	11,000	14,000	18,000
R17 (735cc twin)	4,000	6,000	**10,000**	**12,000**	**15,000**	**20,000**
1937						
R20 (192cc single)	1,400	2,100	3,200	4,200	5,600	7,000
R35 (342cc twin)	1,800	2,700	4,100	5,400	7,200	9,000
R4 (398cc single)	3,800	5,700	8,600	11,000	15,000	19,000
R5 (494cc twin)	2,200	3,300	5,000	6,600	8,800	11,000
R6 (598cc twin)	2,000	3,000	4,500	6,000	8,000	10,000
R17 (735cc twin) (434-3 yrs)	3,400	5,100	**10,000**	**12,000**	**15,000**	**20,000**
R12 (745cc twin)	2,600	3,900	5,900	7,800	11,000	13,000
1938						
R20 (192cc single) (5,000-2 yrs)	1,400	2,100	3,200	4,200	5,600	7,000
R23 (247cc single)	1,400	2,100	3,100	4,100	5,500	6,900
R35 (342cc twin)	1,800	2,700	5,500	7,000	9,000	11,000
R51 (494cc twin)	**3,400**	**5,100**	**7,700**	**10,000**	**14,000**	**17,000**
R66 (597cc twin)	3,400	5,100	7,700	10,000	14,000	17,000
R61 (599cc twin)	1,600	2,400	3,600	4,800	6,400	8,000
R12 (745cc twin)	2,400	3,600	5,400	7,200	9,600	12,000
R71 (745cc twin)	3,000	4,500	6,800	9,000	12,000	15,000
1939						
R23 (247cc single)	1,400	2,100	3,100	4,100	5,500	6,900
R35 (342cc single)	1,800	2,700	4,100	5,400	7,200	9,000
R51 (494cc twin)	**3,400**	**5,100**	**7,700**	**10,000**	**14,000**	**17,000**
R61 (597cc twin)	2,400	3,600	5,400	7,200	9,600	12,000
R66 597cc twin)	3,200	4,800	7,200	9,600	13,000	16,000
R12 745cc twin)	2,400	3,600	5,400	7,200	9,600	12,000
R71 (745cc twin)	3,000	4,500	6,800	9,000	12,000	15,000
1940						
R23 (247cc single) (8,021-3 yrs)	1,400	2,100	3,100	4,100	5,500	6,900
R35 (342cc single) (15,386-4 yrs)	1,800	2,700	4,100	5,400	7,200	9,000
R51 (494cc twin) (3,775-3 yrs)	**3,400**	**5,100**	**7,700**	**10,000**	**14,000**	**17,000**
R61 (597cc twin)	2,200	3,300	5,000	6,600	8,800	11,000
R66 (597cc twin)	3,200	4,800	7,200	9,600	13,000	16,000
R12 (745cc twin)	2,400	3,600	5,400	7,200	9,600	12,000
R71 (745cc twin)	3,400	5,100	7,700	10,000	14,000	17,000
1941						
R61 (597cc twin) (3,747-4yrs)	2,200	3,300	5,000	6,600	8,800	11,000
R66 (597cc twin) (1,669-4 yrs)	3,200	4,800	7,200	9,600	13,000	16,000
R12 (745cc twin)	2,400	3,600	5,400	7,200	9,600	12,000
R71 (745cc twin) (3,458-4 yrs)	3,400	4,500	5,500	8,000	12,000	14,000
R75 (745cc twin)	2,800	4,200	6,300	8,400	11,000	14,000
1942						
R12 (745cc twin) (36,000-8 yrs)	2,400	3,600	5,400	7,200	9,600	12,000
R75 (745cc twin)	2,800	4,200	6,300	8,400	11,000	14,000
1943						
R75 (745cc twin)	2,800	4,200	6,300	8,400	11,000	14,000
1944						
R75 (745cc twin) (18,000-4 yrs)	2,800	4,200	6,300	8,400	11,000	14,000
1948						
R24 (247cc single)	1,300	2,000	2,900	3,900	5,200	6,500
1949						
R24 (247cc single)	1,300	2,000	2,900	3,900	5,200	6,500
1950						
R24 (247cc single) (12,020-3 yrs)	1,300	2,000	2,900	3,900	5,200	6,500
R25 (247cc single)	1,200	1,800	2,700	3,600	4,800	6,000

	6	5	4	3	2	1
R51/2 (494cc twin)	2,000	3,000	4,500	6,000	8,000	10,000
1951						
R25 (247cc single) (23,040-2 yrs)	1,200	1,800	2,700	3,600	4,800	6,000
R25/2 (247cc single)	1,200	1,800	2,700	3,600	4,800	6,000
R51/2 (494cc twin) (5,000-2 yrs)	2,000	3,000	4,500	6,000	8,000	10,000
R51/3 (494cc twin)	2,500	4,000	7,500	10,000	13,000	16,000
R67 (594cc twin) (1,470)	1,600	2,400	3,600	4,800	6,400	8,000
1952						
R25/2 (247cc single)	1,200	1,800	2,700	3,600	4,800	6,000
R51/3 (494cc twin)	2,500	4,000	7,500	10,000	13,000	16,000
R67/2 (594cc twin)	1,400	2,100	3,200	4,200	5,600	7,000
R68 (594cc twin)	3,000	4,500	6,800	9,000	12,000	15,000
1953						
R25/2 (247cc single) (38,651-3 yrs)	1,200	1,800	2,700	3,600	4,800	6,000
R25/3 (247cc single)	1,200	1,800	2,700	4,000	5,000	6,500
R51/3 (494cc twin)	2,500	4,000	7,500	10,000	13,000	16,000
R67/2 (594cc twin)	1,400	2,100	3,200	4,200	5,600	7,000
R68 (594cc twin)	3,000	6,000	9,000	12,000	15,000	18,000
1954						
R25/3 (247cc single)	1,200	1,800	2,700	3,600	4,800	6,000
R51/3 (494cc twin) (18,420-4 yrs)	2,400	3,600	5,400	7,200	9,600	12,000
R67/2 (594cc twin) (4,234-3 yrs)	1,400	2,100	3,200	4,200	5,600	7,000
R68 (594cc twin) (1,452-3 yrs)	3,200	4,800	7,200	9,600	13,000	16,000
1955						
R25/3 (247cc single)	1,200	1,800	2,700	3,600	4,800	6,000
R50 (494cc twin)	1,200	1,800	2,700	3,600	4,800	6,000
R67/3 (594cc twin) (700-2 yrs)	1,600	2,400	3,600	4,800	6,400	8,000
R69 (594cc twin)	1,400	2,100	3,200	4,200	5,600	7,000
1956						
R25/3 (247cc single) (47,700-4 yrs)	1,200	1,800	2,700	3,600	4,800	6,000
R26 (247cc single)	1,000	1,500	2,300	3,000	4,000	5,000
R50 (494cc twin)	1,300	2,000	3,000	4,000	6,000	8,000
R60 (594cc twin)	**1,500**	**2,200**	**3,300**	**4,400**	**5,900**	**7,400**
R67/3 (594cc twin)	1,600	2,400	3,600	4,800	6,400	8,000
R69 (594cc twin)	1,400	2,100	4,000	6,000	9,000	12,000
1957						
R50 (494cc twin)	1,300	2,000	3,000	4,000	6,000	8,000
R60 (594cc twin)	1,500	2,200	3,300	4,400	5,900	7,400
R69 (594cc twin)	1,400	2,100	**4,000**	**6,000**	**9,000**	**12,000**
1958						
R26 (247cc single)	1,000	1,500	2,300	3,000	4,000	5,000
R50 (494cc twin)	1,500	2,300	3,400	4,500	6,000	7,500
R60 (594cc twin)	1,500	2,200	3,300	4,400	5,900	7,400
R69 (594cc twin)	1,400	2,100	**4,000**	**6,000**	**9,000**	**12,000**
1959						
R26 (247cc single)	1,000	1,500	2,300	3,000	4,000	5,000
R50 (494cc twin)	1,500	2,300	3,400	4,500	6,000	7,500
R60 (594cc twin)	1,500	2,200	3,300	4,400	5,900	7,400
R69 (594cc twin)	1,400	2,100	**4,000**	**6,000**	**9,000**	**12,000**
1960						
R26 (247cc single) (30,236-5 yrs)	1,000	1,500	2,300	3,000	4,000	5,000
R27 (247cc single)	**1,500**	**2,500**	**3,500**	**5,000**	**6,500**	**8,000**
R50 (494cc twin) (13,510-6 yrs)	1,500	2,300	3,400	4,500	6,000	7,500
R50/2 (494cc twin)	2,400	3,600	5,400	7,200	9,600	12,000
R50S (494cc twin)	2,400	3,600	5,400	7,200	9,600	12,000
R60 (594cc twin) (3,530-5 yrs)	2,000	4,000	6,000	8,000	10,000	12,000
R60/2 (594cc twin)	1,900	2,900	4,300	**6,000**	**9,000**	**12,000**
R69 (594cc twin) (2,956-6 yrs)	2,500	4,000	7,000	10,000	13,000	16,000
R69S (594cc twin)	2,400	3,600	6,000	9,000	12,000	15,000

	6	5	4	3	2	1
1961						
R27 (247cc single)	**1,500**	**2,500**	**3,500**	**5,000**	**6,500**	**8,000**
R50/2 (494cc twin)	2,400	3,600	5,400	7,200	9,600	12,000
R50S (494cc twin)	2,400	3,600	5,400	7,200	9,600	12,000
R60/2 (594cc twin)	1,900	2,900	4,300	**6,000**	**9,000**	**12,000**
R69S (594cc twin)	2,400	3,600	6,000	9,000	12,000	15,000
1962						
R27 (247cc single)	**1,500**	**2,500**	**3,500**	**5,000**	**6,500**	**8,000**
R50/2 (494cc twin)	2,400	3,600	5,400	7,200	9,600	12,000
R50S (494cc twin) (1,634-3 yrs)	2,400	3,600	5,400	7,200	9,600	12,000
R60/2 (594cc twin)	1,900	2,900	4,300	**6,000**	**9,000**	**12,000**
R69S (594cc twin)	2,400	3,600	6,000	9,000	12,000	15,000
1963						
R27 (247cc single)	**1,500**	**2,500**	**3,500**	**5,000**	**6,500**	**8,000**
R50/2 (494cc twin)	2,400	3,600	6,000	9,000	12,000	15,000
R60/2 (594cc twin)	1,900	3,000	4,500	6,000	9,000	12,000
R69S (594cc twin)	2,400	3,600	6,000	9,000	12,000	15,000
1964						
R27 (247cc single)	**1,500**	**2,500**	**3,500**	**5,000**	**6,500**	**8,000**
R50/2 (494cc twin)	2,400	3,600	5,400	7,200	9,600	12,000
R60/2 (594cc twin)	1,900	2,900	4,300	**6,000**	**9,000**	**12,000**
R69S (594cc twin)	2,400	3,600	6,000	9,000	12,000	15,000
1965						
R27 (247cc single)	**1,500**	**2,500**	**3,500**	**5,000**	**6,500**	**8,000**
R50/2 (494cc twin)	2,400	3,600	5,400	7,200	9,600	12,000
R60/2 (594cc twin)	1,900	2,900	4,300	**6,000**	**9,000**	**12,000**
R69S (594cc twin)	2,400	3,600	6,000	9,000	12,000	15,000
1966						
R27 (247cc single) (15,364-7 yrs)	**1,500**	**2,500**	**3,500**	**5,000**	**6,500**	**8,000**
R50/2 (494cc twin)	2,400	4,000	6,000	9,000	12,000	15,000
R60/2 (594cc twin)	1,900	3,000	4,500	6,000	9,000	12,000
R69S (594cc twin) (11,317-10 yrs)	2,400	3,600	6,000	9,000	12,000	15,000
1967						
R50US (294cc twin)	**1,000**	**2,000**	**3,000**	**5,000**	**7,000**	**9,000**
R50/2 (494cc twin)	2,400	3,600	6,000	9,000	12,000	15,000
R60/2 (594cc twin)	1,900	2,900	4,300	6,000	**9,000**	**12,000**
R60US (594cc twin)	1,000	1,500	2,300	3,000	4,000	5,000
R69US (594cc twin)	1,600	2,400	4,000	6,000	8,000	10,000
1968						
R50US (294cc twin)	1,400	2,100	2,000	4,000	6,000	8,000
R50/2 (494cc twin)	2,400	3,600	5,400	7,200	9,600	12,000
R60/2 (594cc twin)	2,400	3,600	5,400	7,200	9,600	12,000
R60US (594cc twin)	1,400	2,100	3,200	4,200	5,600	7,000
R69US (594cc twin) (Incl in R69/S)	1,600	2,400	4,000	6,000	8,000	10,000
1969						
R50US (294cc twin) (Incl in R50/2)	1,400	2,100	3,200	4,200	5,600	7,000
R50/2 (494cc twin) (19,036-10 yrs)	2,400	3,600	5,400	7,200	9,600	12,000
R50/5 (496cc twin)	1,100	1,700	2,500	3,300	4,400	5,500
R60/5 (594cc twin)	900	1,400	2,100	2,800	3,800	4,700
R60/2 (594cc twin) (17,306-10 yrs)	2,400	3,600	5,400	7,200	9,600	12,000
R60US (594cc twin) (Incl in R60/2)	1,400	2,100	3,200	4,200	5,600	7,000
R69US (594cc twin)	1,600	2,400	4,000	6,000	8,000	10,000
R75/5 (745cc twin)	1,000	1,500	2,300	3,000	4,000	5,000
1970						
R50/5 (496cc twin)	1,100	1,700	2,500	3,300	4,400	5,500
R60/5 (594cc twin)	900	1,400	2,100	2,800	3,800	4,700
R75/5 (745cc twin)	1,200	1,800	2,700	3,600	4,800	6,000
1971						
R50/5 (496cc twin)	1,100	1,700	2,500	3,300	4,400	5,500

	6	5	4	3	2	1
R60/5 (594cc twin)	1,000	1,400	2,200	2,900	3,800	4,800
R75/5 (745cc twin)	1,200	1,800	2,700	3,600	4,800	6,000
1972						
R50/5 (496cc twin)	1,100	1,700	2,500	3,300	4,400	5,500
R60/5 (594cc twin)	1,000	1,400	2,200	2,900	3,800	4,800
R75/5 (745cc twin)	1,200	1,800	2,700	3,600	4,800	6,000
1973						
R50/5 (496cc twin) (7,865-5 yrs)	1,100	1,700	2,500	3,300	4,400	5,500
R60/5 (594cc twin) (22,721-5 yrs)	900	1,400	2,000	2,700	3,600	4,500
R75/5 (745cc twin) (38,370-5 yrs)	1,200	1,800	2,700	3,600	4,800	6,000
1974						
R60/6 (599cc twin)	800	1,200	1,800	2,400	3,200	4,000
R75/6 (745cc twin)	800	1,200	1,900	2,500	3,300	4,100
R90/6 (898cc twin)	1,300	2,000	3,000	4,000	6,000	8,000
R90S (898cc twin).	1,900	2,900	4,300	5,700	7,000	9,000
1975						
R60/6 (599cc twin)	800	1,200	2,000	3,000	3,500	4,200
R75/6 (745cc twin)	800	1,200	1,900	2,500	3,300	4,100
R90/6 (898cc twin)	900	1,400	2,500	3,000	3,600	4,500
R90S (898cc twin).	1,900	2,900	4,300	5,700	7,600	9,500
1976						
R60/6 (599cc twin) (13,511-4 yrs)	800	1,200	1,800	2,400	3,200	4,000
R60/7 (599cc twin)	800	1,200	1,800	2,400	3,200	4,000
R75/6 (745cc twin) (17,587-4 yrs)	800	1,200	1,900	2,500	3,300	4,100
R75/7 (745cc twin)	900	1,300	1,900	2,600	3,400	4,300
R75/7 (745cc twin)	900	1,300	1,900	2,600	3,400	4,300
R90/6 (898cc twin) (21,097-4 yrs)	900	1,300	2,000	2,600	3,500	4,400
R90S (898cc twin) (17,465-4 yrs)	1,900	2,900	4,300	5,700	7,600	9,500
R100/7 (980cc twin)	800	1,100	1,700	2,300	3,000	3,800
R100RS (980cc twin)	800	1,200	1,800	2,400	3,200	4,000
R100S (980cc twin)	800	1,100	1,700	2,300	3,000	3,800
1977						
R60/7 (599cc twin)	800	1,200	1,800	2,400	3,200	4,000
R75/7 (745cc twin) (6,264-4 yrs)	800	1,300	1,900	2,500	3,400	4,200
R80/7 (797cc twin)	800	1,200	1,800	2,400	3,200	4,000
R100/7 (980cc twin).	800	1,100	2,000	2,500	3,000	3,800
R100RS (980cc twin)	800	1,200	1,800	2,400	3,200	4,000
R100S (980cc twin)	900	1,500	2,500	3,000	3,800	4,500
1978						
R60/7 (599cc twin)	800	1,200	1,800	2,400	3,200	4,000
R65 (649cc twin)	800	1,100	1,700	2,300	3,000	3,800
R80/7 (797cc twin)	800	1,200	1,800	2,400	3,200	4,000
R100RS (980cc twin)	900	1,400	2,100	2,800	3,800	4,700
R100RT (980cc twin)	900	1,400	2,100	2,800	3,800	4,700
R100S (980cc twin) (11,762-5yrs).	700	1,100	1,600	2,100	2,800	3,500
R100T (980cc twin) (5,463-3 yrs)	700	1,100	1,600	2,100	2,800	3,500
R100/7 (980cc twin) (12,056-5 yrs)	600	1,000	1,400	1,900	2,600	3,200
1979						
R60/7 (599cc twin)	800	1,200	1,800	2,400	3,200	4,000
R65 (649cc twin)	800	1,100	1,700	2,300	3,000	3,800
R80/7 (707cc twin)	800	1,200	1,800	2,400	3,200	4,000
R100RS (980cc twin)	900	1,400	2,100	2,800	3,800	4,700
R100RT (980cc twin)	900	1,400	2,100	2,800	3,800	4,700
R100T (980cc twin)	800	1,200	1,800	2,400	3,200	4,000
1980						
R60/7 (599cc twin)	800	1,200	1,800	2,400	3,200	4,000
R65 (649cc twin)	800	1,100	1,700	2,300	3,000	3,800
R80G/S (797cc twin)	800	1,200	1,800	2,400	3,200	4,000
R80/7 (797cc twin) (18,522-8 yrs).	800	1,200	1,800	2,400	3,200	4,000

	6	5	4	3	2	1
R100RS (980cc twin)	900	1,400	2,100	2,800	3,800	4,700
R100RT (980cc twin)	900	1,400	2,100	2,800	3,800	4,700
R100T (980cc twin)	800	1,200	1,800	2,400	3,200	4,000
1981						
R60/7 (599cc twin)	800	1,200	1,800	2,400	3,200	4,000
R65 (650cc twin)	800	1,200	1,800	2,400	3,200	4,000
R80G/S (800cc twin)	900	1,400	2,100	2,800	3,300	3,900
R100 (1000cc twin)	900	1,400	2,100	2,900	4,000	5,300
R100CS (1000cc twin)	900	1,400	2,100	2,800	3,800	4,700
R100RS (1000cc twin)	900	1,400	2,100	3,500	4,500	5,500
R100RT (1000cc twin)	900	1,400	2,100	2,800	3,800	4,700
1982						
R60/7 (599cc twin) (11,163-7yrs)	800	1,200	1,800	2,400	3,200	4,000
R65 (650cc twin)	700	1,000	1,500	2,000	2,700	3,400
R65LS (650cc twin)	800	1,100	1,700	2,300	3,000	3,800
R100 (1000cc twin)	800	1,400	2,100	2,800	3,900	5,000
R100TR (1000cc twin)	900	1,400	2,100	2,800	3,800	4,700
R100RS (1000cc twin)	900	1,400	2,100	2,800	3,800	4,700
R100RT (1000cc twin)	900	1,400	2,100	2,800	3,800	4,700
1983						
R65 (650cc twin)	700	1,000	1,600	2,200	2,900	3,600
R65LS (650cc twin)	700	1,000	1,600	2,200	2,900	3,600
R80G/S (800cc twin)	800	1,400	2,100	2,800	3,500	4,200
R80ST (800cc twin)	800	1,400	2,100	2,800	3,500	4,200
R80RT (800cc twin)	800	1,400	2,100	2,800	3,600	4,400
R100 (1000cc twin)	900	1,500	2,200	2,900	3,800	4,800
R100S (1000cc twin)	900	1,500	2,200	2,900	3,800	4,800
R100RS (1000cc twin)	900	1,500	2,200	2,900	3,800	4,800
R100RT (1000cc twin)	900	1,500	2,200	2,900	3,800	4,800
1984						
R65 (650cc twin) (29,454-9yrs)	700	1,000	1,600	2,200	2,900	3,700
R65LS (650cc twin)	700	1,000	1,600	2,200	2,900	3,700
R80G/S (800cc twin)	800	1,400	2,100	2,900	3,600	4,300
R80ST (800cc twin) (5,963-3 yrs)	800	1,400	2,100	2,900	3,600	4,300
R80RT (800cc twin)	800	1,400	2,100	2,800	3,600	4,400
R100 (1000cc twin) (10,111-5 yrs)	900	1,500	2,200	2,900	3,800	4,800
R100CS (1000cc twin) (4,038-5 yrs)	900	1,500	2,200	2,900	3,800	4,800
R100RS (1000cc twin) (33,648-9 yrs)	1,000	2,000	3,000	3,900	4,800	5,500
R100RT (1000cc twin) (18,015-7 yrs)	900	1,500	2,200	2,900	3,800	4,800
1985						
R80G/S (800cc twin)	800	1,400	2,100	2,900	3,600	4,300
R80 (800cc twin)	800	1,400	2,100	2,900	3,600	4,300
R80RT (800cc twin) (7,315-3 yrs)	800	1,400	2,100	2,900	3,600	4,300
K100 (987cc four)	900	1,600	2,300	3,000	3,900	4,900
K100RS (987cc four)	900	1,600	2,300	3,000	3,900	4,900
K100RT (987cc four)	900	1,600	2,300	3,000	3,900	4,900
1986						
R65 (650cc twin)	700	1,100	1,700	2,300	3,000	3,800
K75T (750cc triple)	900	1,500	2,200	2,900	3,700	4,500
K75C (750cc triple)	900	1,500	2,200	2,900	3,700	4,500
K75S (750cc triple)	900	1,500	2,200	2,900	3,700	4,500
R80 (800cc twin)	800	1,400	2,100	2,800	3,600	4,400
R80G/S (800cc twin) (21,864-8 yrs)	800	1,400	2,100	2,900	3,600	4,300
R80RT (800cc twin)	800	1,400	2,100	2,800	3,600	4,400
K100 (1000cc four) (12,871-9 yrs)	900	1,600	2,300	3,000	4,000	5,000
K100RS (1000cc four)	900	1,600	2,300	3,000	4,000	5,000
K100RT (1000cc four)	900	1,600	2,300	3,000	4,000	5,000
1987						
R65 (650cc twin)	800	1,200	1,800	2,400	3,200	4,100

	6	5	4	3	2	1
K75C (750cc triple)	900	1,500	2,200	2,900	3,700	4,500
K75S (750cc triple)	900	1,500	2,200	2,900	3,700	4,500
K75T (750cc triple) (Incl in K75C).	900	1,500	2,200	2,900	3,700	4,500
R80 (800cc twin) (13,815-12 yrs)	900	1,500	2,200	2,900	3,800	4,800
R80RT (800cc twin)	1,000	1,700	2,400	2,900	3,800	4,700
K100RS (1000cc four) (34,804-7 yrs)	900	1,600	2,300	3,000	4,000	5,000
K100RT (1000cc four).	900	1,600	2,300	3,000	4,000	5,000
K100LT (1000cc four)	900	1,600	2,300	3,000	4,000	5,000
1988						
K75C (750cc triple)	900	1,500	2,200	2,800	3,700	4,600
K75 (750cc triple)	900	1,500	2,200	2,800	3,700	4,600
K75S (750cc triple)	1,000	1,700	2,400	2,900	3,800	4,700
R100 GS (1000cc twin)	900	1,600	2,300	3,000	4,000	5,000
R100RS (1000cc twin)	900	1,600	2,300	3,000	4,000	5,000
R100RT (1000cc twin)	900	1,600	2,300	3,000	4,000	5,000
K100RS (1000cc four).	900	1,600	2,300	3,000	4,000	5,000
K100RS ABS Spcl Ed (1000cc four)	1,400	2,000	2,600	3,500	4,700	6,000
K100RT (1000cc four) (22,335-7 yrs) . . .	900	1,600	2,300	3,000	4,000	5,000
K100LT (1000cc four) (14,899-6 yrs)	1,400	2,000	2,600	3,500	4,700	6,000
1989						
K75 (750cc triple)	900	1,500	2,200	2,800	3,700	4,600
R100 GS (1000cc twin)	900	1,600	2,300	3,100	4,100	5,100
R100RS (1000cc twin)	900	1,600	2,300	3,100	4,100	5,100
R100RT (1000cc twin)	900	1,600	2,300	3,100	4,100	5,100
K100RS ABS (1000cc four)	1,400	2,000	3,000	4,000	5,000	6,100
K100LT ABS (1000cc four)	1,400	2,000	3,000	4,100	5,100	6,200
1990						
K75 (750cc triple)	1,000	1,700	2,400	2,900	3,800	4,700
K75S (750cc triple)	1,000	1,700	2,400	2,900	3,800	4,700
K75RT (750cc triple)	1,000	1,700	2,400	2,900	3,800	4,700
R100GS (1000cc twin)	900	1,600	2,300	3,100	4,100	5,100
R100GS Paris-Dakar (1000cc twin)	1,000	1,700	2,400	3,200	4,200	5,200
R100RT (1000cc twin)	900	1,600	2,300	3,100	4,100	5,100
K1 (1000cc four) (6,921-6 yrs)	2,000	3,000	4,200	6,000	7,000	9,000
K100LT ABS (1000cc four)	1,400	2,000	3,000	4,100	5,100	6,200
1991						
K75 (750cc triple)	900	1,500	2,200	2,900	3,800	4,800
K75S (750cc triple)	900	1,500	2,200	2,900	3,800	4,800
K75S ABS (750cc triple)	1,000	1,600	2,300	2,900	3,900	4,900
K75RT (750cc triple)	900	1,500	2,200	2,900	3,800	4,800
K75RT ABS (750cc triple).	1,000	1,600	2,300	2,900	3,900	4,900
R100GS (1000cc twin)	1,000	1,700	2,400	3,200	4,200	5,200
R100GS Paris-Dakar (1000cc twin)	1,200	1,800	2,300	3,300	4,300	5,300
R100 (1000cc twin)	1,200	1,800	2,300	3,300	4,300	5,300
R100RT (1000cc twin)	1,200	1,800	2,300	3,300	4,300	5,300
K100RS (1000cc four).	1,200	1,800	2,300	3,300	4,300	5,300
K100RS ABS (1000cc four)	1,400	2,000	2,600	3,500	4,700	6,000
K1 ABS (1000cc four)	2,100	3,200	4,200	5,200	6,200	7,200
K100LT ABS (1000cc four)	1,400	2,000	3,000	4,100	5,100	6,200
1992						
K75C (750cc triplo) (9,566-6 yrs)	900	1,500	2,200	2,900	3,800	4,800
K75 (750cc triple)	900	1,500	2,200	2,900	3,800	4,800
K75RT ABS (750cc triple).	900	1,600	2,300	3,000	4,000	5,000
K75S (750cc triple)	900	1,500	2,200	2,900	3,800	4,800
K75S ABS (750cc triple)	1,000	1,700	2,400	3,200	4,200	5,200
R100GS (1000cc twin)	1,200	1,800	2,300	3,300	4,300	5,300
R100GS Paris-Dakar (1000cc twin)	1,000	1,700	2,400	3,400	4,400	5,400
R100R (1000cc twin)	1,000	1,700	2,400	3,400	4,400	5,400
R100RS Sport (1000cc twin)	1,300	1,900	2,800	3,800	4,800	5,800

	6	5	4	3	2	1
K100RS ABS (1000cc four) (12,666-4 yrs)	1,100	1,800	2,500	3,500	4,500	5,600
K1 ABS (1000cc four)	2,200	3,400	4,400	5,400	6,400	7,400
R100RT (1000cc twin)	1,400	2,000	3,000	4,100	5,100	6,200
K100LT ABS (1000cc four)	1,900	2,700	3,700	4,700	5,700	6,700
1993						
K75 (750cc triple)	900	1,500	2,200	2,900	3,800	4,800
K75RT ABS (750cc triple)	900	1,600	2,300	3,000	4,000	5,000
K75S (750cc triple)	900	1,500	2,200	2,900	3,800	4,800
K75S ABS (750cc triple)	1,000	1,700	2,400	3,200	4,200	5,200
R100GS (1000cc twin)	1,200	1,800	2,300	3,300	4,300	5,300
R100GS Paris-Dakar (1000cc twin)	1,000	1,700	2,400	3,400	4,400	5,400
R100R (1000cc twin)	1,000	1,700	2,400	3,400	4,400	5,400
R100RS w/fairing (1000cc twin)	1,300	1,900	2,800	3,800	4,800	5,800
K1 ABS (1000cc four)	2,200	3,400	4,400	5,400	6,400	7,400
R100RT (1000cc twin)	1,400	2,000	3,000	4,100	5,100	6,200
K1100RS ABS w/fairing (1100cc four)	2,000	3,000	4,000	5,300	6,300	7,300
K1100LT ABS (1100cc four)	1,600	2,600	3,600	4,800	5,800	7,000
1994						
K75 (750cc triple) (18,485-13 yrs)	900	1,500	2,200	2,900	3,800	4,800
K75RT ABS (750cc triple) (21,264-8 yrs)	900	1,600	2,300	3,000	4,000	5,000
K75A (750cc triple)	300	600	900	2,000	2,900	4,000
K75S (750cc triple) (18,649-12 yrs)	900	1,500	2,200	2,900	3,800	4,800
R100R (1000cc twin) (20,589-6 yrs)	1,000	1,700	2,400	3,400	4,400	5,400
R100GS (1000cc twin) (34,007-12 yrs)	1,000	1,700	2,400	3,400	4,400	5,400
R100GS Paris-Dakar (1000cc twin)	1,000	1,700	2,400	3,400	4,400	5,400
R100RT	1,400	2,000	3,000	4,100	5,100	6,200
K1100LT ABS (1100cc four)	1,600	2,600	3,600	4,800	5,800	7,000
K1100RS ABS w/fairing (1100cc four)	2,000	3,000	4,000	5,300	6,300	7,300
R1100RS	1,300	1,900	2,800	3,800	4,800	5,800
R1100RSL	400	600	1,700	3,500	5,200	7,000
1995						
K75 (750cc triple)	600	1,000	1,900	2,800	3,700	4,600
K75/3 (750cc triple)	600	1,000	1,900	3,000	4,100	5,200
K75/3 ABS (750cc triple)	700	1,200	2,200	3,200	4,200	5,200
K75S (750cc triple)	700	1,200	2,400	3,600	4,800	6,000
K75RT ABS (750cc triple)	700	1,200	2,400	3,600	4,800	6,000
R100GS (1000cc twin)	800	1,500	2,600	3,700	4,800	6,000
R100GS Paris-Dakar (1000cc twin)	700	1,200	2,700	4,000	5,300	6,600
R100GS Paris-Dakar Clas (1000cc twin)	800	1,500	2,800	4,100	5,400	6,700
R100RT (1000cc twin)	700	1,200	2,400	3,600	4,800	6,000
R1100GS (1000cc twin)	700	1,200	2,500	3,800	5,100	6,400
R1100GS ABS (1000cc twin)	800	1,500	3,000	4,300	5,600	6,900
R100M Mystic (1000cc twin)	600	1,300	2,500	3,700	4,900	6,100
R100R Classic (1000cc twin)	600	1,300	2,500	3,700	4,900	6,100
R1100R (1100cc twin)	600	1,100	2,300	3,500	4,700	5,900
R1100RA/S ABS (1100cc twin)	700	1,200	2,400	3,600	4,800	6,000
R1100R ABS (1100cc twin)	700	1,400	2,500	3,600	4,700	5,800
R1100RS ABS Special Edition (1100cc twin)	600	1,300	2,500	3,700	4,900	6,100
R1100RS ABS (1100cc twin)	600	1,300	2,500	3,700	4,900	6,100
R1100RSL ABS Special Edition (1100cc twin)	600	1,300	2,800	4,300	5,800	7,300
R1100RSL ABS (1100cc twin)	600	1,300	2,800	4,300	5,800	7,300
K1100LT ABS (1100cc four)	700	1,400	2,800	4,200	5,600	7,000
K1100RS ABS w/fairing (1100cc four)	600	1,300	2,800	4,300	5,800	7,300
R1100RT (1100cc twin)	600	1,300	2,800	4,300	5,800	7,300
R1100RT Classic Edition (1100cc twin)	700	1,400	2,900	4,400	5,900	7,400

	6	5	4	3	2	1
BRIDGESTONE						
1963						
Bridgestone 7 (48cc single)	300	500	700	1,000	1,300	1,600
1964						
50 Homer (48cc single)	300	500	800	1,000	1,400	1,700
Bridgestone 7 (48cc single)	300	500	700	1,000	1,300	1,600
Bridgestone 90 (88cc single)	400	600	1,000	1,300	1,700	2,100
1965						
50 Sport (48cc single)	300	500	800	1,000	1,400	1,700
50 Homer (48cc single)	300	500	800	1,000	1,400	1,700
60 Sport (60cc single)	400	600	900	1,100	1,500	1,900
90 Deluxe (88cc single)	400	600	900	1,200	1,600	2,000
90 Mountain (88cc single)	400	600	900	1,200	1,600	2,000
90 Racer (88cc single)	400	600	900	1,200	1,600	2,000
90 Sport (88cc single)	400	600	1,000	1,300	1,700	2,100
1966						
50 Sport (48cc single)	300	500	800	1,000	1,400	1,700
50 Homer (48cc single)	300	500	800	1,000	1,400	1,700
60 Sport (60cc single)	400	600	900	1,100	1,500	1,900
90 Deluxe (88cc single)	400	600	900	1,200	1,600	2,000
90 Mountain (88cc single)	400	600	900	1,200	1,600	2,000
90 Racer (88cc single)	400	600	900	1,200	1,600	2,000
90 Sport (88cc single)	400	600	1,000	1,300	1,700	2,100
DT 175 (177cc dual twin)	600	900	1,300	1,700	2,300	2,900
1967						
50 Sport (48cc single)	300	500	800	1,000	1,400	1,700
50 Homer (48cc single)	300	500	800	1,000	1,400	1,700
60 Sport (60cc single)	400	600	900	1,100	1,500	1,900
90 Deluxe (88cc single)	400	600	900	1,200	1,600	2,000
90 Mountain (88cc single)	400	600	900	1,200	1,600	2,000
90 Racer (88cc single)	400	700	1,000	1,300	1,800	2,200
90 Sport (88cc single)	400	600	900	1,200	1,600	2,000
90 Trail (88cc single)	400	600	1,000	1,300	1,700	2,100
DT 175 (177cc dual twin)	600	900	1,300	1,700	2,300	2,900
Hurricane Scrambler (177 cc dual twin) . . .	600	900	1,300	1,700	2,300	2,900
1968						
50 Sport (48cc single)	300	500	800	1,000	1,400	1,700
50 Step-thru (48cc single)	300	500	800	1,000	1,400	1,700
60 Sport (60cc single)	400	500	800	1,100	1,400	1,800
90 Deluxe (88cc single)	400	600	900	1,200	1,600	2,000
90 Mountain (88cc single)	400	600	900	1,200	1,600	2,000
90 Racer (88cc single)	400	700	1,000	1,300	1,800	2,200
90 Sport (88cc single)	400	600	1,000	1,300	1,700	2,100
90 Trail (88cc single)	400	600	1,000	1,300	1,700	2,100
DT 175 (177cc dual twin)	600	900	1,300	1,700	2,300	2,900
Hurricane Scrambler (177 cc dual twin) . . .	600	900	1,300	1,700	2,300	2,900
350 GTR (345cc twin)	800	1,200	1,800	2,300	3,100	3,900
1969						
60 Sport (60cc single)	400	600	900	1,100	1,500	1,900
SR 90 (90cc single)	400	700	1,000	1,300	1,800	2,200
SR 100 (100cc single)	900	1,400	2,000	2,700	3,600	4,500
100 GP (100cc single)	500	800	1,100	1,500	2,000	2,500
100 TMX (100cc single)	500	800	1,200	1,600	2,200	2,700
SR 175 (175cc twin)	1,400	2,100	3,200	4,200	5,600	7,000
350 GTR (345cc twin)	800	1,200	1,800	2,300	3,100	3,900
350 GTO (345cc twin)	1,000	1,500	2,300	3,000	4,000	5,000
1970						
60 Sport (60cc single)	400	600	900	1,100	1,500	1,900
SR 90 (90cc single)	400	700	1,000	1,300	1,800	2,200

	6	5	4	3	2	1
SR 100 (100cc single)	900	1,400	2,000	2,700	3,600	4,500
100 Sport (100cc single)	600	800	1,200	1,600	2,200	2,700
350 GTR (345cc twin)	800	1,200	1,800	2,300	3,100	3,900
350 GTO (345cc twin)	1,000	1,500	2,300	3,000	4,000	5,000
1971						
SR 90 (90cc single)	400	700	1,000	1,300	1,800	2,200
SR 100 (100cc single)	900	1,400	2,000	2,700	3,600	4,500
350 GTR (345cc twin)	800	1,200	1,800	2,300	3,100	3,900
350 GTO (345cc twin)	1,000	1,500	2,300	3,000	4,000	5,000

BROUGH SUPERIOR

	6	5	4	3	2	1
1921						
Mk. I (side-valve J.A.P. twin, 976cc)	8,000	12,000	18,000	24,000	32,000	40,000
1922						
Mk. I (side-valve J.A.P. twin, 976cc)	8,000	12,000	18,000	24,000	32,000	40,000
SS80 (side valve J.A.P. twin, 976cc)	8,000	12,000	18,000	24,000	32,000	40,000
1923						
Mk. I (side-valve J.A.P. twin, 976cc)	8,000	12,000	18,000	24,000	32,000	40,000
SS80 (side valve J.A.P. twin, 976cc)	9,000	13,000	19,000	25,000	34,000	43,000
1924						
Mk. I (side-valve J.A.P. twin, 976cc)	8,000	12,000	18,000	24,000	32,000	40,000
SS80 (side valve J.A.P. twin, 976cc)	9,000	13,000	19,000	25,000	34,000	43,000
SS100 (OHV J.A.P. twin, 984cc)	31,000	50,000	75,000	100K	150K	200K
1925						
SS80 (side valve J.A.P. twin, 976cc)	9,000	14,000	20,000	27,000	36,000	45,000
SS100 (OHV J.A.P. twin, 984cc)	31,000	50,000	75,000	100K	150K	200K
1926						
SS80 (side valve J.A.P. twin, 976cc)	9,000	14,000	20,000	27,000	36,000	45,000
SS100 (OHV J.A.P. twin, 984cc)	31,000	50,000	75,000	100K	150K	200K
Model 680 (OHV J.A.P. twin, 676cc)	9,000	14,000	20,000	27,000	36,000	45,000
1927						
SS80 (side valve J.A.P. twin, 976cc)	9,000	14,000	20,000	27,000	36,000	45,000
SS100 (OHV J.A.P. twin, 984cc)	31,000	50,000	75,000	100K	150K	200K
Model 680 (OHV J.A.P. twin, 676cc)	9,000	14,000	20,000	27,000	36,000	45,000
1928						
SS80 (side valve J.A.P. twin, 976cc)	9,000	14,000	20,000	27,000	36,000	45,000
SS100 (OHV J.A.P. twin, 984cc)	31,000	50,000	75,000	100K	150K	200K
Model 680 (OHV J.A.P. twin, 676cc)	9,000	14,000	20,000	27,000	36,000	45,000
1929						
SS80 (side valve J.A.P. twin, 976cc)	9,000	14,000	20,000	27,000	36,000	45,000
SS100 (OHV J.A.P. twin, 984cc)	31,000	50,000	75,000	100K	150K	200K
Model 680 (OHV J.A.P. twin, 676cc)	9,000	14,000	20,000	27,000	36,000	45,000
1930						
SS80 (side valve J.A.P. twin, 976cc)	9,000	14,000	20,000	27,000	36,000	45,000
SS100 (OHV J.A.P. twin, 984cc)	29,000	50,000	75,000	100K	150K	200K
Model 680 (OHV J.A.P. twin, 676cc)	9,000	14,000	20,000	27,000	36,000	45,000
1931						
SS80 (side valve J.A.P. twin, 976cc)	9,000	14,000	20,000	27,000	36,000	45,000
SS100 (OHV J.A.P. twin, 984cc)	29,000	44,000	65,000	87,000	120K	150K
Model 680 (OHV J.A.P. twin, 676cc)	9,000	13,500	20,250	30,000	40,000	50,000
1932						
SS80 (side valve J.A.P. twin, 976cc)	9,000	14,000	20,000	27,000	36,000	45,000
SS100 (OHV J.A.P. twin, 984cc)	29,000	50,000	75,000	100K	150K	200K
Model 680 (OHV J.A.P. twin, 676cc)	9,000	13,500	20,250	27,000	36,000	45,000
1933						
SS80 (side valve J.A.P. twin, 976cc)	9,000	14,000	20,000	27,000	36,000	45,000
SS100 (OHV J.A.P. twin, 984cc)	29,000	50,000	75,000	100K	150K	200K
Model 680 (OHV J.A.P. twin, 676cc)	9,000	13,500	20,250	27,000	36,000	45,000
Model 1150 (side-valve J.A.P. twin, 1150cc)	7,000	10,000	15,000	23,000	32,000	40,000

	6	5	4	3	2	1
1934						
SS80 (side valve J.A.P. twin, 976cc) (630 from 1921-34)	9,000	14,000	20,000	27,000	36,000	45,000
SS100(OHV J.A.P. twin, 984cc).	29,000	50,000	75,000	100K	150K	200K
Model 680 (OHV J.A.P. twin, 676cc)	9,000	13,500	20,250	27,000	36,000	45,000
Model 1150 (side-valve J.A.P. twin, 1150cc)	7,000	10,000	15,000	20,000	27,000	35,000
1935						
SS80 (side valve Matchless twin, 998cc) . .	12,000	18,000	27,000	36,000	48,000	60,000
SS100(OHV J.A.P. twin, 984cc).	29,000	50,000	75,000	100K	150K	200K
Model 680 (OHV J.A.P. twin, 676cc)	9,000	14,000	20,000	27,000	36,000	45,000
Model 1150 (side-valve J.A.P. twin, 1150cc)	7,000	10,000	15,000	20,000	27,000	35,000
1936						
SS80 (side valve Matchless twin, 998cc) . .	12,000	18,000	27,000	36,000	48,000	60,000
SS100 (OHV Matchless twin, 998cc)	25,000	50,000	75,000	100K	150K	200K
Model 1150 (side-valve J.A.P. twin, 1150cc)	7,000	10,000	15,000	20,000	27,000	35,000
1937						
SS80 (side valve Matchless twin, 998cc) . .	12,000	18,000	27,000	36,000	48,000	60,000
SS100 (OHV Matchless twin, 998cc)	25,000	50,000	75,000	100K	150K	200K
Model 1150 (side-valve J.A.P. twin, 1150cc)	7,000	10,000	15,000	20,000	27,000	35,000
1938						
SS80 (side valve Matchless twin, 998cc) . .	12,000	18,000	27,000	36,000	48,000	60,000
SS100 (OHV Matchless twin, 998cc)	25,000	50,000	75,000	100K	150K	200K
Model 1150 (side-valve J.A.P. twin, 1150cc)	6,000	9,000	14,000	18,000	24,000	30,000
1939						
SS80 (side valve Matchless twin, 998cc) (460 from 1935-39)	12,000	18,000	27,000	36,000	48,000	60,000
SS100 (OHV Matchless twin, 998cc)	25,000	50,000	75,000	100K	150K	200K
Model 1150 (side-valve J.A.P. twin, 1150cc)	8,000	11,000	17,000	23,000	31,000	40,000
BSA						
1916						
Model K	1,500	3,000	6,000	9,000	12,000	15,000
1921						
Model H 557.	1,500	2,500	5,000	8,000	11,000	14,000
1924						
Single Valve.	3,000	6,000	9,000	12,000	15,000	18,000
1930						
A-2 (150cc single).	1,100	1,700	2,500	3,400	4,500	5,600
B-3 (250cc single).	1,200	1,700	2,600	3,500	4,600	5,800
B-4 (250cc single).	1,200	1,700	2,600	3,500	4,600	5,800
L-11 (350cc single).	1,200	1,800	2,700	3,600	4,800	6,000
L-5 (350cc single).	1,200	1,800	2,700	3,600	4,800	6,000
L-6 (350cc single).	1,200	1,800	2,700	3,600	4,800	6,000
S-12 (500cc single).	1,200	1,800	2,800	3,700	4,900	6,100
S-13 Deluxe (500cc single)	1,200	1,900	2,800	3,700	5,000	6,200
S-18 Light (500cc single)	1,300	1,900	2,900	3,800	5,100	6,400
S-19 Light (500cc single)	1,300	1,900	2,900	3,800	5,100	6,400
S-7 (500cc single).	1,300	1,900	2,900	3,800	5,100	6,400
S-9 Deluxe (500cc single)	1,300	1,900	2,900	3,800	5,100	6,400
H-10 Deluxe (550cc single)	1,400	2,000	3,100	4,100	5,400	6,800
H-8 (550cc single)	1,400	2,000	3,100	4,100	5,400	6,800
E-14 (750cc twin)	1,400	2,100	3,200	4,200	5,600	7,000
G-15 (1000cc twin)	2,000	3,000	4,500	6,000	8,000	10,000
G-16 World Tour (1000cc twin)	2,000	3,000	4,500	6,000	8,000	10,000
1931						
B-1 (250cc single).	1,200	1,700	2,600	3,500	4,600	5,800
B-2 (250cc single).	1,200	1,700	2,600	3,500	4,600	5,800
B-3 (250cc single).	1,200	1,800	2,700	3,600	4,800	6,000
L-4 (350cc single).	1,200	1,800	2,800	3,700	4,900	6,100
L-5 Deluxe (350cc single)	1,200	1,800	2,800	3,700	4,900	6,100

	6	5	4	3	2	1
L-6 Deluxe (350cc single)	1,200	1,900	2,800	3,700	5,000	6,200
S-10 Deluxe (500cc single)	1,200	1,900	2,800	3,700	5,000	6,200
S-7 (500cc single)	1,200	1,900	2,800	3,700	5,000	6,200
S-9 (500cc single)	1,200	1,900	2,800	3,700	5,000	6,200
H-8 (550cc single)	1,400	2,000	3,100	4,100	5,400	6,800
E-11 (750cc twin, 3-gal.tank)	1,400	2,100	3,200	4,200	5,600	7,000
1932						
B-1 (250cc single)	1,200	1,700	2,600	3,500	4,600	5,800
L-2 (350cc single)	1,300	2,000	2,900	3,900	5,200	6,500
L-3 (350cc single)	1,300	2,000	2,900	3,900	5,200	6,500
L-4 Deluxe (350cc single)	1,300	2,000	2,900	3,900	5,200	6,500
L-5 Blue Star (350cc single)	1,500	2,200	3,300	4,400	5,900	7,400
L-5 Deluxe (350cc single)	1,300	2,000	2,900	3,900	5,200	6,500
S-8 Deluxe (500cc single)	1,200	1,900	2,800	3,700	5,000	6,200
W-6 (500cc single)	1,200	1,900	2,800	3,700	5,000	6,200
W-7 Blue Star (500cc single)	1,900	2,900	4,300	5,700	7,600	9,500
H-9 Deluxe (550cc single)	1,400	2,000	3,100	4,100	5,400	6,800
G-10 (1000cc twin)	2,000	3,000	4,500	6,000	8,000	10,000
1933						
B-1 (250cc single)	1,200	1,800	2,700	3,600	4,800	6,000
B-2 S.P. (250cc single)	1,200	1,800	2,700	3,600	4,800	6,000
B-3 Blue Star Jr. (250cc single)	1,200	1,800	2,700	3,600	4,800	6,000
R-4 (350cc single)	1,300	2,000	3,000	4,000	5,300	6,600
R-5 Blue Star (350cc single)	1,500	2,200	3,300	4,400	5,900	7,400
W-6 (500cc single)	1,200	1,900	2,800	3,700	5,000	6,200
W-6 Post Office (500cc single)	1,200	1,900	2,800	3,700	5,000	6,200
W-7 (500cc single)	1,200	1,900	2,800	3,700	5,000	6,200
W-8 Blue Star (500cc single)	1,900	2,900	4,300	5,700	7,600	9,500
W-9 Special (500cc single)	1,300	2,000	2,900	3,900	5,200	6,500
M-10 (600cc single)	1,300	2,000	2,900	3,900	5,200	6,500
M-11 (600cc single)	1,300	2,000	2,900	3,900	5,200	6,500
G-13 Light (1000cc twin)	2,000	3,000	4,500	6,000	8,000	10,000
G-13 World Tour (1000cc twin)	2,200	3,300	5,000	6,600	8,800	11,000
G-14 War Office (1000cc twin)	2,200	3,300	5,000	6,600	8,800	11,000
1934						
X-0 (150cc single)	**1,500**	**2,500**	**4,000**	**5,000**	**6,000**	**7,000**
B-1 (250cc single)	1,200	1,800	2,700	3,600	4,800	6,000
B-17 Sports (250cc single)	1,200	1,800	2,700	3,600	4,800	6,000
B-2 (250cc single)	1,200	1,800	2,700	3,600	4,800	6,000
B-3 Blue Star Jr. (250cc single)	1,200	1,800	2,700	3,600	4,800	6,000
R-4 (350cc single)	1,300	2,000	3,000	4,000	5,300	6,600
R-5 Blue Star (350cc single)	1,500	2,300	3,400	4,500	6,000	7,500
R-6 Special (350cc single)	1,300	2,000	3,000	4,000	5,300	6,600
W-7 (500cc single)	1,200	1,800	2,700	3,600	4,800	6,000
W-8 (500cc single)	1,300	2,000	3,000	4,000	5,300	6,600
W-9 Blue Star (500cc single)	1,900	2,900	4,300	5,700	7,600	9,500
W-10 Special (500cc single)	1,300	2,000	2,900	3,900	5,200	6,500
J-11 (500cc single)	1,900	2,900	4,300	5,700	7,600	9,500
M-12 (600cc single)	1,300	2,000	2,900	3,900	5,200	6,500
M-13 (600cc single)	1,300	2,000	2,900	3,900	5,200	6,500
G-14 World Tour (1000cc twin)	2,200	3,300	5,000	6,600	8,800	11,000
1935						
X-0 (150cc single)	**1,500**	**2,500**	**4,000**	**5,000**	**6,000**	**7,000**
B-1 (250cc single)	1,200	1,800	2,700	3,600	4,800	6,000
B-2 (250cc single)	1,200	1,800	2,700	3,600	4,800	6,000
B-3 Deluxe (250cc single)	1,200	1,800	2,700	3,600	4,800	6,000
R-4 Deluxe (350cc single)	1,300	2,000	2,900	3,900	5,200	6,500
R-5 Blue Star (350cc single)	1,400	2,100	3,200	4,200	5,600	7,000
R-17 Twin Port (350cc single)	1,300	2,000	2,900	3,900	5,200	6,500

	6	5	4	3	2	1
W-6 (500cc single)	1,300	2,000	2,900	3,900	5,200	6,500
J-12 (500cc single)	1,900	2,900	4,300	5,700	7,600	9,500
W-7 (500cc single)	1,300	2,000	2,900	3,900	5,200	6,500
W-8 Blue Star (500cc single)	1,900	2,900	4,300	5,700	7,600	9,500
W-9 Speical (500cc single)	1,300	2,000	2,900	3,900	5,200	6,500
M-10 (600cc single)	1,300	2,000	2,900	3,900	5,200	6,500
J-15 War Office (750cc twin)	1,800	2,700	4,100	5,400	7,200	9,000
G-14 (1000cc twin)	2,200	3,300	5,000	6,600	8,800	11,000
1936						
X-0 (150cc single)	**1,500**	**2,500**	**4,000**	**5,000**	**6,000**	**7,000**
B-1 (250cc single)	1,200	1,800	2,700	3,600	4,800	6,000
B-18 Light Deluxe (250cc single)	1,200	1,800	2,700	3,600	4,800	6,000
B-2 (250cc single)	1,200	1,800	2,700	3,600	4,800	6,000
B-3 Deluxe (250cc single)	1,200	1,800	2,700	3,600	4,800	6,000
R-4 Deluxe (350cc single)	1,300	2,000	2,900	3,900	5,200	6,500
R-17 (350cc single)	1,300	2,000	2,900	3,900	5,200	6,500
R-19 Comp. (350cc single)	1,600	2,400	3,600	4,800	6,400	8,000
R-20 New Blue Star (350cc single)	1,400	2,100	3,200	4,200	5,600	7,000
R-5 Empire Star (350cc single)	1,500	2,300	3,400	4,500	6,000	7,500
Q21 New Blue Star (500cc single)	2,200	3,300	5,000	6,600	8,800	11,000
Q7 (500cc single)	1,600	2,400	3,600	4,800	6,400	8,000
Q8 Empire Star (500cc single)	2,000	3,000	4,500	6,000	8,000	10,000
J-12 (500cc single)	2,200	3,300	5,000	6,600	8,800	11,000
W-6 (500cc single)	1,200	1,800	2,700	3,600	4,800	6,000
M-10 (600cc single)	1,300	2,000	3,000	4,000	5,400	6,700
Y-13 (750cc twin)	2,400	3,600	5,400	7,200	9,600	12,000
G-14 (1000cc twin)	2,200	3,300	5,000	6,600	8,800	11,000
1937						
B20 Tourer (250cc single)	1,200	1,800	2,700	3,600	4,800	6,000
B21 Sports (250cc single)	1,200	1,800	2,700	3,600	4,800	6,000
B22 Empire star (250cc single)	1,300	2,000	2,900	3,900	5,200	6,500
B23 Tourer (350cc single)	1,200	1,800	2,700	3,600	4,800	6,000
B24 Empire Star (350cc single)	1,500	2,300	3,400	4,500	6,000	7,500
B25 Comp,. (350cc single)	1,600	2,400	3,600	4,800	6,400	8,000
B26 Sports (350cc single)	1,400	2,200	3,200	4,300	5,800	7,200
M19 Deluxe (350cc single)	1,200	1,800	2,700	3,600	4,800	6,000
M20 Tourer (500cc single)	1,100	1,700	2,500	3,300	4,400	5,500
M22 Sports (500cc single)	1,200	1,800	2,800	3,700	4,900	6,100
M23 Empire Star (500cc single)	1,800	2,700	4,050	5,400	7,200	9,000
M21 Tourer (600cc Single)	1,200	1,800	3,000	4,000	6,000	8,000
Y13 (750cc twin)	2,400	3,600	5,400	7,200	9,600	12,000
G14 (1000cc twin)	2,200	3,300	5,000	6,600	8,800	11,000
1938						
B20 Tourer (250cc single)	1,200	1,800	2,700	3,600	4,800	6,000
B21 Sports (250cc single)	1,200	1,800	2,700	3,600	4,800	6,000
B22 Empire star (250cc single)	1,300	2,000	2,900	3,900	5,200	6,500
C10 (250cc single)	900	1,400	2,000	2,700	3,600	4,500
C11 (250cc single)	900	1,400	2,000	2,700	3,600	4,500
B23 Tourer (350cc single)	1,300	2,000	2,900	3,900	5,200	6,500
B24 Empire Star (350cc single)	1,600	2,400	3,600	4,700	6,300	7,900
B25 Comp,. (350cc single)	1,700	2,600	3,800	5,100	6,800	8,500
B26 Sports (350cc single)	1,400	2,200	3,200	4,300	5,800	7,200
M19 Deluxe (350cc single)	1,100	1,700	2,500	3,300	4,400	5,500
M22 Sports (500cc single)	1,200	1,800	2,800	3,700	4,900	6,100
M23 Empire Star (500cc single)	1,800	2,700	5,000	7,000	9,000	11,000
M24 Gold Star (500cc single)	2,000	3,000	4,500	6,000	8,000	10,000
M21 Tourer (600cc Single)	1,200	1,700	2,600	3,500	4,600	5,800
Y13 (750cc twin)	2,200	3,300	5,000	6,600	8,800	11,000
G14 (1000cc twin)	2,200	3,300	5,000	6,600	8,800	11,000

	6	5	4	3	2	1
B31 Plunger (350cc single)	1,000	1,500	**2,500**	**4,000**	**5,500**	**7,000**
B32 Comp (350cc single)	1,200	1,700	2,600	3,500	4,600	5,800
B32 Comp Plunger (350cc single)	1,200	1,700	2,600	3,500	4,600	5,800
B32GS Gold Star (350cc single)	2,200	3,300	5,000	6,600	8,800	11,000
B32GS Gold Star Plunger (350cc single) . .	2,200	3,300	5,000	6,600	8,800	11,000
A7 (500cc twin)	2,000	3,000	4,500	6,000	8,000	10,000
A7Plunger (500cc twin)	2,000	3,000	4,500	6,000	8,000	10,000
A7S Star Plunger (500cc twin)	2,000	3,000	4,500	6,000	8,000	10,000
B33 (500cc single)	2,000	3,000	4,500	6,000	8,000	10,000
B33 Plunger (500cc single)	2,000	3,000	4,500	6,000	8,000	10,000
B34 Comp. (500cc single).	1,200	2,000	3,500	5,000	6,500	8,000
B34 Comp Plunger (500cc single).	1,200	2,000	3,500	5,000	6,500	8,000
B34GS Gold Star (500cc single)	3,400	5,100	7,700	10,000	14,000	17,000
B34GS Gold Star Plunger (500cc single) . .	3,400	5,100	7,700	10,000	14,000	17,000
M20 (500cc single)	1,000	1,400	2,200	2,900	3,800	4,800
M20 Plunger (500cc single)	1,000	1,400	2,200	2,900	3,800	4,800
M33 (500cc single)	1,000	1,500	2,300	3,100	4,100	5,100
M33 Plunger (500cc single)	1,000	1,500	2,300	3,100	4,100	5,100
M21 (600cc single)	1,000	1,500	2,200	2,900	3,900	4,900
M21 Plunger (600cc single)	1,000	1,500	2,200	2,900	3,900	4,900
A10 Golden Flash (650cc twin)	2,000	3,000	4,500	6,000	8,000	10,000
A10 Golden Flash Plunger (650cc twin) . . .	2,000	3,000	4,500	6,000	8,000	10,000
1952						
D1 Bantam w/WIPAC (125cc single)	600	900	1,300	1,700	2,300	2,900
D1 Bantam w/Lucas (125cc single)	600	900	1,300	1,700	2,300	2,900
D1 Bantam Plunger w/WIPAC (125cc single)	600	900	1,300	1,700	2,300	2,900
D1 Bantam Plunger w/Lucas (125cc single).	600	900	1,300	1,700	2,300	2,900
D1 Bantam Plunger GPO (125cc single) . .	600	900	1,400	1,800	2,400	3,000
C10 (250cc single)	600	900	1,400	1,800	2,400	3,000
C10 Plunger (250cc single)	600	900	1,400	1,800	2,400	3,000
C11 (250cc single)	600	900	1,400	1,800	2,400	3,000
C11 Plunger (250cc single)	600	900	1,400	1,800	2,400	3,000
B31 (350cc single)	1,000	1,500	2,200	2,900	3,900	4,900
B31 Plunger (350cc single)	1,000	1,500	**2,500**	**4,000**	**5,500**	**7,000**
B32 Comp (350cc single)	1,200	1,700	2,600	3,500	4,600	5,800
B32 Comp Plunger (350cc single).	1,200	1,700	2,600	3,500	4,600	5,800
B32GS Gold Star (350cc single)	2,200	3,300	5,000	6,600	8,800	11,000
B32GS Gold Star Plunger (350cc single) . .	2,200	3,300	5,000	6,600	8,800	11,000
B32GS Gold Star Clubman (350cc single) .	2,700	4,100	6,100	8,100	11,000	14,000
B32GS Gold Star Clubman Plunger (350cc single)	2,700	4,100	6,100	8,100	11,000	14,000
A7 (500cc twin)	2,000	3,000	4,500	6,000	8,000	10,000
A7Plunger (500cc twin)	2,000	3,000	4,500	6,000	8,000	10,000
A7S Star Plunger (500cc twin)	2,000	3,000	4,500	6,000	8,000	10,000
B33 (500cc single)	2,000	3,000	4,500	6,000	8,000	10,000
B33 Plunger (500cc single)	2,000	3,000	4,500	6,000	8,000	10,000
B34 Comp. (500cc single).	1,200	2,000	4,000	6,000	7,500	9,000
B34 Comp Plunger (500cc single).	1,200	2,000	4,000	6,000	7,500	9,000
B34GS Gold Star (500cc single)	3,400	5,100	7,700	10,000	14,000	17,000
B34GS Gold Star Plunger (500cc single) . .	3,400	5,100	7,700	10,000	14,000	17,000
M20 (500cc single)	1,000	1,500	2,300	3,100	4,100	5,100
M20 Plunger (500cc single)	1,000	1,400	2,200	2,900	3,800	4,800
M33 (500cc single)	1,000	1,500	2,300	3,000	4,000	5,000
M33 Plunger (500cc single)	1,000	1,500	2,300	3,000	4,000	5,000
M21 (600cc single)	1,000	1,500	2,200	2,900	3,900	4,900
M21 Plunger (600cc single)	1,000	1,500	2,200	2,900	3,900	4,900
A10 Golden Flash (650cc twin)	2,000	3,000	4,500	6,000	8,000	10,000
A10 Golden Flash Plunger (650cc twin) . . .	2,000	3,000	4,500	6,000	8,000	10,000

	6	5	4	3	2	1
1953						
D1 Bantam w/WIPAC (125cc single)	600	900	1,300	1,700	2,300	2,900
D1 Bantam w/Lucas (125cc single)	600	900	1,300	1,700	2,300	2,900
D1 Bantam Plunger w/WIPAC (125cc single)	600	900	1,300	1,700	2,300	2,900
D1 Bantam Plunger w/Lucas (125cc single). .	600	900	1,300	1,700	2,300	2,900
D1 Bantam Plunger GPO (125cc single)	600	900	1,400	1,800	2,400	3,000
C10 (250cc single)	600	800	1,200	1,600	2,200	2,700
C10 Plunger (250cc single)	600	800	1,200	1,600	2,200	2,700
C11 (250cc single)	600	800	1,200	1,600	2,200	2,700
C11 Plunger (250cc single)	600	800	1,200	1,600	2,200	2,700
B31 (350cc single)	1,000	1,400	1,800	2,900	3,800	4,800
B31 Plunger (350cc single)	1,000	1,400	**2,500**	**4,000**	**5,500**	**7,000**
B32 Comp (350cc single)	1,200	1,700	2,600	3,500	4,600	5,800
B32 Comp Plunger (350cc single).	1,200	1,700	2,600	3,500	4,600	5,800
B32GS Gold Star (350cc single)	2,600	3,900	5,900	7,800	10,000	13,000
B32GS Gold Star Plunger (350cc single) . .	2,600	3,900	5,900	7,800	10,000	13,000
A7 (500cc twin)	2,000	3,000	4,500	6,000	8,000	10,000
A7 Plunger (500cc twin)	2,000	3,000	4,500	6,000	8,000	10,000
A7S Star Plunger (500cc twin)	2,000	3,000	4,500	6,000	8,000	10,000
B33 (500cc single)	2,000	3,000	4,500	6,000	8,000	10,000
B33 Plunger (500cc single)	2,000	3,000	4,500	6,000	8,000	10,000
B34 Comp. (500cc single).	1,200	2,000	3,500	5,000	6,500	8,000
B34 Comp Plunger (500cc single).	1,200	2,000	3,500	5,000	6,500	8,000
B34GS Gold Star (500cc single)	3,600	5,400	8,100	11,000	14,000	18,000
B34GS Gold Star Plunger (500cc single) . .	3,600	5,400	8,100	11,000	14,000	18,000
M20 (500cc single)	1,000	1,600	2,300	3,100	4,200	5,200
M20 Plunger (500cc single)	1,000	1,400	2,100	2,800	3,800	4,700
M33 (500cc single)	1,000	1,500	2,300	3,000	4,000	5,000
M33 Plunger (500cc single)	1,000	1,500	2,300	3,000	4,000	5,000
M21 (600cc single)	1,000	1,500	2,200	2,900	3,900	4,900
M21 Plunger (600cc single)	1,000	1,500	2,200	2,900	3,900	4,900
A10 Golden Flash (650cc twin)	2,000	3,000	4,500	6,000	8,000	10,000
A10 Golden Flash Plunger (650cc twin) . .	2,000	3,000	4,500	6,000	8,000	10,000
A10SF Super Flash Plunger (650cc twin) . .	1,100	2,000	3,500	6,000	9,000	12,000
1954						
D1 Bantam w/direct elec. (125cc single) . .	600	900	1,300	1,700	2,300	2,900
D1 Bantam w/batt. (125cc single)	600	900	1,300	1,700	2,300	2,900
D1 Bantam Plunger w/direc elec (125cc single)	600	900	1,300	1,700	2,300	2,900
D1 Bantam Plunger w/batt. (125cc single) .	600	900	1,300	1,700	2,300	2,900
D1 Bantam Comp. Plunger (125cc single) .	600	900	1,400	1,800	2,400	3,000
D1 Bantam Plunger GPO (125cc single) . .	600	900	1,300	1,700	2,300	2,900
D3 Bantam w/direct elec. (153cc single) . .	600	900	1,300	1,700	2,300	2,900
D3 Bantam w/batt. (153cc single)	600	900	1,300	1,700	2,300	2,900
D3 Bantam Plunger w/direct elec. (150cc single)	600	900	1,300	1,700	2,300	2,900
D3 Bantam Plunger w/batt (150cc single). .	600	900	1,300	1,700	2,300	2,900
D3 Bantam Comp. Plunger (150cc single). .	600	900	1,350	1,800	2,400	3,000
C10L (250cc single).	600	800	1,400	2,100	2,800	3,500
C11G (250cc single)	600	800	1,400	2,100	2,800	3,500
C11G Plunger (250cc single)	600	800	1,400	2,100	2,800	3,500
C11G Rigid (250cc single)	600	800	1,400	2,100	2,800	3,500
B31 (350cc single)	1,000	1,400	2,100	2,800	3,800	4,700
B31 Plunger (350cc single)	1,000	1,400	**2,500**	**4,000**	**5,500**	**7,000**
B32 Comp (350cc single)	1,200	1,800	2,700	3,500	4,700	5,900
B32GS Gold Star (350cc single)	2,600	3,900	5,900	7,800	10,000	13,000
B32GS Gold Star New Clubman (350cc single)	2,600	3,900	5,900	7,800	10,000	13,000

	6	5	4	3	2	1
A7Plunger (500cc twin)	2,000	3,000	4,500	6,000	8,000	10,000
A7 (500cc single)	2,000	3,000	4,500	6,000	8,000	10,000
A7S Star Plunger (500cc twin)	2,000	3,000	4,500	6,000	8,000	10,000
A7SS Shooting Star (500cc twin)	2,000	3,000	4,500	6,000	8,000	10,000
B33 (500cc single)	2,000	3,000	4,500	6,000	8,000	10,000
B33 Plunger (500cc single)	2,000	3,000	4,500	6,000	8,000	10,000
B34 Comp. (500cc single)	1,200	2,000	3,500	5,000	6,500	8,000
B34GS Gold Star (500cc single)	3,600	5,400	8,100	11,000	14,000	18,000
B34GS Gold Star New Clubman (500cc single)	3,600	5,400	8,100	11,000	14,000	18,000
B34GS Gold Star Daytona (500cc single) . .	3,600	5,400	8,100	11,000	14,000	18,000
M20 (500cc single)	900	1,400	2,100	2,800	3,800	4,700
M20 Plunger (500cc single)	900	1,400	2,100	2,800	3,800	4,700
M33 (500cc single)	900	1,400	2,200	2,900	3,800	4,800
M33 Plunger (500cc single)	900	1,400	2,200	2,900	3,800	4,800
M21 (600cc single)	900	1,400	2,100	2,800	3,700	4,600
M21 Plunger (600cc single)	900	1,400	2,100	2,800	3,700	4,600
A10 Golden Flash Plunger (650cc twin) . . .	2,000	3,000	4,500	6,000	8,000	10,000
A10SF Super Flash Plunger (650cc twin) . .	2,000	3,000	4,500	6,000	8,000	10,000
A10SF Super Flash (650cc twin)	1,100	2,000	3,500	6,000	9,000	12,000
A10R Road Rocket (650cc twin)	2,000	3,000	4,500	6,000	8,000	10,000
1955						
D1 Bantam w/direct elec. (125cc single) . .	600	800	1,300	1,700	2,200	2,800
D1 Bantam w/batt. (125cc single)	600	800	1,300	1,700	2,200	2,800
D3 Bantam w/direct elec. (153cc single) . .	600	800	1,300	1,700	2,200	2,800
D3 Bantam w/batt. (153cc single)	600	800	1,300	1,700	2,200	2,800
C10L (250cc single)	600	800	1,400	2,100	2,800	3,500
C11G (250cc single)	600	800	1,400	2,100	2,800	3,500
B31 (350cc single)	900	1,400	2,500	4,000	5,500	7,000
B32 Comp (350cc single)	1,400	2,000	3,100	4,100	5,400	6,800
B32GS Gold Star (350cc single)	2,600	3,900	5,900	7,800	10,000	13,000
B32GS Gold Star Clubman (350cc single) .	2,600	3,900	5,900	7,800	10,000	13,000
A7 (500cc single)	2,000	3,000	4,500	6,000	8,000	10,000
A7SS Shooting Star (500cc twin)	2,000	3,000	4,500	6,000	8,000	10,000
B33 (500cc single)	2,000	3,000	4,500	6,000	8,000	10,000
B34 Comp. (500cc single)	1,200	2,000	3,500	5,000	6,500	8,000
B34GS Gold Star (500cc single)	3,600	5,400	8,100	11,000	14,000	18,000
B34GS Gold Star New Clubman (500cc single)	3,600	5,400	8,100	11,000	14,000	18,000
M20 (500cc single)	900	1,400	2,100	2,800	3,800	4,700
M20 Plunger (500cc single)	900	1,400	2,100	2,800	3,800	4,700
M33 (500cc single)	900	1,400	2,100	2,800	3,800	4,700
M33 Plunger (500cc single)	900	1,400	2,100	2,800	3,800	4,700
M21 (600cc single)	900	1,400	2,100	2,700	3,600	4,600
M21 Plunger (600cc single)	900	1,400	2,100	2,700	3,600	4,600
A10 Golden Flash Plunger (650cc twin) . . .	2,000	3,000	4,500	6,000	8,000	10,000
A10 Golden Flash (650cc twin)	2,000	3,000	4,500	6,000	8,000	10,000
A10R Road Rocket (650cc twin)	2,000	3,000	4,500	6,000	8,000	10,000
1956						
D1 Bantam w/direct elec. (125cc single) . .	600	800	1,300	1,700	2,200	2,800
D1 Bantam w/batt. (125cc single)	600	800	1,300	1,700	2,200	2,800
D3 Bantam w/direct elec. (153cc single) . .	600	800	1,300	1,700	2,200	2,800
D3 Bantam w/batt. (153cc single)	600	800	1,300	1,700	2,200	2,800
C10L (250cc single)	600	800	1,400	2,100	2,800	3,500
C11G (250cc single)	600	800	1,400	2,100	2,800	3,500
C12 (250cc single)	600	800	1,400	2,100	2,800	3,500
B31 (350cc single)	900	1,400	2,000	2,700	3,600	4,500
B32 Comp (350cc single)	1,200	1,900	2,800	3,700	5,000	6,200

	6	5	4	3	2	1
B32GS Gold Star (350cc single)	2,600	3,900	5,900	7,800	10,000	13,000
A7 (500cc single)	2,000	3,000	4,500	6,000	8,000	10,000
A7SS Shooting Star (500cc twin)	2,000	3,000	4,500	6,000	8,000	10,000
B33 (500cc single)	2,000	3,000	4,500	6,000	8,000	10,000
B34 Comp. (500cc single)	1,200	2,000	3,500	5,000	6,500	8,000
DBD34 Gold Star (500cc single)	4,000	6,000	11,000	16,000	21,000	26,000
DBD34 Gold Star Rigid US (500cc single) .	4,000	6,000	11,000	16,000	21,000	26,000
M33 (500cc single)	900	1,400	2,100	2,800	3,800	4,700
M33 Plunger (500cc single)	900	1,400	2,100	2,800	3,800	4,700
M21 (600cc single)	900	1,400	2,000	2,700	3,600	4,500
M21 Plunger (600cc single)	900	1,400	2,000	2,700	3,600	4,500
A10 Golden Flash Plunger (650cc twin) . . .	2,000	3,000	4,500	6,000	8,000	10,000
A10 Golden Flash (650cc twin)	2,000	3,000	4,500	6,000	8,000	10,000
A10R Road Rocket (650cc twin)	2,000	3,000	4,500	6,000	8,000	10,000
1957						
Dandy (70cc single)	400	600	1,000	1,300	1,700	2,100
Dandy w/Lucas (70cc single)	400	600	1,000	1,300	1,700	2,100
D1 Bantam w/direct elec. (125cc single) . .	600	800	1,300	1,700	2,200	2,800
D1 Bantam w/batt. (125cc single)	600	800	1,300	1,700	2,200	2,800
D3 Bantam w/direct elec. (153cc single) . .	600	800	1,300	1,700	2,200	2,800
D3 Bantam w/batt. (153cc single)	600	800	1,300	1,700	2,200	2,800
C10L (250cc single)	600	800	1,400	2,100	2,800	3,500
C12 (250cc single)	600	800	1,400	2,100	2,800	3,500
B31 (350cc single)	900	1,400	2,000	2,700	3,600	4,500
B32 Comp (350cc single)	1,200	1,800	2,700	3,600	4,800	6,000
B32GS Gold Star (350cc single)	2,600	3,900	5,900	7,800	10,000	13,000
A7 (500cc twin)	2,000	3,000	4,500	6,000	8,000	10,000
A7SS Shooting Star (500cc twin)	2,000	3,000	4,500	6,000	8,000	10,000
B33 (500cc single)	2,000	3,000	4,500	6,000	8,000	10,000
B34 Comp. (500cc single)	1,400	2,000	3,500	5,000	6,500	8,000
DBD34 Gold Star (500cc single)	4,000	6,000	11,000	16,000	21,000	26,000
DBD34 Gold Star Rigid US (500cc single) .	4,000	6,000	11,000	16,000	21,000	26,000
M33 (500cc single)	900	1,400	2,100	2,800	3,800	4,700
M33 Plunger (500cc single)	900	1,400	2,100	2,800	3,800	4,700
M21 (600cc single)	900	1,400	2,000	2,700	3,600	4,500
M21 Plunger (600cc single)	900	1,400	2,000	2,700	3,600	4,500
A10 Golden Flash Plunger (650cc twin) . . .	2,000	3,000	4,500	6,000	8,000	10,000
A10 Golden Flash (650cc twin)	2,000	3,000	4,500	6,000	8,000	10,000
A10R Road Rocket (650cc twin)	2,000	3,000	4,500	6,000	8,000	10,000
A10S Spitfire Scrambler (650cc twin)	1,500	3,000	5,000	7,000	**10,000**	**13,000**
1958						
Dandy (70cc single)	400	600	1,000	1,300	1,700	2,100
Dandy w/Lucas (70cc single)	400	600	1,000	1,300	1,700	2,100
D1 Bantam w/direct elec. (125cc single) . .	600	800	1,200	1,600	2,200	2,700
D1 Bantam w/batt. (125cc single)	600	800	1,200	1,600	2,200	2,700
D5 Bantam w/direct elec. (175cc single) . .	600	800	1,200	1,600	2,200	2,700
D5 Bantam w/batt. (175cc single)	600	800	1,200	1,600	2,200	2,700
C12 (250cc single)	600	800	1,400	2,100	2,800	3,500
B31 (350cc single)	900	1,400	2,000	2,700	3,600	4,500
A7 (500cc twin)	2,000	3,000	4,500	6,000	8,000	10,000
A7SS Shooting Star (500cc twin)	2,000	3,000	4,500	6,000	8,000	10,000
B33 (500cc single)	2,000	3,000	4,500	6,000	8,000	10,000
DBD34 Gold Star (500cc single)	4,000	8,000	13,000	18,000	23,000	28,000
M21 (600cc single)	900	1,400	2,000	2,700	3,600	4,500
M21 Plunger (600cc single)	900	1,400	2,000	2,700	3,600	4,500
A10 Golden Flash (650cc twin)	2,000	3,000	4,500	6,000	8,000	10,000
A10R Road Rocket (650cc twin)	2,000	3,000	4,500	6,000	8,000	10,000
A10S Spitfire Scrambler (650cc twin)	1,200	2,000	4,000	**7,000**	**10,000**	**13,000**

	6	5	4	3	2	1
1959						
Dandy (70cc single)	400	600	900	1,200	1,600	2,000
Dandy w/Lucas (70cc single)	400	600	900	1,200	1,600	2,000
D1 Bantam w/direct elec. (125cc single)	600	800	1,200	1,600	2,200	2,700
D1 Bantam w/batt. (125cc single)	600	800	1,200	1,600	2,200	2,700
D7 Bantam w/direct elec. (175cc single)	600	800	1,200	1,600	2,200	2,700
D7 Bantam w/batt. (175cc single)	600	800	1,200	1,600	2,200	2,700
C15 Star (250cc single)	600	900	1,400	1,800	2,400	3,000
C15 Scrambler (250cc single)	1,000	2,000	3,000	4,000	5,000	6,000
C15 Trails (250cc single)	700	1,100	1,600	2,100	2,800	3,500
B31 (350cc single)	800	1,300	1,900	2,500	3,400	4,200
B34GS Gold Star (350cc single)	1,800	2,700	4,100	5,400	7,200	9,000
A7 (500cc twin)	2,000	3,000	4,500	6,000	8,000	10,000
A7SS Shooting Star (500cc twin)	2,000	3,000	4,500	6,000	8,000	10,000
B33 (500cc single)	2,000	3,000	4,500	6,000	8,000	10,000
DBD34 Gold Star (500cc single)	3,800	6,000	10,000	15,000	18,000	22,000
DBD34 Gold Star Catalina (500cc single)	3,800	6,000	10,000	14,000	18,000	22,000
M21 (600cc single)	900	1,400	2,000	2,700	3,600	4,500
M21 Plunger (600cc single)	900	1,400	2,000	2,700	3,600	4,500
A10 Golden Flash (650cc twin)	2,000	3,000	4,500	6,000	8,000	10,000
A10R Super Rocket (650cc twin)	2,000	3,000	4,500	6,000	9,000	12,000
A10S Spitfire Scrambler (650cc twin)	1,200	2,000	4,000	**7,000**	**10,000**	**13,000**
1960						
Dandy (70cc single)	400	600	900	1,200	1,600	2,000
Dandy w/Lucas (70cc single)	400	600	900	1,200	1,600	2,000
D1 Bantam w/direct elec. (125cc single)	600	800	1,200	1,600	2,200	2,700
D1 Bantam w/batt. (125cc single)	600	800	1,200	1,600	2,200	2,700
D7 Bantam w/direct elec. (175cc single)	600	800	1,200	1,600	2,200	2,700
D7 Bantam w/batt. (175cc single)	600	800	1,200	1,600	2,200	2,700
C15 Star (250cc single)	600	900	1,400	1,800	2,400	3,000
C15 Scrambler (250cc single)	1,000	2,000	3,000	4,000	5,000	6,000
C15 Trails (250cc single)	700	1,100	1,600	2,100	2,800	3,500
A7 (500cc twin)	2,000	3,000	4,500	6,000	8,000	10,000
A7SS Shooting Star (500cc twin)	2,000	3,000	4,500	6,000	8,000	10,000
B33 (500cc single)	2,000	3,000	4,500	6,000	8,000	10,000
DBD34 Gold Star (500cc single)	3,800	5,700	8,600	11,000	15,000	19,000
DBD34 Gold Star Catalina (500cc single)	3,800	6,000	10,000	14,000	18,000	22,000
M21 (600cc single)	900	1,400	2,000	2,700	3,600	4,500
M21 Plunger (600cc single)	900	1,400	2,000	2,700	3,600	4,500
A10 Golden Flash (650cc twin)	2,000	3,000	4,500	6,000	8,000	10,000
A10R Super Rocket (650cc twin)	2,000	3,000	4,500	6,000	9,000	12,000
A10S Spitfire Scrambler (650cc twin)	1,200	2,000	4,000	**7,000**	**10,000**	**13,000**
1961						
Dandy (70cc single)	400	600	900	1,200	1,600	2,000
Dandy w/Lucas (70cc single)	400	600	900	1,200	1,600	2,000
D1 Bantam w/direct elec. (125cc single)	600	800	1,200	1,600	2,200	2,700
D1 Bantam w/batt. (125cc single)	600	800	1,200	1,600	2,200	2,700
D7 Bantam w/direct elec. (175cc single)	600	800	1,200	1,600	2,200	2,700
D7 Bantam w/batt. (175cc single)	600	800	1,200	1,600	2,200	2,700
C15 Star (250cc single)	600	900	1,400	1,800	2,400	3,000
C15 SS80 Sports Start 80 (250cc single)	600	900	1,400	1,800	2,400	3,000
C15 Scrambler (250cc single)	1,000	2,000	3,000	4,000	5,000	6,000
C15 Trails (250cc single)	700	1,100	1,600	2,200	2,900	3,600
B40 Star (350cc single)	700	1,500	2,500	3,500	4,000	4,500
A7 (500cc twin)	2,000	3,000	4,500	6,000	8,000	10,000
A7 Shooting Star (500cc twin)	2,000	3,000	4,500	6,000	8,000	10,000
DBD34 Gold Star (500cc single)	3,800	6,000	9,000	12,000	16,000	20,000
DBD34 Gold Star Catalina (500cc single)	3,800	6,000	10,000	14,000	18,000	22,000
M21 (600cc single)	900	1,400	2,000	2,700	3,600	4,500

	6	5	4	3	2	1
A10 Golden Flash (650cc twin)	2,000	3,000	4,500	6,000	8,000	10,000
A10R Super Rocket (650cc twin)	2,000	3,000	4,500	6,000	9,000	12,000
A10S Spitfire Scrambler (650cc twin)	1,200	2,000	4,000	**7,000**	**10,000**	**13,000**
1962						
Dandy (70cc single)	400	600	900	1,200	1,600	2,000
Dandy w/Lucas (70cc single)	400	600	900	1,200	1,600	2,000
D1 Bantam w/direct elec. (125cc single) . .	600	800	1,200	1,600	2,200	2,700
D1 Bantam w/batt. (125cc single)	600	800	1,200	1,600	2,200	2,700
D7 Bantam w/direct elec. (175cc single) . .	600	800	1,200	1,600	2,200	2,700
D7 Bantam w/batt. (175cc single)	600	800	1,200	1,600	2,200	2,700
C15 Star (250cc single)	600	900	1,400	1,800	2,400	3,000
C15 SS80 Sports Start 80 (250cc single) . .	600	900	1,400	1,800	2,400	3,000
C15 Scrambler (250cc single)	1,000	2,000	3,000	4,000	5,000	6,000
C15 Trails (250cc single)	700	1,100	1,600	2,200	2,900	3,600
C15 Scrambler Special (250cc single) . . .	700	1,100	1,600	2,200	2,900	3,600
C15 Trails Special (250cc single)	700	1,100	1,600	2,200	2,900	3,600
B40 (350cc single)	700	1,500	2,500	3,500	4,000	4,500
B40 SS90 Sports Star 90 (350cc single) . .	600	700	1,400	1,900	2,600	3,200
A50 Star (500cc twin)	1,000	2,000	3,000	4,000	5,000	6,000
DBD34 Gold Star (500cc single)	3,800	5,700	8,600	11,000	15,000	19,000
DBD34 Gold Star Catalina (500cc single) . .	3,800	6,000	10,000	14,000	18,000	22,000
M21 (600cc single)	900	1,400	2,000	2,700	3,600	4,500
A10 Golden Flash (650cc twin)	2,000	3,000	4,500	6,000	8,000	10,000
A10R Super Rocket (650cc twin)	2,000	3,000	4,500	6,000	9,000	12,000
A10S Spitfire Scrambler (650cc twin)	1,200	2,000	4,000	**7,000**	**10,000**	**13,000**
A10RGS Rocket Gold Star (650cc twin). . .	4,000	6,000	9,000	12,000	16,000	20,000
A65 Star (650cc twin)	**1,000**	**2,000**	**3,000**	**4,000**	**5,000**	**6,000**
1963						
D1 Bantam w/direct elec. (125cc single) . .	600	800	1,200	1,600	2,200	2,700
D1 Bantam w/batt. (125cc single)	600	800	1,200	1,600	2,200	2,700
D7 Bantam w/direct elec. (175cc single) . .	600	800	1,200	1,600	2,200	2,700
D7 Bantam w/batt. (175cc single)	600	800	1,200	1,600	2,200	2,700
D7 Bantam US. (175cc single)	600	800	1,200	1,600	2,200	2,700
D7 Bantam US w/batt. (175cc single)	600	800	1,200	1,600	2,200	2,700
D7 Bantam Police (175cc single)	600	800	1,200	1,600	2,200	2,700
D7 Bantam Trail (175cc single)	600	800	1,200	1,600	2,200	2,700
C15 Star (250cc single)	600	900	1,400	1,800	2,400	3,000
C15 Police (250cc single)	700	1,100	1,600	2,200	2,900	3,600
C15 SS80 Sports Start 80 (250cc single) . .	600	900	1,400	1,800	2,400	3,000
C15 Scrambler (250cc single)	1,000	2,000	3,000	4,000	5,000	6,000
C15 Star US (250cc single)	700	1,100	1,600	2,200	2,900	3,600
C15 Starfire Roadster (250cc single)	700	1,100	1,600	2,200	2,900	3,600
C15 Trails (250cc single)	700	1,100	1,600	2,200	2,900	3,600
C15 Trials Pastoral (250cc single).	700	1,100	1,600	2,200	2,900	3,600
B40 Star (350cc single)	700	1,500	2,500	3,500	4,000	4,500
B40 SS90 Sports Star 90 (350cc single) . .	600	700	1,400	1,900	2,600	3,200
B40 Star US (350cc single)	700	1,000	1,500	2,000	2,700	3,400
A50 Star (500cc twin)	1,000	2,000	3,000	4,000	5,000	6,000
DBD34 Gold Star Clubman (500cc single) .	3,800	5,700	8,600	11,000	15,000	19,000
DBD34 Gold Star Catalina (500cc single) . .	3,800	6,000	10,000	14,000	18,000	22,000
M21 (600cc single)	900	1,400	2,000	2,700	3,600	4,500
A10 Golden Flash (650cc twin)	2,000	3,000	4,500	6,000	8,000	10,000
A10R Super Rocket (650cc twin)	2,000	3,000	4,500	6,000	9,000	12,000
A10S Spitfire Scrambler (650cc twin)	1,200	2,000	4,000	**7,000**	**10,000**	**13,000**
A10RGS Rocket Gold Star (650cc twin). . .	4,000	6,000	9,000	12,000	16,000	20,000
A65 Star (650cc twin)	**1,000**	**2,000**	**3,000**	**4,000**	**5,000**	**6,000**
1964						
Beagle (75cc single).	300	500	700	900	1,200	1,500

	6	5	4	3	2	1
Starlite 75 (75cc single)	300	500	700	900	1,200	1,500
D1 Bantam Plunger GPO (125cc single) . .	600	800	1,200	1,600	2,200	2,700
D7 Bantam w/direct elec. (175cc single) . .	600	800	1,200	1,600	2,200	2,700
D7 Bantam w/batt. (175cc single)	600	800	1,200	1,600	2,200	2,700
D7 Bantam US. (175cc single)	600	800	1,200	1,600	2,200	2,700
D7 Bantam US w/batt. (175cc single)	600	800	1,200	1,600	2,200	2,700
D7 Bantam Trail (175cc single)	600	800	1,200	1,600	2,200	2,700
C15 Star (250cc single)	600	900	1,400	1,800	2,400	3,000
C15 SS80 Sports Start 80 (250cc single) . .	600	900	1,400	1,800	2,400	3,000
C15 Police (250cc single)	700	1,100	1,600	2,100	2,800	3,500
C15 Star US (250cc single)	700	1,100	1,600	2,200	2,900	3,600
C15 Scrambler (250cc single)	1,000	2,000	3,000	4,000	5,000	6,000
C15 Starfire Roadster (250cc single)	700	1,100	1,600	2,200	2,900	3,600
C15 Trails (250cc single)	700	1,100	1,600	2,200	2,900	3,600
C15 Trials Pastoral (250cc single)	700	1,100	1,600	2,200	2,900	3,600
B40 Star (350cc single)	700	1,500	2,500	3,500	4,000	4,500
B40 Police (350cc single)	700	1,000	1,500	2,000	2,700	3,400
B40 Super Star US (350cc single)	700	1,000	1,500	2,000	2,700	3,400
B40 SS90 Sports Star 90 (350cc single) . .	600	700	1,400	1,900	2,600	3,200
B40 Enduro Star US (350cc single)	700	1,100	1,600	2,200	2,900	3,600
A50 Star (500cc twin)	1,000	2,000	3,000	4,000	5,000	6,000
A50C Cyclone (500cc twin)	900	1,400	2,000	3,000	4,500	6,000
A65 Star (650cc twin)	900	1,400	2,000	3,000	4,500	6,000
A65R Rocket (650cc twin).	1,000	1,500	2,300	3,500	5,000	6,500
A65T Thunderbolt Rocket (650cc twin) . . .	1,100	1,700	2,500	3,400	4,500	5,600
A65L Lightning (650cc twin).	1,500	3,000	4,500	6,000	7,500	9,000
A65SH Spitfire Hornet (650cc twin)	1,000	2,000	3,500	6,000	8,000	10,000
1965						
Beagle (75cc single).	300	500	700	900	1,200	1,500
Starlite 75 (75cc single)	300	500	700	900	1,200	1,500
D1 Bantam Plunger GPO (125cc single) . .	600	800	1,200	1,600	2,200	2,700
D7 Bantam w/direct elec. (175cc single) . .	600	800	1,200	1,600	2,200	2,700
D7 Bantam w/batt. (175cc single)	600	800	1,200	1,600	2,200	2,700
D7 Bantam Pastoral (175cc single)	600	800	1,200	1,600	2,200	2,700
D7 Bantam Trail Bonc (175cc single)	600	800	1,200	1,600	2,200	2,700
C15 Star (250cc single)	600	900	1,400	1,800	2,400	3,000
C15 Star US (250cc single)	600	900	1,400	1,800	2,400	3,000
C15 Police (250cc single)	600	900	1,400	1,800	2,400	3,000
C15 SS80 Sports Start 80 (250cc single) . .	600	900	1,400	1,800	2,400	3,000
C15 Scrambler (250cc single).	1,000	2,000	3,000	4,000	5,000	6,000
C15 Starfire Roadster (250cc single)	700	1,100	1,600	2,200	2,900	3,600
C15 Trails (250cc single)	600	700	1,400	1,900	2,600	3,200
C15 Trails Cat (250cc single)	600	700	1,400	1,900	2,600	3,200
C15 Trials Pastoral (250cc single).	600	700	1,400	1,900	2,600	3,200
B40 Star (350cc single)	700	1,500	2,500	3,500	4,000	4,500
B40 Police (350cc single)	700	1,000	1,500	2,000	2,700	3,400
B40 SS90 Sports Star 90 (350cc single) . .	1,000	1,600	2,300	3,100	4,200	5,200
B40 Enduro Star US (350cc single)	700	1,100	1,600	2,200	2,900	3,600
B40 Sportsman US (350cc single)	700	1,000	1,500	2,000	2,700	3,400
A50 Star (500cc twin)	1,000	2,000	3,000	4,000	5,000	6,000
A50 Cyclone Comp UK (500cc twin)	900	1,400	2,000	3,000	4,500	6,000
A50 Cyclone UK (500cc twin)	900	1,400	2,000	3,000	4,500	6,000
A50C Cyclone (500cc twin)	900	1,400	2,000	3,000	4,500	6,000
A50CC Cyclone Comp (500cc twin).	1,000	1,500	2,200	3,500	5,000	6,500
A65 Star (650cc twin)	900	1,400	2,000	3,000	4,500	6,000
A65 Lightning (650cc twin)	1,200	1,800	2,700	3,600	**5,000**	**6,500**
A65 Lightning Clubman (650cc twin)	1,200	2,500	4,000	5,500	7,000	8,500
A65L Lightning Rocket (650cc twin).	2,000	3,500	5,000	6,500	8,000	10,000

	6	5	4	3	2	1
A65R Rocket (650cc twin)	1,000	1,500	2,300	3,000	4,000	5,000
A65SH Spitfire Hornet (650cc twin)	1,000	2,500	4,000	6,000	8,000	10,000
1966						
D7 Silver Bantam (175cc single)	600	800	1,200	1,600	2,200	2,700
D7 Bantam Deluxe (175cc single)	600	800	1,200	1,600	2,200	2,700
D7 Bantam Silver Deluxe (175cc single)	600	800	1,200	1,600	2,200	2,700
D7 Bantam GPO (175cc single)	600	800	1,200	1,600	2,200	2,700
C15 Star (250cc single)	600	900	1,400	1,900	2,500	3,100
C15 Sportsman (250cc single)	600	900	1,400	1,800	2,400	3,000
B40 Star (350cc single)	700	1,500	2,500	3,500	4,000	4,500
B40 Star Mod (350cc single)	700	1,000	1,500	2,000	2,700	3,400
B44 Victor Grand Prix (441cc single)	1,000	2,000	4,000	6,000	8,000	10,000
B44 Victor Enduro (441cc single)	700	1,100	1,600	3,000	4,500	6,000
A50R Royal Star (500cc twin)	800	1,300	2,000	3,000	4,000	5,000
A50W Wasp (500cc Twin)	800	1,200	1,800	3,000	4,500	6,000
A65T Thunderbolt (650cc twin)	1,100	1,700	2,500	3,500	5,000	6,500
A65L Lightning (650cc twin)	1,200	1,800	2,700	3,600	**5,000**	**6,500**
A65LC Lightning Clubman(650cc twin)	1,200	1,900	2,800	3,700	5,000	6,200
A65S Spitfire Mk II (650cc twin)	1,500	3,000	4,500	**7,000**	**10,000**	**13,000**
A65H Hornet (650cc twin)	1,000	2,000	4,000	6,000	8,000	10,000
1967						
D10 Bantam Silver (175cc single)	600	800	1,200	1,600	2,200	2,700
D10 Bantam GPO (175cc single)	600	800	1,200	1,600	2,200	2,700
D10 Bantam Supreme (175cc single)	600	800	1,200	1,600	2,200	2,700
D10 Bantam Sport (175cc single)	600	800	1,300	1,700	2,200	2,800
D10 Bushman (175cc single)	600	800	1,300	1,700	2,200	2,800
D10 Bushman Pastoral (175cc single)	600	800	1,300	1,700	2,200	2,800
B25 Starfire US (250cc single)	800	1,500	2,000	2,500	3,000	4,000
C15 Star (250cc single)	600	900	1,400	1,800	2,400	3,000
C15 Police (250cc single)	600	900	1,400	1,800	2,400	3,000
C15 Sportsman (250cc single)	700	1,000	1,500	2,000	2,600	3,300
C25 Barracuda (250cc single)	700	1,000	1,500	2,000	2,700	3,400
B40 Star (350cc single)	700	1,500	2,500	3,500	4,000	4,500
B40 Military (350cc single)	700	1,000	1,500	2,000	2,700	3,400
B44 Victor Grand Prix (441cc single)	1,000	2,000	4,000	6,000	8,000	10,000
B44 Victor Enduro (441cc single)	700	1,100	2,000	3,000	4,000	5,000
B44 Victor Roadster (441cc single)	700	1,100	1,600	2,400	3,200	4,000
A50R Royal Star (500cc twin)	800	1,500	2,100	2,700	3,600	4,500
A50W Wasp (500cc Twin)	800	1,200	1,800	3,000	4,500	6,000
A65T Thunderbolt (650cc twin)	1,100	1,700	2,500	3,500	5,000	6,500
A65L Lightning (650cc twin)	1,200	1,800	2,700	3,600	**5,000**	**6,500**
A65S Spitfire Mk II (650cc twin)	1,500	3,000	4,500	**7,000**	**10,000**	**13,000**
A65H Hornet (650cc twin)	1,000	2,000	4,000	6,000	8,000	10,000
1968						
D13 Bantam Supreme (175cc single)	600	800	1,200	1,600	2,200	2,700
D13 Bantam Sports (175cc single)	600	800	1,200	1,600	2,200	2,700
D13 Bantam Bushman (175cc single)	600	800	1,200	1,600	2,200	2,700
D14/4 Bantam (175cc single)	600	800	1,200	1,800	2,500	3,500
D14/4 Sports (175cc single)	600	800	1,200	1,600	2,200	2,700
D14/4 Bantam Bushman (175cc single)	600	800	1,300	1,700	2,200	2,800
B25 Starfire US (250cc single)	800	1,500	2,000	2,500	3,000	4,000
B25 Fleetstar (250cc single)	600	800	1,200	1,600	2,200	2,700
B40 Military (350cc single)	700	1,000	1,500	2,000	2,700	3,400
B44 Shooting Star (441cc single)	1,000	2,000	3,000	4,000	5,000	6,000
B44 Victor Special (441cc single)	1,000	2,000	3,000	4,000	5,500	7,000
A50R Royal Star (500cc twin)	800	1,300	2,000	3,000	4,000	5,000
A50W Wasp (500cc Twin)	800	1,200	1,800	3,000	4,500	6,000
A65T Thunderbolt (650cc twin)	1,100	1,700	2,500	4,000	6,000	8,000

	6	5	4	3	2	1
A65L Lightning (650cc twin)	1,200	1,800	2,700	3,600	**5,000**	6,500
A65F Firebird Scrambler (650cc twin)	1,200	1,800	3,000	4,000	5,500	7,000
A65S Spitfire Mk IV (650cc twin)	1,500	3,000	4,500	7,000	10,000	13,000
1969						
B175 Bantam (175cc single)	600	800	1,200	1,600	2,200	2,700
B175 Bantam Bushman (175cc single)	600	900	1,350	1,800	2,400	3,000
B25 Starfire (250cc single)	800	1,500	2,000	2,500	3,000	4,000
B25FS Fleetstar (250cc single)	600	800	1,200	1,600	2,200	2,700
B40 Military (350cc single)	700	1,000	1,500	2,000	2,700	3,400
B40 Roughrider (350cc single)	700	1,000	1,500	2,000	2,700	3,400
B44SS Shooting Star (441cc single)	1,000	2,000	3,000	4,000	5,000	6,000
B44VS Victor Special (441cc single)	1,200	2,000	3,000	4,000	5,500	7,000
A50 Royal Star (500cc twin).	900	1,400	2,000	3,000	4,000	5,000
A65T Thunderbolt (650cc twin)	1,100	1,700	2,500	4,000	6,000	8,000
A65L Lightning (650cc twin).	1,200	1,800	2,700	3,600	**5,000**	6,500
A65F Firebird Scrambler (650cc twin)	1,200	1,800	3,000	4,000	5,500	7,000
A75 Rocket III (750cc triple).	2,000	3,500	**6,000**	10,000	14,000	18,000
1970						
B175 Bantam (175cc single)	600	800	1,200	1,600	2,200	2,700
B175 Bantam Bushman (175cc single)	600	900	1,350	1,800	2,400	3,000
B25 Starfire (250cc single)	800	1,500	2,000	2,500	3,000	4,000
B25FS Fleetstar (250cc single)	600	1,000	1,400	1,900	2,600	3,200
B40 Military (350cc single)	700	1,000	1,500	2,000	2,700	3,300
B44 Shooting Star (441cc single)	1,000	2,000	3,000	4,000	5,000	6,000
B44 Victor Special (441cc single)	900	2,000	3,000	4,000	5,500	7,000
A50 Royal Star (500cc twin)	800	1,200	2,000	3,000	4,000	5,000
A65T Thunderbolt (650cc twin)	1,100	1,700	2,500	4,000	6,000	8,000
A65L Lightning (650cc twin).	1,200	1,800	2,700	3,600	**5,000**	6,500
A65F Firebird Scrambler (650cc twin)	1,200	1,800	3,000	4,000	5,500	7,000
A75 Rocket III (750cc triple).	1,800	2,700	4,100	6,000	9,000	12,000
1971						
B175 Bantam (175cc single)	500	800	1,100	1,500	2,000	2,500
B25 Victor Trail (250cc single)	700	1,100	1,600	2,100	2,800	3,500
B25FS Fleetstar (250cc single)	600	800	1,300	1,700	2,200	2,800
B25SS Gold Star 250 (250cc single)	600	800	1,300	1,700	2,200	2,800
B50 Motorcross (500cc single)	600	1,000	1,600	2,400	3,200	4,000
B50 Victor Trial (500cc single)	600	1,000	2,000	3,000	4,000	5,000
B50SS Gold Star 500 (500cc single)	600	1,000	1,600	2,400	3,200	4,000
A65 Thunderbolt (650cc twin)	1,100	1,700	2,500	3,400	4,500	5,600
A65 Lightning (650cc twin)	1,100	1,700	2,500	3,300	**5,000**	6,500
A65 Firebird Scrambler (650cc twin)	1,100	1,700	3,000	4,000	5,500	7,000
A75 Rocket III (750cc triple).	1,100	2,000	4,000	6,000	8,000	10,000
1972						
Ariel 3 (48cc single)	200	400	500	700	1,000	1,200
B50 Motorcross (500cc single)	600	1,000	1,600	2,400	3,200	4,000
B50 Victor Trial (500cc single)	600	1,000	2,000	3,000	4,000	5,000
B50SS Gold Star 500 (500cc single)	600	1,000	1,600	2,400	3,200	4,000
A65 Thunderbolt (650cc twin)	1,100	1,700	2,500	3,300	4,400	5,500
A65 Lightning (650cc twin)	1,000	1,500	2,300	3,000	4,000	5,000
A70 Lightning 750 (750cc twin)	1,000	2,000	3,500	5,000	6,500	8,000
A75 Rocket III (750cc triple).	1,100	2,000	4,000	6,000	8,000	10,000
1973						
Ariel 3 (48cc single)	200	400	500	700	1,000	1,200
B50 Motorcross (500cc single)	600	1,000	1,600	2,400	3,200	4,000
T65 (660cc Twin)	600	1,000	1,600	2,400	3,200	4,000
1974						
Ariel 3 (48cc single)	200	400	500	700	1,000	1,200

	6	5	4	3	2	1
BUELL						
1987						
RR1000	500	800	2,200	4,600	6,800	9,000
1988						
RR1000	600	900	2,400	4,900	7,300	9,900
1989						
RR1200	300	600	1,500	3,100	4,600	6,100
RS1200	300	500	1,400	2,900	4,400	5,900
1990						
RR1200	300	600	1,600	3,400	5,100	6,800
RS1200	300	600	1,600	3,200	4,800	5,400
1991						
RS1200	300	600	1,700	3,500	5,300	7,100
1992						
RS1200	300	700	1,800	3,700	5,800	6,900
RSS1200	300	600	1,700	3,500	5,200	6,900
1993						
RS1200	300	700	1,900	3,900	5,800	7,700
RSS1200	300	700	1,800	3,800	5,500	7,200
1995						
S2 Thunderbolt w/Fairing	600	1,200	2,100	3,100	4,100	5,500
BULTACO						
1966						
Pursang (250cc.	3,000	4,400	5,400	6,500	9,300	12,000
1968						
Lobito AK (100cc)	1,400	2,300	3,200	4,300	6,400	8,500
Lobito T (100cc).	1,400	2,300	3,200	4,300	6,400	8,500
Sherpa S (125cc)	2,000	2,800	3,400	4,100	5,900	7,500
Campera 4 Speed (175cc)	1,500	2,500	3,500	4,500	5,500	6,500
Mercurio (175cc)	1,500	2,500	3,500	4,500	5,500	6,500
Sherpa S (175cc)	1,500	2,500	3,500	4,500	5,500	6,500
Mercurio (200cc)	600	1,100	1,400	1,600	2,300	3,000
Sherpa S (200cc)	800	1,300	1,900	2,400	3,400	4,400
El Tigre (250cc)	1,100	1,400	1,700	2,000	2,800	3,600
Matador (250cc).	500	1,000	1,700	2,300	3,400	4,500
Metralla (250cc).	2,500	3,200	3,900	4,700	6,900	8,000
Pursang (250cc).	3,000	4,400	5,400	6,500	9,300	12,000
Sherpa T (250cc)	700	1,700	2,800	4,000	5,800	7,500
Bandito (360cc)	1,600	2,200	2,700	3,200	4,600	5,800
Montadero (360cc)	900	1,500	2,700	3,900	5,300	6,500
1969						
Lobito 4 Speed (100cc)	1,400	2,300	3,200	4,300	6,400	8,500
Lobito AK (100cc)	1,400	2,300	3,200	4,300	6,400	8,500
Lobito (125cc).	700	1,100	2,200	3,300	4,000	4,800
Sherpa S (125cc)	1,500	2,800	4,200	5,800	9,000	12,000
Campera 4 Speed (175cc)	1,500	2,500	3,500	4,500	5,500	6,500
Sherpa S (175cc)	1,500	2,500	3,500	4,500	5,500	6,500
El Tigre (200cc)	800	1,300	1,900	2,400	3,400	4,400
Mercurio (200cc)	800	1,300	1,900	2,400	3,400	4,400
Sherpa S (200cc)	800	1,300	1,900	2,400	3,400	4,400
El Tigre (250cc)	1,000	1,400	1,700	2,000	2,800	3,600
Matador 5 Speed III (250cc).	500	1,000	1,700	2,300	3,400	4,500
Metralla (250cc).	1,400	2,300	3,200	4,200	6,100	7,500
Pursang (250cc).	3,000	4,400	5,400	6,500	9,300	12,000
Sherpa T (250cc)	1,000	1,700	2,800	4,000	5,800	7,500
El Bandito (360cc).	1,300	2,200	3,100	4,100	5,900	6,500
El Bandito TT (360cc)	1,300	2,200	3,100	4,100	5,900	6,500
Montadero (360cc)	900	1,500	2,700	3,900	5,300	6,500

	6	5	4	3	2	1
1970						
Lobito (100cc)	1,400	2,300	3,200	4,300	6,400	8,500
Sherpa S (100cc)	500	800	1,000	1,100	1,500	2,000
Lobito (125cc)	700	1,100	2,200	3,300	4,000	4,800
Sherpa S (125cc)	1,500	2,800	4,200	5,800	9,000	12,000
TSS Water Cooled (125cc)	700	1,100	2,200	3,300	4,000	4,800
Campera MK II (175cc)	1,000	1,600	1,900	2,300	3,300	4,500
Sherpa S (175cc)	1,500	2,500	3,500	4,500	5,500	6,500
El Tigre (200cc)	800	1,300	1,900	2,400	3,400	4,400
Mercurio (200cc)	800	1,300	1,900	2,400	3,400	4,400
Sherpa S (200cc)	800	1,300	1,900	2,400	3,400	4,400
El Tigre (250cc)	1,000	1,400	1,700	2,000	2,800	3,600
Matador MK III (250cc)	500	1,000	1,600	2,200	3,400	4,500
Metralla MK III (250cc)	1,800	2,300	3,200	4,200	6,100	7,500
Pursang TT (250cc)	3,000	4,400	5,400	6,500	9,300	12,000
Sherpa T (250cc)	1,000	1,700	2,800	4,000	5,800	7,500
TSS Water Cooled (250cc)	1,000	1,700	2,800	4,000	5,800	7,500
Bandito (360cc)	1,000	1,600	2,400	3,300	5,100	6,500
Bandito TT (360cc)	1,300	1,900	2,700	3,900	5,600	8,000
Montadero (360cc)	900	1,500	2,700	3,900	5,300	6,500
TSS Air Cooled (360cc)	900	1,500	2,700	3,900	5,300	6,500
1971						
Lobito (100cc)	500	800	1,000	1,100	1,500	2,000
Sherpa S (100cc)	1,400	2,300	3,200	4,300	6,400	8,500
Lobito (125cc)	500	800	1,000	1,100	1,500	2,000
Sherpa S (125cc)	1,500	2,800	4,200	5,800	9,000	12,000
TSS Water Cooled (125cc)	700	1,100	2,200	3,300	4,000	4,800
Lobito (175cc)	1,000	1,600	1,900	2,300	3,300	4,500
Sherpa S (175cc)	1,000	1,600	1,900	2,300	3,300	4,500
Campera MK II (175cc)	1,500	2,500	3,500	4,500	5,500	6,500
Sherpa S (200cc)	800	1,300	1,900	2,400	3,400	4,400
El Tigre (200cc)	800	1,300	1,900	2,400	3,400	4,400
Alpina (250cc)	800	1,400	2,400	3,400	4,900	6,400
Mercurio (200cc)	800	1,300	1,900	2,400	3,400	4,400
Matador SD (250cc)	500	1,000	1,600	2,200	3,400	4,500
Metralla (250cc)	1,800	2,300	3,200	4,200	6,100	7,500
Pursang A (250cc)	1,300	1,900	3,500	5,100	6,700	8,200
Pursang E (250cc)	1,300	1,900	3,500	5,100	6,700	8,200
Sherpa T 5 Speed (250cc)	1,000	1,700	2,800	4,000	5,800	7,500
El Tigre (250cc)	1,000	1,400	1,700	2,000	2,800	3,600
Matador MK III (250cc)	500	1,000	1,600	2,200	3,400	4,500
Pursang TT (250cc)	1,600	2,300	3,200	4,200	6,100	7,500
TSS Water Cooled (250cc)	1,000	1,700	2,800	4,000	5,800	7,500
Bandito (360cc)	1,500	2,200	3,200	4,100	5,900	7,500
Bandito TT (360cc)	1,300	1,900	2,700	3,900	5,600	8,000
Montadero (360cc)	900	1,500	2,700	3,900	5,300	6,500
TSS Air Cooled (360cc)	900	1,500	2,700	3,900	5,300	6,500
1972						
Tiron Mini Bike (100cc)	500	800	1,000	1,100	1,500	2,000
Lobito (125cc)	1,200	1,800	2,500	3,300	4,700	6,000
Pursang (125cc)	1,300	1,900	3,200	4,600	6,700	8,500
Sherpa T (125cc)	700	1,100	2,200	3,300	4,000	4,800
Lobito (175cc)	1,100	1,700	2,900	4,100	5,900	7,500
Alpina (250cc)	800	1,400	2,400	3,400	4,900	6,200
Matador SD MK IV (250cc)	1,000	1,700	3,000	4,500	6,000	7,500
Pursang Astro (250cc)	1,300	1,900	3,500	5,100	6,700	8,200
Pursang MK IX (250cc)	1,300	1,900	3,500	5,100	6,700	8,200
Sherpa T (250cc)	1,000	1,700	2,800	4,000	5,800	7,500
Montadero (360cc)	900	1,500	2,700	3,900	5,300	6,500

	6	5	4	3	2	1
Pursang (360cc).	1,000	1,600	2,700	3,800	5,500	6,000
1973						
Tiron Mini Bike (100cc)	500	800	1,000	1,100	1,500	2,000
Alpina (125cc).	500	800	1,300	1,900	2,600	3,300
Pursang MK IX (125cc)	500	800	1,100	1,400	2,000	2,600
Alpina (175cc).	1,000	1,700	2,900	4,100	5,900	7,500
Pursang MK VII (175cc).	900	1,400	2,100	2,800	3,900	5,000
Pursang T (200cc).	1,000	1,500	2,300	3,200	4,600	6,000
Astro (250cc).	500	1,500	3,000	4,500	5,500	6,500
Alpina (250cc).	900	1,400	2,400	3,400	4,900	6,300
Matador SD MK IV (250cc)	1,000	1,700	3,000	4,500	6,000	7,500
Pursang MK IX (250cc)	1,100	1,600	2,700	3,800	5,500	7,000
Sherpa T (250cc)	1,000	1,700	2,800	4,000	5,800	7,500
Astro (350cc).	1,900	2,600	3,600	4,700	6,900	9,000
Alpina (350cc).	800	1,200	1,600	2,000	2,900	3,800
Sherpa T (350cc)	600	1,000	1,700	2,400	3,500	4,500
Pursang (360cc).	1,200	1,900	3,200	4,600	6,700	8,500
1974						
Tiron Mini Bike (100cc)	500	800	1,000	1,100	1,500	2,000
Alpina (125cc).	300	500	1,000	1,500	2,300	3,000
Pursang MK IX (125cc)	500	800	1,100	1,400	2,000	2,600
Alpina (175cc).	300	500	1,000	1,500	2,300	3,000
Pursang MK VI (175cc)	900	1,400	2,100	2,800	3,900	5,000
Pursang T (200cc).	1,000	1,500	2,300	3,200	4,600	6,000
Alpina (250cc).	500	800	1,300	1,800	2,500	3,200
Astro (250cc).	700	1,500	3,000	4,500	5,500	6,500
Matador SD MK IV (250cc)	1,000	1,700	3,000	4,500	6,000	7,500
Pursang MK IX (250cc)	500	1,000	1,500	2,000	3,000	4,000
Sherpa T (250cc)	1,000	1,700	2,800	4,000	5,800	7,500
Alpina (350cc).	800	1,200	1,600	2,000	2,900	3,800
Sherpa T (350cc)	600	1,000	1,700	2,400	3,500	4,500
El Bandito MX (360cc)	1,600	2,200	3,100	4,100	5,900	7,500
Montadero MK II (360cc)	1,000	1,500	2,700	3,900	5,300	6,500
1975						
Pursang MK IX (125cc)	500	800	1,100	1,400	3,000	4,500
Pursang (200cc).	1,000	1,500	2,300	3,200	4,600	6,000
Alpina (250cc).	500	800	1,300	1,800	2,500	3,200
Astro (250cc).	700	1,500	3,000	4,500	5,500	6,500
Frontera MK IX (250cc)	600	1,000	1,500	2,000	3,000	4,000
Matador SD MK IV (250cc)	1,000	1,700	3,000	4,500	6,000	7,500
Pursang (250cc).	1,000	1,600	2,700	3,800	5,500	7,000
Sherpa T (250cc)	1,000	1,700	2,800	4,000	5,800	7,500
Alpina (350cc).	800	1,200	1,600	2,000	2,900	3,800
Astro (350cc).	1,500	2,100	2,900	3,700	5,600	7,500
Sherpa T (350cc)	600	1,000	1,700	2,400	3,500	4,500
Frontera MK IX (360cc)	400	600	1,400	2,100	3,200	4,300
Pursang (360cc).	1,200	1,900	3,200	4,600	6,700	8,500
1976						
Pursang MK IX (125cc)	500	700	1,100	1,400	1,900	2,200
Sherpa T (125cc)	400	600	900	1,100	1,600	2,100
Pursang MK IX (200cc)	900	1,500	2,300	3,200	4,600	5,500
Alpina (250cc).	500	800	1,300	1,800	2,500	3,200
Astro (250cc).	700	1,500	3,000	4,500	5,500	6,500
Frontera MK IX (250cc)	600	900	1,200	1,500	2,100	2,700
Pursang MK IX (250cc)	1,000	1,600	2,700	3,800	5,500	7,000
Sherpa T (250cc)	1,000	1,700	2,800	4,000	5,800	7,500
Alpina (350cc).	800	1,200	1,600	2,000	2,900	3,800
Astro (350cc).	1,500	2,100	2,900	3,900	5,600	7,500
Matador MK IX (350cc)	700	1,000	1,700	2,400	3,500	4,600

	6	5	4	3	2	1
Sherpa T (350cc)	600	1,000	1,700	2,400	3,500	4,500
Frontera (360cc)	500	700	1,300	2,100	3,200	4,300
1977						
Pursang MK IX (125cc)	500	800	1,100	1,400	1,900	2,200
Sherpa T (125cc)	400	600	900	1,100	1,300	1,500
Pursang (200cc)	800	1,300	2,400	3,500	4,700	5,900
Alpina (250cc)	500	800	1,300	1,800	2,500	3,200
Astro (250cc)	800	1,500	3,000	4,500	5,500	6,500
Frontera (250cc)	600	900	1,200	1,500	2,100	2,700
Pursang MK IX (250cc)	1,000	1,600	2,700	3,800	5,500	7,000
Sherpa T (250cc)	1,000	1,700	2,800	4,000	5,800	7,500
Alpina (350cc)	800	1,200	1,600	2,000	2,900	3,800
Matador MK IX (350cc)	500	800	1,000	1,300	1,800	2,300
Sherpa T (350cc)	600	1,000	1,700	2,400	3,500	4,600
Frontera (370cc)	600	900	1,300	1,600	2,300	3,000
Pursang (370cc)	700	1,100	1,900	2,700	3,900	5,000
1978						
Streaker (125cc)	1,200	1,800	2,600	3,500	4,600	5,500
Pursang (200cc)	800	1,300	2,400	3,500	4,700	5,900
Alpina (250cc)	500	800	1,300	1,800	2,500	3,200
Astro (250cc)	800	1,500	3,000	4,500	5,500	6,500
Frontera MK IX (250cc)	600	900	1,500	2,000	2,900	3,800
Metralla (250cc)	700	1,000	1,700	2,400	3,500	4,500
Pursang (250cc)	1,000	1,600	2,700	3,800	5,500	7,000
Alpina (350cc)	800	1,200	1,600	2,000	2,800	3,600
Sherpa T (350cc)	600	1,000	1,700	2,400	3,500	4,600
Frontera MK IX (360cc)	700	1,100	1,700	2,300	3,200	4,100
Pursang (370cc)	700	1,100	1,900	2,700	3,900	5,000
1979						
Alpina (250cc)	500	800	1,300	1,800	2,500	3,200
Astro (250cc)	800	1,500	3,000	4,500	5,500	6,500
Frontera MK XI (250cc)	600	900	1,500	2,000	2,900	3,800
Pursang MK XII (250cc)	1,000	1,600	2,800	4,000	5,800	7,500
Alpina (350cc)	800	1,200	1,600	2,000	2,900	3,800
Sherpa T (350cc)	600	1,000	1,700	2,400	3,500	4,600
Frontera MK XI (370cc)	600	900	1,400	2,200	3,300	4,400
Pursang MK XII Everts (370cc)	900	1,300	2,100	2,900	4,300	5,500
1980						
Astro (250cc)	800	1,200	2,000	2,900	4,300	5,700
Frontera MK XI (250cc)	1,900	2,600	3,300	4,000	5,500	7,000
Sherpa T (350cc)	600	1,000	1,700	2,500	3,500	4,500
1981						
Sherpa T (125cc)	600	1,000	1,600	2,300	2,900	3,500
Astro (250cc)	800	1,500	3,000	4,500	5,500	6,500
Pursang (250cc)	800	1,300	2,400	3,600	5,800	7,500
Sherpa T (250cc)	600	1,000	1,700	2,400	3,200	4,000
Sherpa T (350cc)	700	1,100	1,800	2,500	3,500	4,500
Astro (450cc)	900	1,400	2,100	3,000	4,400	5,800
Pursang (450cc)	1,000	1,500	2,600	3,800	6,000	8,000
1982						
Astro (200cc)	700	1,500	3,000	4,500	5,500	6,500
Sherpa T (200cc)	600	900	1,500	2,300	3,100	3,900
Frontera (250cc)	700	1,300	1,900	2,600	3,400	4,200
Pursang (250cc)	600	1,000	1,800	2,800	4,100	5,400
1983						
Sherpa T (125cc)	700	1,000	1,600	2,300	2,900	3,500
Astro (250cc)	800	1,500	3,000	4,500	5,500	6,500
Pursang (250cc)	800	1,300	2,400	3,600	5,800	7,500
Sherpa T (250cc)	700	1,000	1,600	2,400	3,200	4,000

	6	5	4	3	2	1
Sherpa T (350cc)	800	1,100	1,800	2,500	3,500	4,500
Astro (450cc)	900	1,400	2,100	3,000	4,400	5,800
Pursang (450cc).	1,000	1,500	2,600	3,800	6,000	8,000

CAGIVA

	6	5	4	3	2	1
1981						
WMX 125	300	500	1,500	3,500	4,500	5,500
RXR 250	300	500	1,000	1,500	2,000	2,500
1984						
WMX 125	300	500	1,500	2,500	3,000	3,500
WRX 125	300	500	700	1,300	2,000	2,700
WRX 200	300	500	1,500	2,000	3,000	4,000
WMX 250	300	500	1,500	3,500	4,500	5,500
DG 350	300	500	1,000	1,500	2,500	3,500
MXR 500	300	500	1,500	3,500	4,500	5,500
1985						
WMX 125	300	500	700	1,300	2,000	2,700
Alazzurra 350	300	500	700	1,300	2,000	2,700
WMX 500	300	500	1,500	2,500	3,500	4,500
Elefant 650	300	500	1,600	2,000	3,000	4,000
Alazzurra 650	300	500	1,000	1,500	2,500	3,500
1986						
WMX 125	300	500	700	1,300	2,000	2,700
WMX 500	300	500	1,500	2,000	2,500	3,000
Alazzurra 650	300	500	700	1,300	1,800	2,300
Alazzurra 650SS	300	500	700	1,300	2,000	2,700
Elefant 650	500	800	1,500	2,000	3,000	4,000
F-1 Ducati.	800	1,500	2,500	4,000	5,500	7,000
1987						
WMX 125	300	500	700	1,300	1,800	2,300
Alazzurra 650SS	300	500	700	1,300	2,000	2,700
Alazzurra Sport	300	500	700	1,300	1,800	2,300
Elefant 650	300	500	900	1,400	2,100	2,800
Elefant 650 SE	300	500	1,000	1,500	2,500	3,500
WMX 500	300	500	700	1,300	2,000	2,700
1988						
WMX 125	300	500	700	1,300	1,600	2,000
WRK 125	300	500	700	1,300	1,800	2,300
WMX 250	300	500	700	1,300	2,000	2,700
1989						
WMX 125	300	500	700	1,300	1,800	2,300
WMX 250	300	500	700	1,300	2,000	2,700

CAN AM

	6	5	4	3	2	1
1965						
Bombardier	600	1,000	2,000	3,000	4,000	5,000
1974						
125 MX	1,000	1,600	2,200	2,900	4,500	6,000
125 TNT.	600	900	1,300	1,700	2,500	3,300
175 MX	700	1,100	1,500	1,900	2,800	3,700
175 TNT.	1,200	1,900	2,500	3,300	5,200	7,000
1975						
125 MX-2	1,000	1,400	1,900	2,600	4,000	5,400
125 TNT.	600	900	1,300	1,700	2,600	3,500
175 MX-2	700	1,100	1,500	1,900	2,800	3,700
175 TNT.	1,200	1,900	2,500	3,500	5,300	7,100
250 MX-2	1,900	2,600	3,600	4,800	7,500	9,500
250 TNT.	1,700	2,300	3,100	4,200	6,500	7,800
1976						
175 OR	1,400	2,000	2,800	3,600	5,600	7,600

	6	5	4	3	2	1
175 F3 (175cc single)	3,400	5,100	7,700	10,000	14,000	17,000
200 elite (200cc single)	1,000	1,500	2,300	3,000	4,000	5,000
1960						
Bronco (85cc single)	500	800	1,100	1,500	2,000	2,500
125 F3 (125cc single)	2,400	3,600	5,400	7,200	9,600	12,000
125 Grand Prix (125cc single).	5,200	7,800	18,000	16,000	21,000	26,000
173 F3 (175cc single)	3,400	5,100	7,700	10,000	14,000	17,000
200 Americano (200cc single).	700	1,100	1,600	2,100	2,800	3,500
200 elite (200cc single)	1,000	1,500	2,300	3,000	4,000	5,000
200 Motocross (200cc single)	1,000	1,500	2,300	3,000	4,000	5,000
220 Grand Prix (220cc single).	6,400	9,600	14,000	19,000	26,000	32,000
1961						
Bronco (85cc single)	500	800	1,100	1,500	2,000	2,500
Grand Prix (125cc single)	5,200	7,800	18,000	16,000	21,000	26,000
125 F3 (125cc single)	2,400	3,600	5,400	7,200	9,600	12,000
175 F3 (175cc single)	3,400	5,100	7,700	10,000	14,000	17,000
200 Americano (200cc single).	900	1,400	2,000	2,700	3,600	4,500
200 Elite (200cc single)	1,000	1,500	2,300	3,000	4,000	5,000
200 Motocross (200cc single)	1,000	1,500	2,300	3,000	4,000	5,000
Monza Tourer (250cc single)	800	1,200	1,800	2,400	3,200	4,000
250 F3 (250cc single)	3,400	5,100	7,700	10,000	14,000	17,000
1962						
48 Sport Falcon (48cc single)	600	1,000	1,400	1,900	2,600	3,200
Bronco (85cc single)	500	800	1,100	1,500	2,000	2,500
Diana (250cc single)	1,000	1,500	2,300	3,000	4,000	5,000
250 F3 (250cc single)	3,400	5,100	7,700	10,000	14,000	17,000
Monza Tourer (250cc single)	800	1,200	1,800	2,400	3,200	4,000
250 Scrambler (250cc single)	800	1,100	1,700	2,300	3,000	3,800
1963						
48 Sport Falcon (48cc single)	600	1,000	1,400	1,900	2,600	3,200
Bronco (85cc single)	500	800	1,100	1,500	2,000	2,500
Diana (250cc single)	1,000	1,500	2,300	3,000	4,000	5,000
Monza Tourer (250cc single)	800	1,200	1,800	2,400	3,200	4,000
250 Scrambler (250cc single)	700	1,100	1,600	2,100	2,800	3,500
1964						
48 SL (48cc single)	600	800	1,300	1,700	2,200	2,800
48 Sport Falcon (48cc single)	600	1,000	1,400	1,900	2,600	3,200
Cadet Falcon 100 (98cc single)	600	900	1,300	1,700	2,300	2,900
Mountaineer (98cc single).	600	900	1,400	1,800	2,400	3,000
Diana (250cc single)	1,100	1,700	2,500	3,300	4,400	5,500
Monza Tourer (250cc single)	800	1,200	1,800	2,400	3,200	4,000
250 GT (250cc single).	600	900	1,400	1,800	2,400	3,000
250 Mach 1 (250cc single)	1,100	1,700	2,500	3,300	4,400	5,500
1965						
48 SL (48cc single)	600	800	1,300	1,700	2,200	2,800
48 Sport Falcon (48cc single)	600	1,000	1,400	1,900	2,600	3,200
Cadet Falcon 100 (98cc single)	600	900	1,300	1,700	2,300	2,900
Mountaineer (98cc single).	600	900	1,400	1,800	2,400	3,000
Diana (250cc single)	1,100	1,700	2,500	3,300	4,400	5,500
Monza Tourer (250cc single)	800	1,200	1,800	2,400	3,200	4,000
250 GT (250cc single).	600	900	1,400	1,800	2,400	3,000
250 Mach 1 (250cc single)	1,100	1,700	2,500	3,300	4,400	5,500
1966						
50 SL (50cc single)	600	800	1,300	1,700	2,200	2,800
Cadet Falcon 100 (98cc single)	600	900	1,300	1,700	2,300	2,900
Mountaineer (98cc single).	600	900	1,400	1,800	2,400	3,000
Monza Tourer (250cc single)	800	1,200	1,800	2,400	3,200	4,000
250 GT (250cc single).	600	900	1,400	1,800	2,400	3,000
250 Mach 1 (250cc single)	1,100	1,700	2,500	3,300	4,400	5,500

	6	5	4	3	2	1
1967						
50 SL (50cc single)	600	800	1,300	1,700	2,200	2,800
Cadet Falcon 100 (98cc single)	600	900	1,300	1,700	2,300	2,900
Mountaineer (98cc single).	600	900	1,400	1,800	2,400	3,000
250 GT (250cc single).	600	900	1,400	1,800	2,400	3,000
250 Mach 1 (250cc single)	1,100	1,700	2,500	3,300	4,400	5,500
1968						
50 SL (50cc single)	600	800	1,300	1,700	2,200	2,800
160 Monza Junior (152cc single)	600	900	1,400	1,800	2,400	3,000
250 Mark 3 (250cc single).	800	1,200	1,800	2,600	4,000	5,000
250 Mark 3 Desmo (250cc single).	900	1,400	2,000	2,700	3,600	4,500
250 Street Scrambler (250cc single)	600	900	1,400	1,800	2,400	3,000
350 Mark 3 (340cc single).	900	1,400	2,000	2,700	3,600	4,500
350 Mark 3 Desmo (340cc single).	1,000	1,500	2,300	3,100	4,100	5,100
350 Street Scrambler (340cc single)	700	1,000	1,500	2,000	2,600	3,300
350 Sebring (340cc single)	600	900	1,400	1,800	2,400	3,000
1969						
50 Scrambler (50cc single)	500	700	1,100	1,400	1,900	2,400
50 SL (50cc single)	600	800	1,300	1,700	2,200	2,800
100 Scrambler (100cc single)	400	600	900	1,200	1,600	2,000
160 Monza Junior (152cc single)	600	900	1,400	1,800	2,400	3,000
250 Mark 3 (250cc single).	800	1,200	2,000	3,000	4,000	5,000
250 Mark 3 Desmo (250cc single).	900	1,400	2,000	2,700	3,600	4,500
250 Street Scrambler (250cc single)	600	900	1,400	1,800	2,400	3,000
350 Mark 3 (340cc single).	900	1,400	2,000	2,700	3,600	4,500
350 Mark 3 Desmo (340cc single).	1,000	1,500	2,300	3,100	4,100	5,100
350 Street Scrambler (340cc single)	700	1,000	1,500	2,000	2,600	3,300
350 Sebring (340cc single)	600	900	1,400	1,800	2,400	3,000
1970						
50 Scrambler (50cc single)	500	700	1,100	1,400	1,900	2,400
100 Scrambler (100cc single)	400	600	900	1,200	1,600	2,000
160 Monza Junior (152cc single)	600	900	1,400	1,800	2,400	3,000
250 Mark 3 (250cc single).	800	1,200	1,800	2,400	3,200	4,000
250 Mark 3 Desmo (250cc single).	900	1,400	2,000	2,700	3,600	4,500
250 Street Scrambler (250cc single)	600	900	1,400	1,800	2,400	3,000
350 Mark 3 (340cc single).	900	1,400	2,000	2,700	3,600	4,500
350 Mark 3 Desmo (340cc single).	1,000	1,500	2,300	3,100	4,100	5,100
350 Sebring (340cc single)	700	1,000	1,500	2,000	2,600	3,300
350 Street Scrambler (340cc single)	600	900	1,400	1,800	2,400	3,000
450 Mark 3 (436cc single).	900	1,400	2,100	2,800	3,800	4,700
450 Mark 3 Desmo (436cc single).	1,200	1,900	2,800	3,700	5,000	6,200
1971						
125 Scrambler (125cc single)	400	600	900	1,200	1,600	2,000
250 Mark 3 (250cc single).	800	1,200	1,800	2,400	3,200	4,000
250 Mark 3 Desmo (250cc single).	900	1,400	2,000	2,700	3,600	4,500
250 Street Scrambler (250cc single)	600	900	1,400	1,800	2,400	3,000
350 Mark 3 (340cc single).	900	1,400	2,000	2,700	3,600	4,500
350 Mark 3 Desmo (340cc single).	1,000	1,500	2,300	3,100	4,100	5,100
350 Sebring (340cc single)	600	900	1,400	1,800	2,400	3,000
350 Street Scrambler (340cc single)	700	1,000	1,500	2,000	2,600	3,300
450 Mark 3 (436cc single).	900	1,400	2,100	2,800	3,800	4,700
450 Mark 3 Desmo (436cc single).	1,200	1,900	2,800	3,700	5,000	6,200
750 GT (748cc V-twin)	**2,400**	**3,600**	**5,400**	**7,200**	**9,600**	**12,000**
1972						
250 Mark 3 (250cc single).	800	1,200	1,900	2,500	3,300	4,100
250 Mark 3 Desmo (250cc single).	900	1,400	2,100	2,800	3,800	4,700
250 Street Scrambler (250cc single)	600	900	1,400	1,800	2,400	3,000
350 Mark 3 (340cc single).	900	1,300	2,000	2,600	3,500	4,400
350 Mark 3 Desmo (340cc single).	1,000	1,400	2,200	2,900	3,800	4,800

	6	5	4	3	2	1
350 Desmo Silver Shotgun (340cc single). .	1,100	1,650	2,480	3,300	4,400	5,500
350 Sebring (340cc single)	600	900	1,400	1,800	2,400	3,000
350 Street Scrambler (340cc single)	700	1,000	1,500	2,000	2,600	3,300
450 Mark 3 (436cc single).	900	1,400	2,100	2,800	3,800	4,700
450 Mark 3 Desmo (436cc single).	1,200	1,900	2,800	3,700	5,000	6,200
750 GT (748cc V-twin)	**2,400**	**3,600**	**5,400**	**7,200**	**9,600**	**12,000**
750 Sport (748cc V-twin)	2,400	**4,000**	**7,000**	**12,000**	**17,000**	**22,000**
1973						
250 Mark 3 (250cc single).	800	1,200	1,900	2,500	3,300	4,100
250 Mark 3 Desmo (250cc single).	900	1,400	2,100	2,800	3,800	4,700
250 Street Scrambler (250cc single) . . .	600	900	1,400	1,800	2,400	3,000
350 Mark 3 (340cc single).	900	1,300	2,000	2,600	3,500	4,400
350 Mark 3 Desmo (340cc single).	1,000	1,400	2,200	2,900	3,800	4,800
350 Street Scrambler (340cc single) . . .	700	1,000	1,500	2,000	2,600	3,300
450 Mark 3 (436cc single).	900	1,400	2,100	2,800	3,800	4,700
450 Mark 3 Desmo (436cc single).	1,200	1,900	2,800	3,700	5,000	6,200
750 GT (748cc V-twin)	**2,400**	**3,600**	**5,400**	**7,200**	**9,600**	**12,000**
750 Sport (748cc V-twin)	2,400	**4,000**	**7,000**	**12,000**	**17,000**	**22,000**
750 SS Round Case (748cc V-twin).	7,000	11,000	16,000	21,000	28,000	35,000
1974						
250 Mark 3 (250cc single).	800	1,200	1,900	2,500	3,300	4,100
250 Mark 3 Desmo (250cc single).	900	1,400	2,100	2,800	3,800	4,700
250 Street Scrambler (250cc single) . . .	600	900	1,400	1,800	2,400	3,000
350 Mark 3 (340cc single).	900	1,300	2,000	2,600	3,500	4,400
350 Mark 3 Desmo (340cc single).	1,000	1,400	2,200	2,900	3,800	4,800
350 Street Scrambler (340cc single) . . .	700	1,000	1,500	2,000	2,600	3,300
450 Mark 3 (436cc single).	900	1,400	2,100	2,800	3,800	4,700
450 Mark 3 Desmo (436cc single).	1,200	1,900	2,800	3,700	5,000	6,200
750 GT (748cc V-twin)	**2,400**	**3,600**	**5,400**	**7,200**	**9,600**	**12,000**
750 Sport (748cc V-twin)	2,400	**4,000**	**7,000**	**12,000**	**17,000**	**22,000**
750 SS Round Case (748cc V-twin).	7,000	11,000	16,000	20,000	25,000	30,000
860 GT (864cc V-twin)	900	1,300	2,000	2,600	3,500	4,400
1975						
125 Regolarita (125cc single)	400	700	1,000	1,300	1,800	2,200
GTL 350 (350cc twin)	800	1,100	1,600	2,200	2,900	3,600
GTL 500 (496cc twin)	600	900	1,400	1,900	2,500	3,100
750 SS Square Case (748cc V-twin)	3,000	4,500	6,800	9,000	12,000	15,000
860 GT (864cc V-twin)	900	1,300	2,000	2,600	3,500	4,400
900 SS (864cc V-twin)	3,000	5,000	**10,000**	**15,000**	**20,000**	**25,000**
1976						
125 Regolarita (125cc single)	500	700	1,000	1,400	1,900	2,300
GTL 350 (350cc twin)	700	1,100	1,600	2,100	2,800	3,500
GTL 500 (496cc twin)	600	900	1,400	1,900	2,500	3,100
750 SS Square Case (748cc V-twin)	3,000	4,500	6,800	9,000	12,000	15,000
860 GT (864cc V-twin)	900	1,300	2,000	2,600	3,500	4,400
900 GTS (864cc V-twin).	1,200	1,800	2,700	3,600	4,800	6,000
900 SS (864cc V-twin)	3,000	5,000	**10,000**	**15,000**	**20,000**	**25,000**
1977						
125 Six Days (125cc single).	700	1,100	1,600	2,100	2,800	3,500
GTL 350 (350cc twin)	700	1,100	1,600	2,100	2,800	3,500
Sport Desmo 350 (350cc twin)	700	1,000	1,500	2,000	2,700	3,400
GTL 500 (496cc twin)	600	900	1,350	1,800	2,400	3,000
Sport Desmo 500 (496cc twin)	800	1,100	1,700	2,300	3,000	3,800
750 SS Square Case (748cc V-twin)	3,200	4,800	7,200	9,600	13,000	16,000
Darmah SD (864cc V-twin)	900	1,400	2,000	2,700	3,600	4,500
900 GTS (864cc V-twin).	1,200	1,800	2,700	3,600	4,800	6,000
900 SS (864cc V-twin)	3,000	5,000	**10,000**	**15,000**	**20,000**	**25,000**
1978						
Sport Desmo 350 (350cc twin)	700	1,000	1,500	2,000	2,700	3,400

	6	5	4	3	2	1
Sport Desmo 500 (496cc twin)	800	1,100	1,700	2,300	3,000	3,800
Darmah SD (864cc V-twin)	900	1,400	2,000	2,700	3,600	4,500
900 GTS (864cc V-twin)	1,200	1,800	2,700	3,600	4,800	6,000
900 SS (864cc V-twin)	**3,000**	**5,000**	**10,000**	**15,000**	**20,000**	**25,000**
1979						
GTV 350 (350cc twin)	600	1,000	1,400	1,900	2,600	3,200
Sport Desmo 350 (350cc twin)	700	1,000	1,500	2,000	2,700	3,400
GTV 500 (496cc twin)	700	1,100	1,600	2,100	2,800	3,500
Sport Desmo 500 (496cc twin)	800	1,100	1,700	2,300	3,000	3,800
500 SI Pantah (500cc V-twin)	800	1,100	1,700	2,300	3,000	3,800
Darmah SD (864cc V-twin)	1,000	1,500	2,300	3,000	4,000	5,000
Darmah SD Sport (864cc V-twin)	1,000	**2,000**	**3,000**	**4,000**	**5,500**	**7,000**
Darmah SS (864cc V-twin)	1,100	1,700	2,600	3,400	4,600	5,700
Mike Hailwood Replica (864cc V-twin) . . .	2,400	**4,000**	**8,000**	**12,000**	**16,000**	**20,000**
900 SS (864cc V-twin)	**3,000**	**5,000**	**10,000**	**15,000**	**20,000**	**25,000**
1980						
GTV 350 (350cc twin)	600	1,000	1,400	1,900	2,600	3,200
Sport Desmo 350 (350cc twin)	700	1,000	1,500	2,000	2,700	3,400
GTV 500 (496cc twin)	700	1,100	1,600	2,100	2,800	3,500
Sport Desmo 500 (496cc twin)	800	1,100	1,700	2,300	3,000	3,800
500 SI Pantah (500cc V-twin)	800	1,100	1,700	2,300	3,000	3,800
Darmah SD (864cc V-twin)	1,000	1,500	2,300	3,000	4,000	5,000
Darmah SD Sport (864cc V-twin)	1,000	**2,000**	**3,000**	**4,000**	**5,500**	**7,000**
Darmah SS (864cc V-twin)	1,100	1,700	2,600	3,400	4,600	5,700
Mike Hailwood Replica (864cc V-twin) . . .	2,400	**4,000**	**8,000**	**12,000**	**16,000**	**20,000**
900 SS (864cc V-twin)	**3,000**	**5,000**	**10,000**	**15,000**	**20,000**	**25,000**
1981						
Pantah (500cc twin)	1,500	2,000	3,000	4,800	6,500	7,500
Darmah (900cc twin)	1,500	2,500	4,000	6,000	7,500	9,000
Darmah SS (900cc twin)	2,000	3,000	4,500	5,900	7,900	9,000
Super Sport (900cc twin)	2,400	3,600	5,200	6,550	8,800	10,000
1982						
Pantah (500cc twin)	1,500	2,500	4,000	5,300	7,100	8,500
Darmah (900cc twin)	2,400	3,200	4,200	5,600	7,500	8,700
Darmah SS (900cc twin)	2,000	3,000	4,500	6,100	8,200	9,200
Super Sport (900cc twin)	2,200	3,400	5,000	6,700	9,000	12,000
1986						
F1-S Road Racer (750cc twin)	2,200	2,800	3,500	4,700	6,300	8,000
1987						
Indiana (650cc twin)	1,100	1,600	2,200	2,900	3,600	4,300
Paso (750cc twin)	1,100	1,600	2,200	2,850	4,700	6,400
F1-B Road Racer (750cc twin)	1,400	2,400	3,800	5,000	6,700	7,500
1988						
Paso (750cc twin)	1,200	1,800	2,300	3,000	4,800	6,700
Paso Limited (750cc twin)	1,200	1,800	2,400	3,100	5,100	7,200
F1-B Road Racer (750cc twin)	1,500	2,500	4,000	5,300	7,100	8,500
1990						
750 Sport (750cc twin)	1,400	2,000	2,800	3,700	5,000	6,700
851 Sport (850cc twin)	2,000	3,000	4,400	5,900	8,000	11,000
906 Paso (900cc twin)	1,300	1,900	2,600	3,500	5,100	7,800
1991						
851 Sport (850cc twin)	2,100	3,200	4,700	6,300	8,300	12,000
900 Super Sport (900cc twin)	1,600	2,200	3,000	3,900	5,900	7,900
907 Paso I.E. (900cc twin)	2,000	2,600	3,300	4,400	5,500	8,700
1992						
750SS (750cc twin)	1,500	2,100	2,700	3,600	5,400	7,400
851 Sport (850cc twin)	2,200	3,400	5,100	6,800	10,000	13,000
900 Super Sport (900cc twin)	1,900	2,500	3,200	4,200	6,300	8,500
907 Paso I.E. (900cc twin)	2,200	2,800	3,500	4,600	6,700	9,000

	6	5	4	3	2	1
1993						
750SS (750cc twin)	1,700	2,300	2,900	3,800	5,500	7,500
888SPO (888cc twin)	2,500	4,200	6,300	8,400	10,500	13,000
900 Super Light (900cc twin)	2,000	3,400	5,200	7,000	8,800	11,000
900 Super Sport (900cc twin)	1,900	2,500	3,400	4,500	6,400	8,600
907 Paso I.E. (900cc twin)	2,300	2,900	3,700	5,000	7,000	9,300
M900 (900cc twin).	1,500	2,200	3,000	3,900	4,900	5,900
1994						
888 LTD (900cc twin)	800	1,200	2,100	4,300	6,300	9,100
900 CR (900cc twin)	200	500	1,400	2,900	4,300	5,700
900 SP (900cc twin).	300	600	1,600	3,300	4,900	6,500
E900 (900cc twin)	300	600	1,500	3,000	4,500	6,000
M900 (900cc twin).	1,500	2,200	3,000	3,900	4,900	5,900
916 (916cc twin).	600	900	2,600	5,300	7,800	10,300
1995						
E900 (900cc twin)	600	1,300	2,400	3,500	4,600	5,700
900 CR (900cc twin).	500	1,000	2,100	3,200	4,300	5,400
M900 (900cc twin).	600	1,200	2,300	3,400	4,500	5,600
900 SP (900cc twin).	700	1,300	2,500	3,700	4,900	6,100
916 (916cc twin).	800	1,600	3,300	5,000	6,700	8,000

EXCELSIOR

	6	5	4	3	2	1
1907						
Single	15,000	20,000	26,000	35,000	45,000	55,000
1910						
Single	5,000	10,000	15,000	25,000	35,000	45,000
1911						
Single	10,000	20,000	30,000	40,000	50,000	60,000
Auto-Cycle	10,000	20,000	30,000	50,000	70,000	90,000
30.5 Twin	5,000	10,000	15,000	20,000	26,000	35,000
1913						
Big Valve Twin	15,000	25,000	35,000	50,000	60,000	70,000
1914						
Short Coupled V-Twin.	5,000	10,000	20,000	30,000	40,000	50,000
Twin	10,000	20,000	40,000	60,000	80,000	100K
Auto-Cycle	5,000	10,000	15,000	20,000	26,000	35,000
1917						
Super X Twin	25,000	35,000	45,000	55,000	70,000	90,000
1918						
V-Twin.	10,000	15,000	20,000	25,000	30,000	40,000
1920						
Big Valve Twin	5,000	10,000	20,000	30,000	40,000	50,000
1928						
Super X	4,000	8,000	16,000	24,000	32,000	40,000
1930						
Super X Streamliner.	10,000	20,000	35,000	50,000	65,000	80,000
1938						
Manxman	3,000	6,000	10,000	15,000	20,000	25,000

GAS GAS

	6	5	4	3	2	1
1991						
Delta GT25 (238cc single).	100	200	400	700	1,000	1,300
Delta GT32 (327cc single).	100	200	400	700	1,000	1,300
1992						
Contact GT25 (238cc single)	100	200	400	800	1,100	1,400
Contact GT32 (327cc single)	100	200	400	800	1,100	1,400
1993						
Contact GT12 (124cc single)	100	200	500	800	1,100	1,600
Contact GT16 (143cc single)	100	200	400	900	1,200	1,500
Contact GT25 (238cc single)	100	200	500	900	1,300	1,700
Contact GT32 (327cc single)	100	200	500	900	1,300	1,700

	6	5	4	3	2	1
1994						
Endurocross TT80 (80cc single)	100	300	500	700	900	1,300
Motocross TT80 (80cc single)	100	200	600	800	1,000	1,400
Endurocross TT125 (125cc single)	100	200	400	800	1,200	1,700
Motocross TT125 (125cc single)	100	300	600	900	1,400	1,900
Contact GT16 (143cc single)	100	200	400	900	1,300	1,700
Contact GT25 JT (238cc single)	100	200	500	900	1,400	1,900
Endurocross TT250 (250cc single)	100	200	600	1,100	1,700	2,300
Motocross TT250 (250cc single)	200	500	800	1,100	1,600	2,100
Contact GT32 JT (328cc single)	100	200	500	900	1,400	1,900
1995						
Endurocross TT80 (80cc single)	100	200	300	500	1,000	1,400
Cross CR125 (124cc single)	100	300	600	900	1,400	1,900
Endurocross TT124 (125cc single)	100	300	600	800	1,300	1,800
Contact JT16 (144cc single)	100	300	600	900	1,300	1,800
Contact JT25 (238cc single)	100	300	600	900	1,300	1,800
Cross CR250 (249cc single)	200	500	800	1,100	1,700	2,300
Endurocross TT250 (250cc single)	100	300	600	1,100	1,600	2,100
Contact JT32 (327cc single)	100	300	600	900	1,300	1,800
GREEVES						
1960						
Trials	1,500	3,000	4,000	5,000	6,000	7,000
1962						
MC5	1,000	2,000	3,000	4,000	5,000	6,000
1966						
250cc	750	1,400	2,000	3,000	4,500	6,000
1969						
Ranger	1,500	3,000	4,000	5,000	6,000	7,000
1970						
250 Desert	1,200	1,700	2,300	3,100	4,800	6,500
250 Moto Cross	1,600	2,100	2,800	3,700	5,800	8,000
380 Desert	1,100	1,600	2,100	2,800	4,400	7,000
380 Moto Cross	2,100	2,900	3,900	5,200	8,100	10,000
1971						
250 Desert	1,200	1,700	2,300	3,100	4,800	6,500
250 Moto Cross	1,600	2,100	2,800	3,700	5,800	8,000
380 Desert	1,100	1,600	2,100	2,800	4,400	7,000
380 Moto Cross	2,100	2,900	3,900	5,200	8,100	10,000
1972						
250 Desert	1,200	1,700	2,300	3,100	4,800	6,500
250 Moto Cross	1,600	2,100	2,800	3,700	5,800	8,000
380 Desert	1,100	1,600	2,100	2,800	4,400	7,000
380 Moto Cross	2,100	2,900	3,900	5,200	8,100	10,000
1973						
250 Desert	1,200	1,700	2,300	3,100	4,800	6,500
250 Moto Cross	1,600	2,100	2,800	3,700	5,800	8,000
380 Desert	1,100	1,600	2,100	2,800	4,400	7,000
380 Moto Cross	2,100	2,900	3,900	5,200	8,100	10,000
1974						
250 Desert	1,200	1,700	2,300	3,100	4,800	6,500
250 Moto Cross	1,600	2,100	2,800	3,700	5,800	8,000
380 Desert	1,100	1,600	2,100	2,800	4,400	7,000
380 Moto Cross	2,100	2,900	3,900	5,200	8,100	10,000
1975						
250 Desert	1,200	1,700	2,300	3,100	4,800	6,500
250 Griffon	900	1,400	1,900	2,500	3,900	5,300
380 Desert	1,100	1,600	2,100	2,800	4,400	7,000
380 Griffon	1,400	2,000	3,500	5,000	6,500	8,000

	6	5	4	3	2	1
HARLEY-DAVIDSON						
1903						
Single (24.74ci) (3)	3MM	4.5MM	6MM	9MM	12MM	15MM
1904						
Model 0 (24.74ci) (8)	1MM	1.5MM	2MM	3MM	4MM	5MM
1905						
Model 1 (24.74ci) (16).	500K	750K	1MM	1.5MM	2MM	2.5MM
1906						
Model 2 (24.74 ci) (50)	270K	360K	480K	720K	990K	1.2MM
1907						
Model 3 (24.74ci) (150)	90,000	120K	160K	240K	330K	420K
1908						
Model 4 (26.8ci) (450)	29,000	39,000	52,000	79,000	113K	140K
1909						
5 Single (30ci) (864).	18,000	28,000	40,000	58,000	88,000	120K
5A Single (30ci) (54)	20,000	30,000	42,000	69,000	100K	130K
5B Single (30ci) (168)	18,000	28,000	40,000	58,000	88,000	120K
5C Single (35ci) (36)	20,000	30,000	42,000	69,000	100K	130K
5D Single (50ci) (27)	20,000	30,000	42,000	69,000	100K	130K
1910						
6 Single (35ci) (2,302)	10,000	15,000	24,000	38,000	62,000	85,000
6A Single (35ci) (334)	10,000	15,000	24,000	38,000	62,000	85,000
6B Single (35ci) (443)	10,000	15,000	24,000	38,000	62,000	85,000
6C Single (35ci) (88)	10,000	15,000	24,000	38,000	62,000	85,000
1911						
7 Single (35ci)	9,000	14,000	21,000	31,000	47,000	60,000
7A Single (35ci)	9,000	14,000	21,000	31,000	47,000	60,000
7B Single (35ci)	9,000	14,000	21,000	31,000	47,000	60,000
7C Single (35ci)	9,000	14,000	21,000	31,000	47,000	60,000
7D Twin (49.48ci)	19,000	25,000	43,000	65,000	107K	140K
1912						
8 Single (35ci)	8,000	12,000	19,000	27,000	41,000	55,000
8A Single (35ci)	8,000	12,000	19,000	27,000	41,000	55,000
8D Twin (49.48ci)	12,000	19,000	33,000	48,000	70,000	90,000
X8 Single (35ci)	11,000	15,000	21,000	31,000	47,000	60,000
X8A Single (35ci)	12,000	17,000	24,000	35,000	54,000	65,000
X8D Twin (49.48ci)	15,000	21,000	31,000	47,000	68,000	90,000
X8E Twin (61ci)	14,000	20,000	33,000	47,000	76,000	95,000
1913						
9A Single (35ci) (1,510)	7,000	11,000	16,000	24,000	38,000	50,000
9B Single (35ci) (4,601)	7,000	11,000	16,000	24,000	38,000	50,000
9E Twin (61ci) (6,732).	13,000	19,000	29,000	40,000	63,000	85,000
9F Twin (61ci) (49)	29,000	39,000	52,000	79,000	113K	140K
9G Delivery Twin (61ci)	13,000	19,000	29,000	40,000	63,000	85,000
1914						
10A Single (35ci) (316)	12,000	17,000	23,000	35,000	56,000	75,000
10B Single (35ci) (2,034)	8,000	15,000	25,000	35,000	45,000	55,000
10C Single (35ci) (877)	7,000	10,000	15,000	21,000	34,000	45,000
10E Twin (61ci) (5,055)	12,000	17,000	23,000	35,000	56,000	75,000
10F Twin (61ci) (7,956)	12,000	17,000	23,000	35,000	56,000	75,000
10G Twin (61ci) (171)	29,000	39,000	52,000	79,000	113K	140K
1915						
11B Single (35ci) (670)	7,000	11,000	15,000	22,000	38,000	55,000
11C Single (35ci) (545)	7,000	11,000	15,000	22,000	38,000	55,000
11E Twin (61cici) (1,275)	9,000	12,000	18,000	27,000	43,000	60,000
11F Twin (61ci) (985)	10,000	13,000	20,000	31,000	54,000	75,000
11G Twin (61ci) (93)	10,000	13,000	20,000	31,000	54,000	75,000
11H Twin (61ci) (140)	10,000	13,000	20,000	31,000	54,000	75,000
11J Twin (61ci) (1,719)	11,000	14,000	21,000	32,000	55,000	75,000

	6	5	4	3	2	1
1916						
B Single (35ci) (292)	7,000	11,000	15,000	21,000	34,000	45,000
C Single (35ci) (862)	7,000	11,000	15,000	21,000	34,000	45,000
E Twin (61ci) (252)	9,000	12,000	17,000	28,000	45,000	60,000
F Twin (61ci) (9496)	10,000	13,000	19,000	31,000	48,000	65,000
J Twin (61ci) (5898)	10,000	14,000	19,000	31,000	48,000	65,000
1917						
B Single (35ci) (124)	4,000	6,000	7,000	12,000	23,000	35,000
C Single (35ci) (605)	4,000	6,000	7,000	12,000	23,000	35,000
E Twin (61ci) (68)	4,000	7,000	10,000	20,000	34,000	45,000
F Twin (61ci) (8,527)	4,000	7,000	10,000	20,000	34,000	45,000
J Twin (61ci) (9,180)	4,000	7,000	10,000	20,000	34,000	45,000
1918						
B Single (35ci) (19)	4,000	6,000	7,000	12,000	22,000	32,000
C Single (35ci) (251)	4,000	6,000	7,000	12,000	22,000	32,000
E Twin (61ci) (5)	4,000	7,000	10,000	20,000	34,000	45,000
F Twin (61ci) (11,764)	4,000	7,000	10,000	20,000	34,000	45,000
J Twin (61ci) (6,571)	4,000	7,000	10,000	20,000	34,000	45,000
1919						
F Twin (61ci) (5,064)	4,000	6,000	9,000	16,000	29,000	40,000
J Twin (61ci) (9,941)	4,000	6,000	10,000	16,000	30,000	45,000
1920						
WF (35.64ci twin) (4,459)	4,800	7,200	11,000	14,000	19,000	24,000
WJ (35.64ci twin) (810)	4,800	7,200	11,000	14,000	19,000	24,000
F (60.34ci V-twin) (7,579)	5,000	7,500	11,000	15,000	20,000	25,000
FS (60.34ci V-twin)	5,000	7,500	11,000	15,000	20,000	25,000
J (60.34ci V-twin) (14,192)	10,000	15,000	20,000	25,000	30,000	35,000
JS (60.34ci V-twin)	5,000	7,500	11,000	15,000	20,000	25,000
1921						
WF (35.64ci twin) (1,100)	4,400	6,600	9,900	13,000	18,000	22,000
WJ (35.64ci twin) (823)	4,400	6,600	9,900	13,000	18,000	22,000
CD (37ci single)	4,400	6,600	9,900	13,000	18,000	22,000
F (60.34ci V-twin) (2,413)	5,000	7,500	11,000	15,000	20,000	25,000
FS (60.34ci V-twin)	5,000	7,500	11,000	15,000	20,000	25,000
J (60.34ci V-twin) (4,526)	10,000	15,000	20,000	25,000	30,000	35,000
JS (60.34ci V-twin)	5,000	7,500	11,000	15,000	20,000	25,000
FD (74ci V-twin) (277)	5,100	7,600	15,000	20,000	25,000	30,000
FDS (74ci V-twin)	5,100	7,600	11,000	15,000	20,000	26,000
JD (74ci V-twin) (2,321)	5,100	7,600	11,000	15,000	20,000	26,000
JDS (74ci V-twin)	5,100	7,600	11,000	15,000	20,000	26,000
1922						
WF (35.64ci twin)	4,400	6,600	9,900	13,000	18,000	22,000
WJ (35.64ci twin) (455)	4,400	6,600	9,900	13,000	18,000	22,000
CD (37ci single) (39)	4,400	6,600	9,900	13,000	18,000	22,000
F (60.34ci V-twin) (1,824)	4,600	6,900	10,000	14,000	18,000	23,000
FS (60.34ci V-twin)	4,600	6,900	10,000	14,000	18,000	23,000
J (60.34ci V-twin) (3,183)	10,000	15,000	20,000	25,000	30,000	35,000
JS (60.34ci V-twin)	4,600	6,900	10,000	14,000	18,000	23,000
FD (74ci V-twin) (909)	5,000	7,500	11,000	15,000	20,000	25,000
FDS (74ci V-twin)	5,000	7,500	11,000	15,000	20,000	25,000
JD (74ci V-twin) (3,988)	5,000	7,500	11,000	15,000	20,000	25,000
JDS (74ci V-twin)	5,000	7,500	11,000	15,000	20,000	25,000
1923						
WF (35.64ci twin) (614)	4,400	6,600	9,900	13,000	18,000	22,000
WJ (35.64ci twin) (481)	4,400	6,600	9,900	13,000	18,000	22,000
F (60.34ci V-twin) (2,822)	4,600	6,900	10,000	14,000	18,000	23,000
FS (60.34ci V-twin)	4,600	6,900	10,000	14,000	18,000	23,000
J (60.34ci V-twin) (4,802)	10,000	15,000	20,000	25,000	30,000	35,000
JS (60.34ci V-twin)	5,000	7,500	12,500	15,000	20,000	25,000

	6	5	4	3	2	1
FD (74ci V-twin) (869)	5,000	7,500	11,000	15,000	20,000	25,000
FDS (74ci V-twin)	5,000	7,500	11,000	15,000	20,000	25,000
JD (74ci V-twin) (7,458)	5,000	7,500	11,000	15,000	20,000	25,000
JDS (74ci V-twin)	5,000	7,500	11,000	15,000	20,000	25,000
1924						
FE (60.34ci V-twin)	3,800	5,700	8,600	11,000	15,000	19,000
FES (60.34ci V-twin)	3,800	5,700	8,600	11,000	15,000	19,000
JE (60.34ci V-twin)	4,200	6,300	11,000	15,000	19,000	23,000
JES (60.34ci V-twin)	4,200	6,300	9,500	13,000	17,000	21,000
FD (74ci V-twin)	4,000	6,000	9,000	12,000	16,000	20,000
FDS (74ci V-twin)	4,000	6,000	9,000	12,000	16,000	20,000
FDCA (74ci V-twin)	4,000	6,000	9,000	12,000	16,000	20,000
FDSCA (74ci V-twin)	4,000	6,000	9,000	12,000	16,000	20,000
FDCB (74ci V-twin)	4,000	6,000	9,000	12,000	16,000	20,000
JD (74ci V-twin)	4,600	6,900	10,000	14,000	18,000	23,000
JDS (74ci V-twin)	4,600	6,900	10,000	14,000	18,000	23,000
JDCA (74ci V-twin)	4,600	6,900	10,000	14,000	18,000	23,000
JDSCA (74ci V-twin)	4,600	6,900	10,000	14,000	18,000	23,000
JDCB (74ci V-twin)	4,600	6,900	10,000	14,000	18,000	23,000
1925						
FE (60.34ci V-twin)	3,800	5,700	8,600	11,000	15,000	19,000
FES (60.34ci V-twin)	3,800	5,700	8,600	11,000	15,000	19,000
JE (60.34ci V-twin)	4,200	6,300	9,500	13,000	17,000	21,000
JES 60.34ci V-twin)	4,200	6,300	9,500	13,000	17,000	21,000
FDCB (74ci V-twin)	4,000	6,000	9,000	12,000	16,000	20,000
FDCBS (74ci V-twin)	4,000	6,000	9,000	12,000	16,000	20,000
JDCB (74ci V-twin)	4,600	6,900	10,000	14,000	18,000	23,000
JDCBS (74ci/V—twin)	4,600	6,900	10,000	14,000	18,000	23,000
1926						
A (21.35ci single)	3,200	4,800	7,200	9,600	13,000	16,000
B (21.35ci single)	3,200	4,800	7,200	10,000	14,000	18,000
AA (21.35ci single)	4,000	6,000	9,000	12,000	16,000	20,000
BA (21.35ci single)	4,000	6,000	9,000	12,000	16,000	20,000
S (21.35ci single)	4,400	6,600	9,900	13,000	18,000	22,000
J (60.34ci V-twin)	4,600	6,900	10,000	14,000	18,000	23,000
JS (60.34ci V-twin)	4,600	6,900	10,000	14,000	18,000	23,000
JD (74ci V-twin)	4,600	6,900	10,000	14,000	18,000	23,000
JDS (74ci V-twin)	4,600	6,900	10,000	14,000	18,000	23,000
1927						
A (21.35ci single)	3,200	4,800	7,200	9,600	13,000	16,000
B (21.35ci single)	3,200	4,800	7,200	9,600	13,000	16,000
AA (21.35ci single)	3,900	5,900	8,800	12,000	16,000	20,000
BA (21.35ci single)	4,000	6,000	9,000	12,000	16,000	20,000
S (21.35ci single)	4,400	6,600	9,900	13,000	18,000	22,000
J (60.34ci V-twin)	4,600	6,900	10,000	14,000	18,000	23,000
JS (60.34ci V-twin)	4,600	6,900	10,000	14,000	18,000	23,000
JD (74ci V-twin)	4,600	6,900	10,000	14,000	18,000	23,000
JDS (74ci V-twin)	4,600	6,900	10,000	14,000	18,000	23,000
1928						
B (21.35ci single)	3,000	4,500	6,800	9,000	12,000	15,000
BA (21.35ci single)	3,800	5,700	8,600	11,000	15,000	19,000
J (60.34ci V-twin)	4,600	6,900	10,000	14,000	18,000	23,000
JS (60.34ci V-twin)	4,600	6,900	10,000	14,000	18,000	23,000
JL (60.34ci V-twin)	5,000	7,500	11,000	15,000	20,000	25,000
JH (60.34ci V-twin)	8,400	13,000	19,000	25,000	34,000	42,000
JD (74ci V-twin)	4,600	6,900	10,000	14,000	18,000	23,000
JDS (74ci V-twin)	4,600	6,900	10,000	14,000	18,000	23,000
JDL (74ci V-twin)	5,000	7,500	11,000	15,000	20,000	25,000
JDH (74ci V-twin)	9,000	14,000	20,000	27,000	36,000	45,000

	6	5	4	3	2	1
1929						
B (21.35ci single)	3,000	4,500	6,800	9,000	12,000	15,000
BA (21.35ci single)	3,800	5,700	8,600	11,000	15,000	19,000
C (30.50ci single)	3,400	5,100	7,700	10,000	14,000	17,000
D (45ci V-twin)	3,800	5,700	8,600	11,000	15,000	19,000
DL (45ci V-twin)	4,000	6,000	**10,000**	**15,000**	**20,000**	**25,000**
J (60.34ci V-twin)	4,600	6,900	10,000	14,000	18,000	23,000
JS (60.34ci V-twin)	4,600	6,900	10,000	14,000	18,000	23,000
JH 60.34ci V-twin)	8,400	13,000	19,000	25,000	34,000	42,000
JD 74ci V-twin)	4,600	6,900	10,000	14,000	18,000	23,000
JDS (74ci V-twin)	4,600	6,900	10,000	14,000	18,000	23,000
JDH (74ci V-twin)	10,000	15,000	25,000	30,000	40,000	50,000
1930						
B (21.35ci single)	2,400	3,600	5,400	7,200	9,600	12,000
C (30.50ci single)	2,800	4,200	6,300	8,400	11,000	14,000
D (45ci V-twin)	3,800	5,700	8,600	11,000	15,000	19,000
DS (45ci V-twin)	3,800	5,700	8,600	11,000	15,000	19,000
DL (45ci V-twin)	4,000	6,000	**10,000**	**15,000**	**20,000**	**25,000**
DLD (45ci V-twin)	4,000	6,000	9,000	12,000	16,000	20,000
V (74ci V-twin)	4,400	6,600	9,900	13,000	18,000	22,000
VL (74ci V-twin)	5,000	10,000	15,000	20,000	25,000	30,000
VS (74ci V-twin)	4,400	6,600	9,900	13,000	18,000	22,000
VC (74ci V-twin)	4,400	6,600	9,900	13,000	18,000	22,000
1931						
C (30.50ci single)	2,800	4,200	6,300	8,400	11,000	14,000
D (45ci V-twin)	3,400	5,100	7,700	10,000	14,000	17,000
DS (45ci V-twin)	3,400	5,100	7,700	10,000	14,000	17,000
DL (45ci V-twin)	3,600	5,400	**10,000**	**15,000**	**20,000**	**25,000**
DLD (45ci V-twin)	3,700	5,600	8,300	11,000	15,000	19,000
V (74ci V-twin)	4,400	6,600	9,900	13,000	18,000	22,000
VS (74ci V-twin)	4,400	6,600	9,900	13,000	18,000	22,000
VL (74ci V-twin)	4,800	7,200	11,000	14,000	19,000	24,000
VC (74ci V-twin)	4,000	6,000	9,000	12,000	16,000	20,000
1932						
B (21.35ci single)	2,400	3,600	5,400	7,200	9,600	12,000
C (30.50ci single)	2,800	4,200	6,300	8,400	11,000	14,000
R (45ci V-twin)	2,600	3,900	5,900	7,800	10,000	13,000
RS (45ci V-twin)	2,600	3,900	5,900	7,800	10,000	13,000
RL (45ci V-twin)	2,700	4,100	6,100	8,100	11,000	14,000
RLD (45ci V-twin)	3,000	4,500	6,800	9,000	12,000	15,000
G Servi-Car (45ci V-twin)	**2,000**	**4,000**	**8,000**	**12,000**	**16,000**	**20,000**
GA Servi-Car (45ci V-twin)	**2,000**	**4,000**	**8,000**	**12,000**	**16,000**	**20,000**
GD Servi-Car (45ci V-twin)	**2,000**	**4,000**	**8,000**	**12,000**	**16,000**	**20,000**
GE Servi-Car (45ci V-twin)	**2,000**	**4,000**	**8,000**	**12,000**	**16,000**	**20,000**
V (74ci V-twin)	4,400	6,600	9,900	13,000	18,000	22,000
VS (74ci V-twin)	4,400	6,600	9,900	13,000	18,000	22,000
VL (74ci V-twin)	4,800	7,200	11,000	14,000	19,000	24,000
VC (74ci V-twin)	4,000	6,000	9,000	12,000	16,000	20,000
1933						
B (21.35ci single)	2,400	3,600	5,400	7,200	9,600	12,000
C (30.50ci single)	2,800	4,200	6,300	8,400	11,000	14,000
CB (30.50ci single)	2,800	4,200	6,300	8,400	11,000	14,000
R (45ci V-twin)	2,800	4,200	6,300	8,400	11,000	14,000
RS (45ci V-twin)	2,800	4,200	6,300	8,400	11,000	14,000
RL (45ci V-twin)	3,000	4,500	6,800	9,000	12,000	15,000
RLD (45ci V-twin)	3,000	4,500	6,800	9,000	12,000	15,000
G Servi-Car (45ci V-twin)	**2,000**	**4,000**	**8,000**	**12,000**	**16,000**	**20,000**
GA Servi-Car (45ci V-twin)	**2,000**	**4,000**	**8,000**	**12,000**	**16,000**	**20,000**

	6	5	4	3	2	1
GD Servi-Car (45ci V-twin)	2,000	4,000	8,000	12,000	16,000	20,000
GDT Servi-Car (45ci V-twin)	2,000	4,000	8,000	12,000	16,000	20,000
GE Servi-Car (45ci V-twin)	2,000	4,000	8,000	12,000	16,000	20,000
V (74ci V-twin)	4,400	6,600	9,900	13,000	18,000	22,000
VS (74ci V-twin)	4,400	6,600	9,900	13,000	18,000	22,000
VL (74ci V-twin)	4,800	7,200	11,000	14,000	19,000	24,000
VLD (74ci V-twin)	4,900	7,400	11,000	15,000	20,000	25,000
VC (74ci V-twin)	4,200	6,300	9,500	13,000	17,000	21,000
1934						
B (21.35ci single)	2,400	3,600	5,400	7,200	9,600	12,000
C (30.50ci single)	2,800	4,200	6,300	8,400	11,000	14,000
CB (30.50ci single)	2,800	4,200	6,300	8,400	11,000	14,000
R (45ci V-twin)	2,800	4,200	6,300	8,400	11,000	14,000
RL (45ci V-twin)	3,000	4,500	6,800	9,000	12,000	15,000
RLD (45ci V-twin)	3,300	5,000	7,400	9,900	13,000	17,000
G Servi-Car (45ci V-twin)	2,000	4,000	8,000	12,000	16,000	20,000
GA Servi-Car (45ci V-twin)	2,000	4,000	8,000	12,000	16,000	20,000
GD Servi-Car (45ci V-twin)	2,000	4,000	8,000	12,000	16,000	20,000
GDT Servi-Car (74ci V-twin)	2,000	4,000	8,000	12,000	16,000	20,000
GE Servi-Car (74ci V-twin)	2,000	4,000	8,000	12,000	16,000	20,000
VLD (74ci V-twin)	4,400	6,600	9,900	13,000	18,000	22,000
VD (74ci V-twin)	3,800	5,700	8,600	11,000	15,000	19,000
VDS (74ci V-twin)	3,800	5,700	8,600	11,000	15,000	19,000
VFDS (74ci V-twin)	4,000	6,000	9,000	12,000	16,000	20,000
1935						
R (45ci V-twin)	2,600	3,900	5,900	7,800	10,000	13,000
RL (45ci V-twin)	3,000	4,500	6,800	9,000	12,000	15,000
RS (45ci V-twin)	2,600	3,900	5,900	7,800	10,000	13,000
RLD (45ci V-twin)	3,000	4,500	6,800	9,000	12,000	15,000
RLDR (45ci V-twin)	3,200	4,800	7,200	9,600	13,000	16,000
G Servi-Car (45ci V-twin)	2,000	4,000	8,000	12,000	16,000	20,000
GA Servi-Car (45ci V-twin)	2,000	4,000	8,000	12,000	16,000	20,000
GD Servi-Car (45ci V-twin)	2,000	4,000	8,000	12,000	16,000	20,000
GDT Servi-Car (45ci V-twin)	2,000	4,000	8,000	12,000	16,000	20,000
GE Servi-Car (45ci V-twin)	2,000	4,000	8,000	12,000	16,000	20,000
VD (74ci V-twin)	3,800	5,700	8,600	11,000	15,000	19,000
VDS (74ci V-twin)	3,800	5,700	8,600	11,000	15,000	19,000
VLD (74ci V-twin)	4,400	6,600	9,900	13,000	18,000	22,000
VLDJ (74ci V-twin)	5,000	7,500	11,000	15,000	20,000	25,000
VLDD (80ci V-twin)	5,000	7,500	11,000	15,000	20,000	25,000
VLDS (80ci V-twin)	5,000	7,500	11,000	15,000	20,000	25,000
1936						
R (45ci V-twin)	2,600	3,900	5,900	7,800	10,000	13,000
RL (45ci V-twin)	3,000	4,500	6,800	9,000	12,000	15,000
RLD (45ci V-twin)	3,200	4,800	7,200	9,600	13,000	16,000
RLDR (45ci V-twin)	3,200	4,800	7,200	9,600	13,000	16,000
RS (45ci V-twin)	2,600	3,900	5,900	7,800	10,000	13,000
G Servi-Car (45ci V-twin)	2,000	4,000	8,000	12,000	16,000	20,000
GA Servi-Car (45ci V-twin)	2,000	4,000	8,000	12,000	16,000	20,000
GD Servi-Car (45ci V-twin)	2,000	4,000	8,000	12,000	16,000	20,000
GDT Servi-Car (45ci V-twin)	2,000	4,000	8,000	12,000	16,000	20,000
GE Servi-Car (45ci V-twin)	2,000	4,000	8,000	12,000	16,000	20,000
E (61ci V-twin)	9,400	14,000	21,000	28,000	38,000	47,000
ES (61ci V-twin)	9,400	14,000	21,000	28,000	38,000	47,000
EL (61ci V-twin)	10,000	20,000	30,000	40,000	60,000	80,000
VD (74ci V-twin)	4,000	6,000	9,000	12,000	16,000	20,000
VDS (74ci V-twin)	4,000	6,000	9,000	12,000	16,000	20,000
VLD (74ci V-twin)	4,500	6,800	10,000	14,000	18,000	23,000

	6	5	4	3	2	1
VLH (80ci V-twin)	4,800	7,200	11,000	14,000	19,000	24,000
VHS (80ci V-twin)	4,800	7,200	11,000	14,000	19,000	24,000
1937						
W (45ci V-twin)	2,400	3,600	5,400	7,200	9,600	12,000
WS (45ci V-twin)	2,400	3,600	5,400	7,200	9,600	12,000
WL (45ci V-twin)	2,700	4,100	6,100	8,100	11,000	14,000
WLD (45ci V-twin)	3,000	4,500	6,800	9,000	12,000	15,000
WLDR (45ci V-twin)	3,400	5,100	7,700	10,000	14,000	17,000
G Servi-Car (45ci V-twin)	**2,000**	**4,000**	**8,000**	**12,000**	**16,000**	**20,000**
GA Servi-Car (45ci V-twin)	**2,000**	**4,000**	**8,000**	**12,000**	**16,000**	**20,000**
GD Servi-Car (45ci V-twin)	**2,000**	**4,000**	**8,000**	**12,000**	**16,000**	**20,000**
GDT Servi-Car (45ci V-twin)	**2,000**	**4,000**	**8,000**	**12,000**	**16,000**	**20,000**
GE Servi-Car (45ci V-twin)	**2,000**	**4,000**	**8,000**	**12,000**	**16,000**	**20,000**
E (61ci V-twin)	8,000	12,000	18,000	24,000	32,000	40,000
ES (61ci V-twin)	8,000	12,000	18,000	24,000	32,000	40,000
EL (61ci V-twin)	8,800	13,000	20,000	26,000	35,000	44,000
U (74ci V-twin)	4,400	6,600	9,900	13,000	18,000	22,000
US (74ci V-twin)	4,400	6,600	9,900	13,000	18,000	22,000
UL (74ci V-twin)	5,100	–10,000	**15,000**	20,000	25,000	**30,000**
UH (80ci V-twin)	4,400	6,600	9,900	13,000	18,000	22,000
UHS (80ci V-twin)	4,400	6,600	9,900	13,000	18,000	22,000
ULH (80ci V-twin)	5,000	7,500	11,000	15,000	20,000	25,000
1938						
WL (45ci V-twin)	3,000	4,500	6,800	9,000	12,000	15,000
WLD (45ci V-twin)	3,400	5,100	7,700	10,000	14,000	17,000
WLDR (45ci V-twin)	3,400	5,100	7,700	10,000	14,000	17,000
G Servi-Car (45ci V-twin)	**2,000**	**4,000**	**8,000**	**12,000**	**16,000**	**20,000**
GA Servi-Car (45ci V-twin)	**2,000**	**4,000**	**8,000**	**12,000**	**16,000**	**20,000**
GD Servi-Car (45ci V-twin)	**2,000**	**4,000**	**8,000**	**12,000**	**16,000**	**20,000**
GDT Servi-Car (45ci V-twin)	**2,000**	**4,000**	**8,000**	**12,000**	**16,000**	**20,000**
EL (61ci V-twin)	8,400	13,000	19,000	25,000	34,000	42,000
ES (61ci V-twin)	8,000	12,000	18,000	24,000	32,000	40,000
U (74ci V-twin)	4,000	6,000	9,000	12,000	16,000	20,000
US (74ci V-twin)	4,000	6,000	9,000	12,000	16,000	20,000
UL (74ci V-twin)	4,200	6,300	9,500	13,000	17,000	21,000
UH (80ci V-twin)	4,000	6,000	9,000	12,000	16,000	20,000
UHS (80ci V-twin)	4,000	6,000	9,000	12,000	16,000	20,000
ULH (80ci V-twin)	4,200	6,300	**10,000**	**15,000**	20,000	**25,000**
1939						
WL (45ci V-twin)	3,200	4,700	7,100	9,500	13,000	16,000
WLD (45ci V-twin)	3,400	5,100	7,700	10,000	14,000	17,000
WLDR (45ci V-twin)	3,500	5,300	7,900	11,000	14,000	18,000
G Servi-Car (45ci V-twin)	2,000	**4,000**	**8,000**	**12,000**	**16,000**	**20,000**
GA Servi-Car (45ci V-twin)	2,000	**4,000**	**8,000**	**12,000**	**16,000**	**20,000**
GD Servi-Car (45ci V-twin)	2,000	**4,000**	**8,000**	**12,000**	**16,000**	**20,000**
GDT Servi-Car (45ci V-twin)	2,000	**4,000**	**8,000**	**12,000**	**16,000**	**20,000**
EL (61ci V-twin)	8,400	13,000	19,000	25,000	34,000	42,000
ES (61ci V-twin)	8,000	12,000	18,000	24,000	32,000	40,000
U (74ci V-twin)	4,000	6,000	9,000	12,000	16,000	20,000
US (74ci V-twin)	4,000	6,000	9,000	12,000	16,000	20,000
UL (74ci V-twin)	4,400	6,600	9,900	13,000	18,000	22,000
UH (80ci V-twin)	4,000	6,000	9,000	12,000	16,000	20,000
UHS (80ci V-twin)	4,000	6,000	9,000	12,000	16,000	20,000
ULH (80ci V-twin)	4,200	6,300	9,500	13,000	17,000	21,000
1940						
WL (45ci V-twin)	3,200	4,700	7,100	9,500	13,000	16,000
WLD (45ci V-twin)	3,400	5,100	7,700	10,000	14,000	17,000
WLDR (45ci V-twin)	3,700	5,600	8,300	11,000	15,000	19,000

	6	5	4	3	2	1
G Servi-Car (45ci V-twin)	2,000	**4,000**	8,000	12,000	16,000	20,000
GA Servi-Car (45ci V-twin)	2,000	**4,000**	8,000	12,000	16,000	20,000
GD Servi-Car (45ci V-twin)	2,000	**4,000**	8,000	12,000	16,000	20,000
GDT Servi-Car (45ci V-twin).	2,000	**4,000**	8,000	12,000	16,000	20,000
EL (61ci V-twin).	8,400	13,000	19,000	25,000	34,000	42,000
ES (61ci V-twin).	8,000	12,000	18,000	24,000	32,000	40,000
U (74ci V-twin)	4,000	6,000	9,000	12,000	16,000	20,000
UL (74ci V-twin)	4,200	6,300	**10,000**	**14,000**	17,000	**22,000**
US (74ci V-twin)	4,000	6,000	9,000	12,000	16,000	20,000
UH (80ci V-twin).	3,800	5,700	8,600	11,000	15,000	19,000
ULH (80ci V-twin)	4,200	6,300	9,500	13,000	17,000	21,000
UHS (80ci V-twin)	3,800	5,700	8,600	11,000	15,000	19,000
1941						
WL (45ci V-twin).	3,000	4,500	7,100	9,500	13,000	16,000
WLA (45ci V-twin)	3,400	5,100	7,700	10,000	14,000	17,000
WLD (45ci V-twin)	3,400	5,100	7,700	10,000	14,000	17,000
WLDR (45ci V-twin)	3,600	5,400	8,100	11,000	14,000	18,000
G Servi-Car (45ci V-twin)	2,000	**4,000**	8,000	12,000	16,000	20,000
GA Servi-Car (45ci V-twin)	2,000	**4,000**	8,000	12,000	16,000	20,000
GD Servi-Car (45ci V-twin)	2,000	**4,000**	8,000	12,000	16,000	20,000
GDT Servi-Car (45ci V-twin).	2,000	**4,000**	8,000	12,000	16,000	20,000
EL (61ci V-twin).	8,000	12,000	18,000	24,000	32,000	40,000
ES (61ci V-twin).	7,600	11,000	17,000	23,000	30,000	38,000
U (74ci V-twin)	4,000	7,000	10,000	12,000	16,000	20,000
UL (74ci V-twin)	4,200	6,300	**10,000**	**14,000**	17,000	**22,000**
US (74ci V-twin)	4,000	6,000	9,000	12,000	16,000	20,000
FL (74ci V-twin)	5,800	8,700	13,000	17,000	23,000	29,000
FS (74ci V-twin)	5,500	83,000	12,000	17,000	22,000	28,000
UH (80ci V-twin).	3,800	5,700	8,600	11,000	15,000	19,000
ULH (80ci V-twin)	4,200	6,300	9,500	13,000	17,000	21,000
UHS (80ci V-twin)	3,800	5,700	8,600	11,000	15,000	19,000
1942						
WL (45ci V-twin).	3,200	4,700	7,100	9,500	13,000	16,000
WLA (45ci V-twin)	**5,000**	**8,000**	**12,000**	**16,000**	**20,000**	**25,000**
WLC (45ci V-twin)	3,000	5,100	7,700	10,000	14,000	17,000
WLD (45ci V-twin)	3,400	5,100	7,700	10,000	14,000	17,000
G Servi-Car (45ci V-twin)	2,000	**4,000**	8,000	12,000	16,000	20,000
GA Servi-Car (45ci V-twin)	2,000	**4,000**	8,000	12,000	16,000	20,000
XA (45ci twin)	**4,000**	**8,000**	**12,000**	15,000	18,000	22,000
E (61ci V-twin).	6,800	10,000	15,000	20,000	27,000	34,000
EL (61ci V-twin).	7,000	11,000	16,000	21,000	28,000	35,000
U (74ci V-twin)	3,800	5,700	8,600	11,000	15,000	19,000
UL (74ci V-twin)	4,000	6,000	**10,000**	**14,000**	17,000	**22,000**
F (74ci V-twin)	5,400	8,100	12,000	16,000	22,000	27,000
FL (74ci V-twin)	5,800	8,700	13,000	17,000	23,000	29,000
1943						
WLA (45ci V-twin)	3,400	5,100	7,700	10,000	14,000	17,000
WLC (45ci V-twin).	3,400	5,100	7,700	10,000	14,000	17,000
G Servi-Car (45ci V-twin)	2,000	**4,000**	8,000	12,000	16,000	20,000
GA Servi-Car (45ci V-twin)	2,000	**4,000**	8,000	12,000	16,000	20,000
XA (45ci twin)	**4,000**	**8,000**	**12,000**	15,000	18,000	22,000
E (61ci V-twin).	6,800	10,000	15,000	20,000	27,000	34,000
EL (61ci V-twin).	7,000	11,000	16,000	21,000	28,000	35,000
U (74ci V-twin)	3,800	5,700	8,600	11,000	15,000	19,000
UL (74ci V-twin)	4,000	6,000	**10,000**	**14,000**	17,000	**22,000**
F (74ci V-twin).	5,400	8,100	12,000	16,000	22,000	27,000
FL (74ci V-twin)	5,800	8,700	13,000	17,000	23,000	29,000

	6	5	4	3	2	1
1944						
WLA (45ci V-twin)	3,400	5,100	7,700	10,000	14,000	17,000
WLC (45ci V-twin)	3,400	5,100	7,700	10,000	14,000	17,000
G Servi-Car (45ci V-twin)	2,000	**4,000**	**8,000**	**12,000**	**16,000**	**20,000**
GA Servi-Car (45ci V-twin)	2,000	**4,000**	**8,000**	**12,000**	**16,000**	**20,000**
E (61ci V-twin)	6,500	9,800	15,000	20,000	26,000	33,000
EL (61ci V-twin)	6,800	10,000	15,000	20,000	27,000	34,000
U (74ci V-twin)	3,600	5,400	8,100	11,000	14,000	18,000
UL (74ci V-twin)	4,000	6,000	**10,000**	**14,000**	**17,000**	**22,000**
F (74ci V-twin)	5,400	8,100	12,000	16,000	22,000	27,000
FL (74ci V-twin)	5,800	8,700	13,000	17,000	23,000	29,000
1945						
WL (45ci V-twin)	3,200	4,800	7,200	9,600	13,000	16,000
WLA (45ci V-twin)	3,400	5,100	7,700	10,000	14,000	17,000
G Servi-Car (45ci V-twin)	2,200	**4,000**	**8,000**	**12,000**	**16,000**	**20,000**
GA Servi-Car (45ci V-twin)	2,200	**4,000**	**8,000**	**12,000**	**16,000**	**20,000**
E (61ci V-twin)	6,400	9,600	14,000	19,000	26,000	32,000
EL (61ci V-twin)	6,600	9,900	15,000	20,000	26,000	33,000
ES (61ci V-twin)	6,400	9,600	14,000	19,000	26,000	32,000
U (74ci V-twin)	3,600	5,400	8,100	11,000	14,000	18,000
UL (74ci V-twin)	4,000	6,000	**10,000**	**14,000**	**17,000**	**22,000**
US (74ci V-twin)	3,600	5,400	8,100	11,000	14,000	18,000
F (74ci V-twin)	5,300	8,000	12,000	16,000	21,000	27,000
FL (74ci V-twin)	5,800	8,700	13,050	17,400	23,200	29,000
FS (74ci V-twin)	5,300	8,000	12,000	16,000	21,000	27,000
1946						
WL (45ci V-twin)	3,400	5,100	7,700	10,000	14,000	17,000
G Servi-Car (45ci V-twin)	2,400	3,600	5,400	7,200	9,600	12,000
GA Servi-Car (45ci V-twin)	2,400	3,600	5,400	7,200	9,600	12,000
E (61ci V-twin)	6,000	9,000	13,500	18,000	24,000	30,000
EL (61ci V-twin)	6,400	9,600	14,000	19,000	26,000	32,000
ES (61ci V-twin)	6,000	9,000	13,500	18,000	24,000	30,000
U (74ci V-twin)	5,000	7,000	9,000	13,000	16,000	20,000
UL (74ci V-twin)	4,000	6,000	**10,000**	**14,000**	**17,000**	**22,000**
US (74ci V-twin)	3,600	5,400	8,100	11,000	14,000	18,000
F (74ci V-twin)	5,300	8,000	12,000	16,000	21,000	27,000
FL (74ci V-twin)	5,800	8,700	13,050	17,400	23,200	29,000
FS (74ci V-twin)	5,300	8,000	12,000	16,000	21,000	27,000
1947						
WL (45ci V-twin)	3,400	5,100	7,700	10,000	14,000	17,000
G Servi-Car (45ci V-twin)	2,400	3,600	5,400	7,200	9,600	12,000
GA Servi-Car (45ci V-twin)	2,400	3,600	5,400	7,200	9,600	12,000
E (61ci V-twin)	5,600	8,400	13,000	17,000	22,000	28,000
EL (61ci V-twin)	5,900	8,900	13,000	18,000	24,000	30,000
FS (61ci V-twin)	5,600	8,400	13,000	17,000	22,000	28,000
U (74ci V-twln)	3,600	5,400	8,100	11,000	14,000	18,000
UL (74ci V-twin)	3,600	5,400	**10,000**	**14,000**	**17,000**	**22,000**
US (74ci V-twin)	3,600	5,400	8,100	11,000	14,000	18,000
F (74ci V-twin)	5,200	7,800	12,000	16,000	21,000	26,000
FL (74ci V-twin)	5,600	8,400	13,000	17,000	22,000	28,000
FS (74ci V-twin)	5,200	7,800	12,000	16,000	21,000	26,000
1948						
S Hummer (125cc single)	1,400	2,100	4,000	5,000	6,000	7,500
WL (45ci V-twin)	3,300	5,000	7,400	9,900	13,000	17,000
G Servi-Car (45ci V-twin)	2,400	3,600	5,400	7,200	9,600	12,000
GA Servi-Car (45ci V-twin)	2,400	3,600	5,400	7,200	9,600	12,000
E (61ci V-twin)	4,100	6,200	9,200	12,000	16,000	21,000
EL (61ci V-twin)	4,200	6,300	9,500	13,000	17,000	21,000

	6	5	4	3	2	1
ES (61ci V-twin)	4,100	6,200	9,200	12,000	16,000	21,000
U (74ci V-twin)	3,200	4,800	7,200	9,600	13,000	16,000
UL (74ci V-twin)	3,500	5,200	**10,000**	**14,000**	**17,000**	**22,000**
US (74ci V-twin)	3,200	4,800	7,200	9,600	13,000	16,000
F (74ci V-twin)	5,200	7,800	12,000	16,000	21,000	26,000
FL (74ci V-twin)	5,600	8,400	13,000	17,000	22,000	28,000
FS (74ci V-twin)	5,200	7,800	12,000	16,000	21,000	26,000
1949						
S Hummer (125cc single)	1,400	2,100	3,200	4,200	5,600	7,000
WL (45ci V-twin)	3,300	5,000	7,400	9,900	13,000	17,000
G Servi-Car (45ci V-twin)	2,600	3,900	5,900	7,800	10,000	13,000
GA Servi-Car (45ci V-twin)	2,600	3,900	5,900	7,800	10,000	13,000
E (61ci V-twin)	3,800	5,700	8,600	11,000	15,000	19,000
EL (61ci V-twin)	4,200	6,300	9,500	13,000	17,000	21,000
ES (61ci V-twin)	3,800	5,700	8,600	11,000	15,000	19,000
EP (61ci V-twin)	4,000	5,900	8,900	12,000	16,000	20,000
ELP (61ci V-twin)	4,100	6,200	9,200	12,000	16,000	21,000
F Hydra-Glide (74ci V-twin)	4,200	6,300	9,500	13,000	17,000	21,000
FL Hydra-Glide (74ci V-twin)	4,700	7,100	11,000	14,000	19,000	24,000
FS Hydra-Glide (74ci V-twin)	4,200	6,300	9,500	13,000	17,000	21,000
FP Hydra-Glide (74ci V-twin)	4,300	6,500	9,700	13,000	17,000	22,000
FLP Hydra-Glide (74ci V-twin)	4,800	7,200	11,000	14,000	19,000	24,000
1950						
S Hummer (125cc single)	1,400	2,100	3,200	4,200	5,600	7,000
WL (45ci V-twin)	3,300	5,000	7,400	9,900	13,000	17,000
G Servi-Car (45ci V-twin)	2,600	3,900	7,000	10,000	13,000	16,000
GA Servi-Car (45ci V-twin)	2,600	3,900	5,900	7,800	10,000	13,000
E (61ci V-twin)	4,200	6,300	9,500	13,000	17,000	21,000
EL (61ci V-twin)	4,200	6,300	9,500	13,000	17,000	21,000
ES (61ci V-twin)	4,200	6,300	9,500	13,000	17,000	21,000
F Hydra-Glide (74ci V-twin)	4,200	6,300	9,500	13,000	17,000	21,000
FL Hydra-Glide (74ci V-twin)	4,500	6,800	10,000	15,000	20,000	25,000
FS Hydra-Glide (74ci V-twin)	4,200	6,300	9,500	13,000	17,000	21,000
1951						
S Hummer (125cc single)	1,400	2,500	4,000	5,000	6,500	8,000
WL (45ci V-twin)	3,300	5,000	7,400	9,900	13,000	17,000
G Servi-Car (45ci V-twin)	2,600	3,900	5,900	7,800	10,000	13,000
GA Servi-Car (45ci V-twin)	2,600	3,900	5,900	7,800	10,000	13,000
EL (61ci V-twin)	4,200	6,300	9,500	13,000	17,000	21,000
ELS (61ci V-twin)	4,200	6,300	9,500	13,000	17,000	21,000
FL Hydra-Glide (74ci V-twin)	4,300	6,500	8,000	12,000	16,000	20,000
FLS Hydra-Glide (74ci V-twin)	4,300	6,500	9,700	13,000	17,000	22,000
1952						
S Hummer (125cc single)	900	1,400	2,000	2,700	3,600	4,500
K (45ci V-twin)	2,900	4,400	6,500	8,700	12,000	15,000
G Servi-Car (45ci V-twin)	2,600	3,900	5,900	7,800	10,000	13,000
GA Servi-Car (45ci V-twin)	2,600	3,900	5,900	7,800	10,000	13,000
EL (61ci V-twin)	4,200	6,300	10,000	15,000	20,000	25,000
ELF (61ci V-twin)	4,200	6,300	10,000	15,000	20,000	25,000
ELS (61ci V-twin)	4,200	6,300	9,500	13,000	17,000	21,000
FL Hydra-Glide (74ci V-twin)	4,200	6,300	9,500	13,000	17,000	21,000
FLF Hydra-Glide (74ci V-twin)	4,300	6,500	9,700	13,000	17,000	22,000
FLS Hydra-Glide (74ci V-twin)	4,200	6,300	9,500	13,000	17,000	21,000
1953						
ST Hummer (165cc single)	1,000	1,500	2,300	3,000	4,000	5,000
K (45ci V-twin)	2,900	4,400	6,500	8,700	12,000	15,000
G Servi-Car (45ci V-twin)	2,600	3,900	5,900	7,800	10,000	13,000
GA Servi-Car (45ci V-twin)	2,600	3,900	5,900	7,800	10,000	13,000
FL Hydra-Glide (74ci V-twin)	4,200	6,300	9,500	13,000	17,000	21,000

	6	5	4	3	2	1
FLF Hydra-Glide (74ci V-twin).	4,100	6,100	9,100	12,000	16,000	20,000
FLE Hydra-Glide (74ci V-twin).	4,200	6,300	9,500	13,000	17,000	21,000
FLEF Hydra-Glide (74ci V-twin)	4,100	6,100	9,100	12,000	16,000	20,000
1954						
ST Hummer (165cc single)	1,000	2,000	3,000	4,000	5,000	6,000
STU Hummer (165cc single)	1,000	2,000	3,000	4,000	5,000	6,000
G Servi-Car (45ci V-twin)	2,600	3,900	5,900	7,800	10,000	13,000
GA Servi-Car (45ci V-twin)	2,600	3,900	5,900	7,800	10,000	13,000
KH (55ci V-twin).	**4,000**	**6,000**	**8,000**	**10,000**	**14,000**	**18,000**
FL Hydra-Glide (74ci V-twin)	4,600	6,900	10,000	14,000	18,000	23,000
FLF Hydra-Glide (74ci V-twin).	4,200	6,300	9,500	13,000	17,000	21,000
FLE Hydra-Glide (74ci V-twin).	4,600	6,900	10,000	14,000	18,000	23,000
FLEF Hydra-Glide (74ci V-twin)	4,200	6,300	9,500	13,000	17,000	21,000
1955						
B Hummer (125cc single)	900	1,400	2,000	2,700	3,600	4,500
ST Hummer (165cc single)	1,000	1,500	2,300	3,000	4,000	5,000
STU Hummer (165cc single)	1,000	1,500	2,300	3,000	4,000	5,000
G Servi-Car (45ci V-twin)	2,600	3,900	5,900	7,800	10,000	13,000
GA Servi-Car (45ci V-twin)	2,600	3,900	5,900	7,800	10,000	13,000
KH (55ci V-twin).	2,800	4,200	6,300	8,400	11,000	14,000
KHK (55ci V-twin).	3,000	4,500	6,800	9,000	12,000	15,000
FL Hydra-Glide (74ci V-twin)	4,000	6,000	9,000	12,000	16,000	20,000
FLE Hydra-Glide (74ci V-twin).	4,000	6,000	9,000	12,000	16,000	20,000
FLEF Hydra-Glide (74ci V-twin)	3,800	5,700	8,600	11,000	15,000	19,000
FLF Hydra-Glide (74ci V-twin).	3,800	5,700	8,600	11,000	15,000	19,000
FLH Hydra-Glide (74ci V-twin)	4,100	6,200	9,200	12,000	16,000	21,000
FLHF Hydra-Glide (74ci V-twin)	4,000	6,000	9,000	12,000	16,000	20,000
1956						
B Hummer (125cc single)	900	1,400	2,000	2,700	3,600	4,500
ST Hummer (165cc single)	1,000	1,500	2,300	3,000	4,000	5,000
STU Hummer (165cc single)	1,000	1,500	2,300	3,000	4,000	5,000
G Servi-Car (45ci V-twin)	2,600	3,900	5,900	7,800	10,000	13,000
GA Servi-Car (45ci V-twin)	2,600	3,900	5,900	7,800	10,000	13,000
KH (55ci V-twin).	2,800	4,200	6,300	8,400	11,000	14,000
KHK (55ci V-twin).	3,000	5,000	7,000	10,000	13,000	16,000
FL Hydra-Glide (74ci V-twin)	4,000	6,000	9,000	12,000	16,000	20,000
FLE Hydra-Glide (74ci V-twin).	4,000	6,000	9,000	12,000	16,000	20,000
FLEF Hydra-Glide (74ci V-twin)	3,800	5,700	8,600	11,000	15,000	19,000
FLF Hydra-Glide (74ci V-twin).	3,800	5,700	8,600	11,000	15,000	19,000
FLH Hydra-Glide (74ci V-twin)	4,100	6,200	9,200	12,000	16,000	21,000
FLHF Hydra-Glide (74ci V-twin)	4,000	6,000	9,000	12,000	16,000	20,000
1957						
B Hummer (125cc single)	900	1,400	2,000	2,700	3,600	4,500
ST Hummer (165cc single)	1,000	1,500	2,300	3,000	4,000	5,000
STU Hummer (165cc single)	1,000	1,500	2,300	3,000	4,000	5,000
G Servl-Car (45ci V-twin)	2,600	3,900	5,900	7,800	10,000	13,000
GA Servi-Car (45ci V-twin)	2,600	3,900	5,900	7,800	10,000	13,000
XL Sportster (55ci V-twin)	3,000	6,000	9,000	13,000	16,000	19,000
FL Hydra-Glide (74ci V-twin)	4,200	6,300	9,500	13,000	17,000	21,000
FLF Hydra-Glide (74ci V-twin)	4,000	6,000	9,000	12,000	16,000	20,000
FLH Hydra-Glide (74ci V-twin)	4,200	6,300	9,500	13,000	17,000	21,000
FLHF Hydra-Glide (74ci V-twin)	4,000	6,000	9,000	12,000	16,000	20,000
1958						
B Hummer (125cc single)	800	1,200	1,800	2,400	3,200	4,000
ST Hummer (165cc single)	800	1,200	1,800	2,400	3,200	4,000
STU Hummer (165cc single)	800	1,200	1,800	2,400	3,200	4,000
G Servi-Car (45ci V-twin)	2,600	3,900	5,900	7,800	10,000	13,000
GA Servi-Car (45ci V-twin)	2,600	3,900	5,900	7,800	10,000	13,000
XL Sportster (55ci V-twin)	2,000	3,000	4,500	6,000	8,000	10,000

	6	5	4	3	2	1
XLH Sportster (55ci V-twin)	2,500	4,000	5,500	7,000	9,000	12,000
XLC Sportster (55ci V-twin)	2,200	3,300	5,000	6,600	8,800	11,000
XLCH Sportster (55ci V-twin)	2,300	3,500	5,200	6,900	9,200	12,000
FL Duo-Glide (74ci V-twin)	3,500	6,000	9,000	12,000	15,000	18,000
FLF Duo-Glide (74ci V-twin)	4,000	6,000	9,000	12,000	16,000	20,000
FLH Duo-Glide (74ci V-twin)	4,200	6,300	9,500	13,000	17,000	21,000
FLHF Duo-Glide (74ci V-twin)	4,000	6,000	9,000	12,000	16,000	20,000
1959						
B Hummer (125cc single)	900	1,300	1,900	2,600	3,400	4,300
ST Hummer (165cc single)	800	1,200	1,800	2,300	3,100	3,900
STU Hummer (165cc single)	800	1,200	1,800	2,300	3,100	3,900
G Servi-Car (45ci V-twin)	2,600	3,900	5,900	7,800	10,000	13,000
GA Servi-Car (45ci V-twin)	2,600	3,900	5,900	7,800	10,000	13,000
XL Sportster (55ci V-twin)	2,000	3,000	4,500	6,000	8,000	10,000
XLH Sportster (55ci V-twin)	2,200	3,300	5,000	6,600	8,800	11,000
XLCH Sportster (55ci V-twin)	2,300	3,500	5,200	6,900	9,200	12,000
FL Duo-Glide (74ci V-twin)	3,500	6,000	9,000	12,000	15,000	18,000
FLF Duo-Glide (74ci V-twin)	4,000	6,000	9,000	12,000	16,000	20,000
FLH Duo-Glide (74ci V-twin)	4,200	6,300	9,500	13,000	17,000	21,000
FLHF Duo-Glide (74ci V-twin)	4,000	6,000	9,000	12,000	16,000	20,000
1960						
A Topper (165cc single)	1,000	1,500	2,300	3,000	4,000	5,000
AU Topper (165cc single)	900	1,400	2,000	2,700	3,600	4,500
BT Pacer (165cc single)	500	800	1,100	1,500	2,000	2,500
BTU Pacer (165cc single)	500	800	1,100	1,500	2,000	2,500
G Servi-Car (45ci V-twin)	2,400	3,600	5,400	7,200	9,600	12,000
GA Servi-Car (45ci V-twin)	2,400	3,600	5,400	7,200	9,600	12,000
XLH Sportster (55ci V-twin)	2,200	3,300	5,000	6,600	8,800	11,000
XLCH Sportster (55ci V-twin)	2,300	3,500	5,200	6,900	9,200	12,000
FL Duo-Glide (74ci V-twin)	4,200	6,300	9,500	13,000	17,000	21,000
FLF Duo-Glide (74ci V-twin)	4,000	6,000	9,000	12,000	16,000	20,000
FLH Duo-Glide (74ci V-twin)	4,200	6,300	9,500	13,000	17,000	21,000
FLHF Duo-Glide (74ci V-twin)	4,000	6,000	9,000	12,000	16,000	20,000
1961						
AH Topper (165cc single)	900	1,400	2,100	2,800	3,800	4,700
AU Topper (165cc single)	900	1,400	2,000	2,700	3,600	4,500
BT Pacer (165cc single)	700	1,000	1,500	2,000	3,000	4,000
BTU Pacer (165cc single)	700	1,000	1,500	2,000	3,000	4,000
C Sprint (250cc single)	700	1,100	1,600	2,100	2,800	3,500
G Servi-Car (45ci V-twin)	2,500	4,000	6,000	9,000	12,000	15,000
GA Servi-Car (45ci V-twin)	2,400	3,600	5,400	7,200	9,600	12,000
XLH Sportster (55ci V-twin)	2,200	3,300	5,000	6,600	8,800	11,000
XLCH Sportster (55ci V-twin)	2,200	3,300	5,000	6,600	8,800	11,000
FL Duo-Glide (74ci V-twin)	4,200	6,300	9,500	13,000	17,000	21,000
FLF Duo-Glide (74ci V-twin)	4,000	6,000	9,000	12,000	16,000	20,000
FLH Duo-Glide (74ci V-twin)	4,200	6,300	9,500	13,000	17,000	21,000
FLHF Duo-Glide (74ci V-twin)	4,000	6,000	9,000	12,000	16,000	20,000
1962						
AH Topper (165cc single)	900	1,400	2,100	2,800	3,800	4,700
AU Topper (165cc single)	900	1,400	2,000	2,700	3,600	4,500
BTF Ranger (165cc single)	600	900	1,400	1,800	2,400	3,000
BTU Pacer (165cc single)	700	1,000	1,500	2,000	2,700	3,400
BT Pacer (175cc single)	700	1,000	1,500	2,000	2,700	3,400
BTH Scat (175cc single)	700	1,100	1,600	2,100	2,800	3,500
C Sprint (250cc single)	700	1,100	1,700	2,200	3,000	3,700
CH Sprint (250cc single)	800	1,200	1,800	2,300	3,100	3,900
G Servi-Car (45ci V-twin)	2,400	3,600	5,400	7,200	9,600	12,000
GA Servi-Car (45ci V-twin)	2,400	3,600	5,400	7,200	9,600	12,000
XLH Sportster (55ci V-twin)	2,400	3,600	5,400	7,200	9,600	12,000

	6	5	4	3	2	1
XLCH Sportster (55ci V-twin)	2,400	3,600	5,400	7,200	9,600	12,000
FL Duo-Glide (74ci V-twin)	4,200	6,300	9,500	13,000	17,000	21,000
FLF Duo-Glide (74ci V-twin).	4,000	6,000	9,000	12,000	16,000	20,000
FLH Duo-Glide (74ci V-twin)	4,200	6,300	9,500	13,000	17,000	21,000
FLHF Duo-Glide (74ci V-twin)	4,000	6,000	9,000	12,000	16,000	20,000
1963						
AH Topper (165cc single)	900	1,400	2,100	3,000	4,000	6,000
AU Topper (165cc single).	900	1,400	2,000	3,000	4,000	6,000
BT Pacer (175cc single).	700	1,000	1,500	2,500	3,500	5,000
BTU Pacer (165cc single).	700	1,000	1,500	2,500	3,500	5,000
BTH Scat (175cc single)	700	1,100	1,600	2,100	2,800	3,500
C Sprint (250cc single)	700	1,100	1,700	2,200	3,000	3,700
CH Sprint (250cc single)	800	1,200	1,800	2,300	3,100	3,900
G Servi-Car (45ci V-twin)	2,400	3,600	5,400	7,200	9,600	12,000
GA Servi-Car (45ci V-twin)	2,400	3,600	5,400	7,200	9,600	12,000
XLH Sportster (55ci V-twin)	2,400	3,600	5,400	7,200	9,600	12,000
XLCH Sportster (55ci V-twin)	2,400	3,600	5,400	7,200	9,600	12,000
FL Duo-Glide (74ci V-twin)	4,200	6,300	9,500	13,000	17,000	21,000
FLF Duo-Glide (74ci V-twin).	4,000	6,000	9,000	12,000	16,000	20,000
FLH Duo-Glide (74ci V-twin)	4,200	6,300	9,500	13,000	17,000	21,000
FLHF Duo-Glide (74ci V-twin)	4,000	6,000	9,000	12,000	16,000	20,000
1964						
AH Topper (165cc single)	900	1,400	2,100	3,000	4,000	6,000
AU Topper (165cc single).	1,000	1,500	2,200	3,000	4,000	6,000
BT Pacer (175cc single).	700	1,000	1,500	2,500	3,500	5,000
BTU Pacer (165cc single).	700	1,000	1,500	2,500	3,500	5,000
BTH Scat (175cc single)	700	1,100	1,600	2,100	2,800	3,500
C Sprint (250cc single)	800	1,100	1,700	2,300	3,000	3,800
CH Sprint (250cc single)	800	1,200	1,800	2,400	3,200	4,000
GE Servi-Car (45ci V-twin)	2,200	3,300	5,000	6,600	8,800	11,000
XLH Sportster (55ci V-twin)	2,400	3,600	5,400	7,200	9,600	12,000
XLCH Sportster (55ci V-twin)	2,400	3,600	5,400	7,200	9,600	12,000
FL Duo-Glide (74ci V-twin)	4,200	6,300	9,500	13,000	17,000	21,000
FLF Duo-Glide (74ci V-twin).	4,000	6,000	9,000	12,000	16,000	20,000
FLH Duo-Glide (74ci V-twin)	4,200	6,300	9,500	13,000	17,000	21,000
FLHF Duo-Glide (74ci V-twin)	4,000	6,000	9,000	12,000	16,000	20,000
1965						
M50 (50cc single)	1,000	2,000	3,000	4,000	5,000	6,000
AH Topper (165cc single)	900	1,400	2,100	2,800	3,800	4,700
BT Pacer (175cc single).	700	1,000	2,500	3,000	3,500	4,000
BTH Scat (175cc single)	700	1,100	1,600	2,100	2,800	3,500
C Sprint (250cc single)	800	1,200	1,800	2,400	3,200	4,000
CH Sprint (250cc single)	800	1,200	1,800	2,400	3,200	4,000
GE Servi-Car (45ci V-twin)	2,200	3,300	5,000	6,600	8,800	11,000
XLH Sportster (55ci V-twin)	2,400	3,600	5,400	7,200	9,600	12,000
XLCH Sportster (55ci V-twin)	2,400	3,600	5,400	7,200	9,600	12,000
FLB Electra-Glide (74ci V-twin)	4,200	6,300	9,500	13,000	17,000	21,000
FLFB Electra-Glide (74ci V-twin)	4,000	6,000	9,000	12,000	16,000	20,000
FLHB Electra-Glide (74ci V-twin)	4,200	6,300	9,500	13,000	17,000	21,000
FLHFB Electra-Glide (74ci V-twin)	4,000	6,000	9,000	12,000	16,000	20,000
1966						
M50 (50cc single)	1,000	2,000	3,000	4,000	5,000	6,000
MS (50cc single)	600	900	1,400	1,900	2,500	3,100
BTH Bobcat (175cc single)	600	900	1,400	1,800	2,400	3,000
C Sprint (250cc single)	800	1,200	1,800	2,400	3,200	4,000
CH Sprint (250cc single)	800	1,200	1,800	2,400	3,200	4,000
GE Servi-Car (45ci V-twin)	2,200	3,300	5,000	6,600	8,800	11,000
XLH Sportster (55ci V-twin)	2,200	3,300	5,000	6,600	8,800	11,000
XLCH Sportster (55ci V-twin)	2,200	3,300	5,000	6,600	8,800	11,000

	6	5	4	3	2	1
FLB Electra-Glide (74ci V-twin)	3,400	5,100	7,700	10,000	14,000	17,000
FLFB Electra-Glide (74ci V-twin)	3,300	5,000	7,400	9,900	13,000	16,000
FLHB Electra-Glide (74ci V-twin)	3,400	5,100	7,700	10,000	14,000	17,000
FLHFB Electra-Glide (74ci V-twin)	3,300	5,000	7,400	9,900	13,000	16,000
1967						
M (65cc single)	600	900	1,400	1,800	2,400	3,000
MS (65cc single)	600	900	1,400	1,900	2,500	3,100
SS Sprint (250cc single).	800	1,300	1,900	2,500	3,400	4,200
CH Sprint (250cc single).	800	1,200	1,800	2,400	3,200	4,000
GE Servi-Car (45ci V-twin)	2,200	3,300	5,000	6,600	8,800	11,000
XLH Sportster (55ci V-twin)	2,200	3,300	6,000	7,200	8,800	11,000
XLCH Sportster (55ci V-twin)	2,200	3,300	5,000	6,600	8,800	11,000
FLB Electra-Glide (74ci V-twin)	3,400	5,100	7,700	10,000	14,000	17,000
FLFB Electra-Glide (74ci V-twin)	3,300	5,000	7,400	9,900	13,000	16,000
FLHB Electra-Glide (74ci V-twin)	3,400	5,100	7,700	10,000	14,000	17,000
FLHFB Electra-Glide (74ci V-twin)	3,300	5,000	7,400	9,900	13,000	16,000
1968						
M (65cc single)	600	900	1,400	1,800	2,400	3,000
MS (65cc single)	600	900	1,400	1,900	2,500	3,100
ML Rapido (125cc single)	700	1,000	1,500	2,000	2,700	3,400
SS Sprint (250cc single).	800	1,300	1,900	2,500	3,400	4,200
CH Sprint (250cc single).	800	1,200	1,800	2,400	3,200	4,000
GE Servi-Car (45ci V-twin)	2,100	3,200	4,700	6,300	8,400	11,000
XLH Sportster (55ci V-twin)	1,900	2,900	4,300	5,700	7,600	10,000
XLCH Sportster (55ci V-twin)	2,200	3,300	5,000	6,600	8,800	11,000
FLB Electra-Glide (74ci V-twin)	3,200	4,700	7,100	9,500	13,000	16,000
FLFB Electra-Glide (74ci V-twin)	3,000	4,500	6,800	9,000	12,000	15,000
FLHB Electra-Glide (74ci V-twin)	3,200	4,700	8,000	11,000	15,000	18,000
FLHFB Electra-Glide (74ci V-twin)	3,000	4,500	6,800	9,000	12,000	15,000
1969						
M (65cc single)	600	900	1,400	1,800	2,400	3,000
MS (65cc single)	600	900	1,400	1,800	2,400	3,000
ML Rapido (125cc single)	700	1,000	1,500	2,000	2,600	3,300
MLS Rapido Scrambler (125cc single) . . .	700	1,000	1,500	2,000	2,700	3,400
SS Sprint (350cc single).	800	1,200	1,800	2,400	3,200	4,000
ERS Sprint (350cc single).	800	1,300	2,000	3,000	4,000	5,000
GE Servi-Car (45ci V-twin)	2,000	3,000	4,500	6,000	8,000	10,000
XLH Sportster (55ci V-twin)	1,900	3,000	5,000	7,000	9,000	11,000
XLCH Sportster (55ci V-twin)	2,200	3,300	4,950	6,600	8,800	11,000
FLB Electra-Glide (74ci V-twin)	3,200	4,700	7,100	9,500	13,000	16,000
FLFB Electra-Glide (74ci V-twin)	3,000	4,500	6,800	9,000	12,000	15,000
FLHB Electra-Glide (74ci V-twin)	3,200	4,700	7,100	9,500	13,000	16,000
FLHFB Electra-Glide (74ci V-twin)	3,000	4,500	6,800	9,000	12,000	15,000
1970						
MS Leggero (65cc single)	600	900	1,300	1,700	2,300	2,900
MSR Baja 100 (100cc single)	700	1,000	1,500	2,000	2,700	3,400
MLS Scrambler (125cc single)	700	1,000	1,600	2,100	2,800	3,500
SS Sprint (350cc single).	800	1,200	1,800	2,400	3,200	4,000
ERS Sprint (350cc single).	800	1,200	1,900	2,500	3,300	4,100
GE Servi-Car (45ci V-twin)	2,000	3,000	4,500	6,000	8,000	10,000
XLH Sportster (55ci V-twin)	1,800	2,700	4,050	5,400	7,200	9,000
XLCH Sportster (55ci V-twin)	2,000	3,000	4,500	6,000	8,000	10,000
FLB Electra-Glide (74ci V-twin)	2,900	4,400	6,500	8,700	12,000	15,000
FLFB Electra-Glide (74ci V-twin)	2,800	4,200	6,300	8,400	11,200	14,000
FLHB Electra-Glide (74ci V-twin)	2,900	4,400	6,500	9,200	12,000	15,000
FLHFB Electra-Glide (74ci V-twin)	2,800	4,200	6,300	8,400	11,200	14,000
1971						
MS (65cc single)	600	800	1,200	1,600	2,200	2,700
MSR Baja 100 (100cc single)	600	800	1,300	1,700	2,200	2,800

	6	5	4	3	2	1
MLS Scrambler (125cc single)	600	800	1,300	1,700	2,200	2,800
SS Sprint (350cc single).	800	1,100	1,700	2,300	3,000	3,800
SX Sprint (350cc single).	800	1,200	1,800	2,400	3,200	4,000
ERS Sprint (350cc single).	800	1,200	1,800	2,400	3,200	4,000
GE Servi-Car (45ci V-twin)	2,000	3,000	4,500	6,000	8,000	10,000
XLH Sportster (55ci V-twin)	1,600	2,400	3,600	4,800	6,400	8,000
XLCH Sportster (55ci V-twin)	1,600	2,400	**4,000**	**6,000**	**8,000**	**10,000**
FX Electra-Glide (74ci V-twin)	2,500	3,800	5,600	7,500	10,000	13,000
FLP Electra-Glide (74ci V-twin)	2,900	4,400	6,500	8,700	12,000	15,000
FLPF Electra-Glide (74ci V-twin)	2,800	4,200	6,300	8,400	11,200	14,000
FLH Electra-Glide (74ci V-twin)	2,900	4,400	6,500	8,700	12,000	15,000
FLHF Electra-Glide (74ci V-twin)	2,800	4,200	6,300	8,400	11,200	14,000
1972						
MC (65cc single)	600	800	1,200	1,600	2,200	2,700
MS (65cc single)	600	800	1,200	1,600	2,200	2,700
MSR Baja 100 (100cc single)	600	800	1,300	1,700	2,200	2,800
MLS Scrambler (125cc single)	600	800	1,300	1,700	2,200	2,800
SS Sprint (350cc single).	800	1,100	1,700	2,300	3,000	3,800
SX Sprint (350cc single).	800	1,200	2,000	3,000	4,000	5,000
ERS Sprint (350cc single).	800	1,200	1,800	2,400	3,200	4,000
GE Servi-Car (45ci V-twin)	2,000	3,000	4,500	6,000	9,000	12,000
XLH Sportster (61ci V-twin)	1,600	2,400	4,000	6,000	8,000	11,000
XLCH Sportster (61ci V-twin)	1,600	2,400	**4,000**	**6,000**	**8,000**	**10,000**
FX Super Glide (74ci V-twin)	2,400	3,600	5,400	7,200	9,600	12,000
FLP Electra-Glide (74ci V-twin)	2,600	3,900	5,900	7,800	10,000	13,000
FLPF Electra-Glide (74ci V-twin)	2,500	3,800	5,600	7,500	10,000	13,000
FLH Electra-Glide (74ci V-twin)	2,600	3,900	5,900	7,800	10,000	13,000
FLHF Electra-Glide (74ci V-twin)	2,500	3,800	5,600	7,500	10,000	13,000
1973						
X (90cc single)	200	300	500	800	1,000	1,500
Z (90cc single)	300	500	800	1,000	1,400	1,700
MSR Baja 100 (100cc single)	500	700	1,100	1,400	1,900	2,400
TX (125cc single)	400	600	1,000	1,300	1,700	2,100
S Sprint (350cc single)	600	1,000	1,400	1,900	2,600	3,200
SX Sprint (350cc single).	600	1,000	1,400	2,000	3,000	4,000
GE Servi-Car (45ci V-twin)	2,000	3,000	4,500	6,000	8,000	10,000
XLH Sportster (61ci V-twin)	1,600	2,400	3,600	4,800	6,400	8,000
XLCH Sportster (61ci V-twin)	1,600	2,400	3,600	4,800	6,400	8,000
FX Super Glide (74ci V-twin)	2,200	3,300	5,000	6,600	8,800	11,000
FL Electra-Glide (74ci V-twin)	2,500	3,800	5,600	7,500	10,000	13,000
FLH Electra-Glide (74ci V-twin)	2,500	3,800	5,600	7,500	10,000	13,000
1974						
X (90cc single)	300	500	700	1,000	1,500	2,000
Z (90cc single)	300	500	700	1,000	1,300	1,600
SR (100cc single)	500	700	900	1,200	1,500	2,000
SX (125cc single)	400	600	900	1,200	1,600	2,000
SX (175cc single)	400	700	1,000	1,300	1,800	2,200
SS Sprint (350cc single).	600	1,000	1,400	1,900	2,600	3,200
SX Sprint (350cc single).	600	1,000	1,400	1,900	2,600	3,200
XLH Sportster (61ci V-twin)	1,400	2,100	3,200	4,200	5,600	7,000
XLCH Sportster (61ci V-twin)	1,400	2,100	3,200	4,200	5,600	7,000
FX Super Glide (74ci V-twin)	2,200	3,300	5,000	6,600	8,800	11,000
FXE Super Glide (74ci V-twin)	2,200	3,300	5,000	6,600	8,800	11,000
FLH Electra-Glide (74ci V-twin)	2,300	3,500	5,200	6,900	9,200	12,000
FLHF Electra-Glide (74ci V-twin)	2,300	3,500	5,200	6,900	9,200	12,000
FLP Electra-Glide (74ci V-twin)	2,400	3,600	5,400	7,200	9,600	12,000
1975						
X (90cc single)	200	300	500	700	900	1,100
Z (90cc single)	300	500	700	900	1,200	1,500

	6	5	4	3	2	1
SXT (125cc single)	400	700	1,000	1,300	1,800	2,200
SX (175cc single)	400	600	1,000	1,300	1,700	2,100
SX (250cc single)	500	700	1,400	2,100	2,800	3,500
SS Sprint (250cc single)	500	700	1,100	1,400	1,900	2,400
XLH Sportster (61ci V-twin)	1,400	2,100	3,200	4,200	5,600	7,000
XLCH Sportster (61ci V-twin)	1,400	2,100	3,200	4,200	5,600	7,000
FX Super Glide (74ci V-twin)	2,200	3,300	5,000	6,600	8,800	11,000
FXE Super Glide (74ci V-twin)	2,200	3,300	5,000	6,600	8,800	11,000
FLH Electra-Glide (74ci V-twin)	2,300	3,500	5,200	6,900	9,200	12,000
FLHF Electra-Glide (74ci V-twin)	2,300	3,500	6,000	8,000	11,000	13,000
FLP Electra-Glide (74ci V-twin)	2,400	3,600	5,400	7,200	9,600	12,000
1976						
SS (125cc single)	400	600	1,000	1,300	1,700	2,100
SXT (125cc single)	400	600	1,000	1,300	1,700	2,100
SS (175cc single)	400	600	1,000	1,300	1,700	2,100
SX (175cc single)	400	600	1,000	1,300	1,700	2,100
SS (250cc single)	500	800	1,200	1,600	2,200	2,700
SX (250cc single)	500	800	1,400	2,100	2,800	3,500
XLH Sportster (61ci V-twin)	1,300	2,000	2,900	3,900	5,200	6,500
XLCH Sportster (61ci V-twin)	1,300	2,000	2,900	3,900	5,200	6,500
FX Super Glide (74ci V-twin)	2,200	3,300	5,000	6,600	8,800	11,000
FXE Super Glide (74ci V-twin)	2,200	3,300	5,000	6,600	8,800	11,000
FLH Electra-Glide (74ci V-twin)	2,400	3,600	5,400	7,200	9,600	12,000
1977						
SS (125cc single)	400	600	900	1,200	1,600	2,000
SXT (125cc single)	400	600	900	1,200	1,600	2,000
SS (175cc single)	400	600	900	1,200	1,600	2,000
SS (250cc single)	500	800	1,200	1,600	2,200	2,700
SX (250cc single)	500	800	1,400	2,100	2,800	3,500
XLH Sportster (61ci V-twin)	1,300	2,000	2,900	3,900	5,200	6,500
XLT Sportster (61ci V-twin)	1,300	2,000	2,900	3,900	5,200	6,500
XLCH Sportster (61ci V-twin)	1,300	2,000	2,900	3,900	5,200	6,500
XLCR Sportster (61ci V-twin)	**3,000**	**4,500**	**6,000**	**9,000**	**12,000**	**15,000**
FX Super Glide (74ci V-twin)	2,000	3,000	4,500	6,000	8,000	10,000
FXE Super Glide (74ci V-twin)	2,000	3,000	4,500	6,000	8,000	10,000
FXS Low Rider (74ci V-twin)	2,200	3,300	4,500	6,000	8,000	10,000
FLH Electra-Glide (74ci V-twin)	2,400	3,600	5,400	7,200	9,600	12,000
FLHS Electra-Glide (74ci V-twin)	2,500	3,800	5,600	7,500	10,000	13,000
1978						
SS (125cc single)	400	600	1,000	1,300	1,700	2,100
XLH Sportster (61ci V-twin)	1,300	2,000	2,900	3,900	5,200	6,500
XLH Sportster (61ci V-twin, 75th Anniversary)	1,300	2,000	2,900	3,900	5,200	6,500
XLT Sportster (61ci V-twin)	1,300	2,000	2,900	3,900	5,200	6,500
XLCH Sportster (61ci V-twin)	1,300	2,000	2,900	3,900	5,200	6,500
XLCR Sportster (61ci V-twin)	**3,000**	**4,500**	**6,000**	**9,000**	**12,000**	**15,000**
FX Super Glide (74ci V-twin)	2,000	3,000	4,500	6,000	8,000	10,000
FXE Super Glide (74ci V-twin)	2,000	3,000	4,500	6,000	8,000	10,000
FXS Low Rider (74ci V-twin)	2,200	3,300	5,000	6,600	8,800	11,000
FLH Electra-Glide (74ci V-twin, 75th Anniversary)	2,300	3,500	5,200	6,900	9,200	12,000
FLH-80 Electra-Glide (80ci V-twin)	2,000	3,000	4,500	6,000	8,000	10,000
1979						
XLS Sportster (61ci V-twin)	1,300	2,000	2,900	3,900	5,200	6,500
XLH Sportster (61ci V-twin)	1,300	2,000	2,900	3,900	5,200	6,500
XLCH Sportster (61ci V-twin)	1,300	2,000	2,900	3,900	5,200	6,500
FXE Super Glide (74ci V-twin)	2,000	3,000	4,500	6,000	8,000	10,000
FXS-74 Super Glide (74ci V-twin)	2,000	3,000	4,500	6,000	8,000	10,000
FXS-80 Super Glide (80ci V-twin)	2,000	3,000	4,500	6,000	8,000	10,000
FXEF-74 Fat Bob (74ci V-twin)	2,300	3,500	5,200	6,900	9,200	12,000

	6	5	4	3	2	1
FXEF-80 Fat Bob (80ci V-twin)	2,300	3,500	5,200	6,900	9,200	12,000
FLH-74 Electra Glide (74ci V-twin)	2,000	3,000	4,500	6,000	8,000	10,000
FXH-80 Electra Glide (80ci V-twin)	2,100	3,200	4,700	6,300	8,400	11,000
FLHC Electra Glide (80ci V-twin)	2,100	3,200	4,700	6,300	8,400	11,000
FLHCE Electra Glide (80ci V-twin)	2,100	3,200	4,700	6,300	8,400	11,000
FLHP-74 Electra Glide (74ci V-twin).	2,200	3,300	5,000	6,600	8,800	11,000
FLH-80 Electra-Glide (80ci V-twin)	2,200	3,300	5,000	6,600	8,800	11,000
1980						
XLS Sportster (61ci V-twin)	1,300	2,000	2,900	3,900	5,200	6,500
XLH Sportster (61ci V-twin)	1,300	2,000	2,900	3,900	5,200	6,500
FXB-80 Super Glide Sturgis (80ci V-twin) .	2,600	3,900	5,900	7,800	10,000	13,000
FXS-74 Super Glide (74ci V-twin)	2,200	3,300	5,000	6,600	8,800	11,000
FXEF-80 Fat Bob (80ci V-twin)	2,300	3,500	5,200	6,900	9,200	12,000
FXS-74 Low Rider (74ci V-twin).	2,000	3,000	4,500	6,000	8,000	10,000
FXS-80 Low Rider (80ci V-twin)	2,000	3,000	4,500	6,000	8,000	10,000
FXWG-80 Wide Glide (80ci V-twin)	2,100	3,200	4,700	6,300	8,400	11,000
FLH-74 Electra Glide (74ci V-twin)	2,000	3,000	4,500	6,000	8,000	10,000
FLH-80 Electra Glide (80ci V-twin)	2,100	3,200	4,700	6,300	8,400	11,000
FLHC-80 Electra Glide Classic (50ci V-twin)	2,100	3,200	4,700	6,300	8,400	11,000
FLHCE-80 Electra Glide Classic (80ci V-twin)	2,100	3,200	4,700	6,300	8,400	11,000
FLHP-74 Electra Glide (74ci V-twin).	2,200	3,300	5,000	6,600	8,800	11,000
FLHP-80 Electra-Glide (80ci V-twin)	2,200	3,300	5,000	6,600	8,800	11,000
FLT Tour Glide (80ci V-twin)	2,000	3,000	4,500	6,000	8,000	10,000
1981						
XLS Sportster (61ci V-twin)	2,300	3,500	5,200	6,900	9,200	12,000
XLH Sportster (61ci V-twin)	1,300	2,000	2,900	3,900	5,200	6,500
FXB Super Glide Sturgis (80ci V-twin) . . .	2,100	3,200	4,700	6,300	8,400	11,000
FXE Super Glide (80ci V-twin)	2,200	3,300	5,000	6,600	8,800	11,000
FXEF Fat Bob (80ci V-twin)	2,300	3,500	5,200	6,900	9,200	12,000
FXWG Wide Glide (80ci V-twin)	2,100	3,200	4,700	6,300	8,400	11,000
FLH Electra Glide (80ci V-twin)	2,200	3,300	5,000	6,600	8,800	11,000
FLH Electra Glide Heritage (80ci V-twin) . .	2,200	3,300	5,000	6,600	8,800	11,000
FLHC Electra Glide Classic (80ci V-twin) . .	2,200	3,300	5,000	6,600	8,800	11,000
FLHCE Electra Glide Classic (80ci V-twin) .	2,200	3,300	5,000	6,600	8,800	11,000
FLHP Electra-Glide (80ci V-twin)	2,200	3,300	5,000	6,600	8,800	11,000
FLT Tour Glide (80ci V-twin)	2,000	3,000	4,500	6,000	8,000	10,000
FLT Tour Glide Classic (80ci V-twin)	2,000	3,000	4,500	6,000	8,000	10,000
1982						
XLH Sportster (61ci V-twin)	1,300	2,000	2,900	3,900	5,200	6,500
XLHA Sportster (61ci V-twin, 25th Anniv) . .	1,500	2,200	3,300	4,400	5,800	7,300
XLS Sportster (61ci V-twin)	1,300	2,000	2,900	3,900	5,200	6,500
XLSA Sportster (61ci V-twin, 25th Anniv) . .	1,500	2,200	3,300	4,400	5,800	7,300
FLH Electra Glide (80ci V-twin)	2,200	3,300	5,000	6,600	8,800	11,000
FLHC Electra Glide Classic (80ci V-twin) . .	2,200	3,300	5,000	6,600	8,800	11,000
FLT Tour Glide (80ci V-twin)	2,000	3,000	4,500	6,000	8,000	10,000
FLT Tour Glide Classic (80ci V-twin)	2,000	3,000	4,500	6,000	8,000	10,000
FXB Super Glide "Sturgis" (80ci V-twin) . .	2,800	4,200	6,300	8,400	11,000	14,000
FXE Super Glide (80ci V-twin)	2,200	3,300	5,000	6,600	8,800	11,000
FXR Super Glide II (80ci V-twin)	2,200	3,300	5,000	6,600	8,800	11,000
FXRS Super Glide II (80ci V-twin).	2,200	3,300	5,000	6,600	8,800	11,000
FXS Low Rider (80ci V-twin)	2,300	3,500	5,200	6,900	9,200	12,000
FXWG Wide Glide (80ci V-twin).	2,300	3,500	5,200	6,900	9,200	12,000
1983						
XLH Sportster (61ci V-twin)	1,300	2,000	2,900	3,900	5,200	6,500
XLS Sportster (61ci V-twin)	1,300	2,000	2,900	3,900	5,200	6,500
XLX Sportster (61ci V-twin)	1,300	2,000	2,900	3,900	5,200	6,500
XR-1000 Sportster (61ci V-twin).	3,000	5,000	8,000	10,000	13,000	16,000
FLH Electra Glide (80ci V-twin)	2,200	3,300	5,000	6,600	8,800	11,000
FLHT Electra Glide (80ci V-twin)	2,200	3,300	5,000	6,600	8,800	11,000

	6	5	4	3	2	1
FLHTC Electra Glide Classic (80ci V-twin) .	2,200	3,300	5,000	6,600	8,800	11,000
FLT Tour Glide (80ci V-twin)	2,000	3,000	4,500	6,000	8,000	10,000
FLTC Tour Glide Classic (80ci V-twin) . . .	2,000	3,000	4,500	6,000	8,000	10,000
FXDG Super Glide (80ci V-twin)	2,200	3,300	5,000	6,600	8,800	11,000
FXE Super Glide (80ci V-twin)	2,200	3,300	5,000	6,600	8,800	11,000
FXR Super Glide II (80ci V-twin)	2,200	3,300	5,000	6,600	8,800	11,000
FXRS Super Glide II (80ci V-twin).	2,200	3,300	5,000	6,600	8,800	11,000
FXRT Super Glide II Touring (80ci V-twin) .	2,200	3,300	5,000	6,600	8,800	11,000
FXSB Low Rider (80ci V-twin).	2,300	3,500	5,200	6,900	9,200	12,000
FXWG Wide Glide (80ci V-twin).	2,300	3,500	5,200	6,900	9,200	12,000
1984						
XLH Sportster (61ci V-twin).	1,300	2,000	2,900	3,900	5,200	6,500
XLS Sportster (61ci V-twin)	1,300	2,000	2,900	3,900	5,200	6,500
XLX Sportster (61ci V-twin)	1,300	2,000	2,900	3,900	5,200	6,500
XR-1000 Sportster (61ci V-twin).	3,000	5,000	8,000	10,000	13,000	16,000
FLH Electra Glide (80ci V-twin)	2,200	3,300	5,000	6,600	8,800	11,000
FLHT "Last Edition" (80ci V-twin)	2,700	4,100	6,100	8,100	11,000	14,000
FLHTC Electra Glide Classic (80ci V-twin) .	2,200	3,300	5,000	6,600	8,800	11,000
FLTC Tour Glide Classic (80ci V-twin) . . .	2,000	3,000	4,500	6,000	8,000	10,000
FXE Super Glide (80ci V-twin)	2,200	3,300	5,000	6,600	8,800	11,000
FXRDG Disc Glide (80ci V-twin)	2,400	3,600	5,400	7,200	9,600	12,000
FXRP Super Glide (80ci V-twin).	2,200	3,300	5,000	6,600	8,800	11,000
FXRS Low Glide (80ci V-twin).	2,300	3,500	5,200	6,900	9,200	12,000
FXRT Sport Glide (80ci V-twin)	2,400	3,600	5,400	7,200	9,600	12,000
FXSB Low Rider (80ci V-twin)	2,300	3,500	5,200	6,900	9,200	12,000
FXST Softail (80ci V-twin).	2,700	4,100	6,100	8,100	11,000	14,000
FXWG Wide Glide (80ci V-twin).	2,300	3,500	5,200	6,900	9,200	12,000
1985						
XLH Sportster (61ci V-twin).	1,300	2,000	2,900	3,900	5,200	6,500
XLS Sportster (61ci V-twin)	1,300	2,000	2,900	3,900	5,200	6,500
XLX Sportster (61ci V-twin)	1,300	2,000	2,900	3,900	5,200	6,500
FLHTC Electra Glide Classic (80ci V-twin) .	2,000	3,000	4,500	6,000	8,000	10,000
FLTC Tour Glide Classic (80ci V-twin) . . .	2,000	3,000	4,500	6,000	8,000	10,000
FXEF Fat Bob (80ci V-twin)	2,300	3,500	5,200	6,900	9,200	12,000
FXRC Low Glide Custom (80ci V-twin) . . .	2,500	3,800	5,600	7,500	10,000	13,000
FXRP Super Glide (80ci V-twin).	2,200	3,300	5,500	6,600	8,800	11,000
FXRS Low Glide (80ci V-twin).	2,400	3,600	5,400	7,200	9,600	12,000
FXRT Sport Glide (80ci V-twin)	2,400	3,600	5,400	7,200	9,600	12,000
FXSB Low Rider (80ci V-twin).	2,300	3,500	5,200	6,900	9,200	12,000
FXST Softail (80ci V-twin).	2,700	4,100	6,100	8,100	11,000	14,000
FXWG Wide Glide (80ci V-twin).	2,300	3,500	5,200	6,900	9,200	12,000
1986						
XLH-883 Sportster (883cc V-twin).	1,300	2,000	2,900	3,900	5,200	6,500
XLH-1100 Sportster (1100cc V-twin)	1,800	2,700	4,100	5,400	7,200	9,000
FLHT Electra Glide (80ci V-twin)	2,000	3,000	4,500	6,000	8,000	10,000
FLHTC Electra Glide Classic (80ci V-twin) .	2,000	3,000	4,500	6,000	8,000	10,000
FLTC Tour Glide Classic (80ci V-twin) . . .	2,000	3,000	4,500	6,000	8,000	10,000
FXR Super Glide (80ci V-twin)	2,200	3,300	5,000	6,600	8,800	11,000
FXRD Sport Glide Deluxe (80ci V-twin) . . .	2,200	3,300	5,000	6,600	8,800	11,000
FXRP Super Glide (80ci V-twin).	2,200	3,300	5,000	6,600	8,800	11,000
FXRS Low Rider (80ci V-twin).	2,400	3,600	5,400	7,200	9,600	12,000
FXRT Sport Glide (80ci V-twin)	2,200	3,300	5,000	6,600	8,800	11,000
FXST Softail (80ci V-twin)	2,700	4,100	6,100	8,100	11,000	14,000
FXSTC Softail Custom (80ci V-twin)	2,700	4,100	6,100	8,100	11,000	14,000
FXSTH Softail Heritage (80ci V-twin)	2,700	4,100	6,100	8,100	11,000	14,000
1987						
XLH-883 Sportster (883cc V-twin).	1,300	2,000	2,900	3,900	5,200	6,500
XLH-1100 Sportster (1100cc V-twin)	1,700	2,600	3,800	5,100	6,800	8,500

	6	5	4	3	2	1
XLH-1100 Sportster (1100cc V-twin, 30th Anniv)	2,100	3,500	4,700	6,300	8,400	11,000
FLHS Electra Glide Sport (80ci V-twin) . . .	2,000	3,000	4,500	6,000	8,000	10,000
FLHTC Electra Glide Classic (80ci V-twin) .	2,000	3,000	4,500	6,000	8,000	10,000
FLST Heritage Softail (80ci V-twin)	2,300	3,500	5,200	6,900	9,200	12,000
FLSTC Heritage Softail Special (80ci V-twin)	2,300	3,500	5,200	6,900	9,200	12,000
FLTC Tour Glide Classic (80ci V-twin) . . .	2,000	3,000	4,500	6,000	8,000	10,000
FXLR Low Rider Custom (80ci V-twin) . . .	2,400	3,600	5,400	7,200	9,600	12,000
FXLR Low Rider Custom (80ci V-twin, 10th Anniv.)	2,700	4,100	6,100	8,100	11,000	14,000
FXR Super Glide (80ci V-twin)	2,200	3,300	5,000	6,600	8,800	11,000
FXRP Super Glide (80ci V-twin).	2,200	3,300	5,000	6,600	8,800	11,000
FXRS Low Rider (80ci V-twin).	2,400	3,600	5,400	7,200	9,600	12,000
FXRS-SP Low Rider Sport (80ci V-twin) . . .	2,600	3,800	5,700	7,700	10,000	13,000
FXRT Sport Glide (80ci V-twin)	2,200	3,300	5,000	6,600	8,800	11,000
FXST Softail (80ci V-twin).	2,700	4,100	6,100	8,100	11,000	14,000
FXSTC Softail Custom (80ci V-twin)	2,700	4,100	6,100	8,100	11,000	14,000
1988						
XLH-883 Sportster (883cc V-twin).	1,300	2,000	2,900	3,900	5,200	6,500
XLH-883 Sportster Hugger (883cc V-twin) .	1,400	2,100	3,200	4,200	5,600	7,000
XLH-883 Sportster Deluxe (883cc V-twin). .	1,400	2,100	3,200	4,200	5,600	7,000
XLH-1200 Sportster (1200cc V-twin)	2,000	3,000	4,000	5,000	7,000	8,000
FLHS Electra Glide Sport (80ci V-twin) . . .	2,000	3,000	4,500	6,000	8,000	10,000
FLHTC Electra Glide Classic (80ci V-twin) .	2,000	3,000	4,500	6,000	8,000	10,000
FLHTC Electra Glide Classic (80ci V-twin, 85th Anniv.)	2,600	3,900	5,900	7,800	10,000	13,000
FLST Heritage Softail (80ci V-twin)	2,300	3,500	5,200	6,900	9,200	12,000
FLSTC Heritage Softail Custom (80ci V-twin)	2,300	3,500	5,200	6,900	9,200	12,000
FLTC Tour Glide Classic (80ci V-twin) . . .	2,200	3,300	5,000	6,600	8,800	11,000
FLTC Tour Glide Classic (80ci V-twin, 85th Anniv.)	2,600	6,900	5,900	7,800	10,000	13,000
FXLR Low Rider Custom (80ci V-twin) . . .	2,400	3,600	5,400	7,200	9,600	12,000
FXR Super Glide (80ci V-twin)	2,200	3,300	5,000	6,600	8,800	11,000
FXRP Super Glide (80ci V-twin).	2,200	3,300	5,000	6,600	8,800	11,000
FXRS Low Rider (80ci V-twin).	2,400	3,600	5,400	7,200	9,600	12,000
FXRS Low Rider (80ci V-twin, 85th Anniv) .	2,700	4,100	6,100	8,100	11,000	14,000
FXRS-SP Low Rider Sport (80ci V-twin) . .	2,400	3,800	5,700	7,700	10,000	13,000
FXRT Sport Glide (80ci V-twin)	2,200	3,300	5,000	6,600	8,800	11,000
FXST Softail (80ci V-twin).	2,700	4,100	6,100	8,100	11,000	14,000
FXST Softail (80ci V-twin, 85th Anniv.) . . .	2,900	4,400	6,500	8,700	12,000	15,000
FXSTC Softail Custom (80ci V-twin)	2,700	4,100	6,100	8,100	11,000	14,000
1989						
XLH-883 Sportster (883cc V-twin).	1,300	2,000	2,900	3,900	5,200	6,500
XLH-883 Sportster Hugger (883cc V-twin) .	1,400	2,100	3,200	4,200	5,600	7,000
XLH-883 Sportster Deluxe (883cc V-twin). .	1,400	2,100	3,200	4,200	5,600	7,000
XLH-1200 Sportster (1200cc V-twin)	2,000	3,000	4,000	5,000	7,000	8,000
FLHS Electra Glide Sport (80ci V-twin) . . .	2,200	3,300	5,000	6,600	8,800	11,000
FLHTC Electra Glide Classic (80ci V-twin) .	2,200	3,300	5,000	6,600	8,800	11,000
FLHTCU Electra Glide Ultra Classic (80ci V-twin).	2,800	4,200	6,300	8,400	11,000	14,000
FLST Heritage Softail (80ci V-twin)	2,300	3,500	5,200	6,900	9,200	12,000
FLSTC Heritage Softail Custom (80ci V-twin)	2,300	3,500	5,200	6,900	9,200	12,000
FLTC Tour Glide Classic (80ci V-twin) . . .	2,300	3,500	5,200	6,900	9,200	12,000
FLTCU Tour Glide Ultra Classic (80ci V-twin)	2,800	4,200	6,300	8,400	11,000	14,000
FXLR Low Rider Custom (80ci V-twin) . . .	2,400	3,600	5,400	7,200	9,600	12,000
FXR Super Glide (80ci V-twin)	2,200	3,300	5,000	6,600	8,800	11,000
FXRP Super Glide (80ci V-twin).	2,200	3,300	5,000	6,600	8,800	11,000
FXRS Low Rider (80ci V-twin).	2,500	3,800	5,600	7,500	10,000	13,000

	6	5	4	3	2	1
FXRS-C Low Rider Convertible (80ci V-twin)	2,500	3,800	5,600	7,500	10,000	13,000
FXRS-SP Low Rider Sport (80ci V-twin)	2,500	3,800	5,600	7,500	10,000	13,000
FXRT Sport Glide (80ci V-twin)	2,200	3,300	5,000	6,600	8,800	11,000
FXST Softail (80ci V-twin)	2,600	3,900	5,900	7,800	10,000	13,000
FXSTC Softail Custom (80ci V-twin)	2,700	4,100	6,100	8,100	11,000	14,000
FXSTS Springer Softail (80ci V-twin)	2,700	4,100	6,100	8,100	11,000	14,000
1990						
XLH-883 Sportster (883cc V-twin)	1,300	2,000	2,900	3,900	5,200	6,500
XLH-883 Sportster Hugger (883cc V-twin)	1,400	2,100	3,200	4,200	5,600	7,000
XLH-883 Sportster Deluxe (883cc V-twin)	1,400	2,100	3,200	4,200	5,600	7,000
XLH-1200 Sportster (1200cc V-twin)	2,000	3,000	4,000	5,000	7,000	8,000
FLHS Electra Glide Sport (80ci V-twin)	2,200	3,300	5,000	6,600	8,800	11,000
FLHTC Electra Glide Classic (80ci V-twin)	2,200	3,300	5,000	6,600	8,800	11,000
FLHTCU Electra Glide Ultra Classic (80ci V-twin)	2,800	4,200	6,300	8,400	11,000	14,000
FLST Heritage Softail (80ci V-twin)	2,300	3,500	5,200	6,900	9,200	12,000
FLSTC Heritage Softail Custom (80ci V-twin)	2,300	3,500	5,200	6,900	9,200	12,000
FLSTF Fat Boy (80ci V-twin)	2,600	3,900	5,900	7,800	10,000	13,000
FLTC Tour Glide Classic (80ci V-twin)	2,500	3,800	5,600	7,500	10,000	13,000
FLTCU Tour Glide Ultra Classic (80ci V-twin)	2,800	4,200	6,300	8,400	11,000	14,000
FXLR Low Rider Custom (80ci V-twin)	2,400	3,600	5,400	7,200	9,600	12,000
FXR Super Glide (80ci V-twin)	2,200	3,300	5,000	6,600	8,800	11,000
FXRP Super Glide (80ci V-twin)	2,200	3,300	5,000	6,600	8,800	11,000
FXRS Low Rider (80ci V-twin)	2,500	3,800	5,600	7,500	10,000	13,000
FXRS-C Low Rider Convertible (80ci V-twin)	2,500	3,800	5,600	7,500	10,000	13,000
FXRS-SP Low Rider Sport (80ci V-twin)	2,500	3,800	5,600	7,500	10,000	13,000
FXRT Sport Glide (80ci V-twin)	2,200	3,300	5,000	6,600	8,800	11,000
FXST Softail (80ci V-twin)	2,600	3,900	5,900	7,800	10,000	13,000
FXSTC Softail Custom (80ci V-twin)	2,700	4,100	6,100	8,100	11,000	14,000
FXSTS Springer Softail (80ci V-twin)	2,700	4,100	6,100	8,100	11,000	14,000
1991						
XLH-883 Sportster (883cc V-twin)	1,300	2,000	2,900	3,900	5,200	6,500
XLH-883 Sportster Hugger (883cc V-twin)	1,400	2,100	3,200	4,200	5,600	7,000
XLH-883 Sportster Deluxe (883cc V-twin)	1,400	2,100	3,200	4,200	5,600	7,000
XLH-1200 Sportster (1200cc V-twin)	2,000	3,000	4,000	5,000	7,000	8,000
FXR Super Glide (80ci V-twin)	2,200	3,300	5,000	6,600	8,800	11,000
FXRS Low Rider (80ci V-twin)	2,500	3,800	5,600	7,500	10,000	13,000
FXRS-SP Low Rider Sport (80ci V-twin)	2,500	3,800	5,600	7,500	10,000	13,000
FXLR Low Rider Custom (80ci V-twin)	2,400	3,600	5,400	7,200	9,600	12,000
FXRS-C Low Rider Convertible (80ci V-twin)	2,500	3,800	5,600	7,500	10,000	13,000
FXSTC Softail Custom (80ci V-twin)	2,700	4,100	6,100	8,100	11,000	14,000
FLSTF Fat Boy (80ci V-twin)	2,600	3,900	5,900	7,800	10,000	13,000
FXSTS Springer Softail (80ci V-twin)	2,700	4,100	6,100	8,100	11,000	14,000
FLSTC Heritage Softail Custom (80ci V-twin)	2,300	3,500	5,200	6,900	9,200	12,000
FXDB Dyna Sturgis (80ci V-twin)	3,000	5,000	7,000	8,900	12,000	14,000
FLHS Electra Glide Sport (80ci V-twin)	2,200	3,300	5,000	6,600	8,800	11,000
FXRT Sport Glide (80ci V-twin)	2,200	3,300	5,000	6,600	8,800	11,000
FLTC Tour Glide Classic (80ci V-twin)	2,200	3,300	5,000	6,600	8,800	11,000
FLHTC Electra Glide Classic (80ci V-twin)	2,200	3,300	5,000	6,600	8,800	11,000
FLTCU Tour Glide Ultra Classic (80ci V-twin)	2,800	4,200	6,300	8,400	11,000	14,000
FLHTCU Electra Glide Ultra Classic (80ci V-twin)	2,800	4,200	6,300	8,400	11,000	14,000
1992						
XLH-883 Sportster (883cc V-twin)	1,300	2,000	2,900	3,900	5,200	6,500
XLH-883 Sportster Hugger (883cc V-twin)	1,400	2,100	3,200	4,200	5,600	7,000
XLH-883 Sportster Deluxe (883cc V-twin)	1,400	2,100	3,200	4,200	5,600	7,000
XLH-1200 Sportster (1200cc V-twin)	2,000	3,000	4,000	5,000	7,000	8,000
FXR Super Glide (80ci V-twin)	2,200	3,300	5,000	6,600	8,800	11,000
FXRS Low Rider (80ci V-twin)	2,500	3,800	5,600	7,500	10,000	13,000

	6	5	4	3	2	1
FXRS-SP Low Rider Sport (80ci V-twin) . . .	2,500	3,800	5,600	7,500	10,000	13,000
FXLR Low Rider Custom (80ci V-twin) . . .	2,400	3,600	5,400	7,200	9,600	12,000
FXRS-C Low Rider Convertible (80ci V-twin)	2,500	3,800	5,600	7,500	10,000	13,000
FXSTC Softail Custom (80ci V-twin)	2,700	4,100	6,100	8,100	11,000	14,000
FXDC Dyna Custom (80ci V-twin)	2,700	4,100	6,100	8,100	11,000	14,000
FLSTF Fat Boy (80ci V-twin)	2,600	3,900	5,900	7,800	10,000	13,000
FXSTS Springer Softail (80ci V-twin)	2,700	4,100	6,100	8,100	11,000	14,000
FXDB Dyna Daytona (80ci V-twin)	3,000	5,000	7,000	9,200	12,000	14,000
FLSTC Heritage Softail Custom (80ci V-twin)	2,300	3,500	5,200	6,900	9,200	12,000
FXRT Sport Glide (80ci V-twin)	2,200	3,300	5,000	6,600	8,800	11,000
FLHTC Electra Glide Classic (80ci V-twin) .	2,200	3,300	5,000	6,600	8,800	11,000
FLTCU Tour Glide Ultra Classic (80ci V-twin)	2,800	4,200	6,300	8,400	11,000	14,000
FLHTCU Electra Glide Ultra Classic (80ci						
V-twin)	2,800	4,200	6,300	8,400	11,000	14,000
1993						
XLH-883 Sportster (883cc V-twin)	1,500	2,200	3,200	4,400	5,500	6,600
XLH-883 Sportster Hugger (883cc V-twin) .	1,800	2,500	3,500	4,800	5,600	6,700
XLH-883 Sportster Deluxe (883cc V-twin). .	1,900	2,600	3,600	4,900	5,700	6,800
XLH-1200 Sportster (1200cc V-twin)	2,000	2,600	4,100	5,500	6,200	7,000
XLH-1200 Sportster Annversary (1200cc						
V-twin)	2,000	2,600	4,300	5,800	6,300	7,500
FXR Super Glide (80ci V-twin)	2,100	3,200	5,100	7,100	9,600	12,000
FXRS-SP Low Rider Sport (80ci V-twin) . .	2,200	3,300	5,300	7,500	10,100	13,000
FXLR Low Rider Custom (80ci V-twin) . . .	2,300	3,400	5,400	7,600	10,300	13,000
FXDL Dyna Low Rider (80ci V-twin).	2,400	3,500	5,500	7,700	10,500	13,000
FXRS Low Rider Convertible (80ci V-twin) .	2,500	3,600	5,600	7,800	10,600	13,000
FXLR Low Rider Custom Annivesary(80ci						
V-twin).	2,300	3,400	5,400	7,700	10,500	13,000
FXSTC Softail Custom (80ci V-twin)	2,500	4,100	6,200	8,600	11,700	14,000
FXDWG Dyna Wide Glide (80ci V-twin). . .	2,400	4,000	6,000	8,200	11,200	14,000
FXSTS Springer Softail (80ci V-twin)	2,500	4,100	6,200	8,600	11,700	14,000
FLSTF Fat Boy (80ci V-twin)	2,600	4,200	6,300	8,800	12,000	15,000
FLSTC Heritage Softail Custom (80ci V-twin)	2,600	4,200	6,300	8,800	12,000	15,000
FXDWG Dyna Wide Glide Anniversary (80ci						
V-twin).	2,400	4,000	6,000	8,300	11,300	14,000
FLSTN Heritage Nostalgia (80ci V-twin). . .	4,200	6,300	8,400	11,000	14,600	17,000
FLHS Electra Glide Sport (80ci V-twin) . . .	2,200	3,300	5,300	7,500	12,200	15,000
FLHTC Electra Glide Classic (80ci V-twin) .	2,400	4,000	6,000	8,200	11,200	14,000
FLHTC Electra Glide Classic Anniversary						
(80ci V-twin).	2,500	4,100	6,100	8,300	11,300	14,000
FLTCU Tour Glide Ultra Classic (80ci V-twin)	2,400	4,000	6,000	8,200	11,200	14,000
FLHTCU Electra Glide Ultra Classic (80ci						
V-twin).	2,500	4,100	6,100	8,300	11,300	14,000
FLTCU Tour Glide Ultra Classic Anniv (80ci						
V-twin).	2,500	4,100	6,100	8,300	11,300	14,000
FLHTCU Electra Glide Ultra Classic Anniv						
(80ci V-twin).	2,500	4,100	6,200	8,400	11,400	14,000
1994						
XLH-883 Sportster (883cc V-twin).	1,500	2,200	3,200	4,400	5,500	6,600
XLH-883 Sportster Hugger (883cc V-twin) .	1,800	2,500	3,500	4,800	5,600	6,700
XLH-883 Sportster Deluxe (883cc V-twin). .	1,900	2,600	3,600	4,900	5,700	6,800
XLH-1200 Sportster (1200cc V-twin)	2,000	2,600	4,100	5,500	6,200	7,000
FLHR Road King (80ci V-twin)	800	1,200	3,500	7,200	10,500	13,000
FLHTC Electra Glide Classic (80ci V-twin) .	2,400	4,000	6,000	8,200	11,200	14,000
FLHTCU Electra Glide Ultra Classic (80ci						
V-twin).	2,500	4,100	6,100	8,300	11,300	14,000
FLSTC Heritage Softail (80ci V-twin)	2,500	4,100	6,200	8,600	11,700	14,000
FLSTF Fat Boy (80ci V-twin)	2,600	4,200	6,300	8,800	12,000	15,000

	6	5	4	3	2	1
FLSTN Heritage Nostalgia (80ci V-twin). . .	4,200	6,300	8,400	11,000	14,600	17,000
FLTCU Tour Glide Ultra Classic (80ci V-twin)	2,500	4,100	6,100	8,300	11,300	14,000
FXDL Dyna Low Rider (80ci V-twin).	2,400	3,500	5,500	7,700	10,500	13,000
FXDS Convertible Low Rider (80ci V-twin) .	2,000	3,000	4,700	7,200	9,700	12,500
FXDWG Dyna Wide Glide (80ci V-twin). . . .	2,400	4,000	6,000	8,200	11,200	14,000
FXLR Low Rider (80ci V-twin).	2,300	3,400	5,400	7,700	10,500	13,000
FXR Super Glide (80ci V-twin)	2,100	3,200	5,100	7,100	9,600	12,000
FXSTC Softail (80ci V-twin)	2,500	4,100	6,200	8,600	11,700	14,000
FXSTS Springer Softail (80ci V-twin)	2,500	4,100	6,200	8,600	11,700	14,000
1995						
XLH-883 Sportster (883cc V-twin).	900	2,100	3,300	4,500	5,700	7,000
XLH-883 Sportster Hugger (883cc V-twin) .	1,000	2,300	3,600	4,900	5,900	7,000
XLH-883 Sportster Deluxe (883cc V-twin). .	1,100	2,400	3,700	5,000	5,300	7,000
XLH-1200 Sportster (1200cc V-twin)	1,200	2,700	4,200	5,700	6,600	7,500
FXD Dyna Super Glide (80ci V-twin)	1,200	2,200	4,200	6,400	8,600	10,800
FXDL Dyna Low Rider (80ci V-twin).	1,200	2,400	5,400	8,400	11,400	14,500
FXDS Convertible Dyna Low Rider (80ci V-twin). . .	1,100	2,100	4,800	7,500	10,200	13,000
FXSTC Softail Custom (80ci V-twin)	1,500	3,300	6,300	9,300	12,700	16,000
FXSTS Springer Softail (80ci V-twin)	1,500	3,300	6,300	9,300	12,600	16,000
FXDWG Dyna Wide Glide (80ci V-twin) . . .	1,500	3,000	5,900	8,900	12,100	14,500
FLSTF Fat Boy Softail (80ci V-twin).	1,700	3,500	6,500	9,500	12,900	16,000
FLSTN Heritage Softail Special (80ci V-twin)	2,000	4,000	7,200	10,200	13,700	16,500
FXSTSB Bad Boy Softail (80ci V0twin) . . .	1,800	3,500	7,000	10,000	13,400	16,500
FLSTC Heritage Softail (80ci V-twin)	1,800	3,500	6,500	9,500	12,900	16,000
FLHT Electra Glide (80ci V-twin)	1,200	2,500	5,000	8,000	10,900	14,000
FLHR Electra Road King (80ci V-twin) . . .	1,500	3,000	6,000	9,000	12,000	15,000
FLHTC Classic (80ci V-twin)	1,500	3,000	6,000	8,900	12,100	15,000
FLTCU Tour Glide Ultra Classic (80ci V-twin)	1,500	3,000	6,000	9,000	12,200	15,000
FLHTCU Electra Glide Ultra Classic (80ci V-twin).	1,500	3,000	6,000	9,100	12,300	15,000
FLHTCUI Anniversary (80ci V-twin)	1,500	3,100	6,200	9,600	13,100	15,500

HENDERSON

	6	5	4	3	2	1
1920						
Model K (80-cid, inline 4-cyl)	11,000	16,000	24,000	32,000	43,000	54,000
1921						
Model K (80-cid, inline 4-cyl)	11,000	16,000	24,000	32,000	43,000	54,000
1922						
DeLuxe (80-cid, inline 4-cyl).	11,000	16,000	24,000	32,000	42,000	53,000
1923						
DeLuxe (80-cid, inline 4-cyl).	11,000	16,000	24,000	32,000	42,000	53,000
1924						
DeLuxe (80-cid, inline 4-cyl).	11,000	16,000	24,000	32,000	42,000	53,000
1925						
DeLuxe (80-cid, inline 4-cyl).	11,000	16,000	24,000	32,000	42,000	53,000
1926						
DeLuxe (80-cid, inline 4-cyl).	11,000	16,000	24,000	32,000	42,000	53,000
1927						
DeLuxe (80-cid, inline 4-cyl).	11,000	20,000	30,000	35,000	45,000	55,000
1928						
DeLuxe (80-cid, inline 4-cyl).	11,000	20,000	30,000	35,000	45,000	55,000
1929						
Streamline KJ (80-cid, inline 4-cyl)	11,000	17,000	25,000	34,000	45,000	56,000
1930						
Streamline KJ (80-cid, inline 4-cyl)	11,000	17,000	25,000	34,000	45,000	56,000
Streamline KI (high comp.)	12,000	17,000	26,000	35,000	46,000	58,000
1931						
Streamline KJ (80-cid, inline 4-cyl)	11,000	17,000	25,000	35,000	46,000	57,000
Streamline KI (high comp.)	12,000	17,000	26,000	35,000	46,000	58,000

	6	5	4	3	2	1
HODAKA						
1964						
ACE 90 (90cc single)	400	500	800	1,200	1,600	2,000
1965						
ACE 90 (90cc single)	400	500	800	1,200	1,600	2,000
1966						
ACE 90 (90cc single)	400	500	800	1,200	1,600	2,000
1967						
ACE 90 (90cc single)	400	500	800	1,200	1,600	2,000
1968						
ACE 100 (100cc single)	400	500	1,000	1,200	1,600	2,000
1969						
ACE 100A (100cc single)	400	500	800	1,100	1,400	1,800
ACE 100 Super Rat (100cc single)	800	1,200	1,800	2,300	3,100	3,900
1970						
ACE 100B (100cc single)	400	500	800	1,200	1,500	1,900
ACE 100 Super Rat (100cc single)	800	1,300	1,900	2,400	3,200	4,000
1971						
ACE 100B+ (100cc single)	500	700	1,100	1,400	1,900	2,400
ACE 100 Super Rat (100cc single)	800	1,200	1,900	2,500	3,300	4,100
1972						
ACE 100B+ (100cc single)	500	700	1,100	1,400	1,900	2,400
ACE 100 Super Rat (100cc single)	800	1,200	1,900	2,500	3,300	4,100
125 Wombat (125cc single)	500	800	1,200	1,600	2,100	2,600
1973						
100 Dirt Squirt (100cc single)	500	700	1,100	1,400	1,900	2,400
125 Combat Wombat (125cc single)	600	900	1,300	1,700	2,300	2,900
125 Wombat (125cc single)	500	800	1,200	1,600	2,100	2,600
1974						
100 Dirt Squirt (100cc single)	500	700	1,100	1,400	1,900	2,400
100 Road Toad (100cc single)	500	800	1,100	1,500	2,000	2,500
100 Super Rat (100cc single)	800	1,200	1,800	2,300	3,100	3,900
125 Super Combat (125cc single)	900	1,400	2,000	2,700	3,600	4,500
1975						
100 Dirt Squirt (100cc single)	500	800	1,100	1,500	2,000	2,500
100 Road Toad (100cc single)	500	1,000	1,500	2,000	2,500	3,000
1976						
100 Road Toad (100cc single)	500	800	1,100	1,500	2,000	2,500
125 Wombat (125cc single)	600	900	1,300	1,700	2,300	2,900
250 ED (250cc single)	600	1,000	1,400	1,900	2,600	3,200
250 SL (250cc single)	600	900	1,300	1,700	2,300	2,900
1977						
Dirt Squirt 80 (80cc single)	600	900	1,300	1,700	2,300	2,900
175 SL (175cc single)	700	1,100	1,600	2,100	2,800	3,500
250 SL (250cc single)	600	900	1,300	1,700	2,300	2,900
1978						
Dirt Squirt 80 (80cc single)	600	900	1,300	1,700	2,300	2,900
175 SL (175cc single)	700	1,100	1,600	2,100	2,800	3,500
250 SL 70A (250cc single)	600	900	1,300	1,700	2,300	2,900
HONDA						
1959						
C100 Super Cub (49cc single)	600	900	1,400	1,800	2,400	3,000
CA92 Benly Touring 125 (124cc twin) . . .	800	1,200	1,800	2,400	3,200	4,000
CB92 Benly Super Sport 125 (124cc twin) .	2,400	3,600	5,400	7,200	9,600	12,000
CA95 Benly Touring 150 Early (154cc twin) .	800	1,200	1,800	2,400	3,200	4,000
CA71 Dream Touring 250 (247 cc twin) . . .	1,300	2,000	2,900	3,900	5,200	6,500
CE71 Dream Sport 250 (247cc twin)	2,400	3,600	5,400	7,200	9,600	12,000
C76 Dream Touring 300 (305cc twin)	1,300	2,000	2,900	3,900	5,200	6,500
CA76 Dream Touring 300 (305cc twin) . . .	1,300	1,900	2,900	3,800	5,100	6,400

	6	5	4	3	2	1
1960						
C100 Super Cub (49cc single)	600	900	1,400	1,800	2,400	3,000
C102 Super Cub (49cc single)	600	900	1,400	1,800	2,400	3,000
C110 Super Sports Cub (49cc single). . . .	600	900	1,400	1,800	2,400	3,000
CB92 Benly Super Sport 125 (124cc twin) .	2,400	3,600	5,400	7,200	9,600	12,000
CA95 Benly Touring 150 Early (154cc twin)	800	1,200	1,800	2,400	3,200	4,000
CA71 Dream Touring 250 (247cc twin) . . .	1,300	1,950	2,900	3,900	5,200	6,500
CA72 Dream Touring 250 Early (247cc twin)	1,000	1,500	2,300	3,000	4,000	5,000
CE71 Dream Sport 250 (247cc twin)	2,200	3,300	5,000	6,600	8,800	11,000
C76 Dream Touring 300 (305cc twin)	1,300	2,000	2,900	3,900	5,200	6,500
CA76 Dream Touring 300 (305cc twin) . . .	1,200	1,800	2,700	3,600	4,800	6,000
CA77 Dream Touring 305 Early (305cc twin)	900	1,400	2,000	2,700	3,600	4,500
CS76 Dream Sport 300 (305cc twin)	2,200	3,300	5,000	6,600	8,800	11,000
CSA76 Dream Sport 300 (305cc twin) . . .	1,800	2,700	4,100	5,400	7,200	9,000
CSA77 Dream Sport 305 (305cc twin) . . .	1,000	1,500	2,300	3,000	4,000	5,000
1961						
C100 Super Cub (49cc single)	600	900	1,400	1,800	2,400	3,000
C102 Super Cub (49cc single)	600	900	1,400	1,800	2,400	3,000
CA100T Trail 50 (49cc single).	600	900	1,400	1,800	2,400	3,000
C110 Super Sports Cub (49cc single). . . .	600	900	1,400	1,800	2,400	3,000
CB92R Benly SS Racer 125 (124cc twin) . .	4,400	6,600	9,900	13,200	17,600	22,000
CA95 Benly Touring 150 Early (154cc twin).	800	1,200	1,800	2,400	3,200	4,000
CA72 Dream Touring 250 (247cc twin) . . .	1,200	1,800	2,700	3,500	4,700	5,900
CA72 Dream Touring 250 Early (247cc twin)	900	1,400	2,100	2,800	3,800	4,700
CB72 Hawk 250 (247cc twin).	1,000	1,400	2,200	2,900	3,800	4,800
C77 Dream Touring 305 (305cc twin)	800	1,200	2,000	3,000	4,000	5,000
CA77 Dream Touring 305 Early (305cc twin)	900	1,300	2,000	3,000	4,000	5,000
CB77 Super Hawk 305 (305cc twin).	900	**1,500**	**3,000**	**4,000**	**5,000**	**6,000**
CSA77 Dream Sport 305 (305cc twin) . . .	1,000	1,500	2,300	3,000	4,000	5,000
1962						
C100 Super Cub (49cc single)	600	900	1,400	1,800	2,400	3,000
C102 Super Cub (49cc single)	600	900	1,400	1,800	2,400	3,000
C110 Super Sports Cub (49cc single). . . .	600	900	1,400	1,800	2,400	3,000
CA100 Honda 50 (49cc single)	600	900	1,400	1,800	2,400	3,000
CA100T Trail 50 (49cc single).	600	900	1,400	1,800	2,400	3,000
CA102 Honda 50 (49cc single)	600	900	1,400	1,800	2,400	3,000
C110 Sport 50 (49cc single).	600	900	1,400	1,800	2,400	3,000
CA105T Trail 55 (55cc single).	500	800	1,100	1,500	2,000	2,500
CB92R Benly SS Racer 125 (124cc twin) . .	4,400	6,600	9,900	13,200	17,600	22,000
CA95 Benly Touring 150 Early (154cc twin).	800	1,200	1,800	2,400	3,200	4,000
CA72 Dream Touring 250 Early (247cc twin)	900	1,400	2,100	2,800	3,800	4,700
CB72 Hawk 250 (247cc twin).	1,000	1,500	2,300	3,000	4,000	5,000
CL72 Scrambler 250 (247cc twin)	**1,000**	**1,500**	**2,000**	**2,500**	**3,500**	**4,500**
C77 Dream Touring 305 (305cc twin)	800	1,200	1,900	2,500	3,300	4,100
CA77 Dream Touring 305 Early (305cc twin)	900	1,300	1,900	2,600	3,400	4,250
CB77 Super Hawk 305 (305cc twin).	900	**1,500**	**3,000**	**4,000**	**5,000**	**6,000**
CSA77 Dream Sport 305 (305cc twin) . . .	1,000	1,500	2,300	3,000	4,000	5,000
1963						
CA100 Honda 50 (49cc single)	500	800	1,100	1,500	2,000	2,500
CA102 Honda 50 (49cc single)	500	800	1,100	1,500	2,000	2,500
CA110 Sport 50 (49cc single).	600	900	1,400	1,800	2,400	3,000
CA105T Trail 55 (55cc single).	500	750	1,400	1,500	2,000	2,500
C105T Trail 55 (55cc single)	500	750	1,400	1,500	2,000	2,500
CA200 Honda 90 (89cc single)	500	700	1,100	1,400	1,900	2,400
CA95 Benly Touring 150 Early (154cc twin).	800	1,200	1,800	2,400	3,200	4,000
CA95 Benly Touring 150 Late (154cc twin) .	800	1,200	1,800	2,400	3,200	4,000
CA72 Dream Touring 250 Early (247cc twin)	900	1,400	2,100	2,900	3,800	4,700
CA72 Dream Touring 250 Late (247cc twin)	900	1,400	2,100	2,900	3,800	4,700
CB72 Hawk 250 (247cc twin).	800	1,200	1,800	2,400	3,200	4,000

	6	5	4	3	2	1
CL72 Scrambler 250 (247cc twin)	**1,000**	**1,500**	**2,000**	**2,500**	**3,500**	**4,500**
C77 Dream Touring 305 (305cc twin)	800	1,200	2,000	3,000	4,000	5,000
CA77 Dream Touring 305 Early (305cc twin)	900	1,300	2,000	3,000	4,000	5,000
CA77 Dream Touring 305 Late (305cc twin)	900	1,300	2,000	3,000	4,000	5,000
CB77 Super Hawk 305 (305cc twin)	900	**1,500**	**3,000**	**4,000**	**5,000**	**6,000**
CSA77 Dream Sport 305 (305cc twin) . . .	1,000	1,500	2,300	3,000	4,000	5,000
1964						
CA100 Honda 50 (49cc single)	500	800	1,100	1,500	2,000	2,500
CA102 Honda 50 (49cc single)	500	800	1,100	1,500	2,000	2,500
CA110 Sport 50 (49cc single)	500	800	1,100	1,500	2,000	2,500
C105T Trail 55 (55cc single)	500	700	1,100	1,400	1,900	2,400
CA200 Honda 90 (87cc single)	500	700	1,100	1,400	1,900	2,400
CT200 Trail 90 (87cc single)	500	700	1,100	1,400	1,900	2,400
S90 Super 90 (89cc single)	400	600	1,000	1,300	1,700	2,100
CA95 Benly Touring 150 Late (154cc twin) .	**800**	**1,400**	**2,000**	**2,600**	**3,000**	**4,000**
CA72 Dream Touring 250 Late (247cc twin)	900	1,400	2,100	2,900	3,800	4,700
CB72 Hawk 250 (247cc twin)	800	1,200	1,800	2,400	3,200	4,000
CL72 Scrambler 250 (247cc twin)	**1,000**	**1,500**	**2,000**	**2,500**	**3,500**	**4,500**
C77 Dream Touring 305 (305cc twin)	800	1,200	2,000	3,000	4,000	5,000
CA77 Dream Touring 305 Late (305cc twin)	800	1,200	2,000	3,000	4,000	5,000
CB77 Super Hawk 305 (305cc twin)	600	**1,500**	**3,000**	**4,000**	**5,000**	**6,000**
1965						
CA100 Honda 50 (49cc single)	500	800	900	1,200	1,600	2,000
CA102 Honda 50 (49cc single)	500	800	1,100	1,500	2,000	2,500
CA110 Sport 50 (49cc single)	500	800	1,100	1,500	2,000	2,500
C105T Trail 55 (55cc single)	500	700	1,100	1,400	1,900	2,400
S65 Sport 65 (63cc single)	400	600	1,000	1,500	2,000	2,500
CA200 Honda 90 (87cc single)	500	700	1,100	1,400	1,900	2,400
CT200 Trail 90 (87cc single)	400	600	900	1,200	1,600	2,000
S90 Super 90 (89cc single)	400	600	1,000	1,500	2,000	2,500
CA95 Benly Touring 150 Late (154cc twin) .	**800**	**1,400**	**2,000**	**2,600**	**3,000**	**4,000**
CB160 Sport 160 (161cc twin)	400	600	900	1,100	1,500	1,900
CA72 Dream Touring 250 Late (247cc twin)	900	1,400	2,000	2,700	3,600	4,500
CB72 Hawk 250 (247cc twin)	800	1,200	1,800	2,400	3,200	4,000
CL72 Scrambler 250 (247cc twin)	**1,000**	**1,500**	**2,000**	**2,500**	**3,500**	**4,500**
CA77 Dream Touring 305 Late (305cc twin)	800	1,200	2,000	3,000	4,000	5,000
CB77 Super Hawk 305 (305cc twin)	600	**1,500**	**3,000**	**4,000**	**5,000**	**6,000**
CL77 Scrambler 305 (305cc twin)	700	1,100	2,000	3,000	4,000	5,000
CB450 Super Sport 450 (444cc twin)	800	1,200	1,800	2,400	3,200	4,000
1966						
CA100 Honda 50 (49cc single)	400	600	900	1,200	1,600	2,000
CA102 Honda 50 (49cc single)	400	600	900	1,200	1,600	2,000
CA110 Sport 50 (49cc single)	400	600	900	1,200	1,600	2,000
S65 Sport 65 (63cc single)	400	600	1,000	1,500	2,000	2,500
CA200 Honda 90 (87cc single)	400	600	1,000	1,300	1,800	2,200
CT200 Trail 90 (87cc single)	400	600	900	1,200	1,600	2,000
CM91 Honda 90 (89cc single)	400	600	900	1,200	1,600	2,000
CT90 Trail 90 (89cc single)	400	600	900	1,200	1,600	2,000
S90 Super 90 (89cc single)	400	600	1,000	1,500	2,000	2,500
CA95 Benly Touring 150 Late (154cc twin) .	**800**	**1,400**	**2,000**	**2,600**	**3,000**	**4,000**
CA160 Touring 160 (161cc twin)	400	600	900	1,500	2,000	2,500
CB160 Sport 160 (161cc twin)	700	1,000	1,500	2,000	2,500	3,000
CL160 Scrambler 160 (161cc twin)	**1,000**	**2,000**	**3,000**	**4,000**	**5,000**	**6,000**
CA72 Dream Touring 250 Late (247cc twin)	800	1,200	1,800	2,400	3,200	4,000
CB72 Hawk 250 (247cc twin)	800	1,200	1,800	2,400	3,200	4,000
CA77 Dream Touring 305 Late (305cc twin)	800	1,200	1,900	2,500	3,300	4,100
CB77 Super Hawk 305 (305cc twin)	600	1,000	**3,000**	**4,000**	**5,000**	**6,000**
CL77 Scrambler 305 (305cc twin)	800	1,200	2,000	3,000	4,000	5,000
CB450 Super Sport 450 (444cc twin)	**1,000**	**2,000**	**3,500**	**5,000**	**6,500**	**8,000**

	6	5	4	3	2	1
1967						
CA100 Honda 50 (49cc single)	400	600	900	1,200	1,600	2,000
CA102 Honda 50 (49cc single)	400	600	900	1,200	1,600	2,000
CA110 Sport 50 (49cc single)	400	600	900	1,200	1,600	2,000
S65 Sport 65 (63cc single)	400	600	1,000	1,500	2,000	2,500
CL90 Scrambler 90 (89cc single)	400	500	700	1,000	1,400	1,700
CM91 Honda 90 (89cc single).	400	600	900	1,100	1,500	1,900
CT90 Trail 90 (89cc single)	400	600	900	1,200	1,600	2,000
S90 Super 90 (89cc single)	400	600	900	1,200	1,600	2,000
CL125A Scrambler 125 (124cc twin)	400	600	800	1,100	1,400	1,800
SS125A Super Sport 125 (124cc twin) . . .	400	500	800	1,100	1,400	1,800
CA160 Touring 160 (161cc twin)	400	600	1,000	1,500	2,000	2,500
CB160 Sport 160 (161cc twin)	400	600	900	1,100	1,500	1,900
CL160 Scrambler 160 (161cc twin)	1,000	2,000	3,000	4,000	5,000	6,000
CL160D Scrambler 160D (161cc twin) . . .	1,000	2,000	3,000	4,000	5,000	6,000
CA77 Dream Touring 305 Late (305cc twin)	800	1,200	1,900	2,500	3,300	4,100
CB77 Super Hawk 305 (305cc twin). . . .	800	1,200	3,000	4,000	5,000	6,000
CL77 Scrambler 305 (305cc twin).	800	1,200	2,000	3,000	4,000	4,500
CB450 Super Sport 450 (444cc twin)	1,000	2,000	3,500	5,000	6,500	8,000
CB450D Super Sport 450D (444cc twin) . .	800	1,200	1,800	2,400	3,200	4,000
CL450 Scrambler 450 (444cc twin)	−500	−1,000	2,000	3,000	4,000	5,000
1968						
CA100 Honda 50 (49cc single)	400	600	900	1,100	1,500	1,900
CA102 Honda 50 (49cc single)	400	600	900	1,100	1,500	1,900
CA110 Sport 50 (49cc single)	400	600	900	1,200	1,600	2,000
S65 Sport 65 (63cc single)	400	600	1,000	1,500	2,000	2,500
CL90 Scrambler 90 (89cc single)	400	600	900	1,200	1,600	2,000
CL90L Scrambler 90 (89cc single)	400	500	800	1,000	1,400	1,700
CM91 Honda 90 (89cc single).	400	600	900	1,100	1,500	1,900
CT90 Trail 90 (89cc single)	300	500	800	1,000	1,400	1,700
S90 Super 90 (89cc single)	400	600	900	1,200	1,600	2,000
CL125A Scrambler 125 (124cc twin)	400	600	900	1,200	1,600	2,000
SS125A Super Sport 125 (124cc twin) . . .	420	630	950	1,260	1,680	2,100
CA160 Touring 160 (161cc twin)	400	600	900	1,100	1,500	1,900
CB160 Sport 160 (161cc twin)	400	600	900	1,100	1,500	1,900
CL160D Scrambler 160D (161cc twin) . . .	1,000	2,000	3,000	4,000	5,000	6,000
CA175 Touring 175 (174cc twin)	400	500	800	1,100	1,400	1,800
CL175 Scrambler 175 (174cc twin)	400	500	800	1,100	1,400	1,800
CA77 Dream Touring 305 Late (305cc twin)	800	1,200	1,800	2,400	3,200	4,000
CB77 Super Hawk 305 (305cc twin).	900	1,400	3,000	4,000	5,000	6,000
CL77 Scrambler 305 (305cc twin).	800	1,200	1,800	2,400	3,200	4,000
CB350 Super Sport 350 (325cc twin)	700	1,100	1,700	2,200	3,000	3,700
CL350 Scrambler 350 (325cc twin)	700	1,100	1,700	2,200	3,000	3,700
CB450 Super Sport 450 (444cc twin)	800	1,200	1,900	2,500	3,300	4,100
CB450K1 Super Sport 450 (444cc twin). . .	800	1,300	1,900	2,500	3,400	4,200
CL450K1 Scrambler 450 (444cc twin). . . .	−500	−1,000	2,000	3,000	4,000	5,000
1969						
Z50 AK1 Mini Trail (49cc single)	500	1,000	1,500	2,500	3,500	4,500
CA100 Honda 50 (49cc single)	400	500	800	1,100	1,400	1,800
CA102 Honda 50 (49cc single)	400	500	800	1,100	1,400	1,800
CA110 Sport 50 (49cc single)	400	600	900	1,200	1,600	2,000
S65 Sport 65 (63cc single)	400	600	1,000	1,500	2,000	2,500
CL70 Scrambler 70 (72cc single)	400	600	900	1,200	1,600	2,000
CL90 Scrambler 90 (89cc single)	400	600	900	1,200	1,600	2,000
CL90L Scrambler 90 (89cc single)	300	500	800	1,000	1,400	1,700
CM91 Honda 90 (89cc single).	400	600	900	1,100	1,500	1,900
CT90K1 Trail 90 (89cc single).	300	500	800	1,000	1,400	1,700
S90 Super 90 (89cc single)	400	600	900	1,200	1,600	2,000

	6	5	4	3	2	1
SL90 Motosport 90 (89cc single)	400	600	900	1,100	1,500	1,900
CL125A Scrambler 125 (124cc twin)	400	600	900	1,200	1,600	2,000
SS125A Super Sport 125 (124cc twin) . . .	400	600	1,000	1,300	1,700	2,100
CA160 Touring 160 (161cc twin)	400	600	800	1,100	1,500	1,900
CB160 Sport 160 (161cc twin)	400	600	900	1,100	1,500	1,900
CA175 Touring 175 (174cc twin)	300	500	800	1,000	1,400	1,700
CA175K3 Touring 175 (174cc twin).	400	600	900	1,200	1,600	2,000
CB175K3 Super Sport 175 Early (174cc twin)	400	600	1,000	1,500	2,000	2,500
CB175K3 Super Sport 175 Late (174cc twin)	400	600	1,000	1,500	2,000	2,500
CL175 Scrambler 175 (174cc twin)	400	500	800	1,100	1,400	1,800
CL175K3 Scrambler 175 (174cc twin). . . .	400	500	800	1,100	1,400	1,800
CA77 Dream Touring 305 Late (305cc twin)	700	1,100	1,700	2,200	3,000	3,700
CB350 Super Sport 350 (325cc twin) . . .	700	1,100	1,600	2,100	2,800	3,500
CB350K1 Super Sport (325cc)	700	1,100	1,600	2,100	2,800	3,500
CL350 Scrambler 350 (325cc twin)	700	1,100	1,700	2,200	3,000	3,700
CL350K1 Scrambler 350 (325cc twin). . . .	700	1,100	1,700	2,200	3,000	3,700
SL350 Motosport 350 (325cc twin)	400	700	1,000	1,300	1,800	2,200
CB450K1 Super Sport 450 (444cc twin). . .	900	1,400	2,000	2,700	3,600	4,500
CB450K2 Super Sport 450 (444cc twin). . .	800	1,200	1,800	2,400	3,200	4,100
CL450K1 Scrambler 450 (444cc twin). . . .	−500	−1,000	**2,000**	**3,000**	**4,000**	**5,000**
CL450K2 Scrambler 450 (444cc twin). . . .	−500	−1,000	**2,000**	**3,000**	**4,000**	**5,000**
CB750K0 Four Sandcast (736cc four). . . .	4,500	6,500	10,000	13,500	18,000	25,000
CB750K0 Four Diecast (736cc four). . . .	1,800	2,600	3,800	5,000	7,000	10,000
1970						
CA100 Honda 50 (49cc single)	200	400	500	700	1,000	1,200
C70M Honda 70 (72cc single).	300	500	600	900	1,200	1,500
CL70K1 Scrambler 70 (72cc single).	300	400	600	800	1,000	1,300
CT70HK0 (72cc single)	400	700	1,000	2,000	3,000	4,000
CL90L Scrambler 90 (89cc single)	300	500	700	900	1,200	1,500
CT90K2 Trail 90 (89cc single).	300	500	700	900	1,200	1,500
CB100 Super Sport 100 (99cc single) . . .	300	400	600	800	1,000	1,300
CL100 Scrambler 100 (99cc single).	200	300	500	700	900	1,100
SL100 Motosport 100 (99cc single)	200	300	500	700	900	1,100
CA175K3 Touring 175 (174cc twin)	300	400	600	800	1,100	1,400
CB175K4 Super Sport 175 (174cc twin). . .	300	500	1,000	1,500	2,000	2,500
CL175K3 Scrambler 175 (174cc twin). . . .	300	400	700	1,000	1,300	1,600
CL175K4 Scrambler 175 (174cc twin). . . .	300	400	600	800	1,100	1,400
SL175 Motosport 175 (174cc twin)	400	500	800	1,100	1,400	1,800
CB350K2 Super Sport350 (325cc twin) . . .	600	900	1,300	1,700	2,300	2,900
CL350K2 Scrambler 350 (325cc twin). . . .	600	900	**1,400**	**2,100**	**2,800**	**3,500**
SL350 Motosport 350 (325cc twin)	600	800	1,400	2,000	2,800	3,500
SL350K1 Motosport 350 (325cc twin)	600	800	1,300	1,700	2,200	2,800
CB450K3 Super Sport 450 (444cc twin). . .	600	1,000	1,400	1,900	2,600	3,200
CL450K3 Scrambler 450 (444cc twin). . . .	−500	1,000	**2,000**	**3,000**	**4,000**	**5,000**
CB750K0 750 Four (736cc four).	1,800	2,600	3,800	5,000	6,800	8,500
1971						
C70M Honda 70 (72cc single).	300	500	600	900	1,200	1,500
CL70K2 Scrambler 70 (72cc single).	200	300	400	600	800	1,000
SL70 Motosport 70 (72cc single)	200	300	500	600	800	1,100
SL70K1 Motosport 70 (72cc single)	200	300	500	600	800	1,000
CT90K2 Trail 90 (89cc single)	300	400	600	800	1,100	1,400
CB100K1 Super Sport 100 (99cc single) . .	200	400	500	700	1,000	1,200
CL100K1 Scrambler 100 (99cc single) . . .	300	400	600	800	1,000	1,300
CL100S Scrambler 100S (99cc single) . . .	300	400	600	800	1,000	1,300
SL100K1 Motosport 100 (99cc single) . . .	300	400	600	800	1,000	1,300
SL125 Motosport 125 (122cc single)	300	400	600	800	1,100	1,400
CB175K5 Super Sport 175 (174cc twin). . .	300	500	1,000	1,500	2,000	2,500
CL175K5 Scrambler 175 (174cc twin). . . .	300	400	600	800	1,100	1,400

	6	5	4	3	2	1
SL175K1 Motosport 175 (174cc twin)	300	400	600	800	1,100	1,400
CB350K3 Super Sport 350 (325cc twin). . .	600	800	1,200	1,600	2,500	3,000
CL350K3 Scrambler 350 (325cc twin). . .	600	800	**1,400**	**2,100**	**2,800**	**3,500**
SL350K1 Motosport 350 (325cc twin)	600	800	1,400	2,100	2,800	3,500
CB450K4 Super Sport 450 (444cc twin). . .	600	1,000	1,400	1,900	2,600	3,200
CL450K2 Scrambler 450 (444cc twin). . . .	–500	1,000	**2,000**	**3,000**	**4,000**	**5,000**
CB500 500 Four (498cc four)	700	1,100	1,600	2,100	2,800	3,500
CB750K1 750 Four (736cc four).	1,800	2,600	3,800	5,000	6,800	8,500
1972						
C70K1 Honda 70 (72cc single)	200	300	400	600	800	1,000
CL70K1 Scrambler 70 (72cc single).	200	300	400	600	800	1,000
SL70 Motosport 70 (72cc single)	200	300	400	600	800	1,000
SL70K1 Motosport 70 (72cc single)	200	300	400	600	800	1,000
CT90K4 Trail 90 (89cc single).	300	500	1,000	1,500	2,000	2,500
CB100K2 Super Sport 100 (99cc single) . . .	300	500	600	900	1,200	1,500
CL100K2 Scrambler 100 (99cc single) . . .	200	300	500	700	900	1,100
CL100S2 Scrambler 100S (99cc single). . .	200	400	500	700	900	1,200
SL100K2 Motosport 100 (99cc single) . . .	200	400	500	700	900	1,200
SL125K1 Motosport 125 (122cc single) . . .	200	400	600	800	1,100	1,400
CB175K6 Super Sport 175 (174cc twin). . .	200	500	1,000	1,500	2,000	2,500
CL175K6 Scrambler 175 (174cc twin) . . .	200	400	500	1,000	1,500	2,000
SL175K1 Motosport 175 (174cc twin)	200	400	500	700	900	1,200
XL250 Motosport 250 (248cc single)	400	600	800	1,000	1,300	1,600
CB350K4 Super Sport 350 (325cc twin). . .	400	500	1,000	1,500	2,000	2,500
CL350K4 Scrambler 350 (325cc twin). . .	**400**	**700**	**1,400**	**2,100**	**2,800**	**3,500**
SL350K2 Motosport 350 (325cc twin)	400	500	800	1,100	1,400	1,800
CB350F (347cc four)	500	700	1,100	1,500	2,000	3,000
CB450K5 Super Sport 450 (444cc twin). . .	400	600	900	1,200	1,600	2,000
CL450K5 Scrambler 450 (444cc twin). . . .	**500**	**1,000**	**2,000**	**3,000**	**4,000**	**5,000**
CB500K1 500 Four (498cc four).	600	1,000	1,400	1,900	2,600	3,200
CB750K2 750 Four (736cc four).	1,800	2,600	3,800	5,000	6,800	8,500
1973						
C70K1 Honda 70 (72cc single)	200	300	400	600	800	1,000
CL70K3 Scrambler 70 (72cc single).	200	300	400	600	800	1,000
CT70K2 (72cc single)	400	700	1,000	2,000	3,000	4,000
XR75 (72cc single)	200	300	400	600	800	1,000
CT90K4 Trail 90 (89cc single).	300	400	800	1,200	1,600	2,000
CL100S3 Scrambler 100S (99cc single). . .	200	300	500	600	800	1,000
SL100K3 Motosport 100 (99cc single) . . .	200	300	500	600	800	1,000
CB125S (122cc single)	300	500	800	1,200	1,600	2,000
CL125S Scrambler 125 (122cc single) . . .	200	400	500	700	900	1,100
SL125K2 Motosport 125 (122cc single) . . .	200	500	800	1,200	1,600	2,000
TL 125 Trails 125 (122cc single)	200	300	500	700	900	1,100
XL175 (173cc single)	300	**600**	**900**	**1,200**	**1,600**	**2,000**
CB175K7 Super Sport 175 (174cc twin). . .	200	400	500	700	1,000	1,200
CL175K7 Scrambler 175 (174cc twin). . .	200	400	500	700	1,000	1,200
CR250M Elsinore (248cc single)	500	800	1,500	2,000	3,000	4,000
XL250 Motosport 250 (248cc single) . . .	300	400	1,000	1,500	2,000	2,500
CB350G Super Sport 350 (325cc twin) . . .	400	500	800	1,100	1,400	1,800
CB350K4 Super Sport 350 (325cc twin). . .	400	500	**1,000**	**1,500**	**2,000**	**2,500**
CL350K5 Scrambler 350 (325cc twin) . . .	600	900	**1,400**	**2,100**	**2,800**	**3,500**
SL350K2 Motosport 350 (325cc twin)	400	600	1,000	1,500	2,000	2,500
CB350F (347cc four)	400	700	1,000	1,500	2,000	3,000
CB450K6 Super Sport 450 (444cc twin). . .	700	1,000	1,500	2,000	2,500	3,000
CL450K5 Scrambler 450 (444cc twin). . . .	**500**	**1,000**	**2,000**	**3,000**	**4,000**	**5,000**
CB500K2 500 Four (498cc four).	600	900	1,400	1,800	2,400	3,000
CB750K3 750 Four (736cc four).	1,600	2,400	3,500	4,800	6,500	8,000

	6	5	4	3	2	1
1974						
MR50 Elsinore (49cc single)	200	300	500	700	900	1,100
XL70 (72cc single)	200	400	500	700	1,000	1,200
XR75K1 (72cc single)	200	300	600	900	1,200	1,500
CT90K5 Trail 90 (89cc single)	200	400	800	1,200	1,600	2,000
XL100 Motosport 100 (99cc single)	200	400	500	700	1,000	1,200
CB125S1 Scrambler 125 (122cc single)	300	500	800	1,200	1,600	2,000
CL125S1 Scrambler 125 (122cc single)	300	500	700	900	1,100	1,300
TL125K1 Trails 125 (122cc single)	200	300	500	700	900	1,100
XL125 (122cc single)	200	400	500	700	1,000	1,200
CR125M Elsinore (123cc single)	300	500	1,000	1,500	2,000	2,500
MT125 Elsinore (123cc single)	300	400	600	800	1,000	1,300
XL175K1 (173cc single)	300	**600**	**900**	**1,200**	**1,600**	**2,000**
CB200 (198cc twin)	200	400	500	700	1,000	1,200
CL200 Scrambler (198cc twin)	200	400	500	700	1,000	1,200
CR250M Elsinore (248cc single)	500	800	1,500	2,000	3,000	4,000
MT250 Elsinore (248cc single)	300	400	700	900	1,200	1,500
XL250K1 Motosport (248cc single)	300	500	1,000	1,500	2,000	2,500
CB350F1 Super Sport 350 (347cc four)	400	600	1,200	1,800	2,400	3,000
XL350 (348cc single)	400	500	800	1,100	1,400	1,800
CB360 (356cc twin)	400	500	**1,000**	**1,500**	**2,000**	**2,500**
CB360G (356cc twin)	400	500	800	1,100	1,400	1,800
CL360 Scrambler 360 (356cc twin)	400	500	1,000	1,500	2,000	2,500
CB450K7 Super Sport 450 (444cc twin)	700	1,000	1,500	2,000	2,500	3,000
CL450K6 Scrambler 450 (444cc twin)	**500**	**1,000**	**2,000**	**3,000**	**4,000**	**5,000**
CB500 500 Four (498cc four)	400	600	900	1,200	1,600	2,000
CB750K4 750 Four (736cc four)	1,600	2,400	3,500	4,800	6,500	8,000
1975						
MR50K1 Elsinore (49cc single)	200	300	500	700	900	1,100
XL70K1 (72cc single)	200	400	500	700	900	1,200
XR75K2 (72cc single)	200	300	400	600	800	1,000
CT90K6 Trail 90 (89cc single)	200	400	800	1,200	1,600	2,000
CB125S2 (122cc single)	200	400	600	900	1,200	1,500
TL125K2 Trails 125 (122cc single)	200	400	600	900	1,200	1,500
XL125K1 (122cc single)	200	400	500	700	1,000	1,200
CR125M1 Elsinore (123cc single)	300	500	1,000	1,500	2,000	2,500
MT125K1 Elsinore (123cc single)	300	400	600	800	1,000	1,300
MR175 (171cc single)	300	400	600	800	1,100	1,400
CB200T (198cc twin)	300	400	600	800	1,100	1,400
CR250M1 Elsinore (248cc single)	500	800	1,500	2,000	3,000	4,000
MT250K1 Elsinore (248cc single)	300	400	700	900	1,200	1,500
TL250 Trails 250 (248cc single)	400	600	1,000	2,000	3,000	4,000
XL250K2 (248cc single)	300	500	700	900	1,200	1,500
XL350K1 (348cc single)	400	500	800	1,200	1,600	2,000
CB360T (356cc twin)	300	500	1,000	1,500	2,000	2,500
CL360K1 Scrambler 380 (356cc twin)	300	500	800	1,000	1,400	1,700
CB400F Super Sport 400 Four (408cc four)	600	900	1,500	2,500	3,500	5,000
CB500T 500 Twin (498cc twin)	**500**	**1,000**	**1,500**	**2,000**	**2,500**	**3,500**
CB550F Super Sport 550 (544cc four)	700	1,000	1,500	2,000	3,000	4,000
CB550K1 550 Four (544cc four)	**800**	**1,200**	**2,000**	**3,000**	**4,000**	**5,000**
CB750F 750 Super Sport (736cc four)	900	1,400	2,000	2,700	3,600	4,500
CB750K5 750 Four (736cc four)	1,200	2,000	3,000	4,200	5,500	7,000
GL1000 Gold Wing (999cc four)	1,000	2,000	3,000	5,000	7,500	10,000
1976						
XL70 (72cc single)	200	300	500	700	900	1,100
XR75 (72cc single)	200	300	400	600	800	1,000
CT90 Trail 90 (89cc single)	200	400	800	1,200	1,600	2,000
XL100 (99cc single)	200	300	500	700	900	1,100

	6	5	4	3	2	1
CR125M Elsinore (123cc single)	300	500	1,000	1,500	2,000	2,500
MT125 Elsinore (123cc single)	300	400	600	800	1,000	1,300
CB125S (124cc single)	200	300	500	700	900	1,100
TL1215S Trails 125 (124cc single)	200	300	500	700	900	1,100
XL125 (124cc single)	200	400	500	700	1,000	1,200
MR175 Elsinore (171cc single)	300	400	600	800	1,100	1,400
XL175 (171cc single)	300	400	600	800	1,000	1,300
CB200T (198cc twin)	300	400	600	800	1,000	1,300
CR250M Elsinore (248cc single)	500	800	1,500	2,000	3,000	4,000
MR250 Elsinore (248cc single)	300	500	700	900	1,200	1,500
MT250 Elsinore (248cc single)	300	400	700	900	1,200	1,500
TL250 Trails 250 (248cc single).	400	600	1,000	2,000	3,000	4,000
XL250 (248cc single)	300	500	1,000	1,500	2,000	2,500
XL350 (348cc single)	600	900	1,200	1,500	2,000	2,500
CB360T (356cc twin)	300	500	800	1,000	1,400	1,700
CJ360T (356cc twin)	300	500	800	1,000	1,400	1,700
CB400F Super Sport 400 Four (408cc four).	500	1,000	1,500	**2,500**	**3,500**	**4,500**
CB500T 500 Twin (498cc twin)	**500**	**1,000**	**1,500**	2,000	2,500	3,500
CB550F Super Sport 550 (544cc four) . . .	400	800	1,500	2,000	2,500	3,000
CB550K 550 Four K (544cc four)	600	800	1,200	1,800	2,500	4,000
CB750F 750 Hondamatic (736cc four) . . .	1,000	1,500	2,000	2,500	3,000	3,500
CB750F 750 Super Sport (736cc four) . . .	600	900	1,400	1,800	2,400	3,000
CB750K 750 Four K (736cc four)	1,200	2,000	3,000	4,200	5,500	7,000
GL1000 Gold Wing (999cc four).	1,000	2,000	3,000	4,200	5,500	7,000
GL1000LTD Gold Wing Limited Edition						
(999cc four)	1,000	1,500	2,000	3,000	4,000	5,000
1977						
XR75 (72cc single)	200	300	400	600	800	1,000
XL75 (75cc single)	200	300	500	700	900	1,100
CT90 Trail 90 (89cc single)	200	400	800	1,200	1,600	2,000
XL100 (99cc single)	200	300	500	700	900	1,100
CR125M Elsinore (123cc single)	300	500	1,000	1,500	2,000	2,500
CT125 Trail 125 (123cc single)	200	400	500	700	1,000	1,200
MT125R Elsinore (123cc single)	200	400	500	700	1,000	1,200
XL125 (124cc single)	200	400	500	700	1,000	1,200
MR175 Elsinore (171cc single)	300	400	600	800	1,100	1,400
XL175 (171cc single)	200	400	500	700	1,000	1,200
XL350 (348cc single)	300	500	700	1,000	1,300	1,600
CJ360T (356cc twin)	300	500	800	1,000	1,400	1,700
CB400F Super Sport 400 Four (408cc four).	400	600	1,000	1,500	2,000	2,500
CB550F Super Sport 550 (544cc four) . . .	400	600	1,000	1,200	1,600	2,000
CB550K 550 Four K (544cc four)	400	600	1,000	1,200	1,600	2,000
CB750A 750 Hondamatic (736cc four) . . .	600	900	1,500	2,000	3,000	4,000
CB750F 750 Super Sport (736cc four) . . .	600	900	1,400	1,800	2,400	3,000
CB750K 750 Four K (736cc four)	600	900	1,400	1,800	2,400	3,000
GL1000 Gold Wing (999cc four).	700	1,000	1,500	2,500	4,000	5,000
1978						
XR75 (72cc single)	200	300	400	600	800	1,000
XL75 (75cc single)	200	300	500	600	800	1,000
CT90 Trail 90 (89cc single)	200	400	800	1,200	1,600	2,000
XL100 (99cc single)	200	300	500	700	900	1,100
CB125S (122cc single)	200	300	500	700	900	1,100
CR125M Elsinore (123cc single)	300	500	1,000	1,500	2,000	2,500
MT125R Elsinore (123cc single)	200	400	500	700	1,000	1,200
XL125 (124cc single)	200	400	500	700	1,000	1,200
XL175 (173cc single)	200	400	500	700	1,000	1,200
CM185T Twinstar (181cc twin)	200	400	500	700	1,000	1,200
CR250R Elsinore (247cc single)	**900**	**1,500**	**2,000**	**2,500**	**3,500**	**5,000**

	6	5	4	3	2	1
XL250S (249cc single)	300	500	700	900	1,200	1,500
XL350 (348cc single)	300	500	700	1,000	1,300	1,600
CB400A Hawk Hondamatic (395cc twin) . .	400	600	900	1,200	1,600	2,000
CB400TI Hawk I (395cc twin)	300	500	700	1,000	1,300	1,600
CB400TII Hawk II (395cc twin)	300	500	800	1,000	1,300	1,700
CX500 (496cc V-twin)	300	500	700	1,000	1,300	1,700
CB550K 550 Four K (544cc four)	300	500	800	1,000	1,400	1,700
CB750K 750 Hondamatic (736cc four) . . .	600	900	1,300	1,800	2,500	3,000
CB750F 750 Super Sport (736cc four) . . .	600	800	1,200	1,700	2,200	2,800
CB750K 750 Four K (736cc four)	600	800	1,200	1,700	2,200	2,800
GL1000 Gold Wing (999cc four)	600	1,000	1,400	1,900	2,600	3,200
1979						
XL75 (75cc single)	200	300	400	500	700	900
XR80 (80cc single)	200	300	400	600	800	1,000
CT90 Trail 90 (89cc single)	200	400	800	1,200	1,600	2,000
XL100S (99cc single)	200	300	400	600	800	1,000
CB125S (122cc single)	200	300	500	700	900	1,100
CR125R Elsinore (124cc single)	300	500	1,000	1,500	2,000	2,500
XL125S (124cc single)	200	300	500	700	900	1,100
XL185S (180cc single)	200	400	500	700	1,000	1,200
XR185 (180cc single)	200	400	500	700	1,000	1,200
CM185T Twinstar (181cc twin)	200	400	500	700	1,000	1,200
CR250R Elsinore (247cc single)	900	1,500	2,000	2,500	**3,500**	**5,000**
XL250S (249cc single)	300	400	600	800	1,100	1,400
XR250 (249cc single)	300	500	700	1,000	1,300	1,600
CB400TI Hawk I (395cc twin)	300	500	700	1,000	1,300	1,600
CB400TII Hawk II (395cc twin)	300	500	800	1,000	1,300	1,700
CM400A Hondamatic (395cc twin)	400	600	900	1,200	1,600	2,000
CM400T (395cc twin)	400	600	1,000	1,300	1,700	2,100
CX500 (496cc V-twin)	300	500	800	1,000	1,400	1,700
CX500C Custom (496cc V-twin)	300	500	800	1,000	1,400	1,700
XL500S (498cc single)	300	500	700	1,000	1,300	1,600
XR500 (498cc single)	300	500	700	1,000	1,300	1,600
CB650 (627cc four)	300	500	800	1,000	1,400	1,700
CB750F 750 Super Sport (736cc four) . . .	600	1,000	1,400	1,900	2,600	3,200
CB750K 750 Four K (736cc four)	500	800	1,200	1,600	2,200	2,700
CB750K Limited Edition (749cc four)	600	900	1,400	1,800	2,400	3,000
GL1000 Gold Wing (999cc four)	600	1,000	2,000	4,000	6,000	8,000
CBX Super Sport (1047cc six)	2,000	2,800	4,300	6,000	9,000	**12,000**
1980						
C70 Passport (72cc single)	200	300	400	600	900	1,200
CR80R Elsinore (80cc single)	200	300	400	600	800	1,000
XL80S (80cc single)	200	300	400	600	800	1,000
XR80 (80cc single)	200	300	400	600	800	1,000
XL100S (99cc single)	200	300	400	600	800	1,000
CT110 Trail 110 (105cc single)	200	300	500	600	800	1,000
CB125S (124cc single)	200	300	500	700	900	1,100
CR125R Elsinore (124cc single)	300	500	1,000	1,500	2,000	2,500
XL125S (124cc single)	200	300	500	700	900	1,100
XL185S (180cc single)	200	400	500	700	1,000	1,200
CM200T Twinstar (194cc twin)	200	400	500	700	1,000	1,200
XR200 (195cc single)	300	400	600	800	1,100	1,400
CR250R Elsinore (247cc single)	400	600	**1,000**	**2,000**	**3,500**	**5,000**
XL250S (249cc single)	300	400	600	800	1,100	1,400
XR250 (249cc single)	300	500	700	1,000	1,300	1,600
CB400T Hawk (395cc twin)	300	500	700	1,000	1,300	1,600
CM400A Hondamatic (395cc twin)	400	600	900	1,100	1,500	1,900
CM400E (395cc twin)	400	600	900	1,200	1,600	2,000

	6	5	4	3	2	1
CM400T (395cc twin)	400	600	900	1,200	1,600	2,000
CX500C Custom (496cc V-twin)	300	500	800	1,000	1,400	1,700
CX500D Deluxe (496cc V-twin)	300	500	800	1,000	1,400	1,700
XL500S (498cc single)	300	500	700	900	1,200	1,500
XR500 (498cc single)	300	500	700	900	1,200	1,500
CB650 (627cc four)	300	500	700	1,000	1,400	1,700
CB650C 650 Custom (627cc four)	300	500	700	1,000	1,300	1,600
CB750C 750 Custom (749cc four)	500	800	1,100	1,500	2,000	2,500
CB750F 750 Super Sport (736cc four)	600	1,000	1,400	1,900	2,600	3,200
CB750K 750 Four K (736cc four)	500	800	1,100	1,500	2,000	2,500
CB900C 900 Custom (902cc four)	500	800	1,100	1,500	2,000	2,500
CBX Super Sport (1047cc six)	2,000	2,800	4,300	5,700	7,500	9,500
GL1100 Gold Wing (1085cc four)	700	1,100	1,600	2,100	2,800	3,500
GL1100I Gold Wing Interstate (1085cc four)	800	1,300	1,900	2,500	3,400	4,200
1981						
C70 Passport (72cc single)	200	300	400	600	900	1,200
C80R Elsinore (80cc single)	200	300	400	600	800	1,000
XL80S (80cc single)	200	300	400	600	800	1,000
XR80 (80cc single)	200	300	400	600	800	1,000
XL100S (99cc single)	200	300	400	600	800	1,000
XR100 (99cc single)	200	300	500	700	900	1,100
CT110 Trail 110 (105cc single)	200	300	500	600	800	1,000
CR125R Elsinore (123cc single)	300	400	600	800	1,100	1,400
CB125S (124cc single)	200	300	500	700	900	1,100
XL125S (124cc single)	200	300	500	700	900	1,100
XL185S (180cc single)	200	400	500	700	1,000	1,200
CM200T Twinstar (194cc twin)	200	400	500	700	1,000	1,200
XR200 (195cc single)	300	400	600	800	1,100	1,400
XR200R (195cc single)	300	500	800	1,000	1,400	1,700
CR250R Elsinore (246cc single)	400	600	900	1,200	1,600	2,000
XL250S (249cc single)	300	400	600	800	1,100	1,400
XR250R (249cc single)	400	600	900	1,100	1,500	1,900
CB400T Hawk (395cc twin)	400	500	800	1,100	1,400	1,800
CM400A Hondamatic (395cc twin)	400	600	900	1,200	1,600	2,000
CM400C Custom (395cc twin)	400	600	900	1,200	1,600	2,000
CM400E (395cc twin)	400	600	900	1,200	1,600	2,000
CM400T (395cc twin)	400	600	900	1,200	1,600	2,000
CR480R Elsinore (431cc single)	400	700	1,000	1,300	1,800	2,200
CX500C Custom (496cc V-twin)	400	500	800	1,100	1,400	1,800
CX500D Deluxe (496cc V-twin)	400	500	800	1,100	1,400	1,800
GL500 Silver Wing (496cc V-twin)	600	900	1,350	1,800	2,400	3,000
GL500I Silver Wing Interstate (496cc V-twin)	600	900	1,350	1,800	2,400	3,000
XL500S (498cc single)	400	600	900	1,200	1,600	2,000
XR500R (498cc single)	500	800	1,100	1,500	2,000	2,500
CB650 (627cc four)	300	500	800	1,000	1,400	1,700
CB650C 650 Custom (627cc four)	300	500	700	1,000	1,300	1,600
CB750C 750 Custom (749cc four)	400	600	900	1,200	1,600	2,000
CB750F 750 Super Sport (749cc four)	400	700	1,000	1,300	1,800	2,200
CB750K 750 Four K (749cc four)	500	800	1,100	1,500	2,000	2,500
CB900C 900 Custom (902cc four)	600	800	1,300	1,700	2,200	2,800
CB900F 900 Super Sport (902cc four)	600	900	1,400	1,800	2,400	3,000
CBX Super Sport (1,047cc six)	2,000	3,000	4,500	5,500	7,000	9,000
GL1100 Gold Wing (1,085cc four)	700	1,100	1,600	2,100	2,800	3,500
GL1100I Gold Wing Interstate (1,085cc four)	900	1,300	1,900	2,500	2,400	4,200
1982						
MB5 (49cc single)	400	600	800	1,000	1,200	1,500
C70 Passport (72cc single)	200	300	400	600	900	1,200
C80R Elsinore (80cc single)	200	300	400	600	800	1,000

	6	5	4	3	2	1
XL80S (80cc single)	200	300	400	600	800	1,000
XR80 (80cc single)	200	300	400	600	800	1,000
XL100S (99cc single)	200	300	400	600	800	1,000
XR100 (99cc single)	200	300	500	700	900	1,100
CT110 Trail 110 (105cc single)	200	300	500	600	800	1,000
CR125R Elsinore (123cc single)	300	400	600	800	1,100	1,400
CB125S (124cc single)	200	300	500	700	900	1,100
XL125S (124cc single)	200	300	500	700	900	1,100
XL185S (180cc single)	200	400	500	700	1,000	1,200
CM200T Twinstar (194cc twin)	200	400	500	700	1,000	1,200
XR200 (195cc single)	300	400	600	800	1,100	1,400
XR200R (195cc single)	300	500	700	900	1,200	1,500
CM250C 250 Custom (234cc twin)	300	500	700	900	1,200	1,500
CR250R (246cc single)	400	600	900	1,200	1,600	2,000
XL250R (249cc single)	400	600	900	1,100	1,500	1,900
XR250R (249cc single)	400	600	900	1,200	1,500	1,900
CB450SC Nighthawk 450 (447cc twin)	400	600	900	1,200	1,600	2,000
CB450T Hawk (447cc twin)	400	500	800	1,100	1,400	1,800
CM450A Hondamatic (447cc twin)	400	600	900	1,200	1,600	2,000
CM450C Custom (447cc twin)	400	600	900	1,200	1,600	2,000
CM450E (447cc twin)	400	600	900	1,100	1,500	1,900
CR480R (431cc single)	400	600	1,000	1,300	1,700	2,100
CX500C Custom (496cc V-twin)	400	500	800	1,100	1,400	1,800
GL500 Silver Wing (496cc V-twin)	600	900	1,400	1,800	2,400	3,000
GL500I Silver Wing Interstate (496cc V-twin)	600	900	1,400	1,800	2,400	3,000
CX500TC 500 Turbo (497cc turbo V-twin)	1,200	1,800	2,700	3,600	4,800	6,000
FT500 Ascot (498cc single)	900	1,400	2,000	2,700	3,600	4,500
XL500R (498cc single)	400	600	900	1,200	1,600	2,000
XR500R (498cc single)	500	800	1,100	1,500	2,000	2,500
CB650 (627cc four)	500	800	1,100	1,500	2,000	2,500
CB650SC Nighthawk 650 (627cc four)	800	1,100	1,700	2,300	3,000	3,800
VF750C V45 Magna (748cc V-four)	600	1,000	1,400	1,900	2,600	3,200
VF750S V45 Sabre (748cc V-four)	600	1,000	1,400	1,900	2,600	3,200
CB750C 750 Custom (749cc four)	400	600	900	1,200	1,600	2,000
CB750F 750 Super Sport (749cc four)	400	700	1,000	1,300	1,800	2,200
CB750K 750 Four K (749cc four)	500	800	1,100	1,500	2,000	2,500
CB750SC Nighthawk 750 (749cc four)	1,000	1,500	2,300	3,000	4,000	5,000
CB900C 900 Custom (902cc four)	600	800	1,300	1,700	2,200	2,800
CB900F 900 Super Sport (902cc four)	600	900	1,400	1,800	2,400	3,000
CBX Super Sport (1,047cc six)	2,000	3,000	4,500	6,000	8,000	10,000
GL1100 Gold Wing (1,085cc four)	700	1,100	1,600	2,100	2,800	3,500
GL1100 Gold Wing Aspencade (1,085cc four)	900	1,400	2,100	2,800	2,700	4,600
GL1100I Gold Wing Interstate (1,085cc four)	800	1,300	1,900	2,500	3,400	4,200
1983						
CR60R (58cc single)	200	300	500	600	800	1,000
C70 Passport (72cc single)	200	300	400	600	900	1,200
C80R Elsinore (80cc single)	200	300	400	600	800	1,000
XL80S (80cc single)	200	300	400	600	800	1,000
XR80 (80cc single)	200	300	400	600	800	1,000
XL100S (99cc single)	200	300	400	600	800	1,000
XR100 (99cc single)	200	300	500	700	900	1,100
CT110 Trail 110 (105cc single)	200	300	500	600	800	1,000
CR125R (123cc single)	300	400	600	800	1,100	1,400
XL185S (180cc single)	200	400	500	700	1,000	1,200
XL200R (195cc single)	300	400	600	800	1,100	1,400
XR200 (195cc single)	300	500	700	900	1,200	1,500
XR200R (195cc single)	400	600	900	1,100	1,500	1,900

	6	5	4	3	2	1
CM250C 250 Custom (234cc twin)	300	500	700	900	1,200	1,500
CR250R (246cc single)	400	600	900	1,200	1,600	2,000
XL250R (249cc single)	400	600	900	1,100	1,500	1,900
XR350R (339cc single)	400	700	1,000	1,300	1,800	2,200
CB450SC Nighthawk 450 (447cc twin) . . .	400	600	900	1,200	1,600	2,000
CM450A Hondamatic (447cc twin)	500	700	1,000	1,500	2,000	2,500
CM450E (447cc twin)	400	600	900	1,100	1,500	1,900
CR480R (431cc single)	400	600	1,000	1,300	1,700	2,100
VT500C Shadow 500 (491cc V-twin)	400	600	900	1,200	1,600	2,000
FT500 Ascot (498cc single)	900	1,000	1,500	2,000	3,000	4,000
XR500R (498cc single)	500	800	1,100	1,500	2,000	2,500
CB550SC Nighthawk 550 (572cc four) . . .	600	900	1,400	1,900	2,500	3,100
XL600R (589cc single)	400	600	1,000	1,300	1,700	2,100
CB650SC Nighthawk 650 (627cc four) . . .	700	1,100	1,600	2,100	2,800	3,500
CX650C Custom (674cc V-twin)	600	1,000	1,400	1,900	2,600	3,200
CX650T 650 Turbo (674cc turbo V-twin) . .	1,100	2,200	3,300	4,400	5,500	6,500
GL650 Silver Wing (674cc V-twin).	700	1,100	1,600	2,100	2,800	3,500
GL650I Silver Wing Interstate (674cc V-twin)	700	1,100	1,600	2,100	2,800	3,500
VF750C V45 Magna (748cc V-four).	600	1,000	1,400	1,900	2,600	3,200
VF750F V45 Interceptor (748cc V-four) . . .	900	1,500	2,500	3,500	4,500	5,500
VF750S V45 Sabre (748cc V-four)	700	1,000	1,500	2,000	2,700	3,400
VT750C Shadow 750 (749cc V-twin)	700	1,000	1,500	2,000	2,700	3,400
CB750SC Nighthawk 750 (749cc four) . . .	1,000	1,400	2,200	2,900	3,800	4,800
CB1000C 1000 Custom (973cc four)	600	1,500	2,500	3,500	4,500	5,500
CB1100F Super Sport (1,067cc four)	900	1,400	2,100	2,800	3,800	4,700
GL1100 Gold Wing (1,085cc four).	700	1,100	1,600	2,100	2,800	3,500
GL1100A Gold Wing Aspencade (1,085cc four)	900	1,400	2,100	2,800	3,400	4,600
GL1100I Gold Wing Interstate (1,085cc four)	900	1,400	2,100	2,800	3,800	4,700
VF1100 V65 Magna (1,098cc V-four)	700	1,100	1,600	2,100	2,800	3,500
1984						
CR60R (58cc single)	200	300	500	600	800	1,000
CR80R (80cc single)	200	300	500	700	900	1,100
XL80S (80cc single).	200	300	500	600	800	1,000
XR80 (80cc single).	200	300	500	600	800	1,000
XL100S (99cc single)	200	300	500	600	800	1,000
XR100 (99cc single).	200	300	500	600	800	1,000
CT110 Trail 110 (105cc single)	200	300	500	600	800	1,000
CR125R (123cc single)	300	400	600	800	1,100	1,400
CB125S (124cc single)	200	400	500	700	1,000	1,200
XL125S (124cc single)	200	400	500	700	1,000	1,200
XL200R (195cc single)	300	400	600	800	1,100	1,400
XR200 (195cc single)	300	500	700	900	1,200	1,500
XR200R (195cc single)	400	600	900	1,100	1,500	1,900
CR250R (246cc single)	400	600	900	1,200	1,600	2,000
XL250R (249cc single)	400	600	900	1,100	1,500	1,900
XR250R (249cc single)	400	700	1,000	1,300	1,800	2,200
XL350R (339cc single)	400	700	1,000	1,300	1,800	2,200
XR350R (339cc single)	400	700	1,000	1,300	1,800	2,200
CR500R (491cc single)	500	800	1,200	1,600	2,100	2,600
VT500C Shadow 500 (491cc V-twin)	400	600	900	1,200	1,600	2,000
VT500FT Ascott (491cc V-twin)	900	1,400	2,000	2,700	3,600	4,500
VF500C V30 Magna (498cc V-four).	600	800	1,300	1,700	2,200	2,800
VF500F 500 Interceptor (498cc V-four) . . .	600	900	1,400	1,900	2,500	3,100
XR500R (498cc single)	500	700	1,000	1,400	1,800	2,300
XL600R (589cc single)	500	700	1,000	1,400	1,800	2,300
CB650SC Nighthawk 650 (655cc four) . . .	700	1,100	1,600	2,100	2,800	3,500
VT700C Shadow (694cc V-twin)	700	1,000	1,500	2,000	2,700	3,400

	6	5	4	3	2	1
CB700SC Nighthawk S (696cc V-four) . . .	800	1,200	1,800	2,400	3,200	4,000
VF700C Magna (699cc V-four)	600	900	1,400	1,800	2,400	3,000
VF700F Interceptor (699cc V-four) . . .	600	1,000	1,400	1,900	2,600	3,200
VF700S Sabre (699cc V-four).	600	900	1,400	1,800	2,400	3,000
VF750F V45 Interceptor (748cc V-four). .	900	1,300	2,000	2,600	3,500	4,400
VF1000S 1000 Interceptor (998cc V-four).	1,000	1,500	2,300	3,000	4,000	5,000
VF1100 V65 Magna (1,098cc V-four) . . .	700	1,100	1,600	2,100	2,800	3,500
VF1100S V65 Sabre (1,098cc V-four). . .	800	1,200	1,800	2,300	3,100	3,900
GL1200 Gold Wing (1,182cc four).	800	1,100	1,700	2,300	3,000	3,800
GL1200A Gold Wing Aspencade (1,182cc four)	900	1,400	2,100	2,800	3,800	4,700
GL1200I Gold Wing Interstate (1,182cc four)	800	1,300	1,900	2,500	3,400	4,200
1985						
XL80S (80cc single).	200	300	500	600	800	1,000
XR80 (80cc single)	200	300	500	600	800	1,000
CR80R (80cc single)	200	300	500	600	800	1,000
XL100S (99cc single).	200	300	500	600	800	1,000
XR100R (99cc single).	200	300	500	600	800	1,000
CB125S (124cc single).	200	300	500	600	800	1,000
CR125R (123cc single)	300	400	600	800	1,100	1,400
XL125S (124cc single)	200	400	500	700	1,000	1,200
XR200R (195cc single)	300	400	600	800	1,100	1,400
CMX250C Rebel 250 (234cc twin)	300	500	700	900	1,200	1,500
CR250R (246cc single)	400	600	900	1,200	1,600	2,000
XL250R (249cc single)	400	600	900	1,100	1,500	1,900
XR250R (249cc single)	400	600	1,000	1,300	1,700	2,100
XL350R (339cc single)	400	600	1,000	1,300	1,700	2,100
XR350R (339cc single)	500	700	1,100	1,400	1,900	2,400
CB450SC Nighthawk 450 (447cc twin) . . .	400	600	1,000	1,300	1,700	2,100
CR500R (491cc single)	500	700	1,100	1,400	1,900	2,400
VF500C V30 Magna (498cc V-four)	600	800	1,300	1,700	2,200	2,800
VF500F 500 Interceptor (498cc V-four) . . .	600	900	1,400	1,900	2,500	3,100
XL600R (589cc single)	500	700	1,000	1,400	1,800	2,300
XR600R (591cc single)	500	700	1,000	1,400	1,800	2,300
CB650SC Nighthawk 650 (655cc four) . . .	700	1,100	1,600	2,100	2,800	3,500
CB700SC Nighthawk S (696cc V-four) . . .	800	1,100	1,700	2,300	3,000	3,800
VT700C Shadow (694cc V-twin)	700	1,000	1,500	2,000	2,700	3,400
VF700C Magna (699cc V-four)	600	900	1,400	1,900	2,500	3,100
VF700F Interceptor (699cc V-four)	700	1,000	1,500	2,000	2,600	3,300
VF700S Sabre (699cc V-four).	600	900	1,400	2,100	2,800	3,500
VF1000R (998cc V-four)	1,000	1,500	2,300	3,000	4,000	5,000
VF1100 V65 Magna (1,098cc V-four) . . .	700	1,100	1,600	2,100	2,800	3,500
VF1100 S V65 Sabre (1,098cc V-four). . . .	800	1,200	1,800	2,300	3,100	3,900
VT1100C Shadow 1100 (1,099cc V-twin) . .	900	1,300	1,900	2,500	3,400	4,200
GL1200A Gold Wing Aspencade (1,182cc four)	1,000	1,400	2,200	2,900	3,800	4,800
GL1200I Gold Wing Interstate (1,182cc four)	800	1,300	1,900	2,500	3,400	4,200
GL1200 Gold Wing Ltd Edition (1,182cc four)	900	1,400	2,100	2,800	3,700	4,600
1986						
XR80 (80cc single)	200	300	500	600	800	1,000
CR80R (83cc single)	200	300	500	600	800	1,000
XR100R (99cc single).	200	300	500	600	800	1,000
CT110 Trail 110 (105cc single)	200	300	500	600	800	1,000
CR125R (124cc single)	200	400	500	700	1,000	1,200
TLR200 Reflex (195cc single).	200	300	800	1,200	1,600	2,000
XR200R (195cc single)	200	400	500	700	1,000	1,200
TR200 Fat Cat (199cc single)	200	400	700	1,000	1,500	2,000
CMX250C Rebel 250 (234cc twin)	300	400	700	1,000	1,500	2,000

	6	5	4	3	2	1
CMX250CD Rebel 250 (234cc twin).	300	500	700	900	1,200	1,600
CR250R (246cc single)	400	500	800	1,100	1,400	1,800
XL250R (249cc single)	400	500	800	1,100	1,400	1,800
XR250R (249cc single)	400	500	800	1,100	1,400	1,800
CB450SC Nighthawk 450 (447cc twin) . . .	400	600	900	1,200	1,600	2,000
CMX450C Rebel 450 (447cc twin)	300	500	800	1,000	1,400	1,700
CR500R (491cc single)	400	700	1,000	1,300	1,800	2,200
VF500F 500 Interceptor (498cc V-four) . . .	600	900	1,400	1,900	2,500	3,100
XL600R (589cc single)	500	700	1,000	1,400	1,800	2,300
XR600R (591cc single)	500	700	1,000	1,400	1,800	2,300
VT700C Shadow (694cc V-twin)	700	1,100	1,600	2,100	2,800	3,500
CB700SC Nighthawk S (696cc V-four) . . .	800	1,200	1,800	2,300	3,100	3,900
VFR700F Interceptor (699cc V-four)	700	1,000	1,500	2,000	2,700	3,400
VFR700F2 Interceptor (699cc V-four). . . .	800	1,100	1,700	2,300	3,000	3,800
VF700C Magna (699cc V-four)	600	900	1,400	1,900	2,500	3,100
VFR750F Interceptor (748cc V-four)	800	1,200	2,200	3,100	3,800	4,500
VF1000R (998cc V-four)	1,000	1,500	2,300	3,000	4,000	5,000
VF1100 V65 Magna (1,098cc V-four)	700	1,000	1,500	2,000	2,700	3,400
VT1100C Shadow 1100 (1,099cc V-twin) . .	800	1,200	1,900	2,500	3,300	4,100
GL1200A Gold Wing Aspencade (1,182cc four)	900	1,400	2,100	2,800	3,700	4,600
GL1200I Gold Wing Interstate (1,182cc four)	800	1,200	1,800	2,400	3,200	4,000
GL1200SEI Gold Wing Aspencade (1,182cc four)	1,000	1,500	2,200	2,900	3,900	4,900
1987						
XR80 (80cc single)	200	300	500	600	800	1,000
CR80R (83cc single)	200	300	500	600	800	1,000
XR100R (99cc single)	200	300	500	600	800	1,000
CR125R (124cc single)	200	300	500	600	800	1,000
TLR200 Reflex (195cc single).	200	600	800	1,000	1,200	1,400
XR200R (195cc single).	200	400	500	700	1,000	1,200
TR200 Fat Cat (199cc single)	200	400	500	700	1,000	1,200
CMX250C Rebel 250 (234cc twin).	300	400	600	800	1,100	1,400
CR250R (246cc single)	400	500	800	1,100	1,400	1,800
XL250R (249cc single)	400	500	800	1,100	1,400	1,800
XR250R (249cc single)	400	500	800	1,100	1,400	1,800
CMX450C Rebel 450 (447cc twin)	300	500	800	1,000	1,400	1,700
CR500R (491cc single)	400	600	1,000	1,300	1,700	2,100
XL600R (589cc single)	500	700	1,000	1,400	1,800	2,300
XR600R (591cc single)	500	700	1,000	1,400	1,800	2,300
CBR600F Hurricane 600 (598cc four). . . .	600	900	1,400	1,800	2,400	3,000
VT700C Shadow (694cc V-twin)	700	1,000	1,500	2,000	2,600	3,300
VFR700F2 Interceptor (699cc V-four). . . .	700	1,100	1,700	2,200	3,000	3,700
VF700C Magna (699cc V-four)	600	1,000	1,400	2,100	2,800	3,500
CBR1000F 1000 Hurricane (998cc four) . .	800	1,200	1,800	2,400	3,200	4,000
VT1100C Shadow 1100 (1,099cc V-twin) . .	800	1,200	1,800	2,400	3,200	4,000
GL1200A Gold Wing Aspencade (1,182cc four)	900	1,400	2,100	2,800	3,700	4,600
GL1200I Gold Wing Interstate (1,182cc four)	800	1,200	1,800	2,400	3,200	4,000
1988						
XR80 (80cc single)	200	300	500	600	800	1,000
CR80R (83cc single)	200	300	500	600	800	1,000
XR100R (99cc single)	200	300	500	600	800	1,000
CR125R (124cc single)	200	300	500	600	800	1,000
NX125 (124cc single)	200	300	500	600	800	1,000
XR200R (195cc single).	200	300	400	500	700	900
CR250R (246cc single)	200	400	500	700	1,000	1,200
NX250 (249cc single)	200	300	500	700	900	1,100

	6	5	4	3	2	1
VTR250 Interceptor VTR (249cc twin). . . .	300	500	700	900	1,200	1,500
XR250R (249cc single)	300	500	700	1,000	1,300	1,600
CR500R (491cc single)	300	500	700	1,000	1,300	1,600
VT600C Shadow VLX (598cc four)	700	1,100	1,600	2,100	2,800	3,500
XR600R (591cc single)	500	700	1,000	1,400	1,800	2,300
CBR600F Hurricane 600 (598cc four). . . .	600	900	1,400	1,800	2,400	3,000
NX650 (644cc single)	400	700	1,000	1,300	1,800	2,200
NT650 Hawk GT (647cc V-twin).	500	800	1,200	1,600	2,200	2,700
VF750C V45 Magna (748cc V-four).	600	1,000	1,400	1,900	2,600	3,200
VT800C Shadow (800cc V-twin)	1,000	1,500	2,300	3,000	4,000	5,000
CBR1000F 1000 Hurricane (998cc four) . . .	800	1,200	1,900	2,500	3,300	4,100
VT1100C Shadow 1100 (1,099cc V-twin) . .	800	1,200	1,800	2,400	3,200	4,000
GL1500 Gold Wing (1,520cc six)	1,200	1,800	2,700	3,600	4,800	6,000
1989						
CR80R (83cc single)	200	300	500	600	800	1,000
XR100R (99cc single).	200	300	500	600	800	1,000
NX125 (124cc single)	200	300	500	600	800	1,000
CR125R (125cc single)	200	300	500	600	800	1,000
CR250R (246cc single)	200	400	500	700	1,000	1,200
NX250 (249cc single)	200	400	500	700	1,000	1,200
VTR250 VTR (249cc twin).	300	500	700	900	1,200	1,500
XR250R (249cc single)	300	500	700	900	1,200	1,500
CB400F CB1 (399cc four).	400	600	1,000	1,300	1,700	2,100
CR500R (491cc single)	300	500	800	1,000	1,400	1,700
GB500 Tourist Trophy (499cc single)	1,400	2,100	3,100	4,100	5,400	6,800
VT600C Shadow VLX (598cc four)	700	1,100	1,600	2,100	2,800	3,500
XL600V TransAlp (583cc V-twin)	1,000	1,500	2,300	3,000	4,000	5,000
XR600R (591cc single)	500	700	1,000	1,400	1,800	2,300
CBR600F (598cc four)	600	900	1,400	1,800	2,400	3,000
NX650 (644cc single)	400	700	1,000	1,300	1,800	2,200
NT650 Hawk GT (647cc V-twin).	500	800	1,200	1,600	2,500	3,000
PC800 Pacific Coast (800cc V-twin)	800	1,200	1,800	2,400	3,200	4,000
VT1100C Shadow 1100 (1,099cc V-twin) . .	800	1,200	1,800	2,400	3,200	4,000
GL1500 Gold Wing (1,520cc six)	1,200	1,800	2,700	3,600	4,800	6,000
1990						
NS50F (49cc single).	200	300	400	500	600	800
XR80 (80cc single)	200	300	500	600	800	1,000
CR80R (83cc single)	200	300	500	600	800	1,000
XR100R (99cc single).	200	300	500	600	800	1,000
NX125 (124cc single)	200	300	500	600	800	1,000
CR125R (125cc single)	200	300	500	600	800	1,000
XR200R (195cc single)	300	400	500	700	1,000	1,200
CR250R (246cc single)	300	400	500	700	1,000	1,200
NX250 (249cc single)	300	400	500	700	1,000	1,200
VTR250 VTR (249cc twin).	300	500	700	900	1,200	1,500
XR250R (249cc single)	300	500	700	900	1,200	1,500
CB400F CB1 (399cc four)	400	600	1,000	1,300	1,700	2,100
CR500R (491cc single)	300	500	800	1,000	1,400	1,700
GB500 Tourist Trophy (499cc single)	1,400	2,100	3,100	4,100	5,400	6,800
XL600V TransAlp (583cc V-twin)	1,000	1,500	2,300	3,000	4,000	5,000
XR600R (591cc single)	500	700	1,000	1,400	1,800	2,300
CBR600F (598cc four)	600	900	1,400	1,800	2,400	3,000
NT650 Hawk GT (647cc V-twin).	500	800	1,200	1,600	2,200	2,700
VFR750F VFR (748cc V-four).	700	1,000	1,500	2,000	2,700	3,400
VFR750R RC30 (748cc V-four).	1,700	2,600	3,800	5,100	6,800	8,500
PC800 Pacific Coast (800cc V-twin).	800	1,200	1,800	2,400	3,200	4,000
CBR1000F (998cc four).	800	1,200	2,000	3,000	4,000	5,000
VT1100C Shadow 1100 (1,099cc V-twin) . .	800	1,200	1,800	2,400	3,200	4,000

	6	5	4	3	2	1
GL1500 Gold Wing (1,520cc six)	1,200	1,800	2,700	3,600	4,800	6,000
GL1500SE Gold Wing SE (1,520cc six). . .	1,300	2,000	2,900	3,900	5,200	6,500
1991						
ZR50R Mini (50cc single)	200	300	400	700	800	900
CT70 (70cc single)	200	400	600	1,000	1,100	1,300
XR80R (80cc single)	200	300	500	600	800	1,000
CR80R (83cc single)	200	300	500	600	800	1,000
EZ90 Cub (90cc single)	200	400	600	900	1,000	1,200
XR100R (99cc single)	200	300	500	600	800	1,000
CR125R (125cc single)	200	300	500	600	800	1,000
XR200R (195cc single)	200	400	500	700	1,000	1,200
CR250R (246cc single)	200	400	500	700	1,000	1,200
XR250 (249cc single)	300	400	600	800	1,100	1,400
XR250R (249cc single)	300	500	700	900	1,200	1,500
CB250 Nighthawk (250cc twin)	500	700	1,000	1,400	1,700	2,200
CR500R (491cc single)	300	500	800	1,000	1,400	1,700
XR600R (591cc single)	500	700	1,000	1,400	1,800	2,300
VT600C Shadow VLX (598cc four)	600	1,000	1,600	2,200	2,800	3,400
CBR600F2 (598cc four)	600	900	1,400	1,800	2,400	3,000
NT650 Hawk GT (647cc V-twin)	500	800	1,200	1,600	2,200	2,700
VFR750F (748cc V-four)	700	1,000	1,500	2,000	2,700	3,400
CB750 Nighthawk (750cc four)	700	1,100	1,700	2,300	2,900	3,500
CBR1000F (998cc four)	800	1,200	2,000	3,000	4,000	5,000
ST1100 (1,100cc four)	1,200	1,900	2,800	3,800	4,700	5,500
GL1500I Gold Wing Interstate (1,520cc six).	2,000	3,000	4,000	5,300	6,000	6,500
GL1500A Gold Wing Aspencade (1,520cc six).	2,200	3,200	4,300	5,700	6,200	6,800
GL1500SE Gold Wing SE (1,520cc six). . .	2,300	3,300	5,000	6,500	7,000	7,500
1992						
ZR50R Mini (50cc single)	200	300	400	700	800	900
CT70 (70cc single)	200	400	600	1,000	1,100	1,300
CR80R (83cc single)	200	300	500	600	800	1,000
EZ90 Cub (90cc single)	200	400	600	900	1,000	1,200
XR100R (99cc single)	200	300	500	600	800	1,000
CR125R (125cc single)	200	300	500	600	800	1,000
CR250R (246cc single)	200	400	500	700	1,000	1,200
XR250 (249cc single)	300	400	600	800	1,100	1,400
XR250L (249cc single)	300	500	700	900	1,200	1,500
CB250 Nighthawk (250cc twin)	500	700	1,000	1,400	1,700	2,200
CR500R (491cc single)	300	500	800	1,000	1,400	1,700
XR600R (591cc single)	500	700	1,000	1,400	1,800	2,300
VT600C Shadow VLX (598cc twin)	600	1,000	1,600	2,200	2,800	3,400
CBR600F2 (598cc four)	600	900	1,400	1,800	2,400	3,000
VFR750F (748cc V-four)	700	1,000	1,500	2,000	2,700	3,400
CB750 Nighthawk (750cc four)	700	1,100	1,700	2,300	2,900	3,500
VT1100CL Shadow (1,100cc twin)	1,000	1,600	2,200	3,000	3,800	4,600
ST1100 (1,100cc four)	1,200	1,900	2,800	3,800	4,700	5,500
ST1100AL ABS (1,100cc four)	1,300	2,000	2,900	3,900	4,800	5,600
GL1500I Gold Wing Interstate (1,520cc six).	2,100	3,100	4,100	5,500	6,100	6,600
GL1500A Gold Wing Aspencade (1,520cc six).	2,300	3,300	4,500	5,900	6,300	6,900
GL1500SE Gold Wing SE (1,520cc six). . .	2,400	3,500	5,100	6,700	7,200	7,700
1993						
ZR50R Mini (50cc single)	200	300	400	700	800	900
CT70 (70cc single)	200	400	600	1,000	1,100	1,300
ZR80R (80cc single)	300	500	600	700	900	1,100
CR80R (83cc single)	200	300	500	600	800	1,100
EZ90 Cub (90cc single)	200	400	600	900	1,000	1,200
XR100R (99cc single)	200	300	500	600	800	1,000

	6	5	4	3	2	1
CR125R (125cc single)	200	300	500	600	800	1,000
XR200R (200cc single)	300	500	700	900	1,100	1,300
CR250R (246cc single)	200	400	500	700	1,000	1,200
XR250L (249cc single)	300	500	700	900	1,200	1,500
XR250R (249cc single)	300	500	700	900	1,200	1,500
CB250 Nighthawk (250cc twin)	500	700	1,000	1,400	1,700	2,200
CR500R (491cc single)	300	500	800	1,000	1,400	1,700
XR600R (591cc single)	500	700	1,000	1,400	1,800	2,300
VT600C Shadow VLX (598cc twin)	600	1,000	1,600	2,200	2,800	3,400
VT600CD Shadow VLX Deluxe (598cc twin)	700	1,200	1,800	2,400	3,000	3,600
CBR600F2 (598cc four)	600	900	1,400	1,800	2,400	3,000
XR650L (650cc single)	500	800	1,100	1,300	1,500	1,800
VFR750F (748cc V-four)	700	1,000	1,500	2,000	2,700	3,400
CB750 Nighthawk (750cc four)	700	1,100	1,700	2,300	2,900	3,500
CBR900RR (900cc four)	1,400	2,000	2,900	3,800	4,700	5,600
CBR1000F (1000cc four)	1,200	1,800	2,500	3,400	4,300	5,200
VT1100CL Shadow (1,100cc twin)	1,000	1,600	2,200	3,000	3,800	4,600
ST1100 (1,100cc four)	1,200	1,900	2,800	3,800	4,700	5,500
ST1100AL ABS (1,100cc four)	1,300	2,000	2,900	3,900	4,800	5,600
GL1500I2 Gold Wing Interstate (1,520cc six)	2,100	3,100	4,100	5,500	6,100	6,600
GL1500A2 Gold Wing Aspencade (1,520cc six)	2,300	3,300	4,500	5,900	6,300	6,900
GL1500SE Gold Wing SE (1,520cc six). . .	2,400	3,500	5,100	6,700	7,200	7,700
1994						
ZR50R Mini (50cc single)	200	300	400	700	800	900
CT70 (70cc single)	200	400	600	1,000	1,100	1,300
ZR80R (80cc single)	300	500	600	700	900	1,100
CR80R (83cc single)	200	300	· 500	600	800	1,100
EZ90 Cub (90cc single)	200	400	600	900	1,000	1,200
XR100R (99cc single)	200	300	500	600	800	1,000
CR125R (125cc single)	200	300	500	600	800	1,000
XR200R (200cc single)	300	500	700	900	1,100	1,300
CR250R (246cc single)	200	400	500	700	1,000	1,200
XR250L (249cc single)	300	500	700	900	1,200	1,500
XR250R (249cc single)	300	500	700	900	1,200	1,500
CB250 Nighthawk (250cc twin)	500	700	1,000	1,400	1,700	2,200
CR500R (491cc single)	300	500	800	1,000	1,400	1,700
XR600R (591cc single)	500	700	1,000	1,400	1,800	2,300
VT600C Shadow VLX (598cc twin)	600	1,000	1,600	2,200	2,800	3,400
VT600CD Shadow VLX Deluxe (598cc twin)	700	1,200	1,800	2,400	3,000	3,600
CBR600F2 (598cc four)	600	900	1,400	1,800	2,400	3,000
XR650L (650cc single)	500	800	1,100	1,300	1,500	1,800
VF750C Magna (750cc four)	500	900	1,800	2,600	3,400	4,200
VFR750F (748cc V-four)	700	1,000	1,500	2,000	2,700	3,400
RV750R RC45 (750cc four)	2,500	5,000	7,100	9,100	11,675	14,000
PC800 Pacific Coast (800cc V-twin).	500	1,000	1,900	2,800	3,700	4,600
CBR900RR (900cc four)	1,400	2,000	2,900	3,800	4,700	5,600
CB1000 (1000cc four).	500	1,000	1,800	2,700	3,500	4,300
CBR1000F (1000cc four)	1,200	1,800	2,500	3,400	4,300	5,200
VT1100CL Shadow (1,100cc twin)	1,000	1,600	2,200	3,000	3,800	4,600
ST1100 (1,100cc four)	1,200	1,900	2,800	3,800	4,700	5,500
ST1100A ABS-TCS (1,100cc four)	1,300	2,000	2,900	3,900	4,800	5,600
GL1500I Gold Wing Interstate (1,520cc six).	2,100	3,100	4,100	5,500	6,100	6,600
GL1500A Gold Wing Aspencade (1,520cc six)	2,300	3,300	4,500	5,900	6,300	6,900
GL1500SE2 Gold Wing SE (1,520cc six) . .	2,400	3,500	5,100	6,700	7,200	7,700
1995						
ZR50R Mini (50cc single)	200	300	400	700	800	900

	6	5	4	3	2	1
ZR80R (80cc single)	300	500	600	700	900	1,100
CR80R (83cc single)	200	300	500	600	800	1,100
EZ90 Cub (90cc single)	200	400	600	900	1,000	1,200
XR100R (99cc single)	200	300	500	600	800	1,000
CR125R (125cc single)	200	300	500	600	800	1,000
XR200R (200cc single)	300	500	700	900	1,100	1,300
CR250R (246cc single)	200	400	500	700	1,000	1,200
XR250L (249cc single)	300	500	700	900	1,200	1,500
XR250R (249cc single)	300	500	700	900	1,200	1,500
CB250 Nighthawk (250cc twin)	500	700	1,000	1,400	1,700	2,200
CR500R (491cc single)	300	500	800	1,000	1,400	1,700
XR600R (591cc single)	500	700	1,000	1,400	1,800	2,300
VT600C Shadow VLX (598cc twin)	600	1,000	1,600	2,200	2,800	3,400
VT600CD Shadow VLX Deluxe (598cc twin)	700	1,200	1,800	2,400	3,000	3,600
CBR600F3 (598cc four)	600	900	1,400	1,800	2,400	3,000
XR650L (650cc single)	500	800	1,100	1,300	1,500	1,800
VFR750F (748cc V-four)	700	1,000	1,500	2,000	2,700	3,400
CB750 Nighthawk (750cc four)	500	800	1,400	2,000	2,700	3,400
VF750C Magna (750cc four)	500	900	1,800	2,600	3,400	4,200
VF750CD Magna Deluxe (750cc four) . . .	700	1,400	2,000	2,700	3,600	4,500
PC800 Pacific Coast (800cc V-twin) . . .	500	1,000	1,900	2,800	3,700	4,600
CBR900RR (900cc four)	1,400	2,000	2,900	3,800	4,700	5,600
CB1000 (1000cc four)	500	1,000	1,800	2,700	3,500	4,300
CBR1000F (1000cc four)	1,200	1,800	2,500	3,400	4,300	5,200
VT1100 Shadow (1,100cc twin)	1,000	1,600	2,200	3,000	3,800	4,600
VT11A Shadow American Classic (1,100 cc twin)	600	1,200	2,200	3,200	4,200	5,200
ST1100 (1,100cc four)	1,200	1,900	2,800	3,800	4,700	5,500
ST1100A ABS-TCS (1,100cc four)	1,300	2,000	2,900	3,900	4,800	5,600
GL1500I Gold Wing Interstate (1,520cc six) .	2,100	3,100	4,100	5,500	6,100	6,600
GL1500A Gold Wing Aspencade (1,520cc six)	2,300	3,300	4,500	5,900	6,300	6,900
GL1500SE Gold Wing SE (1,520cc six) . . .	2,400	3,500	5,100	6,700	7,200	7,700

HUSABERG

	6	5	4	3	2	1
1990						
501E (501cc single)	100	200	300	500	700	900
1991						
350E (349cc single)	100	200	300	600	900	1,200
501E (504cc single)	100	200	300	600	900	1,200
1992						
350E (349cc single)	100	200	400	700	1,000	1,300
499C (499cc single)	100	200	300	600	900	1,200
501E (501cc single)	100	200	400	800	1,100	1,400
600C (595cc single)	100	200	300	600	900	1,200
1993						
350E (349cc single)	100	200	500	900	1,300	1,700
499C (499cc single)	100	200	400	700	1,000	1,300
501E (501cc single)	100	200	500	900	1,400	1,900
600C (595cc single)	100	200	400	700	1,000	1,300
600E (595cc single)	100	200	500	1,000	1,400	1,800
1994						
350E (349cc single)	100	200	600	1,100	1,600	2,100
501C (501cc single)	100	200	400	900	1,200	1,500
501E (501cc single)	100	200	600	1,100	1,700	2,300
600C (595cc single)	100	200	400	900	1,200	1,500
600E (595cc single)	100	200	600	1,100	1,700	2,300
1995						
FE350 (349cc single)	100	200	400	900	1,500	2,100

	6	5	4	3	2	1
FC501 (501cc single)	100	300	600	1,100	1,700	2,300
FE501 (501cc single)	100	300	600	1,100	1,600	2,100
FC600 (595cc single)	100	300	600	1,200	1,800	2,400
FE600 (595cc single)	100	200	500	1,000	1,600	2,200
HUSQVARNA						
1958						
Corona	600	900	1,200	1,600	2,100	3,000
1966						
Moto Cross (250cc single).	2,400	3,800	5,400	7,000	10,000	14,000
Moto Cross (360cc single).	2,600	4,000	6,000	10,000	15,000	21,000
1967						
Moto Cross (250cc single).	1,300	2,000	2,800	3,600	5,300	7,000
Viking (360cc single)	1,300	2,000	2,800	3,600	5,300	7,000
1968						
Commando T (250cc single)	1,300	2,000	2,800	3,600	5,300	7,000
Moto Cross (250cc single).	1,300	2,000	2,800	3,600	5,300	7,000
Sportsman Enduro (360cc single).	1,300	2,000	2,800	3,600	5,300	7,000
Viking (360cc single)	1,300	2,000	2,800	3,600	5,300	7,000
1969						
Moto Cross (250cc single).	1,300	2,000	2,800	3,600	5,300	7,000
Sportsman Enduro T (250cc single).	1,300	2,000	2,800	3,600	5,300	7,000
Moto Cross (360cc single).	1,300	2,000	2,800	3,600	5,300	7,000
Sportsman Enduro (360cc single).	1,300	2,000	2,800	3,600	5,300	7,000
Moto Cross (400cc single).	1,500	2,200	3,000	4,000	5,500	7,500
1970						
Moto Cross (250cc single).	1,300	2,000	2,800	3,600	5,300	7,000
Sportsman (360cc single)	1,300	2,000	2,800	3,600	5,300	7,000
Viking (360cc single)	1,300	2,000	2,800	3,600	5,300	7,000
Moto Cross (400cc single).	1,500	2,200	3,000	4,000	5,500	7,500
1971						
Moto Cross 4 Speed (250cc single)	1,300	2,000	2,800	3,600	5,300	7,000
Moto Cross 6 Speed (250cc single)	1,300	2,000	2,800	3,600	5,300	7,000
Moto Cross 8 Speed (250cc single)	1,300	2,000	2,800	3,600	5,300	7,000
Enduro C 4 Speed (360cc single)	1,200	1,800	2,400	3,600	4,800	6,000
Enduro C 8 Speed (360cc single)	1,200	1,800	2,400	3,600	4,800	6,000
Moto Cross 4 Speed (360cc single)	1,300	2,000	2,800	3,600	5,300	7,000
Moto Cross 8 Speed (360cc single)	1,300	2,000	2,800	3,600	5,300	7,000
Moto Cross 4 Speed (400cc single)	1,200	1,800	2,400	3,600	4,800	6,000
Moto Cross 8 Speed (400cc single)	1,200	1,800	2,400	3,600	4,800	6,000
1972						
CR (125cc single)	800	1,200	1,700	2,300	3,300	4,300
WR (125cc single).	800	1,200	1,700	2,300	3,300	4,300
CR (250cc single).	500	800	1,000	1,300	1,800	2,300
WR (250cc single).	500	1,000	2,000	3,000	4,000	5,000
Enduro (360cc single)	900	1,400	2,000	2,600	3,700	4,800
CR (400cc single)	800	1,200	1,800	2,300	3,300	4,300
CR (450cc single)	600	900	1,200	1,500	2,100	2,700
WR (450cc single)	600	900	1,200	2,000	3,000	4,000
DM (450cc single)	600	900	1,200	1,500	2,100	2,700
1973						
CR (125cc single)	800	1,200	1,700	2,300	3,300	4,300
WR (125cc single).	800	1,200	1,700	2,300	3,300	4,300
CR (250cc single).	900	1,400	2,100	2,800	3,800	4,800
WR (250cc single).	900	1,400	2,100	2,800	3,800	4,800
WR RT (250cc single).	600	900	1,200	1,500	2,100	2,700
WR RT (360cc single).	900	1,400	2,000	2,600	3,700	4,800
CR (400cc single)	800	1,200	1,800	2,300	3,300	4,300
CR (450cc single)	600	900	1,200	1,500	2,100	2,700
WR (450cc single).	600	900	1,200	1,500	2,100	2,700

	6	5	4	3	2	1
1974						
CR (125cc single)	1,300	2,000	2,800	3,600	5,300	7,000
SC (125cc single)	1,300	2,000	2,800	3,600	5,300	7,000
WR (175cc single)	1,300	2,000	2,800	3,600	5,300	7,000
CR (250cc single)	1,300	2,000	2,800	3,600	5,300	7,000
WR (250cc single)	500	1,500	2,000	3,000	4,000	5,000
RT SK (360cc single)	1,300	2,000	2,800	3,600	5,300	7,000
CR (400cc single)	1,300	2,000	2,800	3,600	5,300	7,000
WR (400cc single)	1,300	2,000	2,800	3,600	5,300	7,000
SC (400cc single)	1,300	2,000	2,800	3,600	5,300	7,000
CR (450cc single)	500	1,500	2,000	3,000	4,000	5,000
WR (450cc single)	500	1,500	2,000	3,000	4,000	5,000
1975						
CC GP (175cc single)	900	1,400	2,000	2,500	3,700	4,900
CR GP (250cc single)	900	1,400	2,100	2,800	3,800	4,800
WR (250cc single)	600	900	1,200	1,500	2,100	2,700
CR GP (360cc single)	900	1,400	2,000	2,600	3,700	4,800
WR (400cc single)	700	1,000	1,300	1,700	2,400	3,100
CR (460cc single)	800	1,200	1,800	2,400	3,300	4,500
1976						
CR (125cc single)	800	1,200	1,700	2,300	3,300	4,300
CC GP (175cc single)	900	1,400	2,000	2,500	3,700	4,900
CR (250cc single)	900	1,400	2,100	2,800	3,800	4,800
WR (250cc single)	600	900	1,200	1,500	2,100	2,700
Automatic (360cc single)	900	1,400	2,000	2,600	3,700	4,800
CR (360cc single)	1,600	2,200	3,000	4,000	5,800	7,500
WR (360cc single)	900	1,400	2,000	2,600	3,700	4,800
1977						
CR (125cc single)	800	1,200	1,700	2,300	3,300	4,300
CR (250cc single)	900	1,400	2,100	2,800	3,800	4,800
WR (250cc single)	600	900	1,200	1,500	2,100	2,700
Automatic (360cc single)	900	1,400	2,000	2,600	3,700	4,800
WR (360cc single)	900	1,400	2,000	2,600	3,700	4,800
CR (390cc single)	900	1,400	2,000	2,600	3,700	4,800
1978						
CR (125cc single)	800	1,200	1,700	2,300	3,300	4,300
CR (250cc single)	900	1,400	2,100	2,800	3,800	4,800
OR (250cc single)	900	1,400	2,100	2,800	3,800	4,800
WR (250cc single)	600	900	1,200	1,500	2,100	2,700
CR (390cc single)	1,300	2,000	2,800	3,600	5,300	7,000
OR (390cc single)	800	1,200	1,700	2,300	3,300	4,300
WR (390cc single)	800	1,200	1,700	2,300	3,300	4,300
1979						
CR (125cc single)	800	1,200	1,700	2,300	3,300	4,300
WR (125cc single)	800	1,200	1,700	2,300	3,300	4,300
CR (250cc single)	600	900	1,200	1,500	2,100	2,700
OR (250cc single)	900	1,400	2,100	2,800	3,800	4,800
WR (250cc single)	600	900	1,200	1,500	2,100	2,700
ACC (390cc single)	1,000	1,600	2,200	2,900	4,100	5,300
CR (390cc single)	1,300	2,000	2,800	3,600	5,300	7,000
OR (390cc single)	800	1,200	1,700	2,300	3,300	4,300
WR (390cc single)	800	1,200	1,700	2,300	3,300	4,300
1980						
CR (125cc single)	800	1,200	1,700	2,300	3,300	4,300
CR (250cc single)	400	600	800	1,000	1,400	2,000
OR (250cc single)	900	1,400	2,100	2,800	3,800	4,800
WR (250cc single)	600	900	1,200	1,500	2,100	2,700
ACC (390cc single)	1,100	1,700	2,400	3,100	4,500	5,900
CR (390cc single)	1,300	2,000	2,800	3,600	5,300	7,000

	6	5	4	3	2	1
OR (390cc single)	800	1,200	1,700	2,300	3,300	4,300
WR (390cc single)	800	1,200	1,700	2,300	3,300	4,300
1981						
CR (125cc single)	800	1,200	1,700	2,300	3,300	4,300
WR (125cc single)	800	1,200	1,700	2,300	3,300	4,300
CR (250cc single)	800	1,200	1,600	2,000	2,400	3,000
WR (250cc single)	800	1,200	1,600	2,000	2,400	3,000
XC (250cc single)	900	1,400	2,100	2,800	3,800	4,800
AE 4 Speed Automatic (420cc single)	900	1,400	2,100	2,800	3,800	4,800
AXC 4 Speed Automatic (420cc single)	900	1,400	2,100	2,800	3,800	4,800
CR (430cc single)	900	1,400	2,100	2,800	3,800	4,800
WR (430cc single)	900	1,400	2,100	2,800	3,800	4,800
XC (430cc single)	900	1,400	2,100	2,800	3,800	4,800
1982						
CR (125cc single)	800	1,200	1,600	2,000	2,400	3,000
WR (125cc single)	800	1,200	1,600	2,000	2,400	3,000
XC (125cc single)	800	1,200	1,600	2,000	2,400	3,000
CR (250cc single)	800	1,200	1,600	2,000	2,400	3,000
WR (250cc single)	800	1,200	1,600	2,000	2,400	3,000
XC (250cc single)	900	1,400	2,100	2,800	3,800	4,800
Automatic (420cc single)	900	1,400	2,100	2,800	3,800	4,800
CR (430cc single)	900	1,400	2,100	2,800	3,800	4,800
WR (430cc single)	900	1,400	2,100	2,800	3,800	4,800
XC (430cc single)	900	1,400	2,100	2,800	3,800	4,800
CR (500cc single)	800	1,200	1,600	2,000	2,400	3,000
1983						
CR (125cc single)	800	1,200	1,600	2,000	2,400	3,000
WR (125cc single)	800	1,200	1,600	2,000	2,400	3,000
XC (125cc single)	800	1,200	1,600	2,000	2,400	3,000
WR (175cc single)	800	1,200	1,600	2,000	2,400	3,000
XC (175cc single)	800	1,200	1,600	2,000	2,400	3,000
CR (250cc single)	800	1,200	1,600	2,000	2,400	3,000
WR (250cc single)	800	1,200	1,600	2,000	2,400	3,000
XC (250cc single)	900	1,400	2,100	2,800	3,800	4,800
WR (430cc single)	800	1,200	1,600	2,000	2,400	3,000
CR (500cc single)	800	1,200	1,600	2,000	2,400	3,000
TC (500cc single)	800	1,200	1,600	2,000	2,400	3,000
XC (500cc single)	800	1,200	1,600	2,000	2,400	3,000
1984						
CR (125cc single)	800	1,200	1,600	2,000	2,400	3,000
WR (125cc single)	800	1,200	1,600	2,000	2,400	3,000
XC (125cc single)	800	1,200	1,600	2,000	2,400	3,000
CR (250cc single)	800	1,200	1,600	2,000	2,400	3,000
WR (250cc single)	800	1,200	1,600	2,000	2,400	3,000
XC (250cc single)	900	1,400	2,100	2,800	3,800	4,800
WR (400cc single)	700	1,000	1,300	1,700	2,400	3,100
AE Automatic (500cc single)	800	1,200	1,600	2,000	2,400	3,000
CR (500cc single)	800	1,200	1,600	2,000	2,400	3,000
WR (500cc single)	800	1,200	1,600	2,000	2,400	3,000
XC (500cc single)	800	1,200	1,600	2,000	2,400	3,000
1985						
CR (125cc single)	300	600	1,000	1,400	1,800	2,200
XC (125cc single)	300	600	1,000	1,400	1,800	2,200
WR (125cc single)	300	700	1,300	1,900	2,600	3,300
CR (250cc single)	400	800	1,400	2,000	2,600	3,300
XC (250cc single)	300	700	1,300	2,000	2,600	3,200
WR (250cc single)	800	1,200	1,600	2,000	2,400	3,000
WR (400cc single)	700	1,000	1,300	1,700	2,400	3,100
AE Automatic (500cc single)	300	700	1,300	2,000	2,800	3,600

	6	5	4	3	2	1
TC (500cc single)	300	700	1,300	2,000	2,700	3,500
CR (500cc single)	800	1,200	1,600	2,000	2,400	3,000
XC (500cc single)	300	700	1,400	2,100	2,800	3,500
TX (510cc single)	300	700	1,300	2,000	2,800	3,600
TE (510cc single)	500	900	1,600	2,300	3,000	3,700
1986						
CR (125cc single)	300	600	1,000	1,400	1,800	2,200
XC (125cc single)	300	600	1,000	1,400	1,800	2,200
WR (125cc single)	300	700	1,300	1,900	2,600	3,300
CR (250cc single)	400	800	1,400	2,000	2,600	3,300
XC (250cc single)	300	700	1,300	2,000	2,600	3,200
WR (250cc single)	800	1,200	1,600	2,000	2,400	3,000
WR (400cc single)	700	1,000	1,300	1,700	2,400	3,100
XC (400cc single)	300	700	1,300	2,000	2,800	3,600
AE Automatic (500cc single)	300	700	1,300	2,000	2,800	3,600
TC (500cc single)	300	700	1,300	2,000	2,700	3,500
CR (500cc single)	800	1,200	1,600	2,000	2,400	3,000
XC (500cc single)	300	700	1,400	2,100	2,800	3,500
TX (510cc single)	300	700	1,300	2,000	2,800	3,600
TE (510cc single)	500	900	1,600	2,300	3,000	3,700
1987						
CR (250cc single)	400	800	1,400	2,000	2,600	3,300
XC (250cc single)	300	700	1,300	2,000	2,600	3,200
WR (250cc single)	300	700	1,300	1,900	2,600	3,300
CR (430cc single)	300	700	1,300	2,000	2,700	3,400
XC (430cc single)	300	700	1,300	2,000	2,700	3,400
WR (430cc single)	300	700	1,300	2,000	2,700	3,400
AE Automatic (430cc single)	300	700	1,300	2,000	2,800	3,600
XC (500cc single)	300	700	1,400	2,100	2,800	3,500
TC (510cc single)	300	700	1,300	2,000	2,700	3,500
TX (510cc single)	300	700	1,300	2,000	2,800	3,600
TE (510cc single)	500	900	1,600	2,300	3,000	3,700
1988						
WRK (125cc single)	400	800	1,200	1,600	2,000	2,200
XC (250cc single)	400	1,000	1,600	2,300	3,000	3,700
WR (250cc single)	800	1,200	1,600	2,200	3,000	3,800
CR (430cc single)	500	1,100	1,600	2,400	3,200	4,000
XC (430cc single)	900	1,400	2,100	2,800	3,400	4,100
WR (430cc single)	500	1,000	1,600	2,400	3,200	4,000
AE Automatic (430cc single)	800	1,200	1,600	2,200	3,200	4,200
TC (510cc single)	500	1,000	2,000	3,000	4,000	5,000
TX (510cc single)	900	1,400	2,100	2,800	3,800	5,000
TE (510cc single)	900	1,400	2,100	2,800	3,800	5,000
1990						
WMX (125cc single)	300	700	1,400	2,100	2,800	3,500
WMX (250cc single)	500	1,000	1,800	2,600	3,400	4,200
WMX (510cc single)	600	1,200	2,000	2,800	3,600	4,400
WXE (125cc single)	600	1,200	2,000	2,800	3,600	4,400
WXE (250cc single)	700	1,400	2,200	3,200	4,200	5,200
WXE (510cc single)	800	1,500	2,500	3,500	4,500	5,500
1991						
WMX (125cc single)	300	700	1,400	2,100	2,800	3,500
WXE (125cc single)	600	1,200	2,000	2,800	3,600	4,400
WMX (250cc single)	500	1,000	1,800	2,600	3,400	4,200
WXE (250cc single)	700	1,400	2,200	3,200	4,200	5,200
WXE (260cc single)	800	1,500	2,500	3,500	4,500	5,500
WXE (350cc single)	900	1,700	2,700	3,700	4,700	5,700
WMX (610cc single)	800	1,500	2,300	3,100	3,900	4,700
WXE (610cc single)	1,000	2,000	3,000	4,000	5,000	6,000

	6	5	4	3	2	1
1992						
WXC (125cc single)	400	800	1,600	2,400	3,200	4,000
WXE (125cc single)	600	1,200	2,000	2,800	3,600	4,400
WXC (250cc single)	600	1,200	2,100	3,000	3,900	4,800
WXE (250cc single)	700	1,400	2,200	3,200	4,200	5,200
WXC (350cc single)	600	1,200	2,100	3,100	4,100	5,100
WXE (350cc single)	800	1,500	2,500	3,500	4,500	5,500
WXC (360cc single)	700	1,400	2,400	3,400	4,400	5,400
WXE (360cc single)	900	1,700	2,700	3,700	4,700	5,700
WXC (610cc single)	900	1,800	2,800	3,800	4,800	5,800
WXE (610cc single)	1,000	2,000	3,000	4,000	5,000	6,000
1993						
WXC (250cc single)	600	1,200	2,100	3,000	3,900	4,800
WXC (350cc single)	600	1,200	2,100	3,100	4,100	5,100
WXC (360cc single)	700	1,400	2,400	3,400	4,400	5,400
WXC (610cc single)	900	1,800	2,800	3,800	4,800	5,800
1994						
WXC (125cc single)	400	800	1,600	2,400	3,200	4,000
WXE (125cc single)	600	1,200	2,000	2,800	3,600	4,400
WXC (250cc single)	600	1,200	2,100	3,000	3,900	4,800
WXE (250cc single)	700	1,400	2,200	3,200	4,200	5,200
WXC (350cc single)	600	1,200	2,100	3,100	4,100	5,100
WXE (350cc single)	700	1,500	2,500	3,500	4,500	5,500
WXC (360cc single)	700	1,400	2,400	3,400	4,400	5,400
WXE (360cc single)	900	1,700	2,700	3,700	4,700	5,700
WXC (610cc single)	900	1,800	2,800	3,800	4,800	5,800
WXE (610cc single)	1,000	2,000	3,000	4,000	5,000	6,000
1995						
WXE (125cc single)	600	1,200	2,000	2,800	3,600	4,400
WXE (250cc single)	700	1,400	2,200	3,200	4,200	5,200
WXE (350cc single)	800	1,500	2,500	3,500	4,500	5,500
WXE (360cc single)	900	1,700	2,700	3,700	4,700	5,700
WXE (610cc single)	1,000	2,000	3,000	4,000	5,000	6,000

INDIAN

	6	5	4	3	2	1
1901						
Single 1.75hp (3) (rare; price TBD)						
1902						
Single 1.75hp (143) (rare; price TBD)						
1903						
Single 1.75hp (376) (rare; price TBD)						
1904						
Single 1.75hp (596) (rare; price TBD)						
1905						
Single 2.25hp (1,181)	6,000	11,000	19,000	33,000	55,000	75,000
1906						
Single 2.5hp (1,698)	6,000	10,000	18,000	30,000	53,000	70,000
1907						
Single 2.25hp (2,176)	6,000	10,000	15,000	28,000	49,000	70,000
Twin 3.5hp (incl. above)	8,000	15,000	26,000	47,000	75,000	95,000
1908						
Single 3.5hp (3,257)	6,000	8,000	13,000	24,000	42,000	60,000
Twin 5hp (incl. above)	7,000	12,000	21,000	38,000	59,000	80,000
1909						
Single 2hp (4,771)	5,000	7,000	12,000	21,000	40,000	60,000
Single 3.5hp (incl. above)	5,000	8,000	13,000	22,000	41,000	60,000
Single 4hp (incl. above)	6,000	9,000	14,000	24,000	42,000	60,000
Twin 5hp (incl. above)	8,000	14,000	21,000	33,000	54,000	70,000
Twin 7hp (incl. above)	9,000	15,000	22,000	34,000	57,000	80,000

	6	5	4	3	2	1
1910 (Model B)						
Single 2.75hp (6,137)	5,000	7,000	11,000	19,000	35,000	50,000
Single 4hp (incl. above)	5,000	8,000	13,000	23,000	39,000	55,000
Twin 5hp (incl. above)	7,000	13,000	20,000	31,000	50,000	70,000
Twin 7hp (incl. above)	8,000	14,000	21,000	32,000	52,000	70,000
1911 (Model C)						
Single 2.75hp (9,763)	5,000	7,000	10,000	19,000	33,000	45,000
Single 4hp (incl. above)	5,000	7,000	12,000	20,000	36,000	50,000
Twin 5hp (incl. above)	6,000	12,000	18,000	29,000	48,000	65,000
Twin 7hp (incl. above)	7,000	13,000	19,000	30,000	50,000	70,000
1912 (Model D)						
Single 4hp (19,500)	5,000	15,000	25,000	35,000	50,000	65,000
Twin 7hp (incl. above)	6,000	11,000	17,000	28,000	48,000	65,000
1913 (Model E)						
Single 4hp (32,000)	4,000	7,000	10,000	19,000	33,000	50,000
Twin 7hp (incl. above)	6,000	10,000	16,000	26,000	41,000	55,000
1914 (Model F)						
Hendee Special 7hp (25,000)	14,000	18,000	49,000	59,000	74,000	90,000
Single 4hp (incl. above)	5,000	7,000	10,000	17,000	32,000	45,000
Twin 7hp (incl. above)	6,000	9,000	15,000	25,000	38,000	50,000
1915						
Hendee Special 7hp (21,000)	14,000	18,000	49,000	59,000	74,000	90,000
Single 4hp (incl. above)	4,000	6,000	10,000	17,000	32,000	45,000
Twin 7hp (incl. above)	6,000	9,000	14,000	24,000	42,000	60,000
1916						
Model K Featherweight 2.5hp (22,000)	6,000	9,000	14,000	24,000	42,000	60,000
Single 4hp (incl. above)	3,000	5,000	8,000	15,000	27,000	40,000
Powerplus (33ci single) (incl. above)	4,000	7,000	11,000	17,000	31,000	45,000
Twin 7hp (incl. above)	5,000	8,000	13,000	20,000	34,000	50,000
Powerplus (61ci twin) (incl. above)	**10,000**	**20,000**	**30,000**	**40,000**	**50,000**	**60,000**
1917						
Single 4hp (20,500)	3,000	5,000	8,000	14,000	26,000	40,000
Powerplus (33ci single) (incl. above)	4,000	7,000	11,000	16,000	29,000	40,000
Twin 2.5hp (incl. above)	4,000	7,000	11,000	17,000	27,000	40,000
Twin 7hp (incl. above)	5,000	8,000	12,000	19,000	32,000	45,000
Model O Light (15.7ci twin) (incl. above)	4,000	6,000	10,000	15,000	22,000	30,000
Powerplus (61ci twin) (incl. above)	**10,000**	**20,000**	**30,000**	**40,000**	**50,000**	**60,000**
1918						
Single 4hp (22,000)	3,000	5,000	8,000	14,000	25,000	35,000
Powerplus (33ci single) (incl. above)	4,000	7,000	10,000	15,000	27,000	40,000
Twin 2.5hp (incl. above)	4,000	7,000	10,000	16,000	26,000	35,000
Twin 7hp (incl. above)	5,000	8,000	11,000	18,000	30,000	45,000
Model O Light (15.7ci twin) (incl. above)	4,000	6,000	9,000	14,000	21,000	30,000
Powerplus (61ci twin) (incl. above)	**10,000**	**20,000**	**30,000**	**40,000**	**50,000**	**60,000**
1919						
Single 4hp (21,500)	3,000	5,000	8,000	14,000	25,000	35,000
Powerplus (33ci single) (incl. above)	4,000	7,000	10,000	15,000	27,000	40,000
Twin 2.5hp (incl. above)	4,000	7,000	10,000	16,000	25,000	35,000
Twin 7hp (incl. above)	5,000	8,000	11,000	18,000	30,000	45,000
Twin Big Valve 8hp (incl. above)	7,000	12,000	20,000	30,000	40,000	50,000
Model O Light (15.7ci twin) (incl. above)	4,000	6,000	9,000	14,000	21,000	30,000
Powerplus (61ci twin) (incl. above)	**10,000**	**20,000**	**30,000**	**40,000**	**50,000**	**60,000**
1920						
Powerplus (33-cid single)	5,000	7,000	11,000	15,000	20,000	25,000
Scout (37-cid V-twin)	**8,000**	**15,000**	**20,000**	**25,000**	**35,000**	**45,000**
Powerplus (61-cid V-twin)	6,000	9,000	13,000	17,000	23,000	29,000
1921						
Powerplus (33-cid single)	5,000	7,000	11,000	15,000	20,000	25,000
Scout (37-cid V-twin)	**8,000**	**15,000**	**20,000**	**25,000**	**35,000**	**45,000**
Powerplus (61-cid V-twin)	6,000	8,000	13,000	17,000	23,000	28,000

	6	5	4	3	2	1
1922						
Powerplus (33-cid single)	4,000	7,000	10,000	13,000	18,000	23,000
Scout (37-cid V-twin)	**8,000**	**15,000**	**20,000**	**25,000**	**35,000**	**45,000**
Powerplus (61-cid V-twin)	6,000	8,000	13,000	17,000	23,000	28,000
Chief (61-cid V-twin).	9,000	13,000	20,000	26,000	35,000	43,000
1923						
Powerplus (33-cid single)	4,000	6,500	1,000	13,000	17,000	22,000
Scout (37-cid V-twin)	6,000	9,000	13,000	17,000	23,000	30,000
Powerplus (61-cid V-twin)	5,000	8,000	12,000	16,000	22,000	28,000
Chief (61-cid V-twin).	8,000	13,000	19,000	25,000	34,000	43,000
Big Chief (74-cid V-twin)	9,000	13,000	20,000	26,000	35,000	44,000
1924						
Powerplus (33-cid single)	4,000	6,000	10,000	13,000	17,000	22,000
Scout (37-cid V-twin)	5,000	8,000	12,000	16,000	21,000	27,000
Powerplus (61-cid V-twin)	5,000	8,000	12,000	16,000	21,000	27,000
Chief (61-cid V-twin).	8,000	13,000	19,000	25,000	34,000	43,000
Big Chief (74-cid V-twin)	9,000	13,000	19,000	25,000	34,000	44,000
1925						
Prince (21-cid single)	4,000	5,000	8,000	11,000	14,000	18,000
Scout (37-cid V-twin)	5,000	7,000	11,000	14,000	19,000	24,000
Chief (61-cid V-twin).	8,000	12,000	18,000	25,000	33,000	42,000
Big Chief (74-cid V-twin)	9,000	13,000	19,000	25,000	34,000	44,000
1926						
Prince (21-cid single)	5,000	7,000	11,000	14,000	19,000	24,000
Scout (37-cid V-twin)	5,000	7,000	11,000	14,000	19,000	24,000
Chief (61-cid V-twin).	8,000	12,000	18,000	25,000	33,000	42,000
Big Chief (74-cid V-twin)	9,000	13,000	19,000	25,000	34,000	44,000
1927						
Prince (21-cid single)	3,000	5,000	8,000	10,000	14,000	17,000
Scout (37-cid V-twin)	4,000	6,000	9,000	13,000	17,000	21,000
Scout (45-cid V-twin)	5,000	7,000	10,000	14,000	18,000	23,000
Chief (61-cid V-twin).	8,000	12,000	18,000	24,000	32,000	40,000
Big Chief (74-cid V-twin)	9,000	13,000	19,000	26,000	34,000	44,000
Indian Ace (78-cid, inline 4-cyl)	10,000	20,000	30,000	40,000	50,000	60,000
1928						
Prince (21-cid single)	3,000	5,000	8,000	10,000	14,000	17,000
101 Scout (37-cid V-twin)	4,000	7,000	12,000	17,000	20,000	25,000
101 Scout (45-cid V-twin)	5,000	7,000	12,000	18,000	24,000	30,000
Chief (61-cid V-twin).	8,000	12,000	18,000	24,000	32,000	40,000
Big Chief (74-cid V-twin)	9,000	13,000	19,000	26,000	35,000	44,000
Indian Ace (78-cid, inline 4-cyl)	10,000	20,000	30,000	40,000	50,000	60,000
1929						
101 Scout (37-cid V-twin)	4,000	7,000	10,000	13,000	18,000	22,000
101 Scout (45-cid V-twin)	5,000	7,000	11,000	15,000	20,000	25,000
Chief (74-cid V-twin).	8,000	12,000	17,000	23,000	31,000	39,000
Model 401 (78-cid, inline 4-cyl)	**15,000**	**30,000**	**40,000**	**50,000**	**60,000**	**70,000**
Model 402 (78-cid, inline 4-cyl)	**15,000**	**30,000**	**40,000**	**50,000**	**60,000**	**70,000**
1930						
101 Scout (37-cid V-twin)	4,000	7,000	10,000	13,000	18,000	22,000
101 Scout (45-cid V-twin)	5,000	7,000	11,000	15,000	20,000	25,000
Chief (74-cid V-twin).	8,000	11,000	17,000	23,000	30,000	38,000
Model 402 (78-cid, inline 4-cyl)	**15,000**	**30,000**	**40,000**	**50,000**	**60,000**	**70,000**
1931						
101 Scout (37-cid V-twin) (4,557)	4,000	7,000	10,000	13,000	18,000	22,000
101 Scout (45-cid V-twin) (incl. above) . . .	5,000	8,000	11,000	15,000	20,000	25,000
Chief (74-cid V-twin) (incl. above)	8,000	11,000	17,000	23,000	30,000	38,000
Model 402 (78-cid, inline 4-cyl) (incl. above)	**15,000**	**30,000**	**40,000**	**50,000**	**60,000**	**70,000**

	6	5	4	3	2	1
1932						
Scout Pony (30-cid, V-twin) (2,360)	3,000	5,000	7,000	10,000	13,000	16,000
Scout (45-cid V-twin) (incl. above)	4,000	6,000	9,000	13,000	17,000	21,000
Chief (74-cid V-twin) (incl. above)	8,000	11,000	17,000	23,000	30,000	39,000
Model 403 (78-cid, inline 4-cyl) (incl. above)	1,000	20,000	30,000	40,000	50,000	60,000
1933						
Junior Scout (30.5-cid V-twin) (1,667)	3,000	5,000	7,000	10,000	13,000	16,000
Standard Scout (45-cid V-twin) (incl. above)	4,000	6,000	9,000	12,000	16,000	20,000
Motoplane (45-cid V-twin) (incl. above) . . .	20,000	30,000	40,000	50,000	60,000	70,000
Chief (74-cid V-twin) (incl. above)	8,000	11,000	17,000	23,000	30,000	38,000
Model 403 (78-cid, inline 4-cyl) (incl. above)	10,000	20,000	30,000	40,000	50,000	60,000
1934						
Junior Scout (30.5-cid V-twin) (2,809)	3,000	5,000	7,000	10,000	13,000	16,000
Standard Scout (45-cid V-twin) (incl. above)	4,000	6,000	9,000	11,000	15,000	19,000
Sport Scout (45-cid V-twin) (incl. above) . .	5,000	7,000	14,000	21,000	28,000	35,000
Chief (74-cid V-twin) (incl. above)	8,000	11,000	17,000	23,000	30,000	38,000
Model 434 (78-cid, inline 4-cyl) (incl. above)	10,000	20,000	30,000	40,000	50,000	60,000
1935						
Junior Scout (30.5-cid V-twin) (3,703)	3,000	5,000	7,000	10,000	13,000	16,000
Standard Scout (45-cid V-twin) (incl. above)	4,000	6,000	9,000	11,000	15,000	19,000
Sport Scout (45-cid V-twin) (incl. above) . .	5,000	7,000	14,000	21,000	28,000	35,000
Chief (74-cid V-twin) (incl. above)	8,000	11,000	17,000	23,000	30,000	38,000
Model 435 (78-cid, inline 4-cyl) (incl. above)	10,000	20,000	30,000	40,000	50,000	60,000
1936						
Junior Scout (30.5-cid V-twin) (5,028)	3,000	5,000	7,000	9,000	12,000	15,000
Scout 45 (45-cid V-twin) (incl. above)	4,000	5,000	8,000	11,000	14,000	18,000
Sport Scout (45-cid V-twin) (incl. above) . .	5,000	7,000	14,000	21,000	28,000	35,000
Chief (74-cid V-twin) (incl. above)	7,000	11,000	17,000	22,000	30,000	38,000
Model 436 (78-cid, inline 4-cyl) (incl. above)	10,000	20,000	30,000	40,000	50,000	60,000
1937						
Junior Scout (30.5-cid V-twin) (6,037)	3,000	6,000	9,000	12,000	15,000	18,000
Scout 45 (45-cid V-twin) (incl. above)	4,000	5,000	8,000	11,000	14,000	18,000
Sport Scout (45-cid V-twin) (incl. above) . .	5,000	7,000	14,000	21,000	28,000	35,000
Chief (74-cid V-twin) (incl. above)	7,000	11,000	17,000	22,000	30,000	38,000
Model 437 (78-cid, inline 4-cyl) (incl. above)	10,000	20,000	30,000	40,000	50,000	60,000
1938						
Junior Scout (30.5-cid V-twin) (3,650)	5,000	7,000	9,000	12,000	15,000	18,000
Sport Scout (45-cid V-twin) (incl. above) . .	5,000	7,000	14,000	21,000	28,000	35,000
Chief (74-cid V-twin) (incl. above)	8,000	12,000	18,000	25,000	33,000	41,000
Model 438 (78-cid, inline 4-cyl) (incl. above)	11,000	20,000	30,000	40,000	50,000	60,000
1939						
Junior Scout (30.5-cid V-twin) (3,012)	4,000	6,000	9,000	12,000	16,000	20,000
Sport Scout (45-cid V-twin) (incl. above) . .	5,000	7,000	14,000	21,000	28,000	35,000
Chief (74-cid V-twin) (incl. above)	8,000	11,000	17,000	23,000	30,000	38,000
Model 439 (78-cid, inline 4-cyl) (incl. above)	10,000	20,000	30,000	40,000	50,000	60,000
1940						
Thirty-fifty (30.5-cid V-twin) (10,431)	3,000	5,000	7,000	9,000	12,000	15,000
Sport Scout (45-cid V-twin) (incl. above) . .	6,000	8,000	14,000	21,000	28,000	35,000
Chief (74-cid V-twin) (incl. above)	8,000	12,000	18,000	23,000	31,000	40,000
Model 440 (78-cid, inline 4-cyl) (incl. above)	11,000	20,000	30,000	40,000	50,000	60,000
1941						
Thirty-fifty (30.5-cid V-twin) (8,739)	3,000	4,000	6,000	8,000	11,000	14,000
Model 741 (30.5-cid V-twin, military) (incl. above)	3,000	4,000	6,000	8,000	11,000	14,000
Sport Scout (45-cid V-twin) (incl. above) . .	6,000	8,000	14,000	21,000	28,000	35,000
Model 640-B (45-cid V-twin, military) (incl. above)	3,000	5,000	7,000	10,000	13,000	16,000
Model 841 (45-cid V-twin, shaft-drive, military) (incl. above)	5,000	10,000	15,000	20,000	25,000	30,000

	6	5	4	3	2	1
Chief (74-cid V-twin) (incl. above)	8,000	12,000	18,000	23,000	31,000	39,000
Model 441 (78-cid, inline 4-cyl) (incl. above)	11,000	20,000	30,000	40,000	50,000	60,000
1942						
Model 741 (30.5-cid V-twin, military) (16,647)	3,000	4,000	6,000	8,000	11,000	14,000
Model 640-B(45-cid V-twin, military) (incl. above)	3,000	5,000	7,000	10,000	13,000	16,000
Model 841 (45-cid V-twin, shaft-drive,military) (incl. above)	5,000	10,000	15,000	20,000	25,000	30,000
Chief (74-cid V-twin) (incl. above)	8,000	12,000	18,000	23,000	31,000	39,000
Chief (74-cid V-twin, military) (incl. above) .	8,000	12,000	18,000	23,000	31,000	39,000
Model 442 (78-cid, inline 4-cyl) (incl. above)	15,000	25,000	35,000	45,000	55,000	65,000
1943						
Model 640-B(45-cid V-twin, military) (16,456)	3,000	5,000	7,000	10,000	13,000	16,000
Model 841 (45-cid V-twin, shaft-drive,military) (incl. above)	5,000	10,000	15,000	20,000	25,000	30,000
Chief (74-cid V-twin, military) (incl. above) .	7,000	10,000	15,000	20,000	27,000	34,000
1944						
Chief (74-cid V-twin, military) (17,006) . . .	6,000	10,000	14,000	19,000	26,000	32,000
1945						
Chief (74-cid V-twin) (2,070)	7,000	11,000	16,000	21,000	28,000	35,000
Chief (74-cid V-twin, military) (incl. above) .	6,000	10,000	14,000	19,000	26,000	32,000
1946						
Chief (74-cid V-twin) (3,621)	7,000	11,000	13,000	16,000	20,000	25,000
1947						
Chief (74-cid V-twin) (11,849)	7,000	11,000	13,000	16,000	20,000	25,000
Chief Roadmaster (74-cid V-twin) (incl. above)	7,000	11,000	16,000	22,000	25,000	30,000
1948						
Chief (74-cid V-twin) (9,000)	7,000	11,000	16,000	19,000	25,000	32,000
Chief Roadmaster (74-cid V-twin)	7,000	11,000	16,000	22,000	25,000	30,000
1949						
Arrow (13-cid single) (incl. above)	2,000	3,000	5,000	10,000	15,000	20,000
Warrior (30.5-cid vertical twin) (incl. above) .	2,000	3,000	6,000	8,000	10,000	12,000
Scout (27-cid vertical twin) (incl. above) . . .	2,000	3,000	5,000	8,000	12,000	15,000
Papoose Scooter	500	700	1,000	1,500	2,500	3,500
1950						
Arrow (13-cid single) (2,000)	2,000	3,000	4,000	**6,000**	**8,000**	**10,000**
Scout (27-cid vertical twin) (incl. above) . . .	2,000	3,000	4,000	6,000	8,000	10,000
Warrior (30.5-cid vertical twin) (incl. above) .	2,000	3,000	**6,000**	**8,000**	**10,000**	**12,000**
Warrior TT (30.5-cid vertical twin) (incl. above)	2,000	3,000	**6,000**	**8,000**	**10,000**	**12,000**
Chief (80-cid V-twin) (incl. above)	8,000	12,000	19,000	25,000	33,000	41,000
1951						
Brave (15-cid single) (500)	1,000	2,000	3,000	4,000	7,000	9,000
Warrior (30.5-cid vertical twin) (incl. above) .	2,000	3,000	**6,000**	**8,000**	**10,000**	**12,000**
Warrior TT (30.5-cid vertical twin) (incl. above)	2,000	3,000	**6,000**	**8,000**	**10,000**	**12,000**
Chief (80-cid V-twin) (incl. above)	8,000	12,000	19,000	25,000	30,000	35,000
1952						
Brave (15-cid single) (500)	1,000	2,000	3,000	4,000	7,000	9,000
Warrior (30.5-cid vertical twin) (incl. above) .	2,000	3,000	**6,000**	**8,000**	**10,000**	**12,000**
Warrior TT (30.5-cid vertical twin) (incl. above)	2,000	3,000	**6,000**	**8,000**	**10,000**	**12,000**
Chief (80-cid V-twin) (incl. above)	8,000	12,000	19,000	25,000	33,000	42,000
1953						
Brave (15-cid single) (2,000)	1,000	2,000	3,000	4,000	7,000	9,000
Chief (80-cid V-twin) (incl. above)	9,000	13,000	20,000	26,000	35,000	44,000

	6	5	4	3	2	1
JAWA						
1936						
Special	1,500	2,500	3,800	5,300	7,000	9,000
1948						
Perek	1,500	3,000	4,500	6,000	7,500	9,000
1955						
Speedway	1,000	2,000	3,000	4,000	5,000	6,000
1957						
175	400	600	1,000	2,000	3,500	5,000
1960						
355	400	600	1,000	2,000	3,500	5,000
1965						
350	500	1,000	2,000	3,000	4,000	5,000
1967						
Junior (250cc)	1,500	3,000	4,200	5,400	6,600	8,000
1969						
Speedway	1,500	3,000	4,200	5,400	6,600	8,000
1970						
Speedway	1,500	3,000	4,200	5,400	6,600	8,000
1972						
250 Twin	400	600	1,000	2,000	3,500	5,000
1973						
125 MX Desert	1,000	1,700	2,300	3,100	4,800	6,500
175 Trial	600	1,000	1,300	1,700	2,600	3,500
250 MX	700	1,200	1,600	2,100	3,400	4,700
400 MX	1,500	2,200	3,000	4,000	6,300	8,600
1974						
125 MX Desert	1,000	1,700	2,300	3,100	4,800	6,500
125 Sport	300	600	800	1,000	1,500	2,000
175 Sport 4 Speed	1,000	1,600	2,200	3,000	4,600	6,200
175 Sport 6 Speed	1,100	1,800	2,400	3,300	4,900	6,800
250 MX Desert	700	1,200	1,700	2,200	3,500	4,800
400 MX Desert	1,500	2,000	2,800	3,700	5,800	8,000
1975						
125 Moto Cross	1,100	1,800	2,500	3,300	5,100	7,000
125 Street	1,000	1,600	2,200	2,900	4,500	6,100
250 Enduro	700	1,200	1,700	2,200	3,500	4,800
250 GP Moto Cross	800	1,300	1,800	2,400	3,800	5,000
250 MX Desert	700	1,200	1,700	2,200	3,500	4,800
400 GP Moto Cross	800	1,300	1,800	2,400	3,800	5,000
400 MX Desert	1,500	2,000	2,800	3,700	5,800	8,000
1976						
250 Enduro	1,100	1,800	2,500	3,300	5,100	7,000
250 Falta GP-C	1,300	2,000	2,700	3,600	5,600	7,600
350 TSII-C	1,700	2,200	3,000	3,800	5,000	6,500
400 Falta GP-C	1,500	2,000	2,800	3,700	5,800	8,000
1977						
175 Enduro	700	1,200	1,700	2,200	3,400	4,600
250 Enduro	1,100	1,800	2,500	3,300	5,100	7,000
250 MX	800	1,300	1,900	2,400	3,800	5,200
1979						
125 MX	900	1,500	2,100	2,800	4,200	5,500
1980						
500 Jawa 894.1	1,100	1,800	2,500	3,300	5,100	7,000
KAWASAKI						
1963						
B8 (125cc single)	700	1,100	1,600	2,100	2,800	3,500
B8T (125cc single)	700	1,100	1,600	2,100	2,800	3,500

	6	5	4	3	2	1
1964						
B8 (125cc single)	600	1,000	1,400	1,900	2,600	3,200
B8T (125cc single)	600	1,000	1,400	1,900	2,600	3,200
SG (250cc single)	700	1,100	1,700	2,200	3,000	3,700
1965						
J1 (85cc single)	400	600	900	1,200	1,600	2,000
J1T (85cc single)	400	600	900	1,200	1,600	2,000
B8 (125cc single)	600	900	1,400	1,800	2,400	3,000
B8T (125cc single)	600	900	1,400	1,800	2,400	3,000
B8S (125cc single)	600	900	1,400	1,900	2,500	3,100
SG (250cc single)	700	1,100	1,700	2,200	3,000	3,700
1966						
M10 (50cc single)	300	500	700	900	1,200	1,500
M11 (50cc single)	300	500	700	900	1,200	1,500
J1 (85cc single)	400	600	800	1,100	1,500	1,900
J1T (85cc single)	400	600	800	1,100	1,500	1,900
J1R (85cc single)	400	600	900	1,200	1,600	2,000
D1 (100cc single)	300	500	800	1,000	1,400	1,700
C1 (120cc single)	400	600	900	1,200	1,600	2,000
C1D (120 cc single)	400	600	900	1,200	1,600	2,000
B1 (125cc single)	400	600	900	1,200	1,600	2,000
B1T (125cc single)	400	600	900	1,200	1,600	2,000
B1TL (125cc single)	400	600	900	1,200	1,600	2,000
B8 (125cc single)	400	700	1,000	1,300	1,800	2,200
B8T (125cc single)	400	700	1,000	1,300	1,800	2,200
B8S (125cc single)	500	700	1,100	1,400	1,900	2,400
F1 (175cc single)	400	700	1,000	1,300	1,800	2,200
F1TR (175cc single)	500	700	1,000	1,400	1,800	2,300
F2 (175cc single)	500	700	1,000	1,400	1,800	2,300
SG (250cc single)	600	900	1,350	1,800	2,400	3,000
W1 (624cc twin)	1,500	2,300	3,600	4,900	6,600	8,500
1967						
M10 (50cc single)	300	500	700	900	1,200	1,500
M11 (50cc single)	300	500	700	900	1,200	1,500
J1D (85cc single)	400	500	800	1,100	1,400	1,800
J1TL (85cc single)	400	500	800	1,100	1,400	1,800
J1TRL (85cc single)	400	600	900	1,200	1,600	2,000
G1M (90cc single)	300	500	800	1,000	1,400	1,700
D1 (100cc single)	300	500	800	1,000	1,400	1,700
C1DL (120 cc single)	400	600	900	1,200	1,600	2,000
C1L (120cc single)	400	600	900	1,200	1,600	2,000
C2SS Roadrunner (120cc single)	400	500	800	1,100	1,400	1,800
C2TR Roadrunner (120cc single)	400	600	900	1,200	1,600	2,000
B1 (125cc single)	400	600	900	1,200	1,600	2,000
B1T (125cc single)	400	600	900	1,200	1,600	2,000
B1TL (125cc single)	400	600	900	1,200	1,600	2,000
F2 (175cc single)	500	700	1,000	1,400	1,800	2,300
F2TR (175cc single)	500	700	1,000	1,400	1,800	2,300
A1 Samurai (247cc twin)	700	1,000	1,600	2,100	2,700	3,300
A1R (247cc twin)	2,000	3,000	4,500	6,000	8,000	10,000
A1SS Samurai (247cc twin)	700	1,000	1,600	2,100	2,700	3,300
SG (250cc single)	600	900	1,400	1,800	2,400	3,000
A7 Avenger (338cc twin)	800	1,200	1,700	2,300	3,000	3,700
A7SS Avenger (338cc twin)	800	1,200	1,700	2,300	3,000	3,700
W1 (624cc twin)	1,500	2,300	3,600	4,900	6,600	8,500
1968						
M10 (50cc single)	300	500	700	900	1,200	1,500
M11 (50cc single)	300	500	700	900	1,200	1,500
J1L (85cc single)	300	500	700	1,000	1,300	1,600

	6	5	4	3	2	1
G1L (90cc single)	300	500	700	1,000	1,300	1,600
G1M (90cc single)	.300	500	700	1,000	1,300	1,600
D1 (100cc single)	400	500	800	1,100	1,400	1,800
C2SS Roadrunner (120cc single)	400	500	800	1,100	1,400	1,800
C2TR Roadrunner (120cc single)	400	600	900	1,200	1,600	2,000
B1L (125cc single)	400	600	900	1,200	1,600	2,000
B1T (125cc single)	400	600	900	1,200	1,600	2,000
B1TL (125cc single)	400	600	900	1,200	1,600	2,000
F2 (175cc single)	400	600	1,000	1,300	1,700	2,100
F3 Bushwacker (175cc single)	500	700	1,000	1,400	1,800	2,300
A1 Samurai (247cc twin)	700	1,000	1,600	2,100	2,700	3,300
A1R (247cc twin)	2,000	3,000	4,500	6,000	8,000	10,000
A1SS Samurai (247cc twin)	700	1,000	1,600	2,100	2,700	3,300
F21M (250cc single)	600	900	1,400	1,800	2,400	3,000
SG (250cc single)	600	900	1,400	1,800	2,400	3,000
A7 Avenger (338cc twin)	800	1,200	1,700	2,300	3,000	3,700
A7SS Avenger (338cc twin)	800	1,200	1,700	2,300	3,000	3,700
W1 (624cc twin)	1,200	2,200	3,400	5,000	6,000	7,000
W1SS (624cc twin)	1,200	2,200	3,400	5,000	6,000	7,000
W2SS Commander (624cc twin)	1,200	2,200	3,400	5,000	6,000	7,000
1969						
M10 (50cc single)	200	400	500	700	1,000	1,200
M11 (50cc single)	200	400	500	700	1,000	1,200
GA1 (90cc single)	300	400	600	800	1,100	1,400
GA2 (90cc single)	300	400	600	800	1,100	1,400
GA3 Street Scrambler (90cc single)	300	400	600	800	1,100	1,400
G1DL (90cc single)	300	500	700	1,000	1,300	1,600
G1TRL (90cc single)	300	500	700	1,000	1,300	1,600
G3SS (90cc single)	300	500	700	1,000	1,300	1,600
G3TR Bushmaster (90cc single)	300	500	700	1,000	1,300	1,600
B1L (125cc single)	300	500	700	900	1,200	1,600
B1T (125cc single)	300	500	700	900	1,200	1,600
B1TL (125cc single)	300	500	700	900	1,200	1,600
F2 (175cc single)	400	600	1,000	1,300	1,700	2,100
F3 Bushwacker (175cc single)	600	900	1,400	1,800	2,400	3,000
A1 Samurai (247cc twin)	700	1,000	1,600	2,100	2,700	3,300
A1SS Samurai (247cc twin)	700	1,000	1,600	2,100	2,700	3,300
F4 Sidewinder (250cc single)	400	700	1,000	1,300	1,800	2,200
F21M (250cc single)	700	1,100	1,600	2,100	2,800	3,500
SG (250cc single)	400	700	1,000	1,300	1,800	2,200
A7 Avenger (338cc twin)	800	1,200	1,700	2,300	3,000	3,700
A7SS Avenger (338cc twin)	800	1,200	1,700	2,300	3,000	3,700
H1 Mach III (498cc triple)	1,500	3,000	4,500	6,000	8,000	10,000
W1SS (624cc twin)	1,200	2,000	3,200	4,100	5,000	6,000
W2SS Commander (624cc twin)	1,200	2,000	3,200	4,100	5,000	6,000
W2TT Commander (624cc twin)	2,600	4,000	6,000	8,000	11,000	13,000
1970						
GA1 (90cc single)	300	400	600	800	1,100	1,400
GA2 (90cc single)	300	400	600	800	1,100	1,400
GA3 Street Scrambler (90cc single)	300	400	600	800	1,100	1,400
G3SS (90cc single)	300	500	700	1,000	1,300	1,600
G3TR Bushmaster (90cc single)	300	500	700	1,000	1,300	1,600
G4TR Trail Boss (100cc single)	300	500	800	1,000	1,400	1,700
G31M Centurian (100cc single)	**1,000**	**2,000**	**3,000**	**4,000**	**5,000**	**6,000**
B1LA (125cc single)	300	500	700	900	1,200	1,500
F3 Bushwacker (175cc single)	600	900	1,400	1,800	2,400	3,000
A1A Samurai (247cc twin)	700	1,000	1,600	2,100	2,700	3,300
A1SSA Samurai (247cc twin)	700	1,000	1,600	2,100	2,700	3,300

	6	5	4	3	2	1
F4 Sidewinder (250cc single)	400	600	900	1,200	1,600	2,000
F21M (250cc single)	700	1,100	1,600	2,100	2,800	3,500
A7A Avenger (338cc twin)	700	1,000	1,600	2,100	2,700	3,300
A7SSA Avenger (338 cc twin)	700	1,000	1,600	2,100	2,700	3,300
F5 Big Horn (350cc single)	400	600	1,000	1,300	1,700	2,100
H1 Mach III (498cc triple)	1,500	2,300	3,300	4,300	5,700	7,100
W1SS (624cc twin)	1,200	2,000	3,200	4,100	5,000	6,000
W2SS Commander (624cc twin)	1,200	2,000	3,200	4,100	5,000	6,000
1971						
GA1A (90cc single)	300	400	600	800	1,100	1,400
GA2A (90cc single)	300	400	600	800	1,100	1,400
G3SS (90cc single)	300	500	700	1,000	1,300	1,600
GA5A (100cc single)	300	500	700	1,000	1,300	1,600
G3TRA (100cc single)	300	500	700	1,000	1,300	1,600
G4TRA Trail Boss (100cc single)	300	500	800	1,000	1,400	1,700
G31M Centurian (100cc single)	**1,000**	**2,000**	**3,000**	**4,000**	**5,000**	**6,000**
F6 (125cc single)	300	500	700	1,000	1,300	1,600
F7 (175cc single)	300	500	800	1,000	1,400	1,700
A1B Samurai (247cc twin)	600	900	1,400	1,800	2,400	3,000
A1SSB Samurai (247cc twin)	600	900	1,400	1,800	2,400	3,000
F8 (250cc single)	500	700	1,100	1,400	1,900	2,400
A7B Avenger (338cc twin)	500	800	1,200	1,600	2,100	2,700
A7SSB Avenger (338 cc twin)	500	800	1,200	1,600	2,100	2,700
F5B Big Horn (350cc single)	400	500	800	1,100	1,400	1,800
H1 Mach III (498cc triple)	1,400	2,100	3,150	4,200	5,600	7,000
W1SS (624cc twin)	1,200	2,000	3,200	4,100	5,000	6,000
1972						
GA1A (90cc single)	300	400	600	800	1,000	1,300
GA2A (90cc single)	300	400	600	800	1,000	1,300
G3SS (90cc single)	200	400	500	700	1,000	1,200
GA5A (100cc single)	300	400	600	800	1,100	1,400
G4TRB Trail Boss (100cc single)	300	400	600	800	1,100	1,400
G5 (100cc single)	200	400	500	700	1,000	1,200
B1LA (125cc single)	200	400	500	700	1,000	1,200
F6A (125cc single)	300	400	600	800	1,000	1,300
F7A (175cc single)	300	500	700	900	1,200	1,500
S1 Mach I (249cc triple)	**800**	**1,200**	**1,600**	**2,500**	**3,200**	**4,000**
F8A Bison (250cc single)	400	600	900	1,200	1,600	2,000
F11 (250cc single)	400	500	800	1,100	1,400	1,800
F9 Big Horn (350cc single)	300	500	700	1,000	1,300	1,600
S2 Mach II (350cc triple)	400	600	3,000	4,000	5,000	6,000
H1B Mach III (498cc triple)	800	1,500	2,400	3,100	3,800	4,500
H2 Mach IV (750cc triple)	2,500	4,000	6,000	8,000	11,000	14,000
1973						
GA1A (90cc single)	200	400	500	700	1,000	1,200
GA2A (90cc single)	200	400	500	700	1,000	1,200
G3SS (90cc single)	200	400	500	700	1,000	1,200
GA5A (100cc single)	300	400	600	800	1,000	1,300
G4TRC Trail Boss (100cc single)	300	400	600	800	1,100	1,400
G7S (100cc single)	200	400	500	700	1,000	1,200
G7T (100cc single)	200	400	500	700	1,000	1,200
B1LA (125cc single)	200	400	500	700	1,000	1,200
F6B (125cc single)	300	400	600	800	1,000	1,300
F7B (175cc single)	300	400	600	800	1,000	1,300
S1A Mach I (249cc triple)	**800**	**1,200**	**1,600**	**2,500**	**3,200**	**4,000**
F11 (250cc single)	400	600	900	1,100	1,500	1,900
F9A Big Horn (350cc single)	400	600	900	1,200	1,600	2,000
S2A Mach II (350cc triple)	500	700	1,000	1,500	2,000	2,500

	6	5	4	3	2	1
F12MX (450cc single)	300	500	800	1,000	1,400	1,700
H1D Mach III (498cc triple)	800	1,500	**3,000**	**4,000**	**5,000**	**6,000**
H2A Mach IV (750cc triple)	1,500	2,000	4,000	6,000	9,000	13,000
Z2 (750cc four)	2,000	5,000	10,000	15,000	20,000	25,000
Z1 (903cc four) (20,000)	4,000	5,000	8,000	12,000	15,000	18,000
1974						
GA1A (90cc single)	200	300	500	700	900	1,100
GA2A (90cc single)	200	300	500	700	900	1,100
G2S (90cc single)	200	400	500	700	1,000	1,200
G2T (90cc single)	200	400	500	700	1,000	1,200
G3SS (90cc single)	200	400	500	700	1,000	1,200
GA5A (100cc single)	300	400	600	800	1,000	1,300
G4TRD Trail Boss (100cc single)	300	400	600	800	1,100	1,400
G5B (100cc single)	200	500	800	1,200	1,600	2,000
G7S (100cc single)	200	400	500	700	1,000	1,200
G7T (100cc single)	200	400	500	700	1,000	1,200
B1LA (125cc single)	300	400	600	800	1,000	1,300
KS125 (125cc single)	200	300	500	700	900	1,100
S1B Mach I (249cc triple)	800	1,200	1,600	2,500	3,200	4,000
F11A (250cc single)	400	600	900	1,100	1,500	1,900
KX250 (250cc single)	400	600	900	1,200	1,600	2,000
F9B Big Horn (350cc single)	400	600	900	1,200	1,600	2,000
KZ400D (400cc twin)	400	600	900	1,100	1,500	1,900
S3 (400cc triple)	800	1,200	1,600	2,500	3,200	4,000
KX450 (450cc single)	400	600	900	1,100	1,600	2,100
H1E Mach III (498cc triple)	800	1,500	**3,000**	**4,000**	**5,000**	**6,000**
H2B Mach IV (750cc triple)	1,500	2,000	4,000	7,000	9,000	12,000
Z2A (750cc four)	1,500	4,000	8,000	12,000	16,000	20,000
Z1A (903cc four) (27,500)	2,800	4,200	6,600	8,200	12,000	14,000
1975						
GA1A (90cc single)	200	300	400	500	700	900
G2T (90cc single)	200	300	400	500	700	900
G3SSE (100cc single)	200	300	500	600	800	1,000
G3T (100cc single)	200	300	500	600	800	1,000
G4TRE Trail Boss (100cc single)	200	300	500	600	800	1,000
G5C (100cc single)	200	300	500	700	900	1,100
G7SA (100cc single)	200	300	500	700	900	1,100
G7TA (100cc single)	200	300	500	700	900	1,100
B1LA (125cc single)	200	400	500	700	1,000	1,200
KD125 (125cc single)	200	300	500	600	800	1,000
KS125A (125cc single)	200	300	500	600	800	1,000
KX125A (125cc single)	200	300	500	700	900	1,100
KD175-A1 (175cc single)	200	400	500	700	1,000	1,200
KD250B1-Mach 1 (249cc triple)	**800**	**1,200**	**1,600**	**2,500**	**3,200**	**4,000**
KT250 (250cc triple)	500	700	**1,000**	**1,500**	**2,000**	**2,500**
KX250-A3 (250cc single)	300	400	600	800	1,000	1,300
KZ400D (398cc twin)	300	400	600	800	1,000	1,300
KZ400S (398cc twin)	300	500	700	900	1,200	1,500
KH400-A3 (400cc triple)	800	1,200	1,600	2,500	3,200	4,000
KX400 (400cc single)	300	500	800	1,000	1,400	1,700
KH500-AB Mach III (498cc triple)	800	1,200	**2,000**	**3,000**	**4,000**	**5,000**
H2C (750cc triple)	1,500	2,000	4,000	7,000	9,000	12,000
Z2B (750cc four)	1,500	4,000	8,000	12,000	16,000	20,000
Z1B (903cc four) (38,200)	2,700	4,000	6,000	8,000	11,000	13,000
1976						
G2T (90cc single)	200	300	400	500	700	900
G3T (100cc single)	200	300	400	500	700	900
G7TA (100cc single)	200	300	500	600	800	1,000

	6	5	4	3	2	1
KE100-A5 (100cc single)	200	300	500	700	900	1,200
KH100-B7 (100cc single)	200	300	500	700	900	1,100
B1LA (125cc single)	200	300	500	700	900	1,100
KD125 (125cc single)	200	300	500	600	800	1,000
KE125-A3 (125cc single)	200	300	500	600	800	1,000
KX125-A3 (125cc single)	200	300	500	600	800	1,000
KD175-A1 (175cc single)	200	400	500	700	1,000	1,200
KE175-B1 (175cc single)	200	400	500	700	1,000	1,200
KH250-A5 (249cc triple)	800	1,200	1,600	2,500	3,200	4,000
KT250 (250cc single)	300	500	1,000	1,500	2,000	2,500
KX250-A3 (250cc single)	200	400	500	700	1,000	1,200
KX400 (398cc single)	300	500	800	1,000	1,400	1,700
KX400-A2 (398cc single)	300	400	600	800	1,000	1,300
KZ400D3 (398cc twin)	300	500	700	900	1,200	1,600
KZ400S2 (398cc twin)	300	500	700	900	1,200	1,600
KH500-A8 (498cc triple)	700	1,000	2,000	3,000	4,000	5,000
KZ750-B1 (750cc twin)	400	600	900	1,200	1,600	2,000
Z750-A4 (750cc four)	1,500	4,000	8,000	12,000	16,000	20,000
KZ900-A4 (903cc four)	1,000	2,000	4,000	5,500	7,000	8,500
KZ900-B1LTD (903cc four)	1,200	2,000	3,000	4,500	6,000	7,000
1977						
KC90-C1 (90cc single)	200	300	400	500	700	900
KE100-A6 (100cc single)	200	300	500	700	900	1,200
KH100-A2 (100cc single)	200	300	500	600	800	1,000
KH100-B8 (100cc single)	200	300	500	600	800	1,000
KH100-C1 (100cc single)	200	300	500	600	800	1,000
KH100-E1ES (100cc single)	200	300	500	600	800	1,000
KC125-A6 (125cc single)	200	300	500	600	800	1,000
KD125-A2 (125cc single)	200	300	500	600	800	1,000
KE125-A4 (125cc single)	200	300	500	600	800	1,000
KH125-A1 (125cc single)	200	300	500	600	800	1,000
KD175-A1 (175cc single)	200	300	500	700	900	1,100
KE175-B2 (175cc single)	200	300	500	700	900	1,100
KZ200 (200cc single)	200	300	500	600	800	1,000
KH250-B2 Mach 1 (249cc triple)	600	900	1,200	2,000	2,700	3,500
KE250-B1 (250cc single)	300	400	600	800	1,000	1,300
KH400-A4 (398cc triple)	600	900	1,200	2,000	2,700	3,500
KZ400-A1 (398cc twin)	300	500	700	900	1,200	1,600
KZ400-D4 (398cc twin)	300	500	700	900	1,200	1,600
KZ400-S3 (398cc twin)	200	400	500	700	1,000	1,200
KZ650 (652cc four)	500	700	1,000	1,400	1,800	2,200
KZ650-B1 (652cc four)	500	700	1,000	1,400	1,800	2,200
KZ750-B2 (750cc twin)	400	500	800	1,100	1,400	1,800
Z750-A5 (750cc four)	1,500	4,000	8,000	12,000	16,000	20,000
KZ900-A5 (903cc four)	1,000	1,500	2,200	2,900	3,600	4,500
KZ1000-A1 (1,015cc four)	1,000	2,000	4,000	5,500	7,000	8,500
KZ1000-B1LTD (1,015cc four)	1,000	1,500	2,200	2,900	3,600	4,500
1978						
KE100-A7 (100cc single)	200	300	500	700	900	1,200
KD125-A2 (125cc single)	200	300	500	600	800	1,000
KE125-A5 (125cc single)	200	300	500	700	900	1,100
KH125-A2 (125cc single)	200	300	500	600	800	1,000
KX125-A3 (125cc single)	200	300	500	600	800	1,000
KD175-A1 (175cc single)	200	300	500	700	900	1,100
KE175-B3 (175cc single)	200	300	500	700	900	1,100
KE250-B2 (250cc single)	300	400	600	800	1,000	1,300
KL250-A1 (250cc single)	200	300	500	700	900	1,100
KX250 (250cc single)	200	300	500	700	900	1,100

	6	5	4	3	2	1
KH400-A5 (398cc triple).	500	700	1,000	1,400	1,800	2,200
KZ400-A2 (398cc twin)	300	500	700	900	1,200	1,600
KZ400-B1 (398cc twin)	300	500	700	900	1,200	1,500
KZ400-C1 (398cc twin)	200	400	500	700	1,000	1,200
KZ650-B2 (652cc four)	400	600	900	1,200	1,600	2,000
KZ650-C2 (652cc four)	400	600	900	1,100	1,600	2,100
KZ650-D1SR (652cc four).	500	600	700	1,200	1,800	2,400
KZ750-B3 (750cc twin)	400	500	800	1,100	1,400	1,800
Z750-D1 (750cc four)	1,500	4,000	8,000	12,000	16,000	20,000
KZ1000-A2 (1,015cc four).	1,000	1,500	**3,000**	**4,000**	**5,500**	**7,000**
KZ1000-D1Z1R (1,015cc four)	1,000	2,000	4,000	6,000	8,000	10,000
KZ1000-D1Z1R Turbo (1,015cc four)	1,500	3,000	6,000	9,000	12,000	15,000
1979						
KE100-A8 (100cc single)	200	300	500	**700**	**900**	**1,200**
KM100-A4 (100cc single)	200	300	500	700	900	1,100
KD125-A2 (125cc single)	200	300	500	600	800	1,000
KE125-A6 (125cc single)	200	300	500	600	800	1,000
KX125-A3 (125cc single)	200	300	500	600	800	1,000
KD175-A4 (175cc single)	200	300	500	600	800	1,000
KZ200-A2 (200cc single)	200	300	500	600	800	1,000
KE250-B3 (250cc single)	200	300	500	700	900	1,100
KL250-A2 (250cc single)	200	300	500	700	900	1,100
KX250 (250cc single)	300	400	600	800	1,000	1,300
KDX400 (398cc single)	300	400	600	800	1,100	1,400
KZ400-B2 (398cc twin)	300	500	700	900	1,200	1,500
KZ650-B3 (652cc four)	400	600	900	1,200	1,600	2,000
KZ650-C3 (652cc four)	400	600	900	1,100	1,600	2,100
KZ650-D2 (652cc four)	500	700	1,100	1,400	1,900	2,400
KZ750-B4 (750cc twin)	200	300	500	700	900	1,100
KZ1000-A3 (1,015cc four).	500	700	1,100	1,400	1,900	2,400
KZ1000-B3LTD (1,015cc four)	600	900	1,400	1,800	2,240	3,000
KZ1000-E1 (1,015cc four)	600	800	1,300	1,700	2,300	2,800
KZ1300-A1 (1,286cc six)	700	1,000	1,500	3,000	4,000	5,000
1980						
KE100-A9 (100cc single)	200	300	400	**700**	**900**	**1,200**
KE125-A7 (125cc single)	200	300	400	500	700	900
KX125-A6 (125cc single)	200	300	400	500	700	900
KDX175-A1 (175cc single)	200	300	500	600	800	1,000
KD175-D2 (175cc single)	200	300	500	600	800	1,000
KZ250-A1 (249cc twin)	300	400	600	800	1,100	1,400
KDX250-A1 (250cc single)	200	300	500	700	900	1,100
KL250-A3 (250cc single)	200	300	500	700	900	1,100
KLX250-A2 (250cc single).	200	300	500	700	900	1,100
KX250-A6 (250cc single)	200	300	500	700	900	1,100
KDX400-A2 (398cc single)	300	400	600	800	1,100	1,400
KX400 (398cc single)	300	500	700	900	1,200	1,500
KX420-A1 (420cc single)	300	500	700	900	1,200	1,500
KZ440-A1 (443cc twin)	300	500	700	1,000	1,300	1,600
KZ440-B1 (443cc twin)	300	500	700	1,000	1,300	1,600
KZ440-D1 (443cc twin)	300	500	700	1,000	1,300	1,600
KZ550-A1 (553cc four)	200	300	400	500	700	900
KZ550-C1 (553cc four)	200	300	400	500	700	900
KZ650-E1LTD (652cc four)	200	300	500	600	800	1,000
KZ650-F1 (652cc four)	200	300	500	600	800	1,000
KZ750-E1 (739cc four)	200	400	500	700	1,000	1,200
KZ750-G1LTD (739cc four)	200	400	500	700	1,000	1,200
KZ750-H1 (739cc four)	200	400	500	700	1,000	1,200
KZ1000-B3LTD (1,015cc four)	600	800	1,500	2,000	2,500	3,000

	6	5	4	3	2	1
KZ1000-D3Z1R (1,015cc four)	600	800	1,300	1,700	2,300	2,800
KZ1000-E3 Shaft (1,015cc four)	600	900	1,400	1,900	2,500	3,100
KZ1000-G1 Classic (1,015cc four)	600	900	1,300	2,000	3,000	4,000
KZ1300-A2 (1,286cc six)	700	1,000	1,500	3,000	4,000	5,000
KZ1300-B2 (1,286cc six)	700	1,000	1,500	3,000	4,000	5,000
1981						
KZ250-D2 CSR (250cc single)	200	300	500	800	1,000	1,300
KZ305-A1 CSR (305cc twin)	200	400	600	900	1,200	1,500
KZ440-B2 STD (440cc twin)	300	500	800	1,000	1,300	1,600
KZ440-A2 LTD (440cc twin)	300	500	800	1,200	1,500	1,900
KZ440-D2 LTD (440cc twin)	300	500	800	1,100	1,500	1,900
KZ550-A2 STD (550cc four)	300	500	800	1,300	1,800	2,300
KZ550-C2 LTD (550cc four)	300	500	800	1,300	1,800	2,400
KZ550-D1 GPZ (550cc four)	500	700	1,100	1,600	2,100	2,600
KZ650-H1 CSR (650cc four)	500	700	1,000	1,400	1,800	2,200
KZ750-E2 STD (750cc four)	500	800	1,100	1,700	2,300	2,900
KZ750-H2 LTD (750cc four)	400	600	1,000	1,600	2,300	3,000
KZ1000-M1 CSR (1,000cc four)	600	900	1,300	2,100	2,900	3,700
KZ1000-K1 LTD (1,000cc four)	800	1,100	1,600	2,200	3,000	3,900
KZ1100-M1 (1,100cc four)	600	800	1,200	2,000	2,800	3,700
KZ1100-J1 STD (1,100cc four)	600	900	1,300	2,100	2,900	3,800
KZ1100-A1 (1,100cc four)	600	900	1,300	2,200	3,100	4,000
KZ1100-B1 GP (1,100cc four)	1,100	1,400	1,900	2,800	3,600	4,400
KZ1300-A3 (1,300cc six)	1,100	1,400	1,900	3,000	4,000	5,000
1982						
AR50-A1 Mini GP (50cc single)	200	300	500	600	700	800
AR80-A1 Mini GP (80cc single)	200	300	500	600	800	900
KZ250-L1 CSR (250cc single)	200	300	600	800	1,100	1,400
KZ305-A2 CSR (305cc twin)	200	400	700	900	1,200	1,500
KZ305-B1 CSR (305cc twin)	200	400	700	1,000	1,300	1,600
KZ440-G1 Sports (440cc twin)	300	500	800	1,100	1,400	1,800
KZ440-A3 LTD (440cc twin)	300	500	800	1,200	1,500	1,900
KZ440-D4 LTD (440cc twin)	300	500	800	1,200	1,600	2,000
KZ550-A3 Sports (550cc four)	300	500	800	1,300	1,800	2,400
KZ550-C3 LTD (550cc four)	300	500	800	1,400	1,900	2,500
KZ550-H1 GPZ (550cc four)	500	700	1,100	1,600	2,100	2,700
KZ650-H2 CSR (650cc four)	500	700	1,100	1,400	1,800	2,200
KZ750-E3 Sports (750cc four)	500	800	1,100	1,700	2,300	3,000
KZ750-H3 LTD (750cc four)	400	600	1,000	1,700	2,400	3,100
KZ750-M1 CSR Twin (750cc twin)	400	600	1,000	1,400	1,800	2,300
KZ750-R1 GPZ (750cc four)	700	1,000	1,400	2,000	2,600	3,300
KZ750-N1 Spectre (750cc four)	500	700	1,100	1,800	2,600	3,400
KZ1000-M2 CSR (1,000cc four)	700	1,000	1,400	1,800	2,600	3,500
KZ1000-J2 Sports (1,000cc four)	700	1,000	1,400	2,100	2,900	3,700
KZ1000-K2 LTD (1,000cc four)	1,000	1,300	1,800	2,500	3,200	3,900
KZ1000-R1 (1,000cc four)	2,000	2,400	3,100	3,400	4,000	4,400
KZ1100-A2 Sports (1,100cc four)	700	1,000	1,300	2,100	3,100	4,100
KZ1100-D1 Spectre (1,100cc four)	700	1,000	1,500	2,400	3,300	4,300
KZ1100-B2 GPZ (1,100cc four)	1,100	1,400	2,000	2,800	3,600	4,400
KZ1300-A4 Sports (1,300cc six)	1,200	1,600	2,100	3,100	4,100	5,200
1983						
KZ250-W1 LTD (250cc single)	300	500	700	1,000	1,500	2,000
EX305-B1 GPZ (305cc twin)	200	400	700	1,000	1,300	1,800
KZ440-D5 LTD (440cc twin)	500	700	1,000	1,500	2,000	2,500
KZ550-A4 Sports (550cc four)	400	600	800	1,300	1,800	2,400
KZ550-C4 LTD (550cc four)	300	500	800	1,300	1,900	2,500
KZ550-M1 LTD (550cc four)	400	700	900	1,400	2,000	2,600
KZ550-F1 Spectre (550cc four)	400	600	900	1,500	2,100	2,700
KZ550-H2 GPZ (550cc four)	500	700	1,100	1,600	2,200	2,800

	6	5	4	3	2	1
KZ650-H3 CSR (650cc four)	500	700	1,100	1,500	2,000	2,500
KZ750-K1 LTD (750cc four)	400	600	1,000	1,400	1,900	2,400
KZ750-I4 LTD (750cc four)	500	700	1,000	1,700	2,400	3,100
KZ750-L3 Sports (750cc four)	500	700	1,100	1,700	2,400	3,100
KZ750-F1 LTD (750cc four)	500	700	1,100	1,700	2,400	3,200
KZ750-N2 Spectre (750cc four)	500	700	1,100	1,800	2,600	3,400
ZX750-A1 GPZ (750cc four)	700	1,000	1,400	2,000	2,700	3,400
KZ1000-R2 Replica (1000cc four)	2,000	2,400	3,200	3,500	3,800	4,200
KZ1100-A3 (1,100cc four)	600	900	1,400	2,300	3,200	4,100
KZ1100-L1 LTD (1,100cc four)	700	1,000	1,500	2,300	3,200	4,100
KZ1100-D2 Spectre (1,100cc four)	800	1,000	1,600	2,500	3,400	4,300
ZX1100-A1 GPZ (1,100cc four)	1,100	1,500	2,000	2,800	3,600	4,500
ZN1300-A Voyager (1,300cc six)	1,900	2,300	3,050	4,200	5,600	7,000
1984						
KZ550-F2 LTD (550cc four)	400	600	900	1,500	2,100	2,800
ZX550-A1 GPZ (550cc four)	500	800	1,100	1,700	2,300	2,900
KZ700-A1 Sports (700cc four)	500	800	1,100	1,800	2,400	3,000
ZN700-A1 LTD (700cc four)	800	1,100	1,500	2,100	2,600	3,100
ZX750-A2 GPZ (750cc four)	700	1,000	1,400	2,200	2,900	3,700
ZX750-E1 Turbo (750cc four)	1,300	1,700	2,300	3,500	4,200	4,800
ZX900-A1 Ninja (900cc four)	800	1,100	1,600	2,500	3,400	4,400
KZ1000-P3 Police (1,000cc four)	800	1,100	1,500	2,500	3,500	4,500
ZN1100-B1 LTD (1,100cc four)	700	1,000	1,400	2,400	3,400	4,400
ZX1100-A2 GPZ (1,100cc four)	1,100	1,500	2,000	2,800	3,900	4,800
ZN1300-A2 Voyager (1,300cc six)	1,000	1,300	3,100	4,200	5,600	7,000
1985						
KX60-B1 (60cc single)	200	400	600	700	800	900
KDX80-C2 (80cc single)	200	400	500	600	700	800
KX80-E3 (80cc single)	200	400	700	800	900	1,100
KX125-D1 (125cc single)	300	500	800	1,200	1,600	2,000
KDX200-A3 (200cc single)	300	500	800	1,100	1,400	1,800
KL250-D2 KLR (250cc single)	300	500	800	1,200	1,600	2,000
KX250-D1 (250cc single)	400	600	900	1,500	2,000	2,500
EN450-A1 454 LTD (450cc twin)	700	900	1,200	1,400	1,700	2,000
KX500-B1 (500cc single)	400	600	900	1,500	2,100	2,700
ZX550-A2 GPZ (550cc four)	500	800	**1,400**	**2,100**	**2,800**	**3,500**
KL600-B1 KLR (600cc single)	400	600	900	1,500	2,000	2,500
ZX600-A1 Ninja R (600cc four)	600	900	1,300	2,000	2,600	3,300
ZN700-A2 LTD (700cc four)	700	1,100	1,500	2,000	2,600	3,100
VN700-A1 Vulcan (700cc twin)	800	1,100	1,600	2,100	2,700	3,300
ZX750-A3 GPZ (750cc four)	700	1,000	1,400	2,100	2,800	3,500
ZX750-E2 Turbo (750cc four)	1,400	2,000	2,800	3,500	4,000	5,000
XL900-A1 Eliminator (900cc four)	1,300	1,700	2,400	3,100	3,800	4,500
ZX900-A2 Ninja (900cc four)	900	1,200	1,600	2,600	3,600	4,600
ZN1100-B2 LTD (1,100cc four)	700	1,000	1,400	2,400	3,400	4,550
ZN1300-A3 Voyager (1,300cc six)	1,000	1,300	3,100	4,200	5,600	7,000
1986						
KX60-B2 Mini (60cc single)	200	400	600	700	800	900
KD80-M7 (80cc single)	200	300	400	500	600	700
KDX80-C3 Mini (80cc single)	200	400	600	700	800	900
KX80-G1 Mini (80cc single)	200	400	700	800	1,000	1,100
KE100-B5 (100cc single)	200	400	700	800	900	1,000
KX125-E1 (125cc single)	400	600	900	1,300	1,700	2,100
KDX200-C1 (200cc single)	300	500	800	1,100	1,500	1,900
EX250-E1 Ninja (250cc twin)	500	800	1,100	1,500	1,900	2,300
KL250-D3 KLR (250cc single)	400	600	900	1,300	1,700	2,100
KX250-D2 (250cc single)	500	700	1,000	1,500	2,000	2,600
EN450-A2 454 LTD (450cc twin)	600	900	1,300	1,600	1,900	2,200
KX500-B2 (500cc single)	500	700	1,000	1,600	2,200	2,800

	6	5	4	3	2	1
KL600-B2 KLR (560cc single).	400	600	1,000	1,500	2,000	2,600
ZL600-A1 (600cc four).	700	1,000	1,400	2,100	2,800	3,500
ZX600-A2 Ninja R (600cc four).	700	1,000	1,400	2,100	2,800	3,600
VN750-A2 Vulcan (750cc twin)	1,100	1,500	2,100	2,500	3,000	3,500
ZL900-A2 Eliminator (900cc four).	1,400	1,800	2,400	3,000	3,500	4,500
ZX900-A3 Ninja (900cc four)	900	1,300	1,700	2,800	3,800	4,800
ZX1000-A1 Ninja R (1,000cc four)	1,200	1,600	2,100	3,200	4,200	5,200
ZG1000-A1 Concours (1,000cc four) . . .	1,200	1,600	2,100	3,300	4,400	5,700
ZG1200-A1 Voyager XII (1,200cc four) . .	1,900	2,400	3,200	4,200	5,600	7,000
ZN1300-A4 Voyager (1,300cc six)	1,900	2,400	3,200	4,200	5,600	7,000
1987						
KX60-B3 (60cc single)	200	400	700	800	900	1,000
KD80-M8 (80cc single)	200	400	600	700	800	900
KDX80-C4 (80cc single).	200	400	700	800	900	1,000
KX80-G2 (80cc single).	300	500	700	900	1,000	1,200
KX80-J2 (80cc single).	300	500	800	900	1,100	1,300
KE100-B6 (100cc single)	200	400	700	800	900	1,000
KX125-E2 (125cc single)	400	600	1,000	1,400	1,800	2,300
KDX200-C2 (200cc single)	300	500	900	1,300	1,700	2,100
EX250-E2 Ninja (250cc twin)	500	800	1,200	1,600	2,000	2,400
KL250D4 KLR (250cc single)	400	600	1,000	1,400	1,800	2,300
KX250-E1 (250cc single)	500	700	1,100	1,700	2,300	2,900
KZ305-B2 LTD (305cc twin).	500	700	1,000	1,300	1,600	1,900
EN450-A3 454 LTD (450cc twin)	600	900	1,300	1,700	2,100	2,500
EX500-A1 (500cc four)	600	900	1,300	1,800	2,300	2,900
KX500-C1 (500cc single)	500	700	1,100	1,700	2,300	3,000
ZL600-A2 (600cc four)	700	1,000	1,400	2,100	2,800	3,500
ZX600-A3 Ninja R (600cc four)	700	1,000	1,500	2,200	3,000	3,800
ZX600-B1 Ninja RX (600cc four)	700	1,000	1,500	2,300	3,100	4,000
KL650-A1 KLR (650cc single).	500	700	1,000	1,700	2,300	3,000
VN750-A3 Vulcan (750cc twin)	1,200	1,600	2,100	2,600	3,200	3,800
ZX750-F1 Ninja R (750cc four)	900	1,200	1,700	2,700	3,800	4,800
ZG1000-A2 Concours (1,000cc four) . . .	1,200	1,600	2,200	3,500	4,900	6,300
ZL1000-A1 (1,000cc four).	1,400	1,900	2,500	3,300	4,100	4,900
ZX1000-A2 Ninja R (1,000cc four)	1,300	1,700	2,200	3,300	4,500	5,700
ZG1200-B1 Voyager XII (1,200cc four) . .	1,900	2,400	3,200	4,200	5,600	7,000
ZN1300-A5 Voyager (1,300cc six)	1,900	2,400	3,200	4,300	5,700	7,200
VN1500-A1 Vulcan 88 (1,500cc twin) . . .	1,300	1,700	2,300	3,400	4,700	5,900
VN1500-B1 Vulcan 88SE (1,500cc twin) . .	1,300	1,700	2,300	3,400	4,700	5,900
1988						
KX60-B4 (60cc single)	200	400	700	900	1,000	1,200
KD80-N1 (80cc single)	200	400	700	800	900	1,000
KDX80-C5 Mini (80cc single)	200	400	700	900	1,000	1,200
KX80-L1 (80cc single).	300	500	800	1,000	1,200	1,400
KX80-N1 (80cc single).	300	500	800	1,000	1,200	1,500
KE100-B7 (100cc single)	300	500	800	900	1,000	1,100
KX125-F1 (125cc single)	500	700	1,000	1,500	2,000	2,500
KDX200-C3 (200cc single)	400	600	900	1,300	1,800	2,200
EL250-B2 Eliminator (250cc twin).	500	800	1,100	1,500	2,000	2,400
EX250-F2 Ninja R (250c twin).	600	800	1,200	1,800	2,300	2,800
KL250-D5 KLR (250cc single).	500	700	1,000	1,500	2,000	2,500
KX250-F1 (250cc single)	500	800	1,200	1,800	2,400	3,100
KZ305-B3 LTD (305cc twin).	500	700	1,000	1,300	1,600	1,900
EN450-A4 454 LTD (450cc twin)	600	900	1,300	1,800	2,200	2,600
EX500-A2 (500cc twin)	600	900	1,300	1,900	2,500	3,100
KX500-D1 (500cc single)	500	800	1,200	1,800	2,500	3,200
ZX600-C1 Ninja R (600cc four)	900	1,200	1,700	2,400	3,200	4,000
KL650-A2 KLR (650cc single).	500	800	1,100	1,700	2,400	3,100

	6	5	4	3	2	1
VN750-A4 Vulcan (750cc twin)	1,200	1,600	2,200	2,800	3,400	4,000
ZX750-F2 Ninja R (750cc four)	1,000	1,300	1,800	3,000	4,000	5,000
ZX1000-B1 Ninja ZX10 (1,000cc four) . . .	1,300	1,800	2,400	3,600	4,800	6,000
ZG1000-A3 Concours (1,000cc four) . . .	1,300	1,700	2,300	3,800	5,300	6,600
ZG1200-B2 Voyager XII (1,200cc four) . . .	2,000	2,500	3,300	4,600	5,900	7,200
ZN1300-A6 Voyager (1,300cc six)	2,000	2,500	3,300	4,700	6,000	7,400
VN1500-A2 Vulcan 88 (1,500cc twin)	1,300	1,800	2,400	3,700	4,900	6,200
VN1500-B2 Vulcan 88SE (1,500cc twin) . .	1,300	1,800	2,400	3,700	4,900	6,200
1989						
KX60 (60cc single)	300	500	800	1,000	1,200	1,500
KD80-N2 (80cc single)	200	400	500	900	1,000	1,200
KD80X Mini (80cc single)	200	400	700	900	1,000	1,200
KX80-L2 (80cc single).	300	500	800	1,200	1,500	1,800
KX80-N2 (80cc single).	300	500	800	1,200	1,500	1,900
KE100-B8 (100cc single)	300	500	800	1,000	1,100	1,300
KX125-G1 (125cc single)	500	800	1,100	1,800	2,400	3,000
KDX200-E1 (200cc single)	400	600	1,000	1,500	2,100	2,700
EL250-B3 Eliminator (250cc twin)	500	800	1,200	1,700	2,200	2,700
EX250-F3 (250cc twin)	600	900	1,300	1,900	2,600	3,300
KL250-D6 KLR (250cc single).	500	700	1,100	1,600	2,200	2,800
KX250-G1 (250cc single)	600	900	1,300	2,000	2,800	3,600
EN450-A45 454 LTD (450cc twin).	600	900	1,300	1,900	2,500	3,100
EX500-A3 (500cc twin)	700	1,000	1,300	1,900	2,600	3,300
KX500-E1 (500cc single)	600	900	1,300	2,100	2,900	3,800
ZX600-C2 Ninja R (600cc four)	900	1,300	1,700	2,600	3,500	4,400
KL650-A3 KLR (650cc single).	500	800	1,300	1,900	2,700	3,500
VN750-A5 Vulcan (750cc twin)	1,300	1,700	2,200	2,900	3,600	4,300
ZX750-F3 Ninja R (750cc four)	1,000	1,400	1,900	3,000	4,100	5,200
ZX750-H1 Ninja ZX7 (750cc four)	1,500	1,900	2,500	3,800	5,000	6,200
ZX1000-B2 Ninja ZX10 (1,000cc four) . . .	1,500	1,900	2,500	3,800	5,000	6,200
ZG1200 Voyager XII (1,200cc four) . . .	2,100	2,600	3,500	4,700	6,000	7,400
VN1500-A3 Vulcan 88 (1,500cc twin)	1,500	1,900	2,500	3,800	5,000	6,300
1990						
KX60-B6 (60cc single)	300	500	800	1,100	1,300	1,600
KX80-L3 (80cc single).	300	500	900	1,200	1,500	1,900
KX80-N3 (80cc single).	400	600	900	1,200	1,600	2,000
KE100-B9 (100cc single)	300	500	800	1,000	1,100	1,300
KX125-H1 (125cc single)	500	800	1,200	1,900	2,500	3,200
KDX200-E2 (200cc single)	500	700	1,100	1,600	2,200	2,800
EX250-F4 Ninja R (250cc twin)	600	900	1,300	2,000	2,700	3,400
KL250-D7 KLR (250cc single).	500	800	1,200	1,700	2,300	2,900
KX250-H1 (250cc single)	700	1,000	1,400	2,200	3,000	3,900
EN450-A6 454 LTD (450cc twin)	700	1,000	1,400	1,900	2,500	3,100
EX500-A4 (500cc twin)	700	1,100	1,500	2,200	2,800	3,400
EN500-A1 Vulcan (500cc twin)	900	1,300	1,800	2,400	3,000	3,700
KX500-E2 (500cc single)	700	1,000	1,400	2,200	3,100	4,000
ZR550-B1 Zephyr (550cc four)	900	1,200	1,700	2,400	3,200	4,000
ZX600-C3 Ninja R (600cc four)	900	1,300	1,800	2,500	3,300	4,500
ZX600-D1 Ninja ZX6 (600cc four)	1,200	1,700	2,300	3,300	4,400	5,500
KL650-A4 KLR (650cc single).	600	900	1,300	2,000	2,800	3,600
KL650-B2 Tengai (650cc single)	600	900	1,300	2,200	3,000	3,900
VN750-A6 Vulcan (750cc twin)	1,200	1,700	2,300	3,000	3,700	4,500
ZX750-F4 Ninja R (750cc four)	1,100	1,500	2,000	3,100	4,200	5,400
ZX750-H2 Ninja ZX7 (750cc four). . . .	1,500	2,000	2,700	4,000	5,200	6,400
KZ1000 Police (1,000cc four)	900	1,300	1,800	3,000	4,000	5,000
ZG1000-A5 Concours (1,000cc four)	1,300	1,800	2,400	3,900	5,400	6,800
ZX1000-B3 Ninja ZX10 (1,000cc four) . . .	1,500	2,000	2,700	4,000	5,300	6,600
ZX1100-C1 Ninja ZX11 (1,100cc four) . . .	1,800	2,300	3,000	4,500	6,000	7,600

	6	5	4	3	2	1
ZG1200 Voyager XII (1,200cc four)	2,000	2,700	3,500	4,700	6,000	7,600
VN1500-B4 Vulcan 88SE (1,500cc twin) . .	1,300	1,900	2,600	3,900	5,200	6,400
VN1500A4 Vulcan 88 (1,500cc twin)	1,300	1,900	2,600	3,900	5,200	6,500
1991						
KX60-B7 (60cc single)	300	500	900	1,100	1,300	1,600
KX80-R1 (80cc single)	400	600	900	1,400	1,700	2,000
KX80-T1 (80cc single).	400	650	900	1,300	1,700	2,100
KE100-B10 (100cc single).	400	600	900	1,000	1,200	1,400
KX125-H2 (125cc single)	600	900	1,300	2,000	2,700	3,300
KDX200-E3 (200cc single)	500	800	1,100	1,700	2,300	2,900
EL250-E1 250HS (250cc twin)	500	800	1,200	1,800	2,400	3,000
KDX250-D1 (250cc single)	500	800	1,200	2,100	3,000	4,000
KL250-D8 KLR (250cc single).	600	900	1,300	1,800	2,300	2,900
KX250-H2 (250cc single)	700	1,000	1,500	2,300	3,100	4,000
EX500-A5 (500cc twin)	800	1,100	1,600	2,200	2,800	3,500
EN500-A2 Vulcan (500cc twin)	1,000	1,400	1,900	2,500	3,100	3,700
KX500-E3 (500cc single)	700	1,100	1,500	2,400	3,200	4,000
ZR550-B2 Zephyr (550cc four)	1,000	1,300	1,800	2,500	3,200	4,000
ZX600-C4 Ninja R (600cc four)	1,000	1,400	1,900	2,800	3,800	4,700
ZX600-D2 Ninja ZX6 (600cc four).	1,300	1,800	2,400	3,500	4,600	5,600
KL650-A5 KLR (650cc single).	700	1,000	1,400	2,100	2,800	3,600
VN750-A7 Vulcan (750cc twin)	1,300	1,800	2,400	3,100	3,800	4,600
ZR750-C1 Zephyr (750cc four)	1,000	1,300	1,900	2,800	3,700	4,700
ZX750-J1 Ninja ZX7 (750cc four)	1,600	2,100	2,800	4,200	5,600	7,000
ZX750-K1 Ninja ZX7R (750cc four)	1,800	2,300	3,100	5,000	7,000	9,000
KZ1000 Police (1,000cc four)	1,100	1,500	2,000	3,000	4,000	5,000
ZG1000-A6 Concours (1,000cc four)	1,300	1,800	2,500	3,900	5,300	6,900
ZX1100-C2 Ninja ZX11 (1,100cc four) . . .	1,900	2,400	3,200	4,800	6,400	8,000
ZG1200 Voyager XII (1,200cc four)	2,000	2,700	3,600	5,000	6,300	7,700
VN1500-A5 Vulcan 88 (1,500cc twin)	1,500	2,000	2,700	3,900	5,400	6,600
1992						
KX60-B8 (60cc single)	400	600	900	1,100	1,400	1,700
KX80-R2 (80cc single)	400	600	1,000	1,300	1,700	2,100
KX80-T2 (80cc single).	400	600	1,000	1,400	1,800	2,200
KE100-B11 (100cc single).	400	600	900	1,100	1,200	1,400
KX125-J1 (125cc single)	700	1,000	1,400	2,100	2,700	3,400
KDX200-E4 (200cc single)	500	800	1,200	1,800	2,400	3,000
EX250-F6 Ninja R (250cc twin)	700	1,000	1,400	2,000	2,500	3,000
KDX250-D2 (250cc single)	600	900	1,300	2,100	3,000	4,000
KL250-D9 KLR (250cc single).	700	1,000	1,400	1,900	2,400	3,000
KX250-J1 (250cc single)	800	1,100	1,500	2,400	3,200	4,200
EX500-A6 (500cc twin)	800	1,200	1,700	2,300	2,900	3,500
EN500-A3 Vulcan (500cc twin)	1,000	1,400	1,900	2,600	3,200	3,800
KX500-E4 (500cc single)	800	1,100	1,600	2,400	3,300	4,200
ZX600-C5 Ninja R (600cc four)	1,100	1,500	2,100	3,000	3,900	4,700
ZX600-D3 Ninja ZX6 (600cc four).	1,400	1,900	2,500	3,500	4,500	5,600
KL650-A6 KLR (650cc single).	800	1,100	1,500	2,200	2,900	3,700
VN750-A8 Vulcan (750cc twin)	1,300	1,800	2,400	3,200	3,900	4,800
ZR750-C2 Zephyr (750cc four)	1,000	1,400	2,000	2,900	3,900	4,800
ZX750-J2 Ninja ZX7 (750cc four)	1,800	2,200	3,000	4,300	5,600	7,000
ZX750-K2 Ninja ZX7R (750cc four)	1,900	2,500	3,300	5,300	7,300	9,400
KZ1000 Police (1,000cc four)	1,100	1,600	2,100	3,000	4,000	5,000
ZG1000-A7 Concours (1,000cc four)	1,400	1,900	2,500	4,000	5,500	7,100
ZX1100-C3 Ninja ZX11 (1,100cc four) . . .	1,900	2,500	3,000	4,000	5,000	7,000
ZG1200 Voyager XII (1,200cc four)	2,200	2,800	3,700	5,100	6,500	8,000
VN1500-A6 Vulcan 88 (1,500cc twin)	1,500	2,000	2,700	4,000	5,300	6,700

	6	5	4	3	2	1
G80C (500cc single)	1,400	2,200	3,200	4,300	5,800	7,200
G80CS (500cc single)	1,600	2,400	3,600	4,700	6,300	7,900
G80S (500cc single)	1,300	2,000	3,000	4,000	5,400	6,700
G9B (545cc twin)	1,300	1,900	2,900	3,800	5,100	6,400
G9BCSR (545cc twin)	1,400	2,100	3,200	4,200	5,600	7,000
1955						
G3L (350cc single)	1,200	1,800	2,800	3,700	4,900	6,100
G3LC (350cc single)	1,300	2,000	2,900	3,900	5,200	6,500
G3LCS (350cc single)	1,400	2,100	3,200	4,200	5,600	7,000
G3LS (350cc single)	1,200	1,800	2,800	3,700	4,900	6,100
G9 (500cc twin)	1,200	1,900	2,800	3,700	5,000	6,200
G9CSR (500cc twin)	1,400	2,100	3,200	4,200	5,600	7,000
G45 (500cc twin)	6,000	9,000	14,000	18,000	24,000	30,000
G80 (500cc single)	1,300	2,000	3,000	4,500	6,000	7,500
G80C (500cc single)	1,400	2,100	3,200	4,300	5,700	7,100
G80CS (500cc single)	1,600	2,400	3,600	4,700	6,300	7,900
G80S (500cc single)	1,300	2,000	3,000	4,000	5,400	6,700
G9B (545cc twin)	1,300	1,900	2,900	3,800	5,100	6,400
G9BCSR (545cc twin)	1,400	2,100	3,200	4,200	5,600	7,000
1956						
G3LCS (350cc single)	1,400	2,100	3,200	4,200	5,600	7,000
G3LS (350cc single)	1,300	2,000	2,900	3,900	5,200	6,500
G9 (500cc twin)	1,200	1,900	2,800	3,700	5,000	6,200
G9CSR (500cc twin)	1,400	2,100	3,200	4,200	5,600	7,000
G45 (500cc twin)	6,600	10,000	15,000	20,000	26,000	33,000
G80CS (500cc single)	1,600	2,400	3,600	4,700	6,300	7,900
G80S (500cc single)	1,300	2,000	3,000	4,000	5,400	6,700
G11 (600cc twin)	1,300	1,900	2,800	3,800	5,000	6,300
G11CSR (600cc twin)	1,400	2,100	3,200	4,200	5,600	7,000
1957						
G3LCS (350cc single)	1,400	2,100	3,200	4,200	5,600	7,000
G3LS (350cc single)	1,300	2,000	2,900	3,900	5,200	6,500
G9 (500cc twin)	1,300	2,000	2,900	3,800	5,100	6,400
G9CSR (500cc twin)	1,400	2,100	3,200	4,200	5,600	7,000
G45 (500cc twin)	6,600	10,000	15,000	20,000	26,000	33,000
G80CS (500cc single)	1,600	2,400	3,600	4,700	6,300	7,900
G80R/R Dirt Tracker (500cc single)	2,400	3,600	5,400	7,200	9,600	12,000
G80S (500cc single)	1,300	2,000	2,900	3,900	5,200	6,500
G11 (600cc twin)	1,300	1,900	2,800	3,800	5,000	6,300
G11CSR (600cc twin)	1,400	2,100	3,200	4,200	5,600	7,000
1958						
G2 (250cc single)	600	900	1,400	1,900	2,500	3,100
G3LCS (350cc single)	1,400	2,100	3,200	4,200	5,600	7,000
G3LS (350cc single)	1,200	1,900	2,800	3,700	5,000	6,200
G9 (500cc twin)	1,200	1,900	2,800	3,700	5,000	6,200
G9CSR (500cc twin)	1,400	2,100	3,200	4,200	5,600	7,000
G45 (500cc twin)	6,600	10,000	15,000	20,000	26,000	33,000
G80CS (500cc single)	1,600	2,400	3,600	4,700	6,300	7,900
G80S (500cc single)	1,300	2,000	2,900	3,900	5,200	6,500
G11 (600cc twin)	1,300	1,900	2,800	3,800	5,000	6,300
G11CS (600cc twin)	1,300	2,000	3,000	4,000	5,400	6,700
G11 CSR (600cc twin)	1,400	2,100	3,200	4,200	5,600	7,000
1959						
G2 (250cc single)	600	900	1,400	1,900	2,500	3,100
G2CS (250cc single)	700	1,100	1,600	2,100	2,800	3,500
G3 (350cc single)	1,200	1,900	2,800	3,700	5,000	6,200
G3C (350cc single)	1,400	2,100	3,200	4,200	5,600	7,000
G3CS (350cc single)	1,400	2,100	3,200	4,300	5,700	7,100
G9 (500cc twin)	1,200	1,900	2,800	3,700	5,000	6,200

	6	5	4	3	2	1
G9CS (500cc twin)	1,400	2,100	3,200	4,200	5,600	7,000
G9CSR (500cc twin)	1,400	2,100	3,200	4,200	5,600	7,000
G45 (500cc twin)	6,600	10,000	15,000	20,000	26,000	33,000
G50 (500cc single)	7,000	11,000	16,000	21,000	28,000	35,000
G80CS (500cc single).	1,600	2,400	3,600	4,700	6,300	7,900
G80S (500cc single).	1,300	2,000	2,900	3,900	5,200	6,500
G80 Typhoon (600cc single)	2,000	3,000	4,500	6,000	8,000	10,000
G12 Deluxe (650cc twin)	1,200	1,800	2,700	3,600	4,800	6,000
G12 (650cc twin)	1,200	1,800	2,700	3,600	4,800	6,000
G12CS (650cc twin).	1,300	2,000	2,900	3,900	5,200	6,500
G12CSR (650cc twin)	1,400	2,100	3,200	4,200	5,600	7,000
1960						
G2 (250cc single)	600	900	1,400	1,900	2,500	3,100
G2CS (250cc single)	700	1,100	1,600	2,100	2,800	3,500
G3 (350cc single)	1,200	1,900	2,800	3,700	5,000	6,200
G3C (350cc single)	1,400	2,100	3,200	4,200	5,600	7,000
G5 (350cc single)	1,100	1,700	2,500	3,300	4,400	5,500
G9 (500cc twin)	1,200	1,900	2,800	3,700	5,000	6,200
G9CSR (500cc twin)	1,400	2,100	3,200	4,200	5,600	7,000
G50 (500cc single)	7,000	11,000	16,000	21,000	28,000	35,000
G80 (500cc single)	1,300	2,000	2,900	3,900	5,200	6,500
G80CS (500cc single).	1,600	2,400	3,600	4,700	6,300	7,900
G80 Typhoon (600cc single)	2,000	3,000	4,500	6,000	8,000	10,000
G12 (650cc twin)	1,200	1,800	2,700	3,600	5,000	6,500
G12 Deluxe (650cc twin)	1,200	1,800	2,700	3,600	4,800	6,000
G12CS (650cc twin).	1,300	2,000	2,900	3,900	5,200	6,500
G12CSR (650cc twin)	1,400	2,100	3,200	4,200	5,600	7,000
1961						
G2 (250cc single)	600	900	1,400	1,900	2,500	3,100
G2CS (250cc single)	700	1,100	1,600	2,100	2,800	3,500
G2S (250cc single)	600	900	1,400	1,900	2,500	3,100
G3 (350cc single)	1,200	1,900	2,800	3,700	5,000	6,200
G3C (350cc single)	1,400	2,100	3,200	4,200	5,600	7,000
G5 (350cc single)	1,100	1,700	2,500	3,300	4,400	5,500
G9 (500cc twin)	1,200	1,900	2,800	3,700	5,000	6,200
G9CSR (500cc twin)	1,400	2,100	3,200	4,200	5,600	7,000
G50 (500cc single)	7,000	11,000	16,000	21,000	28,000	35,000
G80 (500cc single)	1,300	2,000	2,900	3,900	5,200	6,500
G80CS (500cc single).	1,600	2,400	3,600	4,700	6,300	7,900
G80 Typhoon (600cc single)	2,000	3,000	4,500	6,000	8,000	10,000
G12 (650cc twin)	1,200	1,800	2,700	3,600	4,800	6,000
G12 Deluxe (650cc twin)	1,200	1,800	2,700	3,600	4,800	6,000
G12CSR (650cc twin).	1,400	2,100	3,500	4,500	6,000	8,000
1962						
G2 (250cc single)	600	900	1,400	1,900	2,500	3,100
G2CS (250cc single)	700	1,100	1,600	2,100	2,800	3,500
G2CSR (250cc single)	700	1,100	1,600	2,100	2,800	3,500
G2S (250cc single)	600	900	1,400	1,900	2,500	3,100
G3 (350cc single)	1,200	1,900	2,800	3,700	5,000	6,200
G3C (350cc single)	1,400	2,100	3,200	4,200	5,600	7,000
G3S (350cc single)	1,200	1,900	2,800	3,700	5,000	6,200
G5 (350cc single)	1,100	1,600	2,400	3,200	4,300	5,400
G50 (500cc single)	7,000	11,000	16,000	21,000	28,000	35,000
G80 (500cc single)	1,300	2,000	2,900	3,900	5,200	6,500
G80CS (500cc single).	1,600	2,400	3,600	4,700	6,300	7,900
G80 Typhoon (600cc single)	2,000	3,000	4,500	6,000	8,000	10,000
G12 (650cc twin)	1,200	1,800	2,700	3,600	4,800	6,000
G12CSR (650cc twin).	1,200	1,800	2,700	3,600	4,800	6,000

	6	5	4	3	2	1
1963						
G2 (250cc single)	600	900	1,400	1,900	2,500	3,100
G2CSR (250cc single)	700	1,100	1,600	2,100	2,800	3,500
G3 (350cc single)	1,200	1,900	2,800	3,700	5,000	6,200
G3C (350cc single)	1,400	2,100	3,200	4,200	5,600	7,000
G50 (500cc single)	7,000	11,000	16,000	21,000	28,000	35,000
G80 (500cc single)	1,300	2,000	2,900	3,900	5,200	6,500
G80CS (500cc single)	1,600	2,400	3,600	4,700	6,300	7,900
G80 Typhoon (600cc single)	2,000	3,000	4,500	6,000	8,000	10,000
G12 (650cc single)	1,200	1,800	2,700	3,600	4,800	6,000
G12CSR (650cc twin)	1,400	2,100	3,200	4,200	5,600	7,000
G15 (750cc twin)	1,100	1,700	2,500	**4,000**	**6,000**	**8,000**
G15CSR (750cc twin)	1,300	2,000	2,900	3,900	5,200	6,500
1964						
G2CSR (250cc single)	700	1,100	1,600	2,100	2,800	3,500
G3 (350cc single)	1,200	1,900	2,800	3,700	5,000	6,200
G3C (350cc single)	1,300	2,000	3,000	4,000	5,400	6,700
G80 (500cc single)	1,300	2,000	2,900	3,900	5,200	6,500
G80CS (500cc single)	1,600	2,400	3,600	4,700	6,300	7,900
G80 Typhoon (600cc single)	2,000	3,000	4,500	6,000	8,000	10,000
G12 (650cc twin)	1,200	1,800	2,700	3,600	4,800	6,000
G12CSR (650cc twin)	1,400	2,100	3,200	4,400	6,000	7,200
G15 (750cc twin)	1,100	1,700	2,500	**4,000**	**6,000**	**8,000**
G15CSR (750cc twin)	1,300	2,000	2,900	3,900	5,200	6,500
1965						
G2CSR (250cc single)	700	1,100	1,600	2,100	2,800	3,500
G3 (350cc single)	1,200	1,800	2,700	3,600	4,800	6,000
G80 (500cc single)	1,300	2,000	2,900	3,900	5,200	6,500
G80CS (500cc single)	1,600	2,400	3,600	4,700	6,300	7,900
G80 Typhoon (600cc single)	2,000	3,000	4,500	6,000	8,000	10,000
G12 (650cc twin)	1,200	1,800	2,700	3,600	4,800	6,000
G12CSR (650cc twin)	1,400	2,100	3,200	4,200	5,600	7,000
G15 (750cc twin)	1,100	1,700	2,500	**4,000**	**6,000**	**8,000**
G15CSR (750cc twin)	1,300	2,000	2,900	3,900	5,200	6,500
1966						
G2CSR (250cc single)	700	1,100	1,600	2,100	2,800	3,500
G3 (350cc single)	1,200	1,800	2,700	3,600	4,800	6,000
G80 (500cc single)	1,300	2,000	2,900	3,900	5,200	6,500
G85CS (500cc single)	2,000	4,000	6,000	8,000	10,000	12,000
G80 Typhoon (600cc single)	2,000	3,000	4,500	6,000	8,000	10,000
G12 (650cc twin)	1,200	1,800	2,700	3,600	4,800	6,000
G12CSR (650cc twin)	1,400	2,100	3,200	4,200	5,600	7,000
G15 (750cc twin)	1,100	1,700	2,500	**4,000**	**6,000**	**8,000**
G15CSR (750cc twin)	1,300	2,000	2,900	3,900	5,200	6,500
P11 (750cc twin)	1,600	2,400	3,600	4,800	6,400	8,000
1967						
G85CS (500cc single)	2,000	3,000	4,500	6,000	8,000	10,000
G15 (750cc twin)	1,100	1,700	2,500	**4,000**	**6,000**	**8,000**
G15CSR (750cc twin)	1,300	2,000	2,900	3,900	5,200	6,500
1968						
G85CS (500cc single)	2,000	3,000	4,500	6,000	8,000	10,000
G15 (750cc twin)	1,100	1,700	2,500	**4,000**	**6,000**	**8,000**
G15CSR (750cc twin)	1,300	2,000	2,900	3,900	5,200	6,500
1969						
G85CS (500cc single)	2,000	4,000	6,000	8,000	9,000	11,000
G15 (750cc twin)	1,100	1,700	2,500	**4,000**	**6,000**	**8,000**
G15CSR (750cc twin)	1,300	2,000	2,900	3,900	5,200	6,500

	6	5	4	3	2	1
MONTESA						
1968						
Cappra 250	1,300	2,000	2,700	3,600	5,500	7,400
Impala Special 250	1,300	2,000	2,700	3,600	5,500	7,400
La Cros 250	700	1,200	1,600	2,200	3,400	4,600
Scorpion 250	1,300	2,000	2,700	3,600	5,500	7,400
Cappra 360	1,600	2,400	3,300	4,400	6,900	8,400
1969						
Cota 247	900	1,400	2,200	3,000	4,000	6,200
Cappra 5 Speed 250	1,300	2,000	2,700	3,600	5,500	7,400
Cappra 250GP	1,300	2,000	2,700	3,600	5,500	7,400
Cappra 360GP	1,600	2,400	3,300	4,400	6,900	8,400
1970						
Cota 247	900	1,400	2,200	3,000	4,000	6,200
Cappra 5 Speed 250	1,300	2,000	2,700	3,600	5,500	7,400
Cappra 250GP	1,300	2,000	2,700	3,600	5,500	7,400
Cappra 360GP	1,600	2,400	3,300	4,400	6,900	8,400
1971						
Cappra 125MX	900	1,400	1,900	2,600	3,900	5,200
Texas T175	900	1,400	1,900	2,600	3,900	5,200
Texas XLT175.	900	1,400	1,900	2,600	3,900	5,200
Cota 247	900	1,400	2,200	3,000	4,000	6,200
Cappra 5 Speed 250	1,300	2,000	2,700	3,600	5,500	7,400
King Scorpion 250.	1,300	2,000	2,700	3,600	5,500	7,400
Cappra 250GP	1,300	2,000	2,700	3,600	5,500	7,400
Cappra 360GP	1,600	2,400	3,300	4,400	6,900	8,400
1972						
Cota 125	900	1,400	1,900	2,600	3,900	5,200
Capra 125MX	900	1,400	1,900	2,600	3,900	5,200
Cota 247	900	1,400	2,200	3,000	4,000	6,200
King Scorpion 250.	1,300	2,000	2,700	3,600	5,500	7,400
Cappra 250MX	1,300	2,000	2,700	3,600	5,500	7,400
Cota25 50	600	1,100	1,600	2,100	3,300	4,500
1973						
Cota 125	900	1,400	1,900	2,600	3,900	5,200
Cappra 125MX	900	1,400	1,900	2,600	3,900	5,200
Cota 247	900	1,400	2,200	3,000	4,000	6,200
King Scorpion 250.	1,300	2,000	2,700	3,600	5,500	7,400
Cappra 250MX	1,300	2,000	2,700	3,600	5,500	7,400
Cappra 250VR	600	1,200	1,600	2,200	3,400	4,600
Cota25 50	600	1,100	1,600	2,100	3,300	4,500
1974						
Cota 123	900	1,400	1,900	2,600	4,000	5,400
Cota 123T.	900	1,500	2,000	2,700	4,100	5,500
Cota 247	900	1,400	2,200	3,000	4,000	6,200
Cota 247T.	900	1,400	2,200	3,000	4,000	6,200
Enduro 250	1,300	2,000	2,700	3,600	5,500	7,400
King Scorpion 250.	1,300	2,000	2,700	3,600	5,500	7,400
Rapita 250	1,300	2,000	2,700	3,600	5,500	7,400
Cappra 250VR	600	1,200	1,600	2,200	3,400	4,600
Cota 50	600	1,100	1,600	2,100	3,300	4,500
Cota25 50	600	1,100	1,600	2,100	3,300	4,500
1975						
Cota 123	900	1,400	1,900	2,600	4,000	5,400
Cota 123T.	900	1,500	2,000	2,700	4,100	5,500
Cappra 125	1,100	1,800	2,500	3,200	5,100	7,000
Cota 247	900	1,400	2,200	3,000	4,000	6,200
Cota 247T.	900	1,400	2,200	3,000	4,000	6,200
Enduro 250	1,300	2,000	2,700	3,600	5,500	7,400

	6	5	4	3	2	1
King Scorpion 250.	1,300	2,000	2,700	3,600	5,500	7,400
Rapita 250	1,300	2,000	2,700	3,600	5,500	7,400
Cappra 250VR	600	1,200	1,600	2,200	3,400	4,600
Cota 50	600	1,100	1,600	2,100	3,300	4,500
Cota25 50.	600	1,100	1,600	2,100	3,300	4,500
1976						
Cota 123	900	1,400	1,900	2,600	4,000	5,400
Cota 123T.	900	1,500	2,000	2,700	4,100	5,500
Cappra 125	1,100	1,800	2,500	3,200	5,100	7,000
Cota 172	900	1,400	1,900	2,600	3,900	5,200
Cota 247	900	1,400	2,200	3,000	4,000	6,200
Cota 247T.	900	1,400	2,200	3,000	4,000	6,200
Cappra 250	1,300	2,000	2,700	3,600	5,500	7,400
Enduro 250	1,300	2,000	2,700	3,600	5,500	7,400
Cota 348	900	1,400	1,900	2,500	3,900	5,300
Cappra 360	900	1,400	1,900	2,500	3,900	5,300
Cota 25C 50.	600	1,100	1,600	2,100	3,300	4,500
1977						
Cota 123	900	1,400	1,900	2,600	4,000	5,400
Enduro 125	1,100	1,600	2,100	2,800	4,500	6,200
Cappra 125VB	1,100	1,600	2,100	2,800	4,500	6,200
Cota 247	900	1,400	2,200	3,000	4,000	6,200
Cota 247T.	900	1,400	2,200	3,000	4,000	6,200
Cappra 250VB	1,500	2,200	2,900	3,900	5,900	7,900
Cota 25C 50.	600	1,100	1,600	2,100	3,300	4,500
1978						
Cota 123	900	1,400	1,900	2,600	4,000	5,400
Enduro 125H	1,100	1,600	2,100	2,800	4,500	6,200
Cappra 125VB	1,100	1,600	2,100	2,800	4,500	6,200
Cota 247	900	1,400	2,200	3,000	4,000	6,200
Enduro 250HG	1,500	2,200	2,900	3,900	5,900	7,900
Cappra 250VB	1,500	2,200	2,900	3,900	5,900	7,900
Cota 348	900	1,400	1,900	2,500	3,900	5,300
Cota 348T.	900	1,400	1,900	2,500	3,900	5,300
Enduro 360H	900	1,400	1,900	2,500	3,900	5,300
Cappra 360VB	900	1,400	1,900	2,500	3,900	5,300
Cota 49	400	700	900	1,200	1,700	2,200
1979						
Cappra 125VF.	1,100	1,600	2,100	2,800	4,500	6,200
Cota 247C.	900	1,400	2,200	3,000	4,000	6,200
Cappra 250VF.	1,500	2,200	2,900	3,900	5,900	7,900
Cota 348T.	900	1,400	1,900	2,500	3,900	5,300
Cota 349	400	700	900	1,200	1,700	2,200
Enduro 360H	900	1,400	1,900	2,500	3,900	5,300
Cappra 414VF.	400	800	1,300	1,800	2,200	2,600
Cota 49	400	700	900	1,200	1,700	2,200
1980						
Cappra 125VF.	1,100	1,600	2,100	2,800	4,500	6,200
Cota 247C.	900	1,400	2,200	3,000	4,000	6,200
Cappra 250VF.	1,500	2,200	2,900	3,900	5,900	7,900
Cota 348T.	900	1,400	1,900	2,500	3,900	5,300
Cota 349	400	700	900	1,200	1,700	2,200
Enduro 360H	900	1,400	1,900	2,500	3,900	5,300
Cappra 414VF.	400	800	1,300	1,800	2,200	2,600
Cota 49	400	700	900	1,200	1,700	2,200
1981						
Cappra 125VF.	1,100	1,600	2,100	2,800	4,500	6,200
Cappra 250VF.	1,500	2,200	2,900	3,900	5,900	7,900
Cappra 414VF.	400	800	1,300	1,800	2,200	2,600

	6	5	4	3	2	1
Cota 123	400	700	900	1,200	1,700	2,200
Cota 200	400	700	900	1,200	1,700	2,200
Cota 247	400	700	900	1,200	1,700	2,200
Cota 248	400	700	900	1,200	1,700	2,200
Cota 348T	1,000	1,600	2,100	2,800	4,400	6,000
Cota 349	400	700	900	1,200	1,700	2,200
Enduro 250H6.	400	700	900	1,200	1,700	2,200
Enduro 360H6.	400	700	900	1,200	1,700	2,200
1982						
Cappra 250VG	1,500	2,200	2,900	3,900	5,900	7,900
Cappra 414VG	400	800	1,300	1,800	2,200	2,600
Cota 123	400	700	900	1,200	1,700	2,200
Cota 200	400	700	900	1,200	1,700	2,200
Cota 349	400	700	900	1,200	1,700	2,200
Enduro 250H6.	400	700	900	1,200	1,700	2,200
Enduro 360H7.	400	700	900	1,200	1,700	2,200
1983						
Cappra 250VG	1,500	2,200	2,900	3,900	5,900	7,900
Cota 123	400	700	900	1,200	1,700	2,200
Cota 200	400	700	900	1,200	1,700	2,200
Cota 349	400	700	900	1,200	1,700	2,200
Enduro 250H6.	400	700	900	1,200	1,700	2,200
Enduro 360H7.	400	700	900	1,200	1,700	2,200
1984						
Cota 200	100	200	300	400	500	600
Cota 242	100	200	300	400	500	600
Cota 350	100	200	300	400	500	600
Enduro 250 H7	100	200	400	600	800	1,000
Enduro 360 H7	100	200	400	600	800	1,000
1985						
Cota 242	100	200	300	400	500	600
Cota 330	100	200	300	400	500	600
Cota 348	100	200	300	400	500	600
Enduro 250 H7	100	200	400	600	800	1,000
Enduro 360 H7	100	200	400	600	800	1,000
1986						
Cota 123 (125cc single)	100	200	300	400	500	600
Cota 242 (240cc single)	100	200	300	400	500	600
Cota 304 (240cc single)	100	200	300	400	500	600
Cota 330 (330 cc single)	100	200	300	400	500	600
1987						
Cota 242 (240cc single)	100	200	300	400	500	600
Cota 304 (240cc single)	100	200	300	400	500	600
Cota 335 (330cc single)	100	200	300	400	500	600
1988						
Cota 307 (240cc single)	100	200	300	500	700	1,000
1989						
Cota 307 (240cc single)	100	200	300	500	700	1,000
Cota 309 (260cc single)	100	200	300	500	700	1,000
1990						
Cota 309 (260cc single)	100	200	300	500	700	1,000
1991						
Cota 310 (260cc single)	100	200	300	600	900	1,200
1993						
Cota 311 (260cc single)	100	200	400	800	1,100	1,400
1994						
Cota 314 (260cc single)	100	200	500	1,000	1,500	2,000
1995						
Cota 314R (260cc single)	200	400	800	1,300	1,800	2,300

	6	5	4	3	2	1
MOTO GUZZI						
1922						
Normale 500 (498cc single)	6,000	9,000	14,000	18,000	24,000	30,000
1923						
Normale 500 (498cc single)	6,000	9,000	14,000	18,000	24,000	30,000
1924						
Normale 500 (498cc single)	6,000	9,000	14,000	18,000	24,000	30,000
1931						
Sport 15 (498cc single)	2,400	3,600	5,400	7,200	9,600	15,000
1932						
P175 (175cc single)	1,200	1,800	2,700	3,600	4,800	6,000
Sport 15 (498cc single)	2,400	3,600	5,400	7,200	9,600	12,000
1933						
P175 (175cc single)	1,200	1,800	2,700	3,600	4,800	6,000
Sport 15 (498cc single)	2,400	3,600	5,400	7,200	9,600	12,000
1934						
PE250 (238cc single)	1,500	2,300	3,400	4,500	6,000	7,500
Sport 15 (498cc single)	2,400	3,600	5,400	7,200	9,600	12,000
1935						
PE250 (238cc single)	1,500	2,300	3,400	4,500	6,000	7,500
Sport 15 (498cc single)	2,400	3,600	5,400	7,200	9,600	12,000
GTW500 (499cc single)	2,000	3,000	4,500	6,000	8,000	12,000
1936						
PE250 (238cc single)	1,500	2,300	3,400	4,500	6,000	7,500
Sport 15 (498cc single)	2,400	3,600	5,400	7,200	9,600	12,000
GTW500 (499cc single)	2,000	3,000	4,500	6,000	8,000	12,000
1937						
PE250 (238cc single)	1,200	1,800	2,700	3,600	4,800	6,000
Sport 15 (498cc single)	2,000	3,000	4,500	6,000	8,000	10,000
GTW500 (499cc single)	2,000	3,000	4,500	6,000	8,000	10,000
1938						
PE250 (238cc single)	1,200	1,800	2,700	3,600	4,800	6,000
Condor 500 Sport (498cc single)	2,000	3,000	4,500	6,000	8,000	10,000
Sport 15 (498cc single)	1,800	2,700	4,100	5,400	7,200	9,000
GTW500 (499cc single)	1,600	2,400	3,600	4,800	6,400	8,000
1939						
PE250 (238cc single)	1,200	1,800	2,700	3,600	4,800	6,000
Condor 500 Sport (498cc single)	1,900	2,900	4,300	5,700	7,600	9,500
Sport 15 (498cc single)	1,800	2,700	4,100	5,400	7,200	9,000
GTW500 (499cc single)	1,600	2,400	3,600	4,800	6,400	8,000
1940						
GTW500 (499cc single)	1,600	2,400	3,600	4,800	6,400	8,000
1941						
GTW500 (499cc single)	1,600	2,400	3,600	4,800	6,400	8,000
1942						
GTW500 (499cc single)	1,600	2,400	3,600	4,800	6,400	8,000
1943						
GTW500 (499cc single)	1,600	2,400	3,600	4,800	6,400	8,000
Super Alce (500cc single)	2,500	5,000	7,500	10,000	12,500	15,000
1944						
GTW500 (499cc single)	1,600	2,400	3,600	4,800	6,400	8,000
Super Alce (500cc single)	2,500	5,000	7,500	10,000	12,500	15,000
1945						
GTW500 (499cc single)	1,600	2,400	3,600	4,800	6,400	8,000
Super Alce (500cc single)	2,500	5,000	7,500	10,000	12,500	15,000
1946						
Guzzino 65 (64cc single)	400	600	900	1,200	1,600	2,000
Airone 250 Turismo (247cc single)	1,300	2,000	2,900	3,900	5,200	6,500
GTV500 Alloy (499cc single)	2,400	3,600	5,400	7,200	9,600	12,000

	6	5	4	3	2	1
GTW500 (499cc single)	1,600	2,400	3,600	4,800	6,400	12,000
GTW500 Competition (499cc single)	2,000	3,000	4,500	6,000	8,000	10,000
Super Alce (500cc single)	2,500	5,000	7,500	10,000	12,500	15,000
1947						
Guzzino 65 (64cc single)	400	600	900	1,200	1,600	2,000
Airone 250 Turismo (247cc single)	1,300	2,000	2,900	3,900	5,200	6,500
GTV500 Alloy (499cc single)	2,400	3,600	5,400	7,200	9,600	12,000
GTW500 (499cc single)	1,600	2,400	3,600	4,800	6,400	12,000
Super Alce (500cc single)	2,500	5,000	7,500	10,000	12,500	15,000
1948						
Guzzino 65 (64cc single)	400	600	900	1,200	1,600	2,000
Airone 250 Turismo (247cc single)	1,300	2,000	2,900	3,900	5,200	6,500
GTV500 Alloy (499cc single)	2,400	3,600	5,400	7,200	9,600	12,000
GTW500 (499cc single)	1,600	2,400	3,600	4,800	6,400	12,000
Super Alce (500cc single)	2,500	5,000	7,500	10,000	12,500	15,000
1949						
Airone 250 Sport (247cc single)	1,500	2,300	3,400	4,500	6,000	7,500
Airone 250 Turismo (247cc single)	1,300	2,000	2,900	3,900	5,200	6,500
GTV500 Alloy (499cc single)	2,400	3,600	5,400	7,200	10,000	13,000
GTW500 (499cc single)	1,600	2,400	3,600	4,800	6,400	12,000
Super Alce (500cc single)	2,500	5,000	7,500	10,000	12,500	15,000
1950						
Guzzino 65 (64cc single)	400	600	900	1,200	1,600	2,000
Airone 250 Sport (247cc single)	1,500	2,300	3,400	5,000	6,500	8,000
Airone 250 Turismo (247cc single)	1,300	2,000	2,900	3,900	5,200	6,500
Astore 500 (497cc single)	1,700	2,600	3,800	5,100	6,800	8,500
Falcone 500 Sport (498cc single)	1,900	3,000	6,000	9,000	12,000	15,000
Falcone 500 Tourismo (498cc single) . . .	1,800	3,000	6,000	9,000	12,000	15,000
Super Alce (500cc single)	2,500	5,000	7,500	10,000	12,500	15,000
1951						
Guzzino 65 (64cc single)	400	600	900	1,200	1,600	2,000
Airone 250 Sport (247cc single)	1,500	2,300	3,400	4,500	6,000	7,500
Airone 250 Turismo (247cc single)	1,300	2,000	2,900	3,900	5,200	6,500
Astore 500 (497cc single)	1,700	2,600	3,800	5,100	6,800	8,500
Falcone 500 Sport (498cc single)	1,900	3,000	6,000	9,000	12,000	15,000
Falcone 500 Tourismo (498cc single)	1,800	3,000	6,000	9,000	12,000	15,000
Super Alce (500cc single)	2,500	5,000	7,500	10,000	12,500	15,000
1952						
Airone 250 Sport (247cc single)	1,500	2,300	3,400	4,500	6,000	7,500
Airone 250 Turismo (247cc single)	1,300	2,000	2,900	3,900	5,200	6,500
Astore 500 (497cc single)	1,700	2,600	3,800	5,100	6,800	8,500
Falcone 500 Sport (498cc single)	1,900	3,000	6,000	9,000	12,000	15,000
Falcone 500 Tourismo (498cc single) . . .	1,800	3,000	6,000	9,000	12,000	15,000
Super Alce (500cc single)	2,500	5,000	7,500	10,000	12,500	15,000
1953						
Guzzino 65 (64cc single)	400	600	900	1,200	1,600	2,000
Airone 250 Sport (247cc single)	1,500	2,300	3,400	4,500	6,000	7,500
Airone 250 Turismo (247cc single)	1,300	2,000	2,900	3,900	5,200	6,500
Astore 500 (497cc single)	1,700	2,600	3,800	5,100	6,800	8,500
Falcone 500 Sport (490cc single)	1,900	2,900	4,300	5,700	7,600	9,500
Falcone 500 Tourismp (498cc single)	1,800	**3,000**	**6,000**	**9,000**	**12,000**	**15,000**
Super Alce (500cc single)	2,500	5,000	7,500	10,000	12,500	15,000
1954						
Guzzino 65 (64cc single)	400	600	900	1,200	1,600	2,000
Zigolo 100 (98cc single)	600	800	1,300	1,700	2,200	2,800
Airone 250 Sport (247cc single)	1,500	2,300	3,400	4,500	6,000	7,500
Airone 250 Turismo (247cc single)	1,300	2,000	2,900	3,900	5,200	6,500
Astore 500 (497cc single)	1,700	2,600	3,800	5,100	6,800	8,500
Falcone 500 Sport (498cc single)	1,900	2,900	4,300	5,700	7,600	9,500

	6	5	4	3	2	1
Falcone 500 Tourismo (498cc single)	1,800	**3,000**	**6,000**	**9,000**	**12,000**	**15,000**
Super Alce (500cc single)	2,500	5,000	7,500	10,000	12,500	15,000
1955						
Cardellino 65 (64cc single)	400	600	900	1,200	1,600	2,000
Zigolo 100 (98cc single).	600	800	1,300	1,700	2,200	2,800
Airone 250 Sport (247cc single).	1,500	2,300	3,400	4,500	6,000	7,500
Airone 250 Turismo (247cc single)	1,300	2,000	2,900	3,900	5,200	6,500
Falcone 500 Sport (498cc single)	1,900	2,900	4,300	5,700	7,600	9,500
Falcone 500 Tourismo (498cc single)	1,800	**3,000**	**6,000**	**9,000**	**12,000**	**15,000**
Super Alce (500cc single)	2,500	5,000	7,500	10,000	12,500	15,000
1956						
Cardellino 65 (64cc single)	400	600	900	1,200	1,600	2,000
Zigolo 100 (98cc single).	600	800	1,300	1,700	2,200	2,800
Lodola 175 (174cc single).	700	1,100	1,600	2,200	2,900	3,600
Airone 250 Sport (247cc single).	1,500	2,300	3,400	4,500	6,000	7,500
Airone 250 Turismo (247cc single)	1,300	2,000	2,900	3,900	5,200	6,500
Falcone 500 Sport (498cc single)	1,900	2,900	4,300	5,700	7,600	9,500
Falcone 500 Tourismo (498cc single)	1,800	**3,000**	**6,000**	**9,000**	**12,000**	**15,000**
1957						
Cardellino 65 (64cc single)	400	600	900	1,200	1,600	2,000
Zigolo 100 (98cc single).	600	800	1,300	1,700	2,200	2,800
Lodola 175 (174cc single).	700	1,100	1,600	2,200	2,900	3,600
Airone 250 Sport (247cc single).	1,500	2,300	3,400	4,500	6,000	7,500
Airone 250 Turismo (247cc single)	1,300	2,000	2,900	3,900	5,200	6,500
Falcone 500 Sport (498cc single)	1,900	2,900	4,300	5,700	7,600	9,500
Falcone 500 Tourismo (498cc single)	1,800	**3,000**	**6,000**	**9,000**	**12,000**	**15,000**
1958						
Cardellino 65 (64cc single)	400	600	900	1,200	1,600	2,000
Zigolo 100 (98cc single).	600	800	1,300	1,700	2,200	2,800
Lodola 175 (174cc single).	700	1,100	2,000	3,000	4,000	5,000
Falcone 500 Sport (498cc single)	1,900	2,900	4,300	5,700	7,600	9,500
Falcone 500 Tourismo (498cc single)	1,800	**3,000**	**6,000**	**9,000**	**12,000**	**15,000**
1959						
Cardellino 75 (73cc single)	500	800	1,100	1,500	2,000	2,500
Zigolo 110 (110cc single).	600	900	1,350	1,800	2,400	3,000
Lodola 235 (235cc single).	1,300	2,000	2,900	3,900	5,200	6,500
Falcone 500 Sport (498cc single)	1,900	2,900	4,300	5,700	7,600	9,500
Falcone 500 Tourismo (498cc single)	1,600	2,400	3,600	4,800	6,400	8,000
1960						
Cardellino 75 (73cc single)	500	800	1,100	1,500	2,000	2,500
Zigolo 110 (110cc single).	600	900	1,350	1,800	2,400	3,000
Lodola 175 Regolarita (175cc single)	1,600	2,400	3,600	4,800	6,400	8,000
Lodola 235 (235cc single).	1,200	1,800	2,700	3,600	4,800	6,000
Lodola 235 Regolarita (235cc single)	1,700	2,600	3,800	5,100	6,800	8,500
Falcone 500 Sport (498cc single)	1,900	2,900	4,300	5,700	7,600	9,500
Falcone 500 Tourismo (498cc single)	1,600	2,400	3,600	4,800	6,400	8,000
1961						
Cardellino 75 (73cc single)	400	600	900	1,200	1,600	2,000
Zigolo 110 (110cc single).	600	900	1,400	1,800	2,400	3,000
Stornello Sport (125cc single).	700	1,000	1,500	2,000	2,600	3,300
Lodola 175 Regolarita (175cc single)	1,600	2,400	3,600	4,800	6,400	8,000
Lodola 235 (235cc single).	1,200	1,800	2,700	3,600	4,800	6,000
Lodola 235 Regolarita (235cc single)	1,700	2,600	3,800	5,100	6,800	8,500
Falcone 500 Sport (498cc single)	1,900	2,900	4,300	5,700	7,600	9,500
Falcone 500 Tourismo (498cc single)	1,600	2,400	3,600	4,800	6,400	8,000
1962						
Cardellino 75 (73cc single)	400	600	900	1,200	1,600	2,000
Zigolo 110 (110cc single).	600	900	1,400	1,800	2,400	3,000
Stornello Sport (125cc single).	700	1,000	1,500	2,000	2,600	3,300

	6	5	4	3	2	1
Lodola 235 (235cc single)	1,200	1,800	2,700	3,600	4,800	6,000
Falcone 500 Sport (498cc single)	1,900	2,900	4,300	5,700	7,600	9,500
Falcone 500 Tourismo (498cc single)	1,600	2,400	3,600	4,800	6,400	8,000
1963						
Cardellino 75 (73cc single)	400	600	900	1,200	1,600	2,000
Zigolo 110 (110cc single)	600	900	1,400	1,800	2,400	3,000
Lodola 235 (235cc single)	1,200	1,800	2,700	3,600	4,800	6,000
Falcone 500 Sport (498cc single)	1,900	2,900	4,300	5,700	7,600	9,500
Falcone 500 Tourismo (498cc single)	1,600	2,400	3,600	4,800	6,400	8,000
1964						
Cardellino 85 (83cc single)	400	600	900	1,200	1,600	2,000
Zigolo 110 (110cc single)	600	900	1,400	1,800	2,400	3,000
Stornello Sport (125cc single)	700	1,000	1,500	2,000	2,600	3,300
Lodola 235 (235cc single)	1,200	1,800	2,700	3,600	4,800	6,000
Falcone 500 Sport (498cc single)	1,900	2,900	4,300	5,700	7,600	9,500
Falcone 500 Tourismo (498cc single)	1,600	2,400	3,600	4,800	6,400	8,000
1965						
Cardellino 85 (83cc single)	400	600	900	1,200	1,600	2,000
Zigolo 110 (110cc single)	600	900	1,400	1,800	2,400	3,000
Stornello Sport (125cc single)	700	1,000	1,500	2,000	2,600	3,300
Lodola 235 (235cc single)	1,200	1,800	2,700	3,600	4,800	6,000
1966						
Zigolo 110 (110cc single)	600	900	1,400	1,800	2,400	3,000
Stornello Sport (125cc single)	700	1,000	1,500	2,000	2,600	3,300
Lodola 235 (235cc single)	1,200	1,800	2,700	3,600	4,800	6,000
1967						
Zigolo 110 (110cc single)	600	900	1,400	1,800	2,400	3,000
Stornello 125 American (123cc single) . . .	700	1,000	1,500	2,000	2,600	3,300
Stornello 125 Sport (123cc single)	700	1,000	1,500	2,000	2,600	3,300
1968						
Zigolo 110 (110cc single)	600	900	1,400	1,800	2,400	3,000
Stornello 125 American (123cc single) . . .	700	1,000	1,500	2,000	2,600	3,300
Stornello 125 Sport (123cc single)	700	1,000	1,500	2,000	2,600	3,300
V7 700 (703cc twin)	1,500	3,000	4,500	6,000	7,500	9,000
1969						
Stornello 125 American (123cc single) . . .	700	1,000	1,500	2,000	2,600	3,300
Falcone 500 Nuovo (498cc single)	1,100	1,700	2,500	3,400	4,500	5,600
V7 700 (703cc twin)	1,500	2,300	3,400	4,500	6,000	7,500
V7 750 Ambassador (757cc twin)	1,800	2,700	4,100	5,400	7,200	9,000
1970						
Stornello 125 American (123cc single) . . .	700	1,000	1,500	2,000	2,600	3,300
Falcone 500 Nuovo (498cc single)	1,100	1,700	2,500	3,400	4,500	5,600
V7 750 Ambassador (757cc twin)	1,800	2,700	4,100	5,400	7,200	9,000
1971						
Stornello 125 American (123cc single) . . .	700	1,000	1,500	2,000	2,600	3,300
Falcone 500 Nuovo (498cc single)	1,100	1,700	2,500	3,400	4,500	5,600
V7 750 Police (750cc twin)	2,000	3,000	4,500	6,000	8,000	10,000
V7 750 Ambassador (757cc twin)	1,800	2,700	4,100	5,400	7,200	9,000
1972						
Stornello 125 American (123cc single) . . .	700	1,000	1,500	2,000	2,600	3,300
Falcone 500 Nuovo (498cc single)	1,100	1,700	2,500	3,400	4,500	5,600
V7 750 Police (750cc twin)	2,000	3,000	4,500	6,000	8,000	10,000
V7 750 Sport (748cc twin)	2,100	3,200	5,000	7,000	9,000	11,000
Eldorado 850GT (844cc twin)	2,100	3,200	4,700	6,000	8,000	10,000
V850 California (844cc twin)	2,400	3,600	5,400	7,200	9,600	12,000
1973						
Stornello 125 American (123cc single) . . .	700	1,000	1,500	2,000	2,600	3,300
Falcone 500 Nuovo (498cc single)	1,200	1,800	2,700	3,600	4,800	6,000
850 Eldorado LAPD (844cc twin)	2,200	3,300	5,000	6,600	8,800	11,000

	6	5	4	3	2	1
PANTHER						
1935						
250 (250cc single)	2,000	4,000	8,000	10,000	13,000	16,000
1946						
Model 100 (600cc single)	1,600	2,400	4,000	6,000	7,500	9,000
1947						
Model 65 (250cc single)	800	1,200	1,800	2,400	3,200	4,000
Model 75 (350cc single)	900	1,400	2,000	2,700	3,600	4,500
Model 100 (600cc single)	1,600	2,400	4,000	6,000	7,500	9,000
1948						
Model 65 (250cc single)	800	1,200	1,800	2,400	3,200	4,000
Model 75 (350cc single)	900	1,400	2,000	2,700	3,600	4,500
Model 100 (600cc single)	1,600	2,400	4,000	6,000	7,500	9,000
1949						
Model 65 (250cc single)	800	1,200	1,800	2,400	3,200	4,000
Model 75 (350cc single)	900	1,400	2,000	2,700	3,600	4,500
Model 100 (600cc single)	1,600	2,400	4,000	6,000	7,500	9,000
1950						
Model 65 (250cc single)	800	1,200	1,800	2,400	3,200	4,000
Model 75 (350cc single)	900	1,400	2,000	2,700	3,600	4,500
Model 100 (600cc single)	1,600	2,400	4,000	6,000	7,500	9,000
1951						
Model 65 (250cc single)	800	1,200	1,800	2,400	3,200	4,000
Model 75 (350cc single)	900	1,400	2,000	2,700	3,600	4,500
Model 100 (600cc single)	1,600	2,400	4,000	6,000	7,500	9,000
1952						
Model 65 (250cc single)	800	1,200	1,800	2,400	3,200	4,000
Model 75 (350cc single)	900	1,400	2,000	2,700	3,600	4,500
Model 100 (600cc single)	1,600	2,400	4,000	6,000	7,500	9,000
1953						
Model 65 (250cc single)	800	1,200	1,800	2,400	3,200	4,000
Model 75 (350cc single)	900	1,400	2,000	2,700	3,600	4,500
Model 100 (600cc single)	1,600	2,400	4,000	6,000	7,500	9,000
1954						
Model 65 (250cc single)	800	1,200	1,800	2,400	3,200	4,000
Model 75 (350cc single)	900	1,400	2,000	2,700	3,600	4,500
Model 100 (600cc single)	1,600	2,400	4,000	6,000	7,500	9,000
1955						
Model 65 (250cc single)	800	1,200	1,800	2,400	3,200	4,000
Model 75 (350cc single)	900	1,400	2,000	2,700	3,600	4,500
Model 100 (600cc single)	1,600	2,400	4,000	6,000	7,500	9,000
1956						
Model 65 (250cc single)	800	1,200	1,800	2,400	3,200	4,000
Model 75 (350cc single)	900	1,400	2,000	2,700	3,600	4,500
Model 100 (600cc single)	1,600	2,400	4,000	6,000	7,500	9,000
1957						
Model 65 (250cc single)	800	1,200	1,800	2,400	3,200	4,000
Model 75 (350cc single)	900	1,400	2,000	2,700	3,600	4,500
Model 100 (600cc single)	1,600	2,400	4,000	6,000	7,500	9,000
1958						
Model 65 (250cc single)	800	1,200	1,800	2,400	3,200	4,000
Model 75 (350cc single)	900	1,400	2,000	2,700	3,600	4,500
Model 100 (600cc single)	1,600	2,400	4,000	6,000	7,500	9,000
1959						
Model 65 (250cc single)	800	1,200	1,800	2,400	3,200	4,000
Model 75 (350cc single)	900	1,400	2,000	2,700	3,600	4,500
Model 100 (600cc single)	1,600	2,400	4,000	6,000	7,500	9,000
Model 120 (650cc single)	1,600	2,400	3,600	4,800	6,400	8,000

	6	5	4	3	2	1
1960						
Model 65 (250cc single)	800	1,200	1,800	2,400	3,200	4,000
Model 75 (350cc single)	900	1,400	2,000	2,700	3,600	4,500
Model 100 (600cc single)	1,600	2,400	4,000	6,000	7,500	9,000
Model 120 (650cc single)	1,600	2,400	3,600	4,800	6,400	8,000
1961						
Model 65 (250cc single)	800	1,200	1,800	2,400	3,200	4,000
Model 75 (350cc single)	900	1,400	2,000	2,700	3,600	4,500
Model 100 (600cc single)	1,600	2,400	4,000	6,000	7,500	9,000
Model 120 (650cc single)	1,600	2,400	3,600	4,800	6,400	8,000
1962						
Model 65 (250cc single)	800	1,200	1,800	2,400	3,200	4,000
Model 75 (350cc single)	900	1,400	2,000	2,700	3,600	4,500
Model 100 (600cc single)	1,600	2,400	4,000	6,000	7,500	9,000
Model 120 (650cc single)	1,600	2,400	3,600	4,800	6,400	8,000
1963						
Model 100 (600cc single)	1,600	2,400	4,000	6,000	7,500	9,000
Model 120 (650cc single)	1,600	2,400	3,600	4,800	6,400	8,000
1964						
Model 120 (650cc single)	1,600	2,400	3,000	4,800	6,400	8,000
1965						
Model 120 (650cc single)	1,600	2,400	3,600	4,800	6,400	8,000

PENTON

	6	5	4	3	2	1
1970						
MX	600	1,000	1,600	2,200	3,700	5,250
1971						
Six Day (125cc)	500	1,000	1,500	3,000	4,000	5,000
1972						
Berkshire (100cc)	200	400	600	1,400	2,600	3,800
Berkshire Enduro (100cc)	200	400	600	1,400	2,600	3,800
Six Day (125cc)	500	1,000	1,500	3,000	4,000	5,000
Six Day Enduro (125cc)	200	400	600	1,400	2,600	3,800
Jack Piner (175cc)	300	600	900	1,600	2,900	4,200
Jack Piner Enduro (175cc)	300	600	900	1,600	3,100	4,600
1973						
Berkshire (100cc)	200	400	700	1,200	2,600	4,000
Berkshire Enduro (100cc)	200	400	700	1,300	2,800	4,300
Six Day (125cc)	500	1,000	1,500	3,000	4,000	5,000
Six Day Enduro (125cc)	500	1,000	1,500	3,000	4,000	5,000
Jack Piner (175cc)	300	500	800	1,600	2,900	4,200
Jack Piner Enduro (175cc)	300	500	800	1,600	3,100	4,600
Hare Scrambler (250cc)	300	500	800	1,600	3,100	4,600
Hare Scrambler Enduro (250cc)	300	500	900	1,600	3,300	5,000
1974						
Berkshire (97cc)	200	400	700	1,200	2,600	4,000
Berkshire Enduro (97cc)	200	400	700	1,300	2,800	4,300
Six Day (122cc)	500	1,000	2,000	3,500	5,000	6,500
Six Day D (122cc)	500	1,000	2,000	3,500	5,000	6,500
Jack Piner (171cc)	300	500	800	1,600	3,000	4,400
Jack Piner D (171cc)	300	500	900	1,700	3,100	4,700
Jack Piner SS (171cc)	300	500	900	1,700	3,100	4,700
Hare Scrambler (246cc)	500	1,000	2,000	3,500	5,000	6,500
Hare Scrambler D (246cc)	500	1,000	2,000	3,500	5,000	6,500
Mint (400cc)	400	600	900	1,900	3,800	5,700
Mint D (400cc)	400	600	900	2,000	4,000	6,000
1975						
Berkshire D (97cc)	200	400	700	1,300	2,800	4,300
Six Day (122cc)	300	500	800	1,200	3,000	4,800
Six Day D (122cc)	300	500	800	1,600	3,300	5,000

	6	5	4	3	2	1
Jack Piner (171cc)	200	400	800	1,400	2,900	4,400
Jack Piner D (171cc)	200	400	800	1,500	3,100	4,700
Jack Piner SS (171cc)	200	400	800	1,600	3,300	5,000
Hare Scrambler (246cc)	200	400	800	1,500	3,100	4,700
Hare Scrambler D (246cc)	300	500	800	1,600	3,300	5,000
Mint (357cc)	300	500	800	1,900	3,900	5,900
Mint D (357cc)	400	600	900	2,000	4,000	6,000
1976						
Six Day (122cc)	300	500	800	1,200	3,000	4,800
Six Day D (122cc)	300	500	800	1,600	3,300	5,000
Jack Piner (171cc)	200	400	800	1,400	2,900	4,400
Jack Piner D (171cc)	200	400	800	1,500	3,100	4,700
Jack Piner SS (171cc)	200	400	800	1,600	3,300	5,000
Hare Scrambler (246cc)	200	400	800	1,500	3,100	4,700
Hare Scrambler D (246cc)	300	500	800	1,600	3,300	5,000
Mint (357cc)	300	500	800	1,900	3,900	5,900
Mint D (357cc)	400	600	900	2,000	4,000	6,000
1977						
GS6 (250cc)	300	500	800	1,600	3,300	5,000
POPE						
1911						
Single	2,500	5,000	10,000	15,000	20,000	25,000
1912						
Twin	25,000	40,000	55,000	70,000	85,000	100K
1913						
Twin	25,000	40,000	55,000	70,000	85,000	100K
1915						
OHV V-Twin	25,000	40,000	55,000	70,000	85,000	100K
1916						
Twin	25,000	40,000	55,000	70,000	85,000	100K
1918						
18L	10,000	20,000	40,000	60,000	80,000	100K
RICKMAN						
1969						
Metisse	3,000	5,000	7,000	8,500	10,000	12,000
1972						
Rickman Hodaka 100	600	1,100	2,400	4,800	6,500	8,200
Rickman 125E	300	500	1,100	2,100	3,300	4,500
Rickman 125MX	300	500	1,900	3,200	4,400	5,600
Rickman 250MX	300	500	1,900	3,700	4,900	6,100
1973						
Rickman 125MX	300	500	1,400	2,700	3,800	4,900
Rickman 125SD	300	500	1,100	2,100	3,300	4,500
Rickman 250MX	300	500	1,900	3,700	4,900	6,100
1974						
Rickman 125MX	300	500	1,400	2,700	3,800	4,900
Rickman 125SD	300	500	1,100	2,100	3,300	4,500
Rickman 250MXVR	300	500	1,900	3,700	4,900	6,100
1975						
Rickman 125MX	300	500	1,400	2,700	3,800	4,900
Rickman 125SD	300	500	1,100	2,100	3,300	4,500
Rickman 250MXVR	300	500	1,900	3,700	4,900	6,100
1978						
Rickman 750 2A	800	1,500	2,800	6,900	9,200	12,000
1979						
Rickman 1-1 Honda 750	800	1,500	2,900	6,400	8,200	10,500
Rickman CR Honda 750	800	1,500	2,800	6,900	9,300	12,000
Rickman 1-1 Kawasaki 1000	800	1,500	2,800	6,400	8,700	10,000
Rickman CR Kawasaki 1000	800	1,500	2,800	6,900	9,800	12,500

	6	5	4	3	2	1
1980						
Rickman 1-1 Honda 750	800	1,500	2,900	6,400	8,200	10,500
Rickman CR Honda 750	800	1,500	2,800	6,900	9,300	12,000
Rickman 1-1 Kawasaki 1000	800	1,500	2,800	6,400	8,700	10,000
Rickman CR Kawasaki 1000	800	1,500	2,800	6,900	9,800	12,500
1981						
Rickman CRE Honda	800	1,500	2,800	6,900	8,700	10,500
Rickman CRE Kawasaki	800	1,500	2,800	6,900	9,300	12,000
1982						
Rickman CRE Honda	800	1,500	2,800	6,900	9,300	12,000
Rickman CRE Kawasaki	800	1,500	2,800	6,900	8,200	9,500
Rickman CRE Suzuki	800	1,500	2,800	5,300	7,600	10,000
Rickman CRE Honda	800	1,500	2,800	6,400	8,700	10,000
Rickman CRE Kawasaki	800	1,500	2,800	6,400	7,600	8,800
Rickman CRE Suzuki	800	1,500	2,800	5,800	8,200	10,800

ROYAL ENFIELD

	6	5	4	3	2	1
1910						
V-Twin (425cc twin)	25,000	35,000	45,000	55,000	65,000	75,000
1911						
Model 160	20,000	25,000	30,000	35,000	40,000	50,000
V-Twin	25,000	35,000	45,000	55,000	65,000	75,000
1912						
V-Twin	25,000	35,000	45,000	55,000	65,000	75,000
1913						
V-Twin (600cc twin)	25,000	35,000	45,000	55,000	65,000	75,000
1914						
Single (225cc single)	20,000	25,000	30,000	35,000	40,000	50,000
V-Twin (425cc twin)	20,000	25,000	30,000	35,000	40,000	50,000
V-Twin (600cc twin)	20,000	25,000	30,000	35,000	40,000	50,000
1915						
Single (225cc single)	20,000	25,000	30,000	35,000	40,000	50,000
V-Twin (425cc twin)	20,000	25,000	30,000	35,000	40,000	50,000
Inline 3 Cylinder (675 cc triple)	30,000	45,000	60,000	75,000	90,000	125K
1916						
Single (225cc single)	20,000	25,000	30,000	35,000	40,000	50,000
V-Twin (425cc twin)	20,000	25,000	30,000	35,000	40,000	50,000
1917						
RE 2 Stroke	20,000	25,000	30,000	35,000	40,000	50,000
Single (225cc single)	20,000	25,000	30,000	35,000	40,000	50,000
V-Twin (425cc twin)	20,000	25,000	30,000	35,000	40,000	50,000
1918						
Single (225cc single)	20,000	25,000	30,000	35,000	40,000	50,000
V-Twin (425cc twin)	20,000	25,000	30,000	35,000	40,000	50,000
1919						
Single (225cc single)	20,000	25,000	30,000	35,000	40,000	50,000
V-Twin (425cc twin)	20,000	25,000	30,000	35,000	40,000	50,000
1920						
Single (225cc single)	15,000	20,000	25,000	30,000	35,000	40,000
V-Twin (976cc twin)	20,000	25,000	30,000	35,000	40,000	50,000
1921						
Single (225cc single)	15,000	20,000	25,000	30,000	35,000	40,000
V-Twin (976cc twin)	20,000	25,000	30,000	35,000	40,000	50,000
1922						
Single (225cc single)	15,000	20,000	25,000	30,000	35,000	40,000
V-Twin (976cc twin)	20,000	25,000	30,000	35,000	40,000	50,000
1923						
Single (225cc single)	15,000	20,000	25,000	30,000	35,000	40,000
V-Twin (976cc twin)	20,000	25,000	30,000	35,000	40,000	50,000

	6	5	4	3	2	1
1924						
Single (225cc single)	15,000	20,000	25,000	30,000	35,000	40,000
Single (350cc single)	15,000	20,000	25,000	30,000	35,000	40,000
V-Twin (976cc twin)	20,000	25,000	30,000	35,000	40,000	50,000
1925						
Single (225cc single)	15,000	20,000	25,000	30,000	35,000	40,000
V-Twin (976cc twin)	20,000	25,000	30,000	35,000	40,000	50,000
1926						
Single (225cc single)	15,000	20,000	25,000	30,000	35,000	40,000
201A	15,000	20,000	25,000	30,000	35,000	40,000
V-Twin (976cc twin)	20,000	25,000	30,000	35,000	40,000	50,000
1927						
Single (488cc single)	15,000	20,000	25,000	30,000	35,000	40,000
V-Twin (976cc twin)	20,000	25,000	30,000	35,000	40,000	50,000
1928						
Single (225cc single)	15,000	20,000	25,000	30,000	35,000	40,000
V-Twin (976cc twin)	20,000	25,000	30,000	35,000	40,000	50,000
1929						
350SV	15,000	20,000	25,000	30,000	35,000	40,000
Twinport (488cc single)	15,000	20,000	25,000	30,000	35,000	40,000
V-Twin (976cc twin)	20,000	25,000	30,000	35,000	40,000	50,000
1930						
Single (225cc single)	15,000	20,000	25,000	30,000	35,000	40,000
V-Twin (976cc twin)	20,000	25,000	30,000	35,000	40,000	50,000
1931						
Single	15,000	20,000	25,000	30,000	35,000	40,000
V-Twin (976cc twin)	20,000	25,000	30,000	35,000	40,000	50,000
1932						
Bullet	4,000	7,000	10,000	13,000	16,000	20,000
Model K (976cc twin)	20,000	25,000	30,000	35,000	40,000	50,000
1933						
Bullet	4,000	7,000	10,000	13,000	16,000	20,000
Model K (976cc twin)	20,000	25,000	30,000	35,000	40,000	50,000
1934						
Bullet	4,000	7,000	10,000	13,000	16,000	20,000
Model K (976cc twin)	20,000	25,000	30,000	35,000	40,000	50,000
1935						
T (148cc single)	800	1,300	1,900	2,500	3,400	4,200
A (225cc single)	900	1,400	2,000	2,700	3,600	4,500
Bullet (250cc single)	900	1,400	2,000	2,700	3,600	4,500
Bullet (350cc single)	1,000	1,500	2,300	3,000	4,000	5,000
Bullet (500cc single)	1,400	2,100	3,200	4,200	5,600	7,000
1936						
T (148cc single)	800	1,300	1,900	2,500	3,400	4,200
A (225cc single)	900	1,400	2,000	2,700	3,600	4,500
Bullet (250cc single)	900	1,400	2,000	2,700	3,600	4,500
Bullet (350cc single)	1,000	1,500	2,300	3,000	4,000	5,000
Bullet (500cc single)	1,400	2,100	3,200	4,200	5,600	7,000
1937						
T (148cc single)	800	1,300	1,900	2,500	3,400	4,200
A (225cc single)	900	1,400	2,000	2,700	3,600	4,500
Bullet (250cc single)	900	1,400	2,000	2,700	3,600	4,500
Bullet (350cc single)	900	1,400	2,000	2,700	3,600	4,500
Bullet (500cc single)	1,000	1,500	2,200	2,900	3,900	4,900
V-Twin (1140cc twin)	1,000	1,500	2,300	3,000	4,000	5,000
1938						
T (148cc single)	800	1,200	1,800	2,400	3,200	4,000
A (225cc single)	800	1,300	2,000	3,000	4,000	5,000
Bullet (250cc single)	800	1,300	1,900	2,500	3,400	4,200

	6	5	4	3	2	1
Bullet (350cc single)	900	1,400	2,000	2,700	3,600	4,500
Bullet (500cc single)	900	1,400	2,000	2,700	3,600	4,500
K (1,140cc twin)	1,000	1,500	2,300	3,000	4,000	5,000
1939						
T (148cc single)	800	1,200	1,800	2,400	3,200	4,000
A (225cc single)	800	1,300	1,900	2,500	3,400	4,200
Bullet (250cc single)	800	1,300	1,900	2,500	3,400	4,200
Bullet (350cc single)	900	1,400	2,000	2,700	3,600	4,500
Bullet (500cc single)	900	1,400	2,000	2,700	3,600	4,500
K (1,140cc twin)	1,000	1,500	2,300	3,000	4,000	5,000
1940						
A (225cc single)	1,400	2,100	3,200	4,200	5,600	7,000
Bullet (250cc single)	800	1,300	1,900	2,500	3,400	4,200
Bullet (350cc single)	900	1,400	2,000	2,700	3,600	4,500
Bullet (500cc single)	900	1,400	2,000	2,700	3,600	4,500
K (1,140cc twin)	1,000	1,500	2,300	3,000	4,000	5,000
1941						
WP Models (350cc single)	1,100	1,700	2,500	3,300	4,400	5,500
1942						
WP Models (350cc single)	1,100	1,700	2,500	3,300	4,400	5,500
1943						
WP Models (350cc single)	1,100	1,700	2,500	3,300	4,400	5,500
1944						
WP Models (350cc single)	1,100	1,700	2,500	3,300	4,400	5,500
1945						
WP Models (350cc single)	1,100	1,700	2,500	3,300	4,400	5,500
1946						
RE (125cc single)	600	900	1,400	1,800	2,400	3,000
G (350cc single)	900	1,400	2,000	2,700	3,600	4,500
J (500cc twin)	1,400	2,100	3,200	4,200	5,600	7,000
1947						
RE (125cc single)	600	900	1,400	1,800	2,400	3,000
G (350cc single)	900	1,400	2,000	2,700	3,600	4,500
J (500cc twin)	1,400	2,100	3,200	4,200	5,600	7,000
1948						
RE (125cc single)	600	900	1,400	1,800	2,400	3,000
G (350cc single)	900	1,400	2,000	2,700	3,600	4,500
J (500cc twin)	1,400	2,100	3,200	4,200	5,600	7,000
J2 (500cc twin)	1,600	2,300	3,500	4,700	6,200	7,800
1949						
RE (125cc single)	600	900	1,400	1,800	2,400	3,000
G (350cc single)	900	1,400	2,000	2,700	3,600	4,500
Bullet (350cc single)	1,000	1,500	2,300	3,000	4,000	5,000
Bullet (500cc single)	1,400	2,100	3,200	4,200	5,600	7,000
J (500cc twin)	1,400	2,100	3,200	4,200	5,600	7,000
J2 (500cc twin)	1,600	2,300	3,500	4,700	6,200	7,800
1950						
RE (125cc single)	600	900	1,400	1,800	2,400	3,000
G (350cc single)	900	1,400	2,000	2,700	3,600	4,500
Bullet (350cc single)	1,000	1,500	2,300	3,000	4,000	5,000
Bullet (500cc single)	1,200	1,800	2,700	3,600	4,800	6,000
J (500cc twin)	1,200	1,900	2,800	3,700	5,000	6,200
J2 (500cc twin)	1,600	2,300	3,500	4,700	6,200	7,800
1951						
RE (125cc single)	600	900	1,400	1,800	2,400	3,000
RE2 (125cc single)	600	900	1,400	1,800	2,400	3,000
G (350cc single)	900	1,400	2,000	2,700	3,600	4,500
Bullet (350cc single)	1,000	1,500	2,300	3,000	4,000	5,000
Bullet (500cc single)	1,200	1,800	2,700	3,600	4,800	6,000

	6	5	4	3	2	1
J (500cc twin)	1,200	1,900	2,800	3,700	5,000	6,200
J2 (500cc twin)	1,600	2,300	3,500	4,700	6,200	7,800
1952						
RE (125cc single)	600	800	1,300	1,700	2,200	2,800
RE2 (125cc single)	600	800	1,300	1,700	2,200	2,800
G (350cc single)	1,000	1,500	2,300	3,000	4,000	5,000
Bullet (350cc single)	1,000	1,500	2,300	3,000	4,000	5,000
Bullet (500cc single)	1,200	1,800	2,700	3,600	4,800	6,000
J (500cc twin)	1,200	1,800	2,700	3,600	4,800	6,000
J2 (500cc twin)	1,500	2,300	3,400	4,500	6,000	7,500
1953						
RE2 (125cc single)	600	800	1,300	1,700	2,200	2,800
Ensign (148cc single)	600	900	1,400	1,900	2,500	3,100
Bullet (350cc single)	1,000	1,500	2,300	3,000	4,000	5,000
G (350cc single)	1,000	1,400	2,200	2,900	3,800	4,800
Trials (350cc single)	1,600	2,400	3,600	4,800	6,400	8,000
Bullet (500cc single)	1,200	1,800	2,700	3,600	4,800	6,000
J (500cc twin)	1,200	1,800	2,700	3,600	4,800	6,000
J2 (500cc twin)	1,400	2,100	3,200	4,200	5,600	7,000
Meteor (700cc twin)	1,200	1,800	2,700	3,600	4,800	6,000
1954						
RE2 (125cc single)	600	800	1,300	1,700	2,200	2,800
Ensign (148cc single)	600	900	1,400	1,900	2,500	3,100
Clipper (250cc single)	700	1,000	1,800	2,500	3,000	3,500
S (250cc single)	700	1,000	1,500	2,000	2,700	3,400
Bullet (350cc single)	1,000	1,500	2,300	3,000	4,000	5,000
G (350cc single)	1,000	1,400	2,200	2,900	3,800	4,800
Trials (350cc single)	1,600	2,400	3,600	4,800	6,400	8,000
Bullet (500cc single)	1,200	1,800	2,700	3,600	4,800	6,000
J (500cc twin)	1,200	1,800	2,700	3,600	4,800	6,000
J2 (500cc twin)	1,400	2,100	3,200	4,200	5,600	7,000
Meteor (700cc twin)	1,200	1,800	2,700	3,600	4,800	6,000
1955						
Ensign (148cc single)	600	900	1,400	1,900	2,500	3,100
Clipper (250cc single)	700	1,000	1,500	2,000	2,700	3,400
S (250cc single)	700	1,000	1,500	2,000	2,700	3,400
Bullet (350cc single)	1,000	1,500	2,300	3,000	4,000	5,000
Trials (350cc single)	1,600	2,400	3,600	4,800	6,400	8,000
Bullet (500cc single)	1,200	1,800	2,700	3,600	4,800	6,000
J (500cc twin)	1,200	1,800	2,700	3,600	4,800	6,000
J2 (500cc twin)	1,400	2,100	3,200	4,200	5,600	7,000
Meteor (700cc twin)	1,200	1,800	2,700	3,600	4,800	6,000
1956						
Ensign (148cc single)	600	900	1,400	1,900	2,500	3,100
Ensign II (150cc single)	600	900	1,400	1,900	2,500	3,100
Clipper (250cc single)	700	1,100	1,600	2,100	2,800	3,500
Crusader (250cc single)	800	1,200	1,800	2,300	3,100	3,900
Bullet (350cc single)	1,000	1,500	2,300	3,000	4,000	5,000
Trials (350cc single)	1,600	2,400	3,600	4,800	6,400	8,000
Bullet (500cc single)	1,200	1,800	2,700	3,600	4,800	6,000
J2 (500cc twin)	1,400	2,100	3,200	4,200	5,600	7,000
Meteor (700cc twin)	1,100	1,700	2,500	3,300	4,400	5,500
Super Meteor (700cc twin)	1,200	1,800	2,700	4,000	5,500	7,000
1957						
Ensign II (150cc single)	600	900	1,400	1,900	2,500	3,100
Clipper (250cc single)	700	1,100	1,600	2,100	2,800	3,500
Crusader (250cc single)	800	1,200	1,800	2,300	3,100	3,900
Bullet (350cc single)	1,000	1,500	2,300	3,000	4,000	5,000
Trials (350cc single)	1,600	2,400	3,600	4,800	6,400	8,000

	6	5	4	3	2	1
Bullet (500cc single).	1,000	1,500	2,300	3,000	4,000	5,000
J2 (500cc twin)	1,400	2,100	3,200	4,200	5,600	7,000
Meteor (700cc twin)	1,100	1,700	2,500	3,300	4,400	5,500
Super Meteor (700cc twin)	1,200	1,800	2,700	4,000	5,500	7,000
1958						
Ensign II (150cc single)	600	900	1,400	1,900	2,500	3,100
Ensign III (150cc single).	600	900	1,400	1,900	2,500	3,100
Crusader (250cc single).	800	1,200	1,800	2,300	3,100	3,900
Bullet (350cc single).	1,000	1,500	2,300	3,000	4,000	5,000
Clipper (350cc single).	800	1,200	1,800	2,400	3,200	4,000
Trials (350cc single).	1,400	2,100	3,200	4,200	5,600	7,000
Bullet (500cc single).	1,200	1,800	2,700	3,600	4,800	6,000
J2 (500cc twin)	1,400	2,100	3,200	4,200	5,600	7,000
Meteor (700cc twin)	1,100	1,700	2,500	3,300	4,400	5,500
Meteor Air Flow (700cc twin)	1,300	1,900	2,900	3,800	5,100	6,400
Super Meteor (700cc twin)	1,200	1,800	2,700	4,000	5,500	7,000
1959						
Ensign III (150cc single).	600	900	1,400	1,900	2,500	3,100
Prince (150cc single)	600	900	1,400	1,900	2,500	3,100
Crusader (250cc single).	800	1,200	1,800	2,300	3,100	3,900
Bullet (350cc single).	1,000	1,500	2,300	3,000	4,000	5,000
Clipper (350cc single).	800	1,200	1,800	2,400	3,200	4,000
Trials (350cc single).	1,200	1,800	2,700	3,600	4,800	6,000
Bullet (500cc single).	1,200	1,800	2,700	3,600	4,800	6,000
J2 (500cc twin)	1,400	2,100	3,200	4,200	5,600	7,000
Constellation (700cc twin).	1,000	1,600	2,300	3,100	4,200	5,200
Meteor (700cc twin)	1,100	1,700	2,500	3,300	4,400	5,500
Meteor Air Flow (700cc twin)	1,300	1,900	2,900	3,800	5,100	6,400
Meteor Deluxe (700cc twin)	1,100	1,700	2,500	3,300	4,400	5,500
Super Meteor (700cc twin)	1,200	1,800	2,700	4,000	5,500	7,000
1960						
Ensign III (150cc single).	600	900	1,400	1,900	2,500	3,100
Prince (150cc single)	600	900	1,400	1,900	2,500	3,100
Crusader (250cc single).	800	1,200	1,800	2,300	3,100	3,900
Bullet (350cc single).	1,000	1,500	2,300	3,000	4,000	5,000
Clipper (350cc single).	800	1,200	1,800	2,400	3,200	4,000
Trials (350cc single).	1,200	1,800	2,700	3,600	4,800	6,000
Big Head Bullet (500cc single)	1,600	2,400	3,600	4,800	6,400	8,000
Fury (U.S.) (500cc single).	1,300	2,000	2,900	3,900	5,200	6,500
J2 (500cc twin)	1,400	2,100	3,200	4,200	5,600	7,000
Meteor Minor (500cc twin).	1,000	1,600	2,300	3,100	4,200	5,200
Constellation (700cc twin).	1,000	1,600	2,300	3,100	4,200	5,200
Meteor (700cc twin)	1,100	1,700	2,500	3,300	4,400	5,500
Meteor Air Flow (700cc twin)	1,300	1,900	2,900	3,800	5,100	6,400
Meteor Deluxe (700cc twin)	1,100	1,700	2,500	3,300	4,400	5,500
Super Meteor (700cc twin)	1,200	1,800	2,700	4,000	5,500	7,000
1961						
Prince (150cc single)	600	900	1,400	1,900	2,500	3,100
Crusader (250cc single).	800	1,200	1,800	2,300	3,100	3,900
Bullet (350cc single).	1,000	1,500	2,300	3,000	4,000	5,000
Clipper (350cc single).	800	1,200	1,800	2,400	3,200	4,000
Trials (350cc single).	1,200	1,800	2,700	3,600	4,800	6,000
Big Head Bullet (500cc single)	1,600	2,400	3,600	4,800	6,400	8,000
Fury (U.S.) (500cc single).	1,300	2,000	2,900	3,900	5,200	6,500
J2 (500cc twin)	1,400	2,100	3,200	4,200	5,600	7,000
Constellation (700cc twin).	1,000	1,600	2,300	3,100	4,200	5,200
Meteor Deluxe (700cc twin)	1,100	1,700	2,500	3,300	4,400	5,500
Super Meteor (700cc twin)	1,200	1,800	2,700	3,600	4,800	6,000

	6	5	4	3	2	1
1962						
Crusader (250cc single)	700	1,100	1,600	2,200	2,900	3,600
Super 5 (250cc single)	1,300	2,000	2,900	3,900	5,200	6,500
Bullet (350cc single)	1,000	1,500	2,300	3,000	4,000	5,000
Clipper (350cc single)	800	1,200	1,800	2,400	3,200	4,000
Big Head Bullet (500cc single)	1,600	2,400	3,600	4,800	6,400	8,000
Fury (U.S.) (500cc single)	1,300	2,000	2,900	3,900	5,200	6,500
Constellation (700cc twin)	1,000	1,600	2,300	3,100	4,200	5,200
Meteor Deluxe (700cc twin)	1,100	1,700	2,500	3,300	4,400	5,500
Super Meteor (700cc twin)	1,200	1,800	2,700	3,600	4,800	6,000
1963						
Continental (250cc single)	700	1,000	2,000	3,000	4,000	5,000
Super 5 (250cc single)	1,300	2,000	2,900	3,900	5,200	6,500
Bullet (350cc single)	1,000	1,500	2,300	3,000	4,000	5,000
Clipper (350cc single)	800	1,200	1,800	2,400	3,200	4,000
Big Head Bullet (500cc single)	1,600	2,400	3,600	4,800	6,400	8,000
Fury (U.S.) (500cc single)	1,300	2,000	2,900	3,900	5,200	6,500
Interceptor (750cc twin)	1,200	1,800	2,700	4,000	6,000	8,000
1964						
Continental (250cc single)	700	1,000	2,000	3,000	4,000	5,000
GT (250cc single)	700	1,100	1,600	2,200	2,900	3,600
Olympic (250cc single)	600	900	1,400	1,800	2,400	3,000
Super 5 (250cc single)	1,300	2,000	2,900	3,900	5,200	6,500
Turbo Twin (250cc single)	1,400	2,100	3,200	4,200	5,600	7,000
Interceptor (750cc twin)	1,200	1,800	2,700	4,000	6,000	8,000
1965						
Continental (250cc single)	700	1,000	2,000	3,000	4,000	5,000
Crusader (250cc single)	700	1,100	1,600	2,200	2,900	3,600
GT (250cc single)	700	1,100	1,600	2,200	2,900	3,600
Olympic (250cc single)	600	900	1,400	1,800	2,400	3,000
Turbo Twin (250cc single)	1,400	2,100	3,200	4,200	5,600	7,000
Interceptor (750cc twin)	1,200	1,800	2,700	4,000	6,000	8,000
1966						
Crusader Sports (250cc single)	700	1,100	1,600	2,100	2,800	3,500
GT (250cc single)	700	1,100	1,600	2,200	3,000	4,000
Turbo Twin (250cc single)	1,400	2,100	3,200	4,200	5,600	7,000
Interceptor (750cc twin)	1,200	1,800	2,700	4,000	6,000	8,000
1967						
Crusader Sports (250cc single)	700	1,100	1,600	2,100	2,800	3,500
Interceptor (750cc twin)	1,200	1,800	2,700	4,000	6,000	8,000
1968						
Interceptor (750cc twin)	1,200	1,800	2,700	4,000	6,000	8,000
Interceptor II (750cc twin)	1,300	2,000	3,000	4,000	6,000	8,000
1969						
Interceptor II (750cc twin)	1,300	2,000	3,000	4,000	6,000	8,000
1970						
Interceptor II (750cc twin)	1,300	2,000	3,000	4,000	6,000	8,000
1971						
Interceptor II (750cc twin)	1,300	2,000	3,000	4,000	6,000	8,000
SUNBEAM						
1916						
500	2,500	5,000	10,000	15,000	20,000	25,000
1928						
Model 6	7,000	10,000	12,500	15,000	18,000	21,000
1933						
Model 90	6,000	9,000	12,000	15,000	18,000	21,000
1935						
Model 16	3,000	4,000	6,000	8,000	10,000	13,000

	6	5	4	3	2	1
1937						
Light Solo	7,000	10,000	12,500	15,000	18,000	21,000
Model 8	3,500	5,000	7,000	8,800	11,000	14,000
1947						
S7 (487cc twin, shaft drive)	3,000	4,000	6,000	8,000	10,000	13,000
1948						
S7 (487cc twin, shaft drive)	3,000	4,000	6,000	8,000	10,000	13,000
1949						
S7 (487cc twin, shaft drive)	3,000	4,000	6,000	8,000	10,000	13,000
1950						
S7 Deluxe (487cc twin, shaft drive)	3,000	4,000	6,000	8,000	10,000	13,000
S8 (487cc twin, shaft drive)	3,000	4,000	6,000	8,000	10,000	13,000
1951						
S7 Deluxe (487cc twin, shaft drive)	3,000	4,000	6,000	8,000	10,000	13,000
S8 (487cc twin, shaft drive)	3,000	4,000	6,000	8,000	10,000	13,000
1952						
S7 Deluxe (487cc twin, shaft drive)	3,000	4,000	6,000	8,000	10,000	13,000
S8 (487cc twin, shaft drive)	3,000	4,000	6,000	8,000	10,000	13,000
1953						
S7 Deluxe (487cc twin, shaft drive)	3,000	4,000	6,000	8,000	10,000	13,000
S8 (487cc twin, shaft drive)	3,000	4,000	6,000	8,000	10,000	13,000
1954						
S7 Deluxe (487cc twin, shaft drive)	3,000	4,000	6,000	8,000	10,000	13,000
S8 (487cc twin, shaft drive)	3,000	4,000	6,000	8,000	10,000	13,000
1955						
S7 Deluxe (487cc twin, shaft drive)	3,000	4,000	6,000	8,000	10,000	13,000
S8 (487cc twin, shaft drive)	3,000	4,000	6,000	8,000	10,000	13,000
1956						
S7 Deluxe (487cc twin, shaft drive)	3,000	4,000	6,000	8,000	10,000	13,000
S8 (487cc twin, shaft drive)	3,000	4,000	6,000	8,000	10,000	13,000
SUZUKI						
1963						
RM63 (50cc single)	11,000	17,000	25,000	33,000	44,000	55,000
RT63 (124cc twin)	10,000	15,000	22,500	30,000	40,000	50,000
S31 (124cc twin)	200	300	500	700	900	1,100
S250 Colleda (248cc twin)	300	500	700	900	1,200	1,500
TC250 El Camino (248cc twin)	300	500	700	900	1,200	1,500
1964						
M12 Sports 50 (50cc single)	200	300	500	700	900	1,100
K11 Sports 80 (79cc single)	200	300	500	700	900	1,100
T10 (246cc twin)	300	500	700	900	1,200	1,500
1965						
K11 Sports 80 (79cc single)	200	300	400	500	700	900
B100 (118cc single)	200	300	400	500	700	900
S10 (124cc twin)	200	300	500	700	900	1,100
S32 (149cc twin)	200	400	500	700	1,000	1,200
T20 (247cc twin)	300	500	700	900	1,200	1,500
X-6 Super Six (247cc twin)	300	500	700	1,000	1,300	1,600
1966						
M15 (49cc single)	200	300	400	500	700	900
K11 P Challenger (79cc single)	200	300	400	500	700	900
A100 (98cc single)	200	300	400	500	700	900
B120 (118cc single)	200	400	500	700	1,000	1,200
S32 II (149cc twin)	200	400	500	700	1,000	1,200
T20 (247cc twin)	300	500	700	900	1,200	1,500
1967						
RK67 Racer (50cc twin)	9,000	14,000	20,000	27,000	36,000	45,000
K10 P Corsair (79cc single)	200	300	400	500	700	900
K11 P Challenger (79cc single)	200	300	400	500	700	900

	6	5	4	3	2	1
K15 P Hillbilly (79cc single)	300	600	900	1,200	1,500	1,800
A90 (86cc single)	200	300	500	600	800	1,000
A100 Charger (98cc single)	200	300	500	600	800	1,000
AS100 Sierra (98cc single)	200	300	500	600	800	1,000
B100P Magnum (118cc single)	200	300	500	600	800	1,100
BP105 P Bearcat (118cc single)	200	300	500	600	800	1,100
B120 (118cc single)	200	300	500	600	800	1,100
TC120 (118cc single)	200	300	500	600	800	1,100
T125 (124cc twin)	200	400	500	700	1,000	1,200
T200 (196cc single)	200	400	500	700	1,000	1,200
TC200 Stingray (196cc single)	200	400	500	700	1,000	1,200
T20 Super Six (247cc twin)	300	500	700	900	1,200	1,500
T21 Super (247cc twin)	300	500	700	900	1,200	1,500
TC250 Hustler (247cc twin)	700	1,100	1,600	2,100	2,800	3,500
1968						
AC90 (86 single)	200	300	500	600	800	1,100
KT120 Trail (118cc single)	200	300	400	500	700	900
T200 (196cc single)	200	400	500	700	1,000	1,200
TC200 Stingray (196cc single)	200	400	500	700	1,000	1,200
TC250 (247cc twin)	300	500	700	900	1,200	1,500
TM250 (249cc single)	400	700	1,000	1,300	1,800	2,200
T305 (305cc twin)	500	800	1,100	1,500	2,000	2,500
TC305 (305cc twin)	500	800	1,100	1,500	2,000	2,500
T500 Cobra (492cc twin)	600	900	1,400	1,800	2,400	3,000
1969						
AS50 (49cc single)	200	400	700	1,000	1,500	2,000
A95 (69cc single)	300	500	700	1,000	1,300	1,600
T90 Wolf (89cc single)	300	500	700	1,000	1,300	1,600
T125 Stinger (124cc twin)	300	500	1,000	1,500	2,000	2,500
T250 Hustler (247cc twin)	400	700	1,000	1,300	1,800	2,200
TS250 (247cc twin)	400	600	900	1,200	1,600	2,000
T305 Raider (305cc twin)	500	700	1,100	1,440	1,900	2,400
T350 Rebel (315cc twin)	500	800	1,200	1,600	2,100	2,600
T500 II Titan (492cc twin)	700	1,000	1,600	2,000	3,000	4,000
TR500 (500cc twin)	600	900	1,400	1,800	2,400	3,000
1970						
AC50 Maverick (49cc single)	200	400	500	700	1,000	1,200
TC90 Blazer (89cc single)	300	500	700	1,000	1,300	1,600
TS90 Honcho (89cc single)	300	500	700	1,000	1,300	1,600
TC120 II Cat (118cc single)	300	500	700	1,000	1,300	1,600
T125 II Stinger (124cc twin)	300	500	1,000	1,500	2,000	2,500
TS250 II Savage (246cc single)	400	600	900	1,200	1,600	2,000
T250 II Hustler (247cc twin)	400	700	1,000	1,300	1,800	2,200
T350 II Rebel (315cc twin)	500	800	1,200	1,600	2,100	2,600
T500 II Titan (492cc twin)	700	1,000	1,600	2,000	3,000	4,000
1971						
TS50R (49cc single)	300	500	700	900	1,200	1,500
TC90R (89cc single)	300	500	700	1,000	1,300	1,600
TS90R (89cc single)	300	500	700	1,000	1,300	1,600
TC120R (188cc single)	300	500	800	1,000	1,400	1,700
TS125R (123cc single)	300	500	800	1,000	1,400	1,700
TS185R (183cc single)	400	600	900	1,100	1,500	1,900
T250R (246cc single)	400	600	900	1,200	1,600	2,000
TS250R (247cc twin)	500	700	1,000	1,400	1,800	2,300
T350R (315cc twin)	500	800	1,200	1,600	2,100	2,600
T500R Titan (492cc twin)	700	1,000	1,600	2,000	3,000	4,000
1972						
T50J Gaucho (49cc single)	300	400	600	800	1,000	1,300
TC90J Blazer (89cc single)	300	500	700	1,000	1,300	1,600

	6	5	4	3	2	1
TS125J (123cc single)	300	500	800	1,000	1,400	1,700
TS185J Sierra (183cc single)	400	500	800	1,100	1,400	1,800
TS250J Savage (246cc single)	400	600	900	1,100	1,500	1,900
T250J Hustler (247cc twin)	400	600	1,000	1,300	1,700	2,100
GT380J Sebring (371cc triple)	600	900	1,200	1,500	2,000	2,500
TS400J (396cc twin)	400	600	1,000	1,300	1,700	2,100
TS500J Titan (492cc twin).	600	900	1,400	1,800	2,400	3,000
GT550J Indy (543cc triple)	500	800	1,200	1,600	2,100	2,600
GT750J LeMans (739cc triple)	1,500	2,000	3,500	5,000	6,500	8,000
1973						
T50K Gaucho (49cc single)	200	400	500	700	900	1,200
TC100K Blazer (97cc single)	200	400	500	700	1,000	1,200
TS100K Honcho (97cc single).	200	400	500	700	1,000	1,200
TS125K Duster (123cc single)	300	500	800	1,000	1,400	1,700
TS185K Sierra (183cc single).	400	500	800	1,100	1,400	1,800
GT185K Adventurer (184cc twin) . . .	400	500	800	1,100	1,400	1,800
T250K Hustler (247cc twin)	400	700	1,000	1,300	1,800	2,200
TS250K Savage (246cc single)	400	600	900	1,100	1,500	1,900
GT380K Sebring (371cc triple)	600	900	1,200	1,500	2,000	2,500
TS400K (396cc twin)	400	600	1,000	1,300	1,700	2,100
TS500K Titan (492cc twin)	600	900	1,400	1,800	2,400	3,000
GT550K Indy (543cc triple)	500	800	1,200	1,600	2,100	2,600
GT750K LeMans (739cc triple)	1,000	2,000	3,000	4,000	5,000	6,000
1974						
T50L Gaucho (49cc single)	200	400	500	700	900	1,200
TC100L Blazer (97cc single)	200	400	500	700	1,000	1,200
TS100L Honcho (97cc single).	200	400	500	700	1,000	1,200
TS125L Duster (123cc single).	300	500	700	1,000	1,300	1,600
TC185L Ranger (183cc single)	300	500	800	1,000	1,400	1,700
TS185L Sierra (183cc single)	300	500	800	1,000	1,400	1,700
GT185L Adventurer (184cc twin) . . .	400	500	800	1,100	1,400	1,800
T250L Hustler (247cc twin)	400	700	1,000	1,300	1,800	2,200
TS250L Savage (246cc single)	400	600	900	1,100	1,500	1,900
GT380L Sebring (371cc triple)	600	900	1,200	1,500	2,000	2,500
TS400L (396cc twin)	400	600	1,000	1,300	1,700	2,100
TS500L Titan (492cc twin)	600	900	1,400	1,800	2,400	3,000
GT550L Indy (543cc triple)	500	800	1,200	1,600	2,100	2,600
GT750L LeMans (739cc triple)	1,000	2,000	3,000	4,000	5,000	6,000
1975						
TC100M Blazer (97cc single)	200	400	500	700	1,000	1,200
TS100M Honcho (97cc single)	200	400	500	700	1,000	1,200
TS125M Duster (123cc single)	300	500	700	1,000	1,300	1,600
TC185M Ranger (183cc single)	300	500	800	1,000	1,400	1,700
TS185M Sierra (183cc single).	400	600	1,000	1,300	1,700	2,100
GT185M Adventurer (184cc twin)	400	500	800	1,100	1,400	1,800
T250M Hustler (247cc twin)	400	700	1,000	1,300	1,800	2,200
TS250M Savage (246cc single)	400	500	800	1,200	1,600	2,000
GT380M Sebring (371cc triple)	600	900	1,200	1,500	2,000	2,500
TS400M (396cc twin)	400	600	1,000	1,300	1,700	2,100
TS500M Titan (492cc twin)	600	900	1,400	1,800	2,400	3,000
RE5M (497cc single rotary)	1,700	2,300	3,100	4,100	5,200	6,500
GT550M Indy (543cc triple)	500	800	1,200	1,600	2,100	2,600
GT750M LeMans (739cc triple)	900	1,900	2,800	3,700	4,600	5,500
1976						
TC100A Blazer (97cc single)	200	400	500	700	1,000	1,200
TS100A Honcho (97cc single).	200	400	500	700	1,000	1,200
TS125A Duster (123cc single)	300	500	700	1,000	1,300	1,600
TC185A Ranger (183cc single)	300	500	800	1,000	1,400	1,700
TS185A Sierra (183cc single).	300	500	800	1,200	1,600	2,000

	6	5	4	3	2	1
GT185A Adventurer (184cc twin)	400	500	800	1,100	1,400	1,800
T250A Hustler (247cc twin)	400	700	1,000	1,300	1,800	2,200
TS250A Savage (246cc single)	400	500	800	1,100	1,400	1,800
RM370A Cyclone	500	1,200	2,700	3,600	5,500	7,400
GT380A Sebring (371cc triple)	600	900	1,200	1,500	2,000	2,500
TS400A (396cc twin)	400	600	1,000	1,300	1,700	2,100
TS500A Titan (492cc twin)	600	900	1,400	1,800	2,400	3,000
RE5A (497cc single rotary)	1,200	1,800	2,600	3,600	4,700	6,000
GT550A Indy (543cc triple)	500	800	1,200	1,600	2,100	2,600
GT750A LeMans (739cc triple)	900	1,900	2,800	3,700	4,600	5,500
1977						
TC100B Blazer (97cc single)	200	300	500	700	900	1,100
TS100B Honcho (97cc single)	200	300	500	700	900	1,100
TS125B (123cc single)	300	400	600	800	1,100	1,400
TC185B Ranger (183cc single)	300	500	800	1,000	1,400	1,700
TS185B Sierra (183cc single)	300	500	800	1,200	1,600	2,000
GT185B Adventurer (184cc twin)	400	500	800	1,100	1,400	1,800
GT250 (250cc twin)	400	700	1,000	1,300	1,800	2,200
T250B Hustler (247cc twin)	400	700	1,000	1,300	1,800	2,200
TS250B Savage (246cc single)	400	500	800	1,100	1,400	1,800
GT380B Sebring (371cc triple)	600	900	1,200	1,500	2,000	2,500
TS400B Apache (396cc twin)	400	600	900	1,200	1,600	2,000
GS400B (398cc four)	300	500	800	1,000	1,400	1,700
GS400XB (398cc four)	400	600	900	1,100	1,500	1,900
T500B Titan (492cc twin)	500	800	1,300	1,700	2,300	2,800
GT550B Indy (543cc triple)	400	600	1,000	1,300	1,700	2,100
GS550B (549cc four)	400	600	900	1,100	1,500	1,900
GT750B LeMans (739cc triple)	900	1,400	2,000	2,700	3,600	4,500
GS750B (748cc four)	900	1,300	2,000	2,600	3,500	4,400
1978						
TS100C (97cc single)	200	300	500	700	900	1,100
TS125C (123cc single)	200	400	500	700	1,000	1,200
TS185C (183cc single)	300	500	700	900	1,200	1,500
TS250C (246cc single)	400	500	800	1,100	1,400	1,800
DR370C (370cc single)	400	500	800	1,100	1,400	1,800
SP370C (370cc single)	400	500	800	1,100	1,400	1,800
GS400C (398cc four)	300	500	800	1,000	1,400	1,700
GS400XC (398cc four)	400	600	900	1,100	1,500	1,900
GS550C (549cc four)	400	700	1,000	1,300	1,800	2,200
GS550EC (549cc four)	400	700	1,000	1,300	1,800	2,200
GS750C (748cc four)	600	900	1,300	1,700	2,300	2,900
GS750EC (748cc four)	600	900	1,300	1,700	2,300	2,900
GS1000C (997cc four)	600	900	1,400	1,800	2,400	3,000
1979						
TS100N (97cc single)	200	300	400	500	700	900
TS125N (123cc single)	200	300	500	600	800	1,000
TS185N (183cc single)	200	300	500	700	900	1,100
TS250N (246cc single)	300	500	800	1,000	1,400	1,700
DR370N (370cc single)	300	500	700	1,000	1,300	1,600
SP370N (370cc single)	300	500	700	1,000	1,300	1,600
GS425EN (423cc twin)	300	400	600	800	1,100	1,400
GS425LN (423cc twin)	300	400	600	800	1,100	1,400
GS425N (423cc twin)	300	400	600	800	1,100	1,400
GS550EN (549cc four)	400	600	900	1,200	1,600	2,000
GS550LN (549cc four)	400	600	900	1,200	1,600	2,000
GS550N (549cc four)	400	600	900	1,200	1,600	2,000
GS750EN (748cc four)	400	700	1,000	1,300	1,800	2,200
GS750LN (748cc four)	400	700	1,000	1,300	1,800	2,200
GS750N (748cc four)	400	700	1,000	1,300	1,800	2,200

	6	5	4	3	2	1
GS850GN (843cc four)	500	700	1,000	1,400	1,800	2,300
GS1000EN (997cc four)	600	900	1,400	1,800	2,400	3,000
GS1000LN (997cc four)	600	900	1,400	1,800	2,400	3,000
GS1000N (997cc four)	600	900	1,400	1,800	2,400	3,000
GS1000SN (997cc four)	700	1,100	1,600	2,100	2,800	3,500
1980						
DR50T (49cc single)	200	300	400	500	700	900
RM50T (49cc single)	200	300	400	500	700	900
TS100T (97cc single)	200	300	400	500	700	900
RM100T (99cc single)	200	300	400	500	700	900
TS125T (123cc single)	200	300	500	600	800	1,000
RM125T (124cc single)	200	300	500	600	800	1,000
PE175T (172cc single)	200	300	500	600	800	1,100
RS175T (174cc single)	200	300	500	600	800	1,100
TS185T (183cc single)	200	400	500	700	1,000	1,200
PE250T (246cc single)	200	400	500	700	1,000	1,200
RM250T (246cc single)	200	400	500	700	1,000	1,200
RS250T (246cc single)	300	400	600	800	1,100	1,400
TS250T (246cc single)	300	400	600	800	1,100	1,400
GS250TT (247cc four)	300	450	680	900	1,200	1,500
GN400TT (396cc single)	300	400	600	800	1,100	1,400
GN400XT (396cc single)	300	400	600	800	1,100	1,400
DR400T (399cc single)	300	500	700	900	1,200	1,500
RM400T (396cc single)	300	500	800	1,000	1,400	1,700
GS450ET (448cc twin)	300	500	700	900	1,200	1,500
GS450LT (448cc twin)	300	500	700	900	1,200	1,500
GS450ST (448cc twin)	300	500	700	900	1,200	1,500
GS550ET (549cc four)	300	500	800	1,000	1,400	1,700
GS550LT (549cc four)	300	500	800	1,000	1,400	1,700
GS750ET (748cc four)	400	600	900	1,100	1,500	1,900
GS750LT (748cc four)	400	600	900	1,100	1,500	1,900
GS850GLT (843cc four)	400	600	900	1,200	1,600	2,000
GS1000ET (997cc four)	600	900	1,400	1,800	2,400	3,000
GS1000GLT (997cc four)	600	900	1,400	1,800	2,400	3,000
GS1000GT (997cc four)	600	900	1,400	1,800	2,400	3,000
GS1000ST (997cc four)	700	1,000	1,500	2,000	2,700	3,400
GS1100ET (1,074cc four)	700	1,000	15,000	2,000	2,600	3,300
GS1100LT (1,074cc four)	700	1,000	15,000	2,000	2,600	3,300
1981						
GS250T (250cc twin)	300	500	700	800	1,000	1,100
GN400X (400cc single)	300	500	700	800	900	1,000
GN400T (400cc single)	300	500	700	800	1,000	1,100
GS450E (450cc twin)	300	500	900	1,200	1,500	1,800
GS450T (450cc twin)	300	500	900	1,200	1,500	1,800
GS450L (450cc twin)	300	500	900	1,200	1,500	1,800
GS450S (450cc twin)	400	600	900	1,300	1,600	1,900
GS550T (550cc four)	400	600	900	1,400	1,700	2,000
GS550L (550cc four)	400	600	1,000	1,400	1,900	2,400
GS650E (650cc four)	400	600	900	1,500	2,000	2,600
GS650G (650cc four)	400	600	900	1,500	2,100	2,700
GS650GL (650cc four)	400	700	1,100	1,600	2,200	2,800
GS750E (750cc four)	400	700	1,100	1,700	2,300	3,000
GS750L (750cc four)	500	700	1,100	1,600	2,200	2,800
GS850G (850cc four)	500	800	1,100	1,700	2,300	3,000
GS850GL (850cc four)	500	800	1,100	1,900	2,500	3,500
GS1000G (1,000cc four)	600	900	1,300	2,000	3,000	4,000
GS1100GL (1,000cc four)	650	950	1,300	2,000	3,000	4,000
GS1100E (1,100cc four)	800	1,200	2,000	3,000	4,000	5,000

	6	5	4	3	2	1
1982						
GN125 (125cc single)	200	400	700	800	900	1,000
GN250 (250cc single)	300	500	800	1,000	1,200	1,400
GS300L (300cc twin)	300	500	800	1,000	1,300	1,500
GN400T (400cc single)	300	500	800	1,000	1,300	1,600
GS450TX (450cc twin)	400	600	900	1,200	1,400	1,600
GS450T (450cc twin)	400	600	900	1,300	1,500	1,900
GS450E (450cc twin)	300	500	800	1,300	1,500	1,900
GS450L (450cc twin)	400	600	900	1,200	1,500	1,900
GS450GA Automatic (450cc twin)	400	600	900	1,300	1,600	2,000
GS550L (550cc four)	500	700	1,000	1,500	2,000	2,500
GS550M (550cc four)	500	700	1,000	1,500	2,100	2,600
GS650E (650cc four)	400	600	900	1,500	2,100	2,600
GS650G (650cc four)	400	600	900	1,600	2,200	2,800
GS650GL (650cc four)	500	700	1,000	1,600	2,200	2,900
GS750E (750cc four)	500	700	1,100	1,700	2,400	3,100
GS750T (750cc four)	500	700	1,100	1,700	2,300	3,000
GS850G (850cc four)	600	800	1,200	1,900	2,700	3,500
GS850GL (850cc four)	600	800	1,200	2,000	2,800	3,600
GS1000S Katana (1,000cc four)	1,000	1,300	2,000	3,000	4,000	6,000
GS1100E (1,100cc four)	1,000	1,300	1,800	2,300	3,200	4,000
GS1100G (1,100cc four)	700	1,000	1,500	2,300	3,200	4,000
GS1100GL (1,100cc four)	700	1,000	1,500	2,300	3,200	4,000
GS1100GK (1,100cc four)	700	1,000	1,500	2,800	4,000	5,000
1983						
GN125 (125cc single)	200	400	700	800	1,000	1,100
GN250 (250cc single)	300	500	800	1,000	1,300	1,500
GS300L (300cc twin)	300	500	800	1,100	1,300	1,600
GS450TX (450cc twin)	500	700	1,000	1,300	1,600	1,800
GS450E (450cc twin)	400	600	900	1,350	1,700	2,000
GS450L (450cc twin)	400	600	1,000	1,400	1,750	2,000
GS450GA (450cc twin)	500	700	1,000	1,400	1,800	2,100
GS550L Impulse (570cc four)	500	700	1,000	1,600	2,100	2,600
GS550E (570cc four)	500	700	1,000	1,650	2,200	2,800
GS550ES (570cc four)	500	700	1,100	1,800	2,500	3,000
GR650X Tempter (650cc twin)	500	800	1,100	1,400	1,700	2,100
GR650 Tempter (650cc twin)	500	800	1,100	1,500	1,900	2,400
GS650G (670cc four)	500	700	1,000	1,600	2,300	2,900
GS650M Katana (670cc four)	400	600	1,000	1,600	2,300	2,900
GS650GL (670cc four)	500	800	1,100	1,700	2,400	3,000
XN85 Turbo (670cc four)	1,200	1,600	2,100	2,900	3,700	4,700
GS750T (750cc four)	500	800	1,200	1,800	2,400	3,000
GS750E (750cc four)	600	900	1,200	1,900	2,600	3,300
GS750ES (750cc four)	600	900	1,300	2,000	2,800	3,500
GS750S Katana (750cc four)	600	900	1,300	2,000	2,800	3,500
GS850G (850cc four)	600	900	1,300	2,100	2,900	3,600
GS850GL (850cc four)	600	900	1,300	2,100	2,900	3,600
GS1100E (1,075cc four)	1,000	1,300	1,800	2,600	3,300	3,900
GS1100G (1,075cc four)	700	1,000	1,500	2,300	3,200	4,100
GS1100GL (1,075cc four)	700	1,000	1,500	2,300	3,200	4,100
GS1100ES (1,075cc four)	1,000	1,300	1,800	2,500	3,400	4,300
GS1100S Katana (1,075cc four)	700	1,000	1,500	2,500	3,500	4,500
GS1100GK (1,075cc four)	800	1,100	1,500	2,900	4,000	5,000
1984						
GS550ES (575cc four)	500	700	1,100	1,600	2,500	3,100
GS1150ES (1,150cc four)	1,200	1,600	2,200	3,000	3,900	4,800
GS1100GK (1,075cc four)	800	1,100	1,500	3,200	4,300	5,500
1985						
JR50 Mini (50cc single)	200	300	500	600	700	800

	6	5	4	3	2	1
DS80 Mini (80cc single)	200	400	600	700	800	900
RM80 (80cc single)	200	400	700	800	900	1,000
RM125 (125cc single)	300	500	800	1,200	1,500	1,900
DR200 (200cc single)	300	500	800	900	1,100	1,100
RM250 (250cc single)	400	600	900	1,400	1,900	2,500
DR250 (250cc single)	300	500	800	1,200	1,500	1,700
SP250 (250cc single)	300	500	800	1,200	1,500	1,700
GN250 (250cc single)	300	500	800	1,000	1,200	1,400
GS300L (300cc twin)	300	500	800	1,100	1,300	1,500
GS450L (450cc twin)	400	700	1,000	1,200	1,500	1,800
GS450GA (450cc twin)	400	700	1,000	1,400	1,800	2,200
GS550L (570cc four)	400	700	1,000	1,500	2,000	2,500
GS550E (570cc four)	400	700	1,000	1,500	2,100	2,600
GS550ES (570cc four)	400	700	1,100	1,700	2,400	3,100
SP600 (600cc single)	400	600	900	1,400	1,900	2,400
GS700E (700cc four)	700	1,000	1,400	1,800	2,400	3,100
GS700ES (700cc four)	700	1,000	1,400	1,900	2,600	3,300
GV700GL Madura (700cc four)	900	1,200	1,700	2,400	3,000	3,500
GS1150E (1,135cc four)	1,200	1,600	2,100	2,800	3,600	4,400
GS1150ES (1,135cc four)	1,300	1,700	2,300	3,000	3,900	4,800
GV1200GL Madura (1,165 four)	900	1,200	1,700	2,600	3,600	4,500
1986						
JR50 Mini (50cc single)	200	300	400	500	600	700
DS80 Mini (80cc single)	200	400	500	600	700	800
RM80 (80cc single)	200	400	700	800	1,000	1,100
DR100 (100cc single)	200	400	700	800	900	1,100
DR125 (125cc single)	300	500	800	900	1,100	1,300
RM125 (125cc single)	400	600	900	1,300	1,700	2,100
SP125 (125cc single)	300	500	800	900	1,100	1,300
DR200 (200cc single)	300	500	800	1,100	1,300	1,600
SP200 (200cc single)	300	500	800	1,200	1,400	1,600
RM250 (250cc single)	400	600	1,000	1,500	2,000	2,600
GS450L (450cc twin)	400	700	1,000	1,300	1,600	1,900
GS550L (570cc four)	400	700	1,100	1,600	2,200	2,700
GS550ES (570cc four)	400	700	1,100	1,700	2,300	2,900
LS650F Savage (650cc single)	700	1,000	1,500	1,600	1,800	2,000
LS650P Savage (650cc single)	700	1,000	1,500	1,600	1,800	2,000
VS700GLF Intruder (700cc twin)	800	1,100	1,500	2,200	2,800	3,400
VS700GLEF Intruder (700cc twin)	800	1,100	1,600	2,300	2,900	3,600
GSX-R750 (750cc four)	1,300	1,700	2,300	3,100	3,800	4,500
GSX-R750P Ltd Edition (750cc four)	1,400	1,800	2,500	3,800	5,200	6,500
GSX-R1100 (1,050cc four)	1,500	1,900	2,500	3,500	4,500	5,400
GS1150E (1,135cc four)	1,200	1,600	2,200	3,000	3,700	4,600
GV1200GL Madura (1,165 four)	1,000	1,300	1,800	2,700	3,700	4,650
GV1400GT Cavalcade (1,360cc four)	1,500	2,000	2,600	4,000	5,100	6,300
GV1400GD Cavalcade LX (1,360cc four) . .	1,500	2,000	2,700	4,000	5,100	6,300
GV1400GC Cavalcade LXE (1,360cc four) .	1,700	2,200	2,900	4,000	5,100	6,300
1987						
JR50 Mini (50cc single)	200	300	400	500	600	700
RB50 Mini GSX-R50 (50cc single)	400	500	600	700	800	1,000
DS80 Mini (80cc single)	200	400	600	700	800	900
RM80 (80cc single)	300	500	800	900	1,100	1,300
DR100 (100cc single)	200	400	700	900	1,100	1,200
DR125 (125cc single)	300	500	800	1,000	1,200	1,400
RM125 (125cc single)	400	600	1,000	1,400	1,900	2,400
SP125 (125cc single)	300	500	800	1,100	1,300	1,500
DR200 (200cc single)	400	600	900	1,200	1,400	1,700
SP200 (200cc single)	300	600	900	1,200	1,500	1,800

	6	5	4	3	2	1
RM250 (250cc single)	400	700	1,000	1,600	2,300	2,900
GS450L (450cc twin)	400	700	1,000	1,300	1,600	2,000
LS650 Savage (650cc single)	800	1,100	1,500	1,800	2,000	2,300
VS700GLF Intruder (700cc twin)	800	1,100	1,600	2,200	2,900	3,700
VS700GLEF Intruder (700cc twin)	800	1,200	1,600	2,300	3,000	3,800
GSX-R750 (750cc four)	1,500	1,800	2,500	3,200	4,000	4,900
GSX-R1100 (1,050cc four)	1,500	2,000	2,700	3,700	4,800	5,900
VS1400GLF Intruder (1,360cc twin)	1,300	1,700	2,200	3,500	4,700	5,900
GV1400 Cavalcade LX (1,360cc four)	1,600	2,000	2,700	3,900	5,000	6,500
GV1400 Cavalcade LXE (1,360cc four)	1,700	2,200	3,000	4,000	5,100	6,500
1988						
JR50 Mini (50cc single)	200	300	400	500	600	700
DS80 Mini (80cc single)	200	400	700	800	900	1,000
RM80 (80cc single)	300	500	800	1,000	1,200	1,400
DR100 (100cc single)	200	400	700	900	1,100	1,300
DR125 (125cc single)	300	500	800	1,100	1,300	1,500
RM125 (125cc single)	400	700	1,000	1,500	2,000	2,500
SP125 (125cc single)	400	600	900	1,100	1,300	1,600
DR200 (200cc single)	400	600	900	1,300	1,600	1,900
SP200 (200cc single)	400	600	900	1,300	1,600	1,900
GN250 (250cc single)	400	600	900	1,200	1,500	1,800
RM250 (250cc single)	500	800	1,100	1,800	2,400	3,100
GS450L (450cc twin)	500	700	1,100	1,400	1,800	2,200
GSX600F Katana (600cc four)	1,000	1,400	1,900	2,500	3,300	4,000
LS650P Savage (650cc single)	800	1,100	1,600	1,900	2,200	2,500
VS750GLP Intruder (750cc twin)	1,100	1,500	2,000	2,600	3,200	4,000
GSX-R750 (750cc four)	1,500	1,900	2,600	3,400	4,300	5,200
GSX-R1100 (1,050cc four)	1,600	2,100	2,800	3,800	4,900	6,200
GSX1100F Katana (1,125cc four)	1,300	1,700	2,300	3,700	4,800	6,000
VS1400GLP Intruder (1,360cc twin)	1,300	1,700	2,300	3,700	4,800	6,000
GV1400GD Cavalcade LX (1,360cc four)	1,700	2,100	2,800	4,000	5,100	6,500
1989						
JR50 Mini (50cc single)	200	300	500	600	700	800
DS80 Mini (80cc single)	200	400	700	1,000	1,100	1,200
RM80 (80cc single)	300	500	800	1,200	1,500	1,800
DR100 (100cc single)	300	500	800	1,000	1,250	1,500
RM125 (125cc single)	500	800	1,100	1,800	2,400	3,000
RM250 (250cc single)	500	800	1,200	2,000	2,800	3,700
RMX250 (250cc single)	500	800	1,100	2,000	2,900	3,900
GS500E (500cc twin)	600	900	1,400	1,900	2,500	3,000
GSX600F Katana (600cc four)	1,100	1,500	2,000	2,700	3,500	4,400
VS750GLP Intruder (750cc twin)	1,100	1,500	2,100	2,700	3,500	4,300
GSX750F Katana (750cc four)	1,200	1,600	2,200	3,000	4,000	5,300
GSX-R750 (750cc four)	1,700	2,000	2,700	3,600	4,600	5,800
GSX1100F Katana (1,100cc four)	1,400	1,800	2,500	3,500	5,000	6,400
GSX-R1100 (1,100cc four)	1,800	2,200	3,000	4,300	5,400	6,600
VS1400GLP Intruder (1,400cc twin)	1,300	1,700	2,300	3,600	5,200	6,500
GV1400GD Cavalcade LX (1,360cc four)	1,800	2,200	2,900	4,000	5,200	6,500
1990						
JR50 Mini (50cc single)	200	300	500	600	700	800
DS80 Mini (80cc single)	300	500	800	1,000	1,150	1,300
RM80 (80cc single)	400	600	900	1,300	1,700	2,000
DR100 (100cc single)	300	500	800	1,100	1,300	1,500
RM125 (125cc single)	500	800	1,200	1,800	2,500	3,300
DR250 (250cc single)	500	800	1,100	1,800	2,400	3,000
DR250S (250cc single)	500	800	1,200	1,800	2,400	3,000
RM250 (250cc single)	600	900	1,300	2,000	3,000	3,900
RMX250 (250cc single)	500	800	1,200	2,000	3,000	4,000
DR350 (350cc single)	500	800	1,100	1,900	2,500	3,300

	6	5	4	3	2	1
DR350S (350cc single)	500	800	1,200	1,900	2,500	3,300
GS500E (500cc twin)	700	1,000	1,400	1,900	2,500	3,100
DR650S (650cc single)	600	900	1,300	2,000	2,700	3,600
GSX600F Katana (600cc four)	1,100	1,500	2,100	2,800	3,700	4,600
VS750GLP Intruder (750cc twin)	1,200	1,600	2,100	2,800	3,700	4,500
GSX750F Katana (750cc four)	1,400	1,800	2,400	3,300	4,400	5,500
GSX-R750 (750cc four)	1,800	2,200	2,900	4,000	5,000	6,200
VX800 Maurauder (800cc twin)	1,000	1,350	1,800	2,800	3,700	4,600
GSX1100F Katana (1,100cc four)	1,600	1,900	2,600	4,300	5,400	6,600
GSX-R1100 (1,100cc four)	1,900	2,400	3,100	4,300	5,500	7,000
VS1400GLP Intruder (1,400cc twin).	1,400	1,800	2,400	4,000	5,000	6,000
1991						
JR50 Mini (50cc single)	200	400	500	600	700	800
DS80 Mini (80cc single)	300	500	800	1,000	1,100	1,300
RM80 (80cc single)	400	600	900	1,300	1,700	2,100
GN125E (125cc single)	400	600	1,000	1,200	1,500	1,800
RM125 (125cc single)	700	900	1,300	2,000	2,700	3,400
DR250 (250cc single)	500	800	1,200	1,800	2,500	3,100
RM250 (250cc single)	700	1,000	1,400	2,200	3,100	4,000
RMX250 (250cc single)	600	900	1,300	2,100	3,100	4,100
DR350 (350cc single)	600	900	1,200	1,900	2,600	3,400
DR250S (250cc single)	600	900	1,300	1,900	2,500	3,100
DR350S (350cc single)	600	900	1,300	2,000	2,700	3,400
GSF400 Bandit (400cc four).	900	1,200	1,700	2,400	3,100	3,700
GS500E (500cc twin)	800	1,100	1,500	2,000	2,500	3,150
GSX600F Katana (600cc four)	1,200	1,600	2,200	3,000	3,800	4,700
DR650S (650cc single)	700	1,000	1,400	2,200	3,000	3,700
VS750GLP Intruder (750cc twin)	1,200	1,600	2,200	3,000	3,800	4,600
GSX750F Katana (750cc four)	1,600	1,900	2,500	3,300	4,400	5,600
GSX-R750 (750cc four)	1,900	2,300	3,100	4,200	5,300	6,500
VX800 Maurauder (800cc twin)	1,000	1,400	1,900	2,700	3,700	4,700
GSX1100G (1,100cc four).	1,600	2,000	2,700	4,000	5,000	6,000
GSX1100F Katana (1,100cc four).	1,700	2,100	2,800	4,400	5,500	6,800
GSX-R1100 (1,100cc four)	1,900	2,500	3,300	4,500	5,600	7,300
VS1400GLP Intruder (1,400cc twin).	1,400	1,900	2,500	4,100	5,100	6,200
1992						
JR50 Mini (50cc single)	200	400	600	700	800	900
DS80 Mini (80cc single)	300	500	800	1,000	1,200	1,400
RM80 (80cc single)	400	600	1,000	1,400	1,800	2,200
GN125E (125cc single)	500	700	1,000	1,300	1,600	1,900
RM125 (125cc single)	700	1,000	1,400	2,100	2,800	3,500
DR250 (250cc single)	600	900	1,300	1,900	2,500	3,200
DR250S (250cc single)	700	1,000	1,400	2,000	2,600	3,200
RM250 (250cc single)	800	1,100	1,500	2,300	3,200	4,100
RMX250 (250cc single)	700	1,000	1,400	2,200	3,200	4,200
DR350 (350cc single)	600	900	1,300	2,000	2,700	3,500
DR350S (350cc single)	700	1,000	1,400	2,100	2,800	3,500
GSF400 Bandit (400cc four).	1,000	1,300	1,800	2,500	3,200	3,900
GS500E (500cc twin)	800	1,100	1,500	2,100	2,700	3,250
GSX600F Katana (600cc four)	1,300	1,700	2,200	3,000	3,900	4,800
GSX-R600 (600cc four)	1,600	2,000	2,700	3,900	5,000	6,200
DR650S (650cc single)	800	1,100	1,500	2,200	3,000	3,800
GSX750F Katana (750cc four)	1,600	2,000	2,700	3,800	4,800	5,800
GSX-R750 (750cc four)	1,900	2,500	3,300	4,400	5,500	6,700
VS750FLP Intruder (750cc twin)	1,400	1,800	2,500	3,200	4,000	4,800
VX800 Maurauder (800cc twin)	1,100	1,500	2,000	2,900	3,800	4,800
GSX1100G (1,100cc four).	1,700	2,100	2,900	4,000	5,000	6,200
GSX1100F Katana (1,100cc four).	1,700	2,200	2,900	4,400	5,500	7,000

	6	5	4	3	2	1
GSX-R1100 (1,100cc four)	2,000	2,700	3,500	4,600	5,700	7,500
VS1400GLP Intruder (1,400cc twin).	1,600	2,000	2,700	4,100	5,200	6,400
1993						
JR50 Mini (50cc single)	200	400	600	700	800	900
DS80 Mini (80cc single)	300	500	800	1,000	1,200	1,400
RM80 (80cc single)	400	600	1,000	1,400	1,800	2,200
GN125E (125cc single)	500	700	1,000	1,300	1,600	1,900
RM125 (125cc single)	700	1,000	1,400	2,100	2,800	3,500
DR250 (250cc single)	600	900	1,300	1,900	2,500	3,200
DR250SE (250cc single)	700	1,000	1,400	2,000	2,600	3,200
RM250 (250cc single)	800	1,100	1,500	2,300	3,200	4,100
RMX250 (250cc single)	700	1,000	1,400	2,200	3,200	4,200
DR350 (350cc single)	600	900	1,300	2,000	2,700	3,500
DR350S (350cc single)	700	1,000	1,400	2,100	2,800	3,500
GSF400 Bandit (400cc four)	1,000	1,300	1,800	2,500	3,200	3,900
GS500E (500cc twin)	800	1,100	1,500	2,100	2,700	3,250
GSX600F Katana (600cc four)	1,300	1,700	2,200	3,000	3,900	4,800
GSX-R600W (600cc four)	1,600	2,000	2,700	3,900	5,000	6,200
DR650S (650cc single)	600	900	1,200	1,700	2,300	3,000
GSX750F Katana (750cc four)	1,600	2,000	2,700	3,800	4,800	5,800
GSX-R750W (750cc four)	1,900	2,500	3,300	4,400	5,500	6,700
VX800 Maurauder (800cc twin)	1,100	1,500	2,000	2,900	3,800	4,800
VS800GL Intruder (800cc twin)	1,400	1,800	2,500	3,200	4,000	4,800
GSX1100G (1,100cc four)	1,700	2,100	2,900	4,000	5,000	6,200
GSX1100F Katana (1,100cc four)	1,700	2,200	2,900	4,400	5,500	7,000
GSX-R1100W (1,100cc four)	2,000	2,700	3,500	4,600	5,700	7,500
VS1400GLP Intruder (1,400cc twin).	1,600	2,000	2,700	4,100	5,200	6,400
1994						
JR50 Mini (50cc single)	200	400	600	700	800	900
DS80 Mini (80cc single)	300	500	800	1,000	1,200	1,400
RM80 (80cc single)	400	600	1,000	1,400	1,800	2,200
DR125SE (125cc single)	400	600	1,000	1,400	1,800	2,200
GN125E (125cc single)	500	700	1,000	1,300	1,600	1,900
RM125 (125cc single)	700	1,000	1,400	2,100	2,800	3,500
DR250SE (250cc single)	700	1,000	1,400	2,000	2,600	3,200
RM250 (250cc single)	800	1,100	1,500	2,300	3,200	4,100
RMX250 (250cc single)	700	1,000	1,400	2,200	3,200	4,200
DR350 (350cc single)	600	900	1,300	2,000	2,700	3,500
DR350SE (350cc single)	700	1,000	1,400	2,100	2,800	3,500
GS500E (500cc twin)	800	1,100	1,500	2,100	2,700	3,250
GSX600F Katana (600cc four)	−800	1,700	**2,700**	**3,700**	**4,700**	**5,700**
RF600R (600cc four)	700	1,200	1,900	2,600	3,300	4,000
DR650SE (650cc single)	600	900	1,200	1,700	2,300	3,000
GSX750F Katana (750cc four)	−1,000	2,000	**3,200**	**4,400**	**5,600**	**6,800**
GSX-R750W (750cc four)	−1,400	**2,900**	**4,300**	**5,700**	**7,100**	**8,500**
VS800GL Intruder (800cc twin)	−800	**1,900**	**2,900**	**3,900**	**4,900**	**5,900**
RF900R (900cc four)	**1,400**	**2,900**	**4,300**	**5,700**	**7,100**	**8,500**
GSX-R1100W (1,100cc four)	2,000	2,700	3,500	4,600	5,700	7,500
VS1400GLP Intruder (1,400cc twin).	1,600	2,000	2,700	4,100	5,200	6,400
1995						
JR50 Mini (50cc single)	200	400	600	700	800	900
DS80 Mini (80cc single)	300	500	800	1,000	1,200	1,400
RM80 (80cc single)	400	600	1,000	1,400	1,800	2,200
DR125SE (125cc single)	400	600	1,000	1,400	1,800	2,200
GN125E (125cc single)	500	700	1,000	1,300	1,600	1,900
RM125 (125cc single)	700	1,000	1,400	2,100	2,800	3,500
DR250SE (250cc single)	700	1,000	1,400	2,000	2,600	3,200
RM250 (250cc single)	800	1,100	1,500	2,300	3,200	4,100

	6	5	4	3	2	1
RMX250 (250cc single)	700	1,000	1,400	2,200	3,200	4,200
DR350 (350cc single)	600	900	1,300	2,000	2,700	3,500
DR350SE (350cc single)	700	1,000	1,400	2,100	2,800	3,500
GS500E (500cc twin)	800	1,100	1,500	2,100	2,700	3,250
GSX600F Katana (600cc four)	800	1,700	2,700	3,700	4,700	5,700
RF600R (600cc four)	700	1,200	1,900	2,600	3,300	4,000
DR650SE (650cc single)	600	900	1,200	1,700	2,300	3,000
LS650P Savage (650cc single)	500	800	1,600	2,400	3,200	4,000
GSX750F Katana (750cc four)	1,000	2,000	3,200	4,400	5,600	6,800
GSX-R750W (750cc four)	1,400	2,900	4,300	5,700	7,100	8,500
VS800GL Intruder (800cc twin)	800	1,900	2,900	3,900	4,900	5,900
RF900R (900cc four)	1,400	2,900	4,300	5,700	7,100	8,500
GSX-R1100W (1,100cc four)	2,000	2,700	3,500	4,600	5,700	7,500
VS1400GLP Intruder (1,400cc twin)	1,600	2,000	2,700	3,400	5,200	6,400
SWM						
1978						
RS125 GS.	200	500	1,100	1,900	2,900	3,900
RS125 MC	200	500	1,400	2,400	3,900	5,400
RS175 GS.	200	500	100	1,900	2,900	3,900
RS250 GS.	200	500	1,400	2,400	3,900	5,400
RS250 MC	200	500	1,400	2,900	4,400	5,700
320 TL.	200	500	1,400	1,900	2,900	3,900
1979						
SWM 50	200	500	1,000	1,300	1,800	2,300
RS125 GS.	200	500	1,400	1,900	2,900	3,900
RS125 MC	200	500	1,400	2,400	3,400	4,400
RS175 GS.	200	500	1,400	1,900	2,900	3,900
RS175 MC	200	500	1,400	1,900	2,900	3,900
RS250 GS.	200	500	1,400	2,900	3,900	4,900
RS250 MC	200	500	1,400	2,900	4,400	5,700
320 TL.	200	500	1,400	1,900	2,900	3,900
RS350 GS.	200	500	1,400	2,400	3,400	4,400
1980						
50 Automatic	200	300	700	900	1,500	2,100
50 Cross Boy	200	300	700	900	1,500	2,100
125 Enduro	200	500	1,400	2,400	3,400	4,400
125 MX	200	500	1,400	2,900	3,900	4,900
175 Enduro	200	500	1,400	2,400	3,400	4,400
175 Hare Scrambler.	200	500	1,400	2,400	3,400	4,400
250 Enduro	200	500	1,400	2,900	3,900	4,900
250 Hare Scrambler.	200	500	1,400	2,900	3,900	4,900
250 MX	200	500	1,400	2,900	4,400	5,700
320 Trials	200	500	1,400	1,900	2,900	3,900
370 Enduro	200	500	1,400	2,400	3,900	5,400
370 Hare Scrambler.	200	500	1,400	2,400	3,900	5,400
370 MX	200	500	1,400	2,900	4,400	5,700
1981						
RS125 TLNW Trail	200	500	1,400	1,900	2,900	3,900
RS175 GSTF1	200	500	1,400	2,400	3,400	4,400
RS250 GSTF1	200	500	1,400	2,400	3,400	4,400
RS250 MCTF4	200	500	1,400	2,900	4,900	6,900
RS320 TLNW Trail	200	500	1,400	2,400	3,400	4,400
RS440 GSTF1	200	500	1,400	2,900	4,900	6,900
RS440 MCTF1	200	500	1,400	3,400	5,400	7,400
1982						
RS80 TLNW Trail	200	500	900	1,400	2,000	2,600
RS125 GSTF3	200	500	1,400	1,800	2,200	2,600
RS125 TLNW Trail	200	500	1,100	1,500	2,000	2,500

	6	5	4	3	2	1
RS175 GSTF3	200	500	1,400	1,700	2,200	2,700
RS240 TLNW Trail	200	500	1,400	1,900	2,900	3,900
RS250 GSTF3	200	500	1,400	2,400	3,400	4,400
RS250 MCTF6	200	500	1,400	2,900	4,900	6,900
HS320 TLNW Trail	200	500	1,400	2,400	3,400	4,400
RS440 GSTF3	200	500	1,400	2,900	4,900	6,900
RS440 MCTF6	200	500	1,400	3,400	5,400	7,400
1983						
RS125 GS.	200	500	1,400	1,900	2,900	3,900
RS125 MC	200	500	1,400	2,900	3,900	4,900
RS175 GSTF3	200	500	1,400	1,800	2,200	2,600
RS240 TLNW	200	500	1,400	1,900	2,900	3,900
RS250 GS.	200	500	1,400	2,400	4,400	6,400
RS250 MCTF6	200	500	1,400	2,900	4,900	6,900
RS320 TLNW	200	500	1,400	2,400	3,400	4,400
RS350 TLNW Jumbo	200	500	1,400	2,400	3,400	4,400
RS440 GSTF3	200	500	1,400	2,900	4,900	6,900
RS440 MCTF6	200	500	1,400	3,400	5,400	7,400
1984						
MC125 S2.	200	500	1,400	2,900	3,400	3,900
RS240 TLNW	200	500	1,400	1,900	2,900	3,900
GS250 S1.	200	500	1,400	2,400	2,900	3,400
MC250 S2.	200	500	1,400	2,900	3,900	4,900
RS320 TLNW	200	500	1,400	1,900	2,900	3,900
RS350 TLNW	200	500	1,400	2,400	3,400	4,400
TRIUMPH						
1925						
Model W.	2,000	4,000	6,000	8,000	12,000	16,000
1934						
Side Valve 5/3 (350cc single)	2,000	3,000	4,000	5,000	7,500	9,500
1936						
T70 Tiger (250cc single).	1,500	2,300	3,400	4,500	6,000	7,500
T80 Tiger (350cc single).	1,800	2,700	4,100	5,400	7,200	9,000
T90 Tiger (500cc single).	2,600	3,900	5,900	7,800	10,400	13,000
6/1 (650cc twin)	3,600	5,400	8,100	10,800	14,400	18,000
1937						
T70 Tiger (250cc single).	1,500	2,300	3,400	4,500	6,000	7,500
2H (250cc single)	1,400	2,100	3,200	4,200	5,600	7,000
T80 Tiger (350cc single).	1,800	2,700	4,100	5,400	7,200	9,000
3H (350cc single)	1,600	2,500	3,700	4,900	6,600	8,200
3S (350cc single)	1,600	2,500	3,700	4,900	6,600	8,200
T90 Tiger (500cc single).	2,600	3,900	5,900	7,800	10,000	13,000
5H (500cc single)	2,400	3,600	5,400	7,200	9,600	12,000
1938						
T70 Tiger (250cc single).	1,500	2,300	3,400	4,500	6,000	7,500
2H (250cc single)	1,400	2,100	3,200	4,200	5,600	7,000
2HC (250cc single)	1,400	2,200	3,200	4,300	5,800	7,200
T80 Tiger (350cc single).	1,800	2,700	4,100	5,400	7,200	9,000
3H (350cc single)	1,600	2,500	3,700	4,900	6,600	8,200
3S (350cc single)	1,600	2,500	3,700	4,900	6,600	8,200
3SC (350cc single)	1,700	2,600	3,900	5,200	6,900	8,600
T90 Tiger (500cc single).	2,600	3,900	6,000	9,000	12,000	15,000
T100 Tiger (500cc twin)	3,200	5,000	8,000	12,000	16,000	20,000
5H (500cc single)	2,400	3,600	5,400	7,200	9,600	12,000
5T Speed (500cc twin)	4,000	6,000	10,000	14,000	18,000	22,000
6S (600cc twin)	3,600	5,400	8,100	11,000	14,000	18,000
1939						
T70 Tiger (250cc single).	1,500	2,300	3,400	4,500	6,000	7,500
2H (250cc single)	1,400	2,100	3,200	4,200	5,600	7,000

	6	5	4	3	2	1
2HC (250cc single)	1,400	2,200	3,200	4,300	5,800	7,200
T80 Tiger (350cc single).	1,800	2,700	4,100	5,400	7,200	9,000
3H (350cc single)	1,600	2,500	3,700	4,900	6,600	8,200
3S (350cc single)	1,600	2,500	3,700	4,900	6,600	8,200
3SC (350cc single)	1,700	2,600	3,900	5,200	6,900	8,600
T90 Tiger (500cc single).	2,600	3,900	5,900	7,800	10,000	13,000
T100 Tiger (500cc twin)	3,200	5,000	8,000	12,000	16,000	20,000
5H (500cc single)	2,400	3,600	5,400	7,200	9,600	12,000
5S (500cc single)	2,400	3,600	5,400	7,200	9,600	12,000
5T Speed (500cc twin)	4,000	6,000	10,000	14,000	18,000	22,000
6S (600cc twin)	3,600	5,400	8,100	10,800	14,400	18,000
1940						
T70 Tiger (250cc single).	1,500	2,300	3,400	4,500	6,000	7,500
T80 Tiger (350cc single).	1,800	2,700	4,100	5,400	7,200	9,000
3H (350cc single)	1,600	2,500	3,700	4,900	6,600	8,200
3S (350cc single)	1,600	2,500	3,700	4,900	6,600	8,200
3SE (350cc single)	1,600	2,500	3,700	4,900	6,600	8,200
T100 Tiger (500cc twin)	3,200	5,000	8,000	12,000	16,000	20,000
5S (500cc single)	2,400	3,600	5,400	7,200	9,600	12,000
5SE (500cc single)	2,400	3,600	5,400	7,200	9,600	12,000
5T Speed (500cc twin)	4,000	6,000	10,000	14,000	18,000	22,000
1941						
WD/3HW (350cc single).	1,600	2,500	3,700	4,900	6,600	8,200
WD/3SW (350cc single).	1,800	2,700	4,100	5,400	7,200	9,000
WD/5SW (350cc single).	2,400	3,600	5,400	7,200	9,600	12,000
1942						
WD/3HW (350cc single).	1,600	2,500	3,700	4,900	6,600	8,200
WD/3SW (350cc single).	1,800	2,700	4,100	5,400	7,200	9,000
WD/5SW (350cc single).	2,400	3,600	5,400	7,200	9,600	12,000
1943						
WD/3HW (350cc single).	1,600	2,500	3,700	4,900	6,600	8,200
WD/3SW (350cc single).	1,800	2,700	4,100	5,400	7,200	9,000
WD/5SW (350cc single).	2,400	3,600	5,400	7,200	9,600	12,000
1944						
WD/3HW (350cc single).	1,600	2,500	3,700	4,900	6,600	8,200
WD/3SW (350cc single).	1,800	2,700	4,100	5,400	7,200	9,000
WD/5SW (350cc single).	2,400	3,600	5,400	7,200	9,600	12,000
1945						
WD/3HW (350cc single).	1,600	2,500	3,700	4,900	6,600	8,200
WD/3SW (350cc single).	1,800	2,700	4,100	5,400	7,200	9,000
WD/5SW (350cc single).	2,400	3,600	5,400	7,200	9,600	12,000
1946						
3T (350cc single)	1,700	2,600	**4,000**	**6,000**	**9,000**	**12,000**
T100 Tiger (500cc twin)	3,200	5,000	8,000	12,000	16,000	20,000
5T Speed (500cc twin)	3,600	5,000	8,000	12,000	16,000	20,000
1947						
3T (350cc single)	1,700	2,600	**4,000**	**6,000**	**9,000**	**12,000**
T100 Tiger (500cc twin)	3,200	5,000	8,000	12,000	16,000	20,000
5T Speed (500cc twin)	3,600	5,000	8,000	12,000	16,000	20,000
1948						
3T (350cc single)	1,700	2,600	3,800	5,100	6,800	8,500
Grand Prix (500cc twin)	6,200	9,300	14,000	19,000	25,000	31,000
T100 Tiger (500cc twin)	3,000	5,000	7,000	10,000	14,000	18,000
TR5 Trophy (500cc twin)	2,400	4,000	6,000	8,000	11,000	14,000
5T Speed (500cc twin)	4,000	6,000	8,000	11,000	15,000	19,000
1949						
3T (350cc single)	1,700	2,600	3,800	5,100	6,800	8,500
Grand Prix (500cc twin)	6,200	9,300	14,000	19,000	25,000	31,000
TR5 Trophy (500cc twin)	2,400	4,000	6,000	8,000	11,000	14,000

	6	5	4	3	2	1
T100 Tiger (500cc twin)	3,000	5,000	7,000	10,000	14,000	18,000
TRW (500cc twin)	1,200	2,000	3,000	4,000	5,000	7,000
5T Speed (500cc twin)	4,000	6,000	8,000	11,000	15,000	19,000
6T Thunderbird (650cc twin)	2,000	3,000	6,000	9,000	12,000	15,000
1950						
3T (350cc single)	1,700	2,600	3,800	5,100	6,800	8,500
Grand Prix (500cc twin)	6,200	9,300	14,000	19,000	25,000	31,000
T100 Tiger (500cc twin)	4,000	6,000	8,000	11,000	15,000	19,000
TR5 Trophy (500cc twin)	2,400	4,000	6,000	8,000	11,000	14,000
TRW (500cc twin)	1,200	2,000	3,000	4,000	5,000	7,000
5T Speed (500cc twin)	3,400	5,100	7,700	11,000	14,000	18,000
6T Thunderbird (650cc twin)	2,000	3,000	6,000	9,000	12,000	15,000
1951						
3T (350cc single)	1,700	2,600	3,800	5,100	6,800	8,500
T100 Tiger (500cc twin)	3,000	5,000	7,000	10,000	14,000	18,000
TR5 Trophy (500cc twin)	2,400	3,600	6,000	9,000	12,000	15,000
TRW (500cc twin)	1,200	2,000	3,000	4,000	5,000	7,000
5T Speed (500cc twin)	3,400	5,100	7,700	11,000	14,000	18,000
6T Thunderbird (650cc twin)	2,000	3,000	6,000	9,000	12,000	15,000
1952						
T100 Tiger (500cc twin)	2,800	4,200	5,500	7,000	10,000	13,000
TR5 Trophy (500cc twin)	2,400	3,600	6,000	9,000	12,000	15,000
TRW (500cc twin)	1,200	2,000	3,000	4,000	5,000	7,000
5T Speed (500cc twin)	3,400	5,100	7,700	1,000	14,000	18,000
6T Thunderbird (650cc twin)	2,000	3,000	6,000	9,000	12,000	15,000
1953						
T15 Terrier (150cc single)	1,000	1,500	2,300	3,000	4,000	5,000
T100 Tiger (500cc twin)	2,800	4,200	7,000	10,000	13,000	16,000
TR5 Trophy (500cc twin)	2,400	3,600	5,400	7,200	9,600	12,000
TRW (500cc twin)	1,200	1,800	2,700	3,600	4,800	6,000
5T Speed (500cc twin)	3,400	5,100	7,700	**10,000**	14,000	17,000
6T Thunderbird (650cc twin)	2,000	3,000	6,000	9,000	12,000	15,000
1954						
T15 Terrier (150cc single)	1,000	1,500	2,300	3,000	4,000	5,000
T100 Tiger (500cc twin)	2,800	4,200	6,300	8,400	11,200	14,000
TR5 Trophy (500cc twin)	2,200	3,300	5,000	6,600	8,800	11,000
TRW (500cc twin)	1,200	1,800	2,700	3,600	4,800	6,000
5T Speed (500cc twin)	3,200	4,800	7,200	9,600	13,000	16,000
T110 Tiger (650cc twin)	2,800	4,200	6,300	8,400	11,000	14,000
6T Thunderbird (650cc twin)	2,000	3,000	6,000	9,000	12,000	15,000
1955						
T15 Terrier (150cc single)	1,000	1,500	2,300	3,000	4,000	5,000
T100 Tiger (500cc twin)	2,800	4,200	6,300	8,400	11,000	14,000
TR5 Trophy (500cc twin)	2,200	3,300	5,000	7,000	9,000	12,000
TRW (500cc twin)	1,200	1,800	2,700	3,600	4,800	6,000
5T Speed (500cc twin)	3,200	4,800	7,200	9,600	13,000	16,000
T110 Tiger (650cc twin)	2,800	4,200	6,300	8,400	11,000	14,000
6T Thunderbird (650cc twin)	2,000	3,000	6,000	9,000	12,000	15,000
1956						
T15 Terrier (150cc single)	1,000	1,500	2,300	3,000	4,000	5,000
T100 Tiger (500cc twin)	2,800	4,200	6,300	8,400	11,000	14,000
TR5 Trophy (500cc twin)	2,200	3,300	5,000	6,600	8,800	11,000
TRW (500cc twin)	1,200	1,800	2,700	3,600	4,800	6,000
5T Speed (500cc twin)	3,200	4,800	7,200	9,600	13,000	16,000
T110 Tiger (650cc twin)	2,800	4,200	6,300	8,400	11,000	14,000
TR6 Trophy (650cc twin)	2,200	3,300	6,000	9,000	12,000	15,000
6T Thunderbird (650cc twin)	2,000	3,000	6,000	9,000	12,000	15,000
1957						
T20 Tiger Cub (200cc single)	1,000	1,500	2,300	3,500	5,000	7,000

	6	5	4	3	2	1
T20C Tiger Cub (200cc single)	1,000	1,500	2,300	3,500	5,000	7,000
3TA Twenty One (350cc twin).	1,200	1,800	3,000	4,000	6,000	8,000
T100 Tiger (500cc twin).	2,800	4,200	6,300	8,400	11,000	14,000
TR5 Trophy (500cc twin)	2,200	3,300	4,950	6,600	8,800	11,000
TRW (500cc twin)	1,200	1,800	2,700	3,600	4,800	6,000
5T Speed (500cc twin)	3,200	4,800	7,200	9,600	13,000	16,000
T110 Tiger (650cc twin)	2,800	4,200	6,300	8,400	11,000	14,000
TR6 Trophy (650cc twin)	2,200	3,300	5,000	6,600	10,000	14,000
6T Thunderbird (650cc twin)	2,000	3,000	6,000	9,000	12,000	15,000
1958						
T20 Tiger Cub (200cc single)	900	1,400	2,000	3,500	5,000	7,000
T20C Tiger Cub (200cc single)	1,000	1,500	2,300	3,500	5,000	7,000
3TA Twenty One (350cc twin).	1,200	1,800	3,000	4,000	6,000	8,000
T100 Tiger (500cc twin).	2,600	3,900	5,900	7,800	10,000	13,000
TR5 Trophy (500cc twin)	2,200	3,300	5,000	7,000	10,000	13,000
TRW (500cc twin)	1,200	1,800	2,700	3,600	4,800	6,000
5T Speed (500cc twin)	3,000	4,500	6,800	9,000	12,000	15,000
T110 Tiger (650cc twin)	2,800	4,200	6,300	8,400	11,000	14,000
TR6 Trophy (650cc twin)	2,200	3,300	5,000	6,600	10,000	14,000
6T Thunderbird (650cc twin)	2,000	3,000	6,000	9,000	12,000	15,000
1959						
T20 Tiger Cub (200cc single)	900	1,400	2,000	3,500	5,000	7,000
T20C Tiger Cub (200cc single)	1,000	1,500	2,300	3,500	5,000	7,000
3TA Twenty One (350cc twin).	1,200	1,800	3,000	4,000	6,000	8,000
T100 Tiger (500cc twin).	2,600	3,900	5,900	7,800	10,000	13,000
TRW (500cc twin)	1,200	1,800	2,700	3,600	4,800	6,000
5TA Speed (500cc twin).	3,000	4,500	6,800	9,000	12,000	15,000
T110 Tiger (650cc twin)	2,800	4,200	6,300	8,400	11,000	14,000
T120 Bonneville (650cc twin)	4,300	6,300	10,000	15,000	19,000	23,000
TR6 Trophy (650cc twin)	2,200	3,300	5,000	6,600	10,000	14,000
6T Thunderbird (650cc twin)	3,000	4,500	6,000	9,000	12,000	16,000
1960						
T20 Tiger Cub (200cc single)	900	1,400	2,000	3,500	5,000	7,000
T20S Tiger Cub (200cc single)	1,000	1,500	2,300	3,500	5,000	7,000
3TA Twenty One (350cc twin).	1,200	1,800	3,000	4,000	6,000	8,000
T100A Tiger (500cc twin)	2,600	3,900	5,900	7,800	10,000	13,000
TRW (500cc twin)	1,200	1,800	2,700	3,600	4,800	6,000
5TA Speed (500cc twin)	3,000	4,500	6,800	9,000	12,000	15,000
T110 Tiger (650cc twin)	2,800	4,200	6,300	8,400	11,000	14,000
T120 Bonneville (650cc twin)	3,600	5,400	8,100	11,000	14,400	18,000
TR6 Trophy (650cc twin)	2,200	3,300	5,000	6,600	10,000	14,000
6T Thunderbird (650cc twin)	2,000	3,000	4,500	6,000	10,000	14,000
1961						
T20 Tiger Cub (200cc single)	900	1,400	2,000	2,700	3,600	4,500
T20S/L Tiger Cub (200cc single)	900	1,400	2,000	2,700	3,600	4,500
T20T Tiger Cub (200cc single)	900	1,400	2,000	2,700	3,600	4,500
3TA Twenty One (350cc twin).	1,200	1,800	3,000	4,000	6,000	8,000
T100A Tiger (500cc twin)	2,400	3,600	5,400	7,200	9,600	12,000
TRW (500cc twin)	1,200	1,800	2,700	3,600	4,800	6,000
5TA Speed (500cc twin)	2,800	4,200	6,300	8,400	11,000	14,000
T110 Tiger (650cc twin)	2,800	4,200	6,300	8,400	11,000	14,000
T120 Bonneville (650cc twin)	3,600	5,400	8,100	11,000	14,000	18,000
T120R Bonneville (650cc twin)	3,600	5,400	8,100	11,000	14,000	18,000
TR6 Trophy (650cc twin)	2,000	3,000	4,500	6,000	10,000	14,000
6T Thunderbird (650cc twin)	2,000	3,000	4,500	6,000	10,000	14,000
1962						
T20 Tiger Cub (200cc single)	900	1,400	2,000	2,700	3,600	4,500
T20S/H Tiger Cub (200cc single)	900	1,400	2,000	2,700	3,600	4,500
T20S/S Tiger Cub (200cc single)	900	1,400	2,000	2,700	3,600	4,500

	6	5	4	3	2	1
TR20 Tiger Cub (200cc single)	900	1,400	2,000	2,700	3,600	4,500
3TA Twenty One (350cc twin)	1,200	1,800	3,000	4,000	6,000	8,000
T100SS Tiger (500cc twin)	2,400	3,600	5,400	7,200	9,600	12,000
TRW (500cc twin)	1,200	1,800	2,700	3,600	4,800	6,000
5TA Speed (500cc twin)	2,800	4,200	6,300	8,400	11,000	14,000
T120 Bonneville (650cc twin)	3,600	5,400	8,100	10,000	12,000	15,000
T120R Bonneville (650cc twin)	3,600	5,400	8,100	10,000	12,000	15,000
TR6 Trophy (650cc twin)	2,000	3,000	4,500	6,000	8,000	10,000
6T Thunderbird (650cc twin)	2,000	3,000	4,500	6,000	9,000	12,000
1963						
T20 Tiger Cub (200cc single)	900	1,400	2,000	2,700	3,600	4,500
T20S/H Tiger Cub (200cc single)	900	1,400	2,000	2,700	3,600	4,500
T20S/S Tiger Cub (200cc single)	900	1,400	2,000	2,700	3,600	4,500
T90 Tiger (350cc twin)	1,100	1,700	2,500	3,400	4,500	5,600
3TA Twenty One (350cc twin)	1,200	1,800	3,000	4,000	6,000	8,000
T100SC Tiger (500cc twin)	2,200	3,300	5,000	6,600	8,800	11,000
T100SR Tiger (500cc twin)	2,200	3,300	5,000	6,600	8,800	11,000
T100SS Tiger (500cc twin)	2,200	3,300	5,000	6,600	8,800	11,000
TRW (500cc twin)	1,200	1,800	2,700	3,600	4,800	6,000
5TA Speed (500cc twin)	2,800	4,200	6,300	8,400	11,000	14,000
T120 Bonneville (650cc twin)	3,600	5,400	7,000	8,000	11,000	14,000
T120C Bonneville (650cc twin)	3,600	5,400	7,000	8,000	11,000	14,000
T120R Bonneville (650cc twin)	3,600	5,400	7,000	8,000	11,000	14,000
TR6 Trophy (650cc twin)	2,000	3,000	4,500	6,000	8,000	10,000
6T Thunderbird (650cc twin)	2,000	3,000	4,500	6,000	9,000	12,000
1964						
T20 Tiger Cub (200cc single)	900	1,400	2,100	2,800	3,700	4,600
T20S/H Tiger Cub (200cc single)	900	1,400	2,100	2,800	3,700	4,600
T20S/S Tiger Cub (200cc single)	900	1,400	2,100	2,800	3,700	4,600
T90 Tiger (350cc twin)	1,100	1,700	2,500	3,400	4,500	5,600
3TA Twenty One (350cc twin)	1,200	1,800	3,000	4,000	6,000	8,000
T100SC Tiger (500cc twin)	2,000	3,000	4,500	6,000	8,000	10,000
T100SR Tiger (500cc twin)	2,000	3,000	4,500	6,000	8,000	10,000
T100SS Tiger (500cc twin)	2,000	3,000	4,500	6,000	8,000	10,000
5TA Speed (500cc twin)	2,600	3,900	5,900	7,800	10,000	13,000
T120 Bonneville (650cc twin)	3,200	4,800	6,500	8,000	10,000	12,000
T120 Bonneville Thruxton (650cc twin) . . .	4,100	6,200	9,200	12,000	16,000	21,000
T120C Bonneville (650cc twin)	3,200	4,800	6,500	8,000	10,000	12,000
T120R Bonneville (650cc twin)	3,200	4,800	6,500	8,000	10,000	12,000
T120TT Bonneville TT Special (650cc twin),	3,300	4,950	6,500	8,000	10,000	12,000
TR6 Trophy (650cc twin)	2,000	3,000	4,500	6,000	8,000	10,000
TR6S/C Trophy (650cc twin)	2,000	3,000	4,500	6,000	8,000	10,000
TR6S/R Trophy (650cc twin)	2,000	3,000	4,500	6,000	8,000	10,000
TRW (500cc twin)	1,200	1,800	2,700	3,600	4,800	6,000
6T Thunderbird (650cc twin)	2,000	3,000	4,500	6,000	8,000	10,000
1965						
T20 Tiger Cub (200cc single)	900	1,400	2,500	3,000	4,000	5,000
T20S/H Tiger Cub (200cc single)	900	1,400	2,100	2,800	3,700	4,600
T20S/M Tiger Cub (200cc single)	900	1,400	2,100	2,800	3,700	4,600
T20S/S Tiger Cub (200cc single)	900	1,400	2,100	2,800	3,700	4,600
T90 Tiger (350cc twin)	1,100	1,700	2,500	3,400	4,500	5,600
3TA Twenty One (350cc twin)	1,200	1,800	3,000	4,000	6,000	8,000
T100SC Tiger (500cc twin)	2,000	3,000	4,500	6,000	8,000	10,000
T100SR Tiger (500cc twin)	2,000	3,000	4,500	6,000	8,000	10,000
T100SS Tiger (500cc twin)	2,000	3,000	4,500	6,000	8,000	10,000
5TA Speed (500cc twin)	2,600	3,900	5,900	7,800	10,000	13,000
T120 Bonneville (650cc twin)	3,200	4,800	6,500	8,000	10,000	12,000
T120 Bonneville Thruxton (650cc twin) . . .	4,100	6,200	9,200	12,000	16,000	21,000
T120C Bonneville (650cc twin)	3,200	4,800	6,500	8,000	10,000	12,000

	6	5	4	3	2	1
T120R Bonneville (650cc twin)	3,200	4,800	6,500	8,000	10,000	12,000
T120TT Bonneville TT Special (650cc twin).	3,300	4,950	6,500	8,000	10,000	13,000
TR6 Trophy (650cc twin)	2,000	3,000	4,500	6,000	8,000	10,000
TR6S/C Trophy (650cc twin)	2,000	3,000	4,500	6,000	8,000	10,000
TR6S/R Trophy (650cc twin)	2,000	3,000	4,500	6,000	8,000	10,000
TRW (500cc twin).	1,200	1,800	2,700	3,600	4,800	6,000
6T Thunderbird (650cc twin)	2,000	3,000	4,500	6,000	8,000	10,000
1966						
T20 Tiger Cub Bantam (200cc single). . . .	900	1,400	2,000	2,700	3,600	4,500
T20S/H Tiger Cub (200cc single)	900	1,400	2,100	2,800	3,700	4,600
T20S/M Tiger Cub (200cc single)	900	1,400	2,100	2,800	3,700	4,600
T20S/S Tiger Cub (200cc single)	900	1,400	2,100	2,800	3,700	4,600
T90 Tiger (350cc twin)	1,100	1,700	2,500	3,400	4,500	5,600
3TA Twenty One (350cc twin).	1,200	1,800	3,000	4,000	6,000	8,000
T100C Tiger (500cc twin)	1,800	2,700	4,100	5,400	7,200	9,000
T100R Tiger Daytona (500cc twin)	1,800	2,700	4,100	5,400	7,200	9,000
5TA Speed (500cc twin).	2,500	3,800	5,600	7,500	10,000	13,000
T120 Bonneville (650cc twin)	3,200	4,800	6,500	8,000	10,000	12,000
T120R Bonneville (650cc twin)	3,200	4,800	6,500	8,000	10,000	12,000
T120TT Bonneville TT Special (650cc twin).	3,300	5,000	6,500	8,000	10,000	12,000
TR6 Trophy (650cc twin)	2,000	3,000	4,500	6,000	8,000	10,000
TR6C Trophy (650cc twin)	2,000	3,000	4,500	6,000	8,000	10,000
TR6R Trophy (650cc twin)	2,000	3,000	4,500	6,000	8,000	10,000
TR6S/C Trophy (650cc twin)	2,000	3,000	4,500	6,000	8,000	10,000
TR6S/R Trophy (650cc twin)	2,000	3,000	4,500	6,000	8,000	10,000
6T Thunderbird (650cc twin)	2,000	3,000	4,500	6,000	8,000	10,000
1967						
T20S/C Tiger Cub (200cc single)	900	1,400	2,100	3,000	4,500	6,000
T90 Tiger (350cc twin)	1,100	1,700	2,500	3,400	4,500	5,600
T100 Tiger (500cc twin)	1,800	2,700	4,050	5,400	7,200	9,000
T100R Tiger Daytona (500cc twin)	1,900	2,900	4,400	5,800	7,800	9,700
T120 Bonneville (650cc twin)	3,200	4,800	6,500	8,000	10,000	12,000
T120R Bonneville (650cc twin)	3,200	4,800	6,500	8,000	10,000	12,000
T120TT Bonneville TT Special (650cc twin).	3,300	5,000	6,500	8,000	10,000	13,000
TR6 Trophy (650cc twin)	2,000	3,000	4,500	6,000	8,000	10,000
TR6C Trophy (650cc twin)	2,000	3,000	4,500	6,000	8,000	10,000
TR6R Trophy (650cc twin)	2,000	3,000	4,500	6,000	8,000	10,000
1968						
T20S/C Tiger Cub (200cc single)	900	1,400	2,100	3,000	4,500	6,000
TR25W Trophy (250cc single).	800	1,300	1,900	2,500	3,400	4,200
T90 Tiger (350cc twin)	1,100	1,700	2,500	3,400	4,500	5,600
T100C Tiger (500cc twin)	1,800	2,700	4,050	5,400	7,200	9,000
T100R Tiger Daytona (500cc twin)	1,900	2,900	4,400	5,800	7,800	9,700
T100S Tiger (500cc twin)	1,800	2,700	4,050	5,400	7,200	9,000
T120 Bonneville (650cc twin)	1,000	2,500	6,500	8,000	10,000	12,000
T120R Bonneville (650cc twin)	1,000	2,500	6,500	8,000	10,000	12,000
TR6 Trophy (650cc twin)	2,000	3,000	4,500	6,000	8,000	10,000
TR6C Trophy (650cc twin)	2,000	3,000	4,500	6,000	8,000	10,000
TR6R Trophy (650cc twin)	2,000	3,000	4,500	6,000	8,000	10,000
1969						
TR25W Trophy (250cc single).	800	1,300	1,900	2,500	3,400	4,200
T90 Tiger (350cc twin)	1,100	1,700	2,500	3,400	4,500	5,600
T100C Tiger (500cc twin)	1,800	2,700	4,050	5,400	7,200	9,000
T100R Tiger Daytona (500cc twin)	1,900	2,900	4,400	5,800	7,800	9,700
T100S Tiger (500cc twin)	1,800	2,700	4,050	5,400	7,200	9,000
T120 Bonneville (650cc twin)	1,000	2,500	6,500	8,000	10,000	12,000
T120R Bonneville (650cc twin)	1,000	2,500	6,500	8,000	10,000	12,000
TR6 Trophy (650cc twin)	2,000	3,000	4,500	6,000	8,000	10,000
TR6C Trophy (650cc twin)	2,000	3,000	4,500	6,000	8,000	10,000

	6	5	4	3	2	1
TR6R Trophy (650cc twin)	2,000	3,000	4,500	6,000	8,000	10,000
T150 Trident (750cc triple)	1,000	2,500	5,000	6,600	8,800	11,000
1970						
T25SS Street Scrambler (250cc single) . . .	900	1,300	2,000	2,600	3,500	4,400
T25T Blazer (250cc single)	900	1,300	2,000	2,600	3,500	4,400
TR25W Trophy (250cc single).	800	1,300	1,900	2,500	3,400	4,200
T100C (500cc twin)	1,800	2,700	4,050	5,400	7,200	9,000
T100R Tiger Daytona (500cc twin)	1,900	2,900	4,400	6,000	8,000	10,000
T100S Tiger (500cc twin)	1,800	2,700	4,050	5,400	7,200	9,000
T120 Bonneville (650cc twin)	1,000	2,500	6,500	8,000	10,000	12,000
T120R Bonneville (650cc twin)	1,000	2,500	6,500	8,000	10,000	12,000
T120RT Bonneville (U.S.) (650cc twin) . . .	1,000	2,500	6,500	8,000	10,000	12,000
TR6 Trophy (650cc twin)	1,800	2,700	4,100	5,400	7,200	9,000
TR6C Trophy (650cc twin)	1,800	2,700	4,100	5,400	7,200	9,000
TR6R Trophy (650cc twin)	1,800	2,700	4,100	6,000	8,000	10,000
T150 Trident (750cc triple)	1,000	2,500	5,000	6,600	8,800	11,000
1971						
T25SS Street Scrambler (250cc single) . . .	900	1,300	2,000	2,600	3,500	4,400
T25T Blazer (250cc single)	900	1,300	2,000	2,600	3,500	4,400
T100C (500cc twin)	1,900	2,900	4,400	5,800	7,800	9,700
T100R Tiger Daytona (500cc twin)	1,800	2,700	4,050	5,400	7,200	9,000
T120 Bonneville (650cc twin)	1,000	2,500	4,000	6,000	8,000	10,000
T120R Bonneville (650cc twin)	1,000	2,500	4,000	6,000	8,000	10,000
TR6C Trophy (650cc twin)	1,800	2,700	4,100	5,400	7,200	9,000
T150 Trident (750cc triple)	1,000	2,500	5,000	6,600	8,800	11,000
1972						
T100R Tiger Daytona (500cc twin)	1,900	2,900	4,400	5,800	7,800	9,700
T120R Bonneville (650cc twin)	1,000	2,500	4,000	6,000	8,000	10,000
T120RV Bonneville (650cc twin)	1,000	2,500	4,000	6,000	8,000	10,000
T120V Bonneville (650cc twin)	1,000	2,500	4,000	6,000	8,000	10,000
TR6C Trophy (650cc twin)	1,800	2,700	4,100	5,400	7,200	9,000
TR6CV Trophy (650cc twin).	1,800	2,700	4,100	5,400	7,200	9,000
TR6R Trophy Sports (650cc twin)	1,900	2,800	4,200	5,600	7,400	9,300
T150 Trident (750cc triple)	1,000	2,500	4,000	6,000	8,000	10,000
T150V Trident (750cc triple).	1,000	2,500	4,000	6,000	8,000	10,000
1973						
T100R Tiger Daytona (500cc twin)	1,900	2,900	4,400	5,800	7,800	9,700
TR5T Adventurer (500cc twin)	800	1,300	2,000	3,000	4,000	6,000
T120R Bonneville (650cc twin)	1,000	2,500	4,000	6,000	8,000	10,000
T120RV Bonneville (650cc twin)	1,000	2,500	4,000	6,000	8,000	10,000
T120V Bonneville (650cc twin)	1,000	2,500	4,000	6,000	8,000	10,000
TR6C Trophy (650cc twin)	1,800	2,700	4,100	5,400	7,200	9,000
TR6CV Trophy (650cc twin)	1,800	2,700	4,100	5,400	7,200	9,000
TR6R Trophy Sports (650cc twin)	1,900	2,800	4,200	5,600	7,400	9,300
T140RV Bonneville (750cc twin)	1,000	2,000	3,000	5,000	7,500	9,000
T140V Bonneville (750cc twin)	1,000	2,000	3,000	5,000	7,500	9,000
T150V Trident (750cc triple).	1,000	2,500	4,000	5,500	7,000	9,000
TR7RV Tiger (750cc twin).	1,800	2,500	**4,000**	**5,500**	**7,000**	**9,000**
X75 Hurricane (750cc triple).	3,000	**6,000**	**12,000**	**15,000**	**18,000**	**22,000**
1974						
T100R Tiger Daytona (500cc twin)	1,900	2,900	4,400	5,800	7,800	9,700
TR5MX Avenger (500cc twin)	800	1,200	2,000	3,000	4,000	6,000
TR5T Adventurer (500cc twin)	800	1,300	2,000	3,000	4,000	6,000
T120R Bonneville (650cc twin)	2,000	3,000	4,000	6,000	8,000	10,000
T120RV Bonneville (650cc twin)	2,000	3,000	4,000	6,000	8,000	10,000
T120V Bonneville (650cc twin)	2,000	3,000	4,000	6,000	8,000	10,000
T140RV Bonneville (750cc twin)	1,000	2,000	3,000	5,000	7,500	9,000
T140V Bonneville (750cc twin)	1,000	2,000	3,000	5,000	7,500	9,000
T150V Trident (750cc triple).	1,000	2,500	4,000	5,500	7,000	9,000

	6	5	4	3	2	1
TR7RV Tiger (750cc twin)	1,800	2,500	**4,000**	**5,500**	**7,000**	**9,000**
1975						
T120RV Bonneville (650cc twin)	2,000	3,000	4,000	6,000	8,000	10,000
T120V Bonneville (650cc twin)	2,000	3,000	4,000	6,000	8,000	10,000
T140RV Bonneville (750cc twin)	1,000	2,000	3,000	5,000	7,500	9,000
T140V Bonneville (750cc twin)	1,000	2,000	3,000	5,000	7,500	9,000
T150V Trident (750cc triple).	1,000	2,500	4,000	5,500	7,000	9,000
T160 Trident (750cc triple)	1,000	2,500	4,000	5,500	7,000	9,000
TR7RV Tiger (750cc twin).	1,800	2,500	**4,000**	**5,500**	**7,000**	**9,000**
1976						
T140V Bonneville (750cc twin)	1,000	2,000	3,000	5,000	7,500	9,000
T160 Trident (750cc triple)	1,000	2,500	4,000	5,500	7,000	9,000
TR7RV Tiger (750cc twin).	1,800	2,500	**4,000**	**5,500**	**7,000**	**9,000**
1977						
T140J Bonneville Silver Jubilee (750cc twin)	1,000	2,000	3,000	6,000	8,000	10,000
T140V Bonneville (750cc twin)	1,000	2,000	3,000	5,000	7,500	9,000
TR7RV Tiger (750cc twin).	1,300	2,000	**4,000**	**5,500**	**7,000**	**9,000**
1978						
T140E Bonneville (750cc twin)	1,000	2,000	3,000	5,000	7,500	9,000
T140V Bonneville (750cc twin)	1,000	2,000	3,000	5,000	7,500	9,000
TR7RV Tiger (750cc twin).	1,000	2,000	**4,000**	**5,500**	**7,000**	**9,000**
1979						
T140D Bonneville (750cc twin)	1,000	2,000	3,000	5,000	7,500	9,000
T140E Bonneville (750cc twin)	1,000	2,000	3,000	5,000	7,500	9,000
TR7RV Tiger (750cc twin).	1,100	2,000	**4,000**	**5,500**	**7,000**	**9,000**
1980						
T140 Executive Bonneville (750cc twin). . .	1,000	2,000	3,000	5,000	7,500	9,000
T140D Bonneville (750cc twin)	1,000	2,000	3,000	5,000	7,500	9,000
T140E Bonneville (750cc twin)	1,000	2,000	3,000	5,000	7,500	9,000
T140ES Bonneville Electro (750cc twin) . .	1,000	2,000	3,000	5,000	7,500	9,000
TR7RV Tiger (750cc twin).	1,100	2,000	**4,000**	**5,500**	**7,000**	**9,000**
1982						
T140ES Bonneville (750cc twin)	1,000	2,000	3,000	5,000	7,500	9,000
T140ES Royal (750cc twin)	1,000	2,000	3,000	5,000	7,500	9,000
T140ES Executive (750cc twin)	1,000	2,000	3,000	5,000	7,500	9,000
1983						
T140ES Bonneville (750cc twin)	1,000	2,000	3,000	5,000	7,500	9,000
T140TSX (750cc twin).	2,500	3,300	4,300	6,300	8,300	11,000
T140TSS Eight Valve (750cc twin)	2,900	3,900	5,100	7,100	9,000	12,000
T140ES Executive (750cc twin)	1,000	2,000	3,000	5,000	7,500	9,000
1995						
Tiger SE (885cc triple)	1,700	3,500	5,100	6,700	8,300	9,900
Trident 900SA (885cc triple).	1,200	2,400	3,800	5,200	6,600	8,000
Sprint SD (885cc triple)	1,000	2,000	4,000	6,000	8,000	10,000
Thunderbird SJ (885cc triple)	1,000	2,000	4,000	6,000	8,000	10,000
Speed Triple SG (885cc triple)	1,000	2,000	4,000	6,000	8,000	10,500
Daytona 900SC (885cc triple)	1,000	2,000	4,000	6,000	8,500	11,000
Super III SH (885cc triple).	1,500	3,000	4,500	7,500	10,500	13,500
Daytona 1200VS (1,180cc four)	2,000	4,000	6,000	8,000	10,000	12,400
Trophy 900SB (885cc four)	1,000	2,000	4,000	6,000	8,000	10,700
Trophy 1200VA (1,200cc four)	2,000	4,000	6,000	8,000	10,000	12,400

VELOCETTE

	6	5	4	3	2	1
1935						
MSS.	3,000	5,000	7,000	9,500	11,500	13,500
1937						
GTP.	1,000	2,000	4,000	6,000	8,000	10,000
KSS.	3,000	6,000	9,000	12,000	15,000	18,000
1938						
MAC (349cc single)	2,500	4,000	5,300	6,500	8,000	10,000

	6	5	4	3	2	1
1946						
KSS (350cc single)	2,000	3,000	4,500	6,000	8,000	10,000
1947						
KTT (348cc single)	7,000	11,000	16,000	21,000	28,000	35,000
KSS MK II (349cc single)	2,000	3,000	4,500	6,000	8,000	10,000
MAC (349cc single)	1,400	2,100	4,000	5,000	6,000	7,500
1948						
KTT (348cc single)	7,000	11,000	16,000	21,000	28,000	35,000
KSS MK II (349cc single)	2,000	3,000	4,500	6,000	8,000	10,000
MAC (349cc single)	1,400	2,100	4,000	5,000	6,000	7,500
1949						
LE (150cc twin, shaft drive)	700	1,100	1,600	2,100	2,800	3,500
KTT (348cc single)	7,000	11,000	16,000	21,000	28,000	35,000
MAC (349cc single)	1,400	2,100	4,000	5,000	6,000	7,500
1950						
LE (150cc twin, shaft drive)	700	1,100	1,600	2,100	2,800	3,500
KTT (348cc single)	7,000	11,000	16,000	21,000	28,000	35,000
MAC (349cc single)	1,400	2,100	4,000	5,000	6,000	7,500
1951						
LE (200cc twin, shaft drive)	800	1,200	2,000	3,000	4,000	5,000
KTT (348cc single)	7,000	11,000	16,000	21,000	28,000	35,000
MAC (349cc single)	1,400	2,100	4,000	5,000	6,000	7,500
1952						
LE (200cc twin, shaft drive)	800	1,200	2,000	3,000	4,000	5,000
KTT (348cc single)	7,000	11,000	16,000	21,000	28,000	35,000
MAC (349cc single)	1,400	2,100	4,000	5,000	6,000	7,500
1953						
LE (200cc twin, shaft drive)	800	1,200	2,000	3,000	4,000	5,000
KTT (348cc single)	7,000	11,000	16,000	21,000	28,000	35,000
MAC (349cc single)	1,400	2,100	4,000	5,000	6,000	7,500
1954						
LE (200cc twin, shaft drive)	800	1,200	2,000	3,000	4,000	5,000
MAC (349cc single)	1,400	2,100	4,000	5,000	6,000	7,500
MSS (499cc single)	1,600	2,400	3,600	5,000	7,500	9,000
1955						
LE (200cc twin, shaft drive)	800	1,200	2,000	3,000	4,000	5,000
MAC (349cc single)	1,400	2,100	4,000	5,000	6,000	7,500
MSS (499cc single)	1,600	2,400	3,600	5,000	7,500	9,000
1956						
LE (200cc twin, shaft drive)	800	1,200	1,800	2,400	3,200	4,000
MAC (349cc single)	1,400	2,100	4,000	5,000	6,000	7,500
Viper (349cc single)	1,600	2,400	4,000	6,000	8,000	10,000
MSS (499cc single)	1,600	2,400	3,600	5,000	7,500	9,000
Venom (499cc single)	1,700	2,600	3,800	5,100	6,800	8,500
1957						
LE (200cc twin, shaft drive)	800	1,200	2,000	3,000	4,000	5,000
Valiant (200cc twin, shaft drive)	900	1,400	2,000	2,700	3,600	4,500
MAC (349cc single)	1,400	2,100	4,000	5,000	6,000	7,500
Viper (349cc single)	1,600	2,400	4,000	6,000	8,000	10,000
MSS (499cc single)	1,600	2,400	3,600	5,000	7,500	9,000
Venom (499cc single)	1,700	2,600	3,800	5,100	6,800	8,500
1958						
LE (200cc twin, shaft drive)	800	1,200	2,000	3,000	4,000	5,000
Valiant (200cc twin, shaft drive)	900	1,400	2,000	2,700	3,600	4,500
MAC (349cc single)	1,400	2,100	4,000	5,000	6,000	7,500
Viper (349cc single)	1,600	2,400	4,000	6,000	8,000	10,000
MSS (499cc single)	1,600	2,400	3,600	5,000	7,500	9,000
Venom (499cc single)	1,700	2,600	3,800	5,100	6,800	8,500

	6	5	4	3	2	1
1959						
LE (200cc twin, shaft drive)	800	1,200	2,000	3,000	4,000	5,000
Valiant (200cc twin, shaft drive)	900	1,400	2,000	2,700	3,600	4,500
MAC (349cc single)	1,400	2,100	4,000	5,000	6,000	7,500
Viper (349cc single)	1,600	2,400	4,000	6,000	8,000	10,000
MSS (499cc single)	1,600	2,400	3,600	5,000	7,500	9,000
1960						
LE (200cc twin, shaft drive)	800	1,200	2,000	3,000	4,000	5,000
Valiant (200cc twin, shaft drive)	900	1,400	2,000	2,700	3,600	4,500
MAC (349cc single)	1,400	2,100	4,000	5,000	6,000	7,500
Viper (349cc single)	1,600	2,400	4,000	6,000	8,000	10,000
MSS (499cc single)	1,600	2,400	3,600	5,000	7,500	9,000
1961						
LE (200cc twin, shaft drive)	800	1,200	2,000	3,000	4,000	5,000
Valiant (200cc twin, shaft drive)	900	1,400	2,000	2,700	3,600	4,500
Viper (349cc single)	1,600	2,400	4,000	6,000	8,000	10,000
MSS (499cc single)	1,600	2,400	3,600	5,000	7,500	9,000
MSS Scrambler (499cc single)	1,700	2,600	3,800	5,100	6,800	8,500
1962						
LE (200cc twin, shaft drive)	800	1,200	2,000	3,000	4,000	5,000
Valiant (200cc twin, shaft drive)	900	1,400	2,000	2,700	3,600	4,500
Viper (349cc single)	1,600	2,400	4,000	6,000	8,000	10,000
MSS (499cc single)	1,600	2,400	4,000	5,000	7,000	9,000
MSS Scrambler (499cc single)	1,700	2,600	4,000	5,000	7,000	9,000
1963						
LE (200cc twin, shaft drive)	800	1,200	2,000	3,000	4,000	5,000
Valiant (200cc twin, shaft drive)	900	1,400	2,000	2,700	3,600	4,500
Vogue (200cc twin, shaft drive)	800	1,200	1,800	2,400	3,200	4,000
Viper (349cc single)	1,600	2,400	3,600	5,000	7,500	9,000
MSS (499cc single)	1,600	2,400	3,600	4,800	6,400	8,000
MSS Scrambler (499cc single)	1,700	2,600	3,800	5,100	6,800	8,500
1964						
LE (200cc twin, shaft drive)	800	1,200	2,000	3,000	4,000	5,000
Valiant (200cc twin, shaft drive)	900	1,400	2,000	2,700	3,600	4,500
Vogue (200cc twin, shaft drive)	800	1,200	1,800	2,400	3,200	4,000
Viper (349cc single)	1,600	2,400	4,000	6,000	8,000	10,000
MSS (499cc single)	1,600	2,400	3,600	4,800	6,400	8,000
MSS Scrambler (499cc single)	1,700	2,600	3,800	5,100	6,800	8,500
Thruxton (499cc single)	3,500	5,300	10,000	15,000	20,000	25,000
1965						
Viceroy Scooter (200cc single)	900	1,400	2,000	2,700	3,600	4,500
LE (200cc twin, shaft drive)	800	1,200	2,000	3,000	4,000	5,000
Vogue (200cc twin, shaft drive)	900	1,400	2,000	2,700	3,600	4,500
MSS Scrambler (349cc single)	1,600	2,400	3,600	4,800	6,400	8,000
Viper (349cc single)	1,600	2,400	4,000	6,000	8,000	10,000
MSS (499cc single)	1,600	2,400	3,600	4,800	6,400	8,000
MSS Scrambler (499cc single)	1,700	2,600	3,800	5,100	6,800	8,500
Thruxton (499cc single)	3,500	5,300	10,000	15,000	20,000	25,000
1966						
Viceroy Scooter (200cc single)	900	1,400	2,000	2,700	3,600	4,500
LE (200cc twin, shaft drive)	800	1,200	2,000	3,000	4,000	5,000
Vogue (200cc twin, shaft drive)	900	1,400	2,000	2,700	3,600	4,500
MSS Scrambler (349cc single)	1,600	2,400	3,600	4,800	6,400	8,000
Viper Clubman (349cc single)	1,600	2,400	3,600	4,800	6,400	8,000
MK II Venom (499cc single)	1,700	2,600	3,800	5,100	6,800	8,500
MSS (499cc single)	1,600	2,400	3,600	4,800	6,400	8,000
MSS Scrambler (499cc single)	1,700	2,600	3,800	5,100	6,800	8,500
Thruxton (499cc single)	3,500	5,300	10,000	15,000	20,000	25,000

	6	5	4	3	2	1
1967						
LE (200cc twin, shaft drive)	800	1,200	2,000	3,000	4,000	5,000
Vogue (200cc twin, shaft drive)	900	1,400	2,000	2,700	3,600	4,500
MSS Scrambler (349cc single)	1,600	2,400	3,600	4,800	6,400	8,000
Viper Clubman (349cc single)	1,600	2,400	3,600	4,800	6,400	8,000
MK II Venom (499cc single)	1,700	2,600	3,800	5,100	6,800	8,500
MSS (499cc single)	1,600	2,400	4,000	5,500	7,000	8,500
MSS Scrambler (499cc single)	1,700	2,600	4,000	5,500	7,000	8,500
Thruxton (499cc single)	3,500	5,300	10,000	15,000	20,000	25,000
1968						
LE (200cc twin, shaft drive)	800	1,200	2,000	3,000	4,000	5,000
Vogue (200cc twin, shaft drive)	900	1,400	2,000	2,700	3,600	4,500
MSS Scrambler (349cc single)	1,600	2,400	3,600	4,800	6,400	8,000
Viper Clubman (349cc single)	1,600	2,400	3,600	4,800	6,400	8,000
MK II Venom (499cc single)	1,700	2,600	3,800	5,100	6,800	8,500
MSS (499cc single)	1,600	2,400	3,600	4,800	6,400	8,000
MSS Scrambler (499cc single)	1,700	2,600	3,800	5,100	6,800	8,500
Thruxton (499cc single)	3,500	5,300	10,000	15,000	20,000	25,000
1969						
LE (200cc twin, shaft drive)	800	1,200	2,000	3,000	4,000	5,000
MSS Scrambler (349cc single)	1,600	2,400	3,600	4,800	6,400	8,000
Viper Clubman (349cc single)	1,600	2,400	3,600	4,800	6,400	8,000
MK II Venom (499cc single)	1,700	2,600	3,800	5,100	6,800	8,500
Thruxton (499cc single)	3,500	5,300	10,000	15,000	20,000	25,000
1970						
LE (200cc twin, shaft drive)	800	1,200	2,000	3,000	4,000	5,000
MK II Venom (499cc single)	1,700	2,600	3,800	5,100	6,800	8,500
Thruxton (499cc single)	3,500	5,300	10,000	15,000	20,000	25,000
VINCENT						
1934						
Series A Comet (499cc single)	5,000	7,500	11,000	15,000	20,000	25,000
Series A Meteor (499cc single)	4,400	6,600	10,000	13,000	18,000	22,000
1935						
Series A Comet (499cc single)	5,000	7,500	11,000	15,000	20,000	25,000
Series A Comet Special (499cc single)	5,800	8,700	13,000	17,000	23,000	29,000
Series A Meteor (499cc single)	4,400	6,600	10,000	13,000	18,000	22,000
Series A TT Replica (499cc single)	10,000	15,000	25,000	35,000	50,000	65,000
1936						
Series A Comet (499cc single)	5,000	7,500	11,000	15,000	20,000	25,000
Series A Comet Special (499cc single)	5,800	8,700	13,000	17,000	23,000	29,000
Series A Meteor (499cc single)	4,400	6,600	10,000	13,000	18,000	22,000
Series A TT Replica (499cc single)	10,000	15,000	25,000	35,000	50,000	65,000
Series A Rapide (998cc twin)	30,000	45,000	68,000	90,000	120K	150K
1937						
Series A Comet (499cc single)	5,000	7,500	11,000	15,000	20,000	25,000
Series A Comet Special (499cc single)	5,800	8,700	13,000	17,000	23,000	29,000
Series A Meteor (499cc single)	4,400	6,600	10,000	13,000	18,000	22,000
Series A TT Replica (499cc single)	10,000	15,000	25,000	35,000	50,000	65,000
Series A Rapide (998cc twin)	30,000	45,000	68,000	90,000	120K	150K
1938						
Series A Comet (499cc single)	5,000	7,500	11,000	15,000	20,000	25,000
Series A Meteor (499cc single)	4,400	6,600	10,000	13,000	18,000	22,000
Series A TT Replica (499cc single)	10,000	15,000	25,000	35,000	50,000	65,000
Series A Rapide (998cc twin)	30,000	45,000	68,000	90,000	120K	150K
1939						
Series A Comet (499cc single)	5,000	7,500	11,000	15,000	20,000	25,000
Series A Meteor (499cc single)	4,400	6,600	10,000	13,000	18,000	22,000
Series A Rapide (998cc twin)	30,000	45,000	68,000	90,000	120K	150K

	6	5	4	3	2	1
1946						
Series B Rapide (998cc twin)	5,000	7,500	11,000	15,000	20,000	25,000
Series B Rapide Touring (998cc twin). . . .	5,000	7,500	11,000	15,000	20,000	25,000
1947						
Series B Rapide (998cc twin)	5,000	10,000	18,000	25,000	30,000	35,000
Series B Rapide Touring (998cc twin). . . .	5,000	7,500	11,000	15,000	20,000	25,000
1948						
Series B Black Shadow (998cc twin)	15,000	23,000	34,000	45,000	60,000	75,000
Series B Black Shadow Touring (998cc twin)	15,000	23,000	34,000	45,000	60,000	75,000
Series B Rapide (998cc twin)	5,000	**9,000**	**15,000**	**25,000**	**35,000**	**45,000**
Series B Rapide Touring (998cc twin)	5,000	7,500	11,000	15,000	20,000	25,000
Series C Black Lightning (998cc twin). . . .	**50,000**	**75,000**	**100K**	**150K**	**175K**	**200K**
Series C Black Shadow (998cc twin)	10,000	15,000	23,000	30,000	40,000	50,000
Series C Black Shadow Touring (998cc twin)	10,000	15,000	23,000	30,000	40,000	50,000
Series C Rapide (998cc twin)	5,600	8,400	15,000	25,000	35,000	45,000
Series C Rapide Touring (998cc twin). . . .	5,600	8,400	13,000	17,000	22,000	28,000
1949						
Series B Meteor (499cc single)	4,200	6,300	9,500	13,000	17,000	21,000
Series C Comet (499cc single)	2,400	3,600	5,400	7,200	9,600	12,000
Series C Comet Touring (499cc single) . . .	2,400	3,600	5,400	7,200	9,600	12,000
Series C Grey Flash (499cc single)	7,400	11,000	17,000	22,000	30,000	37,000
Series B Black Shadow (998cc twin)	15,000	23,000	34,000	45,000	60,000	75,000
Series B Black Shadow Touring (998cc twin)	15,000	23,000	34,000	45,000	60,000	75,000
Series B Rapide (998cc twin)	6,000	9,000	15,000	25,000	35,000	45,000
Series B Rapide Touring (998cc twin)	6,000	9,000	14,000	18,000	24,000	30,000
Series C Black Lightning (998cc twin). . . .	**50,000**	**75,000**	**100K**	**150K**	**175K**	**200K**
Series C Black Shadow (998cc twin)	6,000	20,000	30,000	40,000	50,000	60,000
Series C Black Shadow Touring (998cc twin)	6,000	9,000	14,000	18,000	24,000	30,000
Series C Rapide (998cc twin)	10,000	15,000	20,000	25,000	35,000	45,000
Series C Rapide Touring (998cc twin). . . .	5,000	7,500	11,000	15,000	20,000	25,000
1950						
Series B Meteor (499cc single)	4,200	6,300	9,500	13,000	17,000	21,000
Series C Comet (499cc single)	3,000	6,000	10,000	13,000	19,000	25,000
Series C Comet Touring (499cc single) . . .	2,800	4,200	7,000	10,000	15,000	20,000
Series C Grey Flash (499cc single)	7,400	11,000	17,000	22,000	30,000	37,000
Series B Black Shadow (998cc twin)	10,000	15,000	23,000	30,000	40,000	50,000
Series B Black Shadow Touring (998cc twin)	10,000	15,000	23,000	30,000	40,000	50,000
Series B Rapide (998cc twin)	6,000	9,000	15,000	25,000	35,000	45,000
Series B Rapide Touring (998cc twin). . . .	6,000	9,000	14,000	18,000	24,000	30,000
Series C Black Lightning (998cc twin). . . .	**50,000**	**75,000**	**100K**	**150K**	**175K**	**200K**
Series C Black Shadow (998cc twin)	6,400	20,000	30,000	40,000	50,000	60,000
Series C Black Shadow Touring (998cc twin)	6,400	9,600	14,000	19,000	26,000	32,000
Series C Rapide (998cc twin)	5,000	7,500	15,000	25,000	35,000	45,000
Series C Rapide Touring (998cc twin). . . .	5,000	7,500	11,000	15,000	20,000	25,000
1951						
Series C Comet (499cc single)	3,000	6,000	10,000	13,000	19,000	25,000
Series C Comet Touring (499cc single) . . .	2,800	4,200	7,000	10,000	15,000	20,000
Series C Grey Flash (499cc single)	7,600	11,000	17,000	23,000	30,000	39,000
Series C Black Lightning (998cc twin). . . .	**50,000**	**75,000**	**100K**	**150K**	**175K**	**200K**
Series C Black Shadow (998cc twin)	10,000	20,000	30,000	40,000	50,000	60,000
Series C Black Shadow Touring (998cc twin)	10,000	15,000	23,000	30,000	40,000	50,000
Series C Rapide (998cc twin)	10,000	16,000	22,000	28,000	35,000	45,000
Series C Rapide Touring (998cc twin). . . .	6,000	9,000	14,000	18,000	24,000	30,000
1952						
Series C Comet (499cc single)	**3,000**	**6,000**	**10,000**	**13,000**	**19,000**	**25,000**
Series C Comet Touring (499cc single) . . .	2,800	4,200	7,000	10,000	15,000	20,000
Series C Black Lightning (998cc twin). . . .	**50,000**	**75,000**	**100K**	**150K**	**175K**	**200K**
Series C Black Shadow (998cc twin)	10,000	20,000	30,000	40,000	50,000	60,000
Series C Black Shadow Touring (998cc twin)	10,000	15,000	23,000	30,000	40,000	50,000

	6	5	4	3	2	1
Series C Rapide (998cc twin)	10,000	15,000	25,000	30,000	35,000	45,000
Series C Rapide Touring (998cc twin). . . .	6,000	9,000	14,000	18,000	24,000	30,000
1953						
Series C Comet (499cc single)	3,000	6,000	10,000	13,000	19,000	25,000
Series C Comet Touring (499cc single) . . .	2,800	4,200	7,000	10,000	15,000	20,000
Series C Black Lightning (998cc twin). . . .	50,000	75,000	100K	150K	175K	200K
Series C Black Shadow (998cc twin)	10,000	20,000	30,000	40,000	50,000	60,000
Series C Black Shadow Touring (998cc twin)	10,000	15,000	23,000	30,000	40,000	50,000
Series C Rapide (998cc twin)	6,000	9,000	14,000	18,000	24,000	30,000
Series C Rapide Touring (998cc twin). . . .	6,000	9,000	14,000	18,000	24,000	30,000
1954						
Firefly	1,500	3,000	6,000	8,000	12,000	15,000
Series C Comet (499cc single)	3,000	6,000	10,000	13,000	19,000	25,000
Series C Comet Touring (499cc single) . . .	2,800	4,200	7,000	10,000	15,000	20,000
Series D Black Lightning (998cc twin)	7,000	11,000	16,000	21,000	28,000	35,000
Series C Black Lightning (998cc twin). . . .	50,000	75,000	100K	150K	175K	200K
Series D Black Prince (998cc twin)	8,000	12,000	18,000	24,000	32,000	40,000
Series C Black Shadow (998cc twin)	10,000	15,000	25,000	40,000	55,000	70,000
Series C Black Shadow Touring (998cc twin)	8,000	12,000	18,000	24,000	32,000	40,000
Series C Rapide (998cc twin)	6,000	9,000	14,000	18,000	24,000	30,000
Series C Rapide Touring (998cc twin). . . .	6,000	9,000	14,000	18,000	24,000	30,000
1955						
Series C Black Lightning (998cc twin). . . .	50,000	75,000	100K	150K	175K	200K
Series D Black Knight (998cc twin)	7,200	11,000	16,000	22,000	29,000	36,000
Series D Black Prince (998cc twin)	7,600	11,000	17,000	23,000	30,000	39,000
Series D Black Shadow (998cc twin)	7,000	11,000	16,000	21,000	28,000	35,000
Series D Rapide (998cc twin)	6,000	9,000	14,000	20,000	30,000	40,000

WHIZZER

	6	5	4	3	2	1
1940						
Schwinn DX	1,500	2,500	3,500	4,500	5,500	7,000
1946						
Schwinn	500	1,000	2,000	3,000	4,000	5,000
1947						
Schwinn	1,000	2,000	3,000	4,000	5,000	6,000
1948						
Pacemaker	2,000	4,000	5,000	7,500	10,000	12,500
1949						
Schwinn	2,000	3,500	5,000	6,500	8,000	10,000
1950						
Schwinn	800	1,500	2,200	2,900	3,600	5,000
Roadmaster	700	1,000	1,300	1,800	2,500	3,500
1951						
Ambassador	1,000	2,000	3,000	4,000	5,000	6,000
1952						
Schwinn	1,500	3,000	4,500	6,000	7,500	9,000
1953						
British Tandem	1,500	3,000	4,500	6,000	7,500	9,000
1955						
Road Runner	1,500	3,000	4,500	6,000	7,500	9,000
1956						
Sportsman	1,000	2,000	3,500	5,000	6,500	8,000
Red Ryder	1,000	2,000	3,000	4,000	5,000	6,000
1957						
Delivery Cycle	400	800	1,600	2,400	3,200	4,000

YAMAHA

	6	5	4	3	2	1
1961						
MF1 (50cc single)	500	800	1,100	1,500	2,000	2,500
MF2 (50cc single)	500	800	1,100	1,500	2,000	2,500
YA2 (125cc single)	500	800	1,100	1,500	2,000	2,500

	6	5	4	3	2	1
YA3 (125cc single)	500	800	1,100	1,500	2,000	2,500
YC1 (175cc single)	500	800	1,200	1,600	2,200	2,700
YD2 (250cc twin)	900	1,400	2,000	2,700	3,600	4,500
YDS1 (250cc twin)	900	1,400	2,000	2,700	3,600	4,500
1962						
MJ2 (55cc single)	400	600	1,000	1,300	1,700	2,100
YA5 (125cc single)	500	800	1,200	1,600	2,100	2,600
YD3 (250cc twin)	900	1,400	2,100	2,800	3,700	4,600
YDS2 (250cctwin)	900	1,400	2,100	2,800	3,700	4,600
1963						
YG1 (73cc single)	500	800	1,200	1,600	2,100	2,600
YG1T (73cc single)	500	800	1,200	1,600	2,100	2,600
YDT1 (250cc twin)	900	1,400	2,100	2,800	3,700	4,600
1964						
MJ2S (55cc single)	400	600	1,000	1,300	1,700	2,100
MJ2T Trail (55cc single)	400	600	1,000	1,300	1,700	2,100
YJ1 (60cc single)	400	600	1,000	1,300	1,700	2,100
MG1T (73cc single)	500	800	1,200	1,600	2,100	2,600
YG1 (73cc single)	500	800	1,100	1,500	2,000	2,500
YA5 (125cc single)	500	800	1,200	1,600	2,100	2,600
YA6 (125cc single)	500	800	1,200	1,600	2,100	2,600
YD3 (250cc twin)	900	1,400	2,100	2,800	3,700	4,600
YDS2 (250cctwin)	1,200	1,800	2,700	3,600	4,800	6,000
TDS3 (250cc twin)	1,400	2,100	3,200	4,200	5,600	7,000
YDT1 (250cc twin)	1,000	1,500	2,300	3,000	4,000	5,000
1965						
U5 (50cc single)	400	600	900	1,200	1,600	2,000
MJ2T (55cc single)	400	600	900	1,200	1,600	2,000
YJ2S (60cc single)	400	600	1,000	1,300	1,700	2,100
YGS1 (73cc single)	500	800	1,100	1,500	2,000	2,500
MG1B (80cc single)	500	800	1,200	1,600	2,100	2,600
YL1 (98cc twin)	600	900	1,350	1,800	2,400	3,000
TD1R (250cc twin)	2,600	3,900	5,900	7,800	10,000	13,000
TD1C (250cc twin)	2,600	3,900	5,900	7,800	10,000	13,000
YD3C Big Bear Scrambler (250cc twin) . . .	1,200	1,800	2,800	3,700	4,900	6,100
YDS3 (250cc twin)	1,400	2,100	3,200	4,200	5,600	7,000
YM1 (305cc twin)	800	1,200	1,800	2,400	3,200	4,000
1966						
US Step Thru (50cc single)	400	600	900	1,200	1,600	2,000
MJ2T Omaha Trail (55cc single)	400	600	900	1,200	1,600	2,000
YJ2 Riverside (60cc single)	400	600	900	1,200	1,600	2,000
YGK Rotary Jet (73cc single)	500	700	1,100	1,400	1,900	2,400
YGTK Trailmaster (73cc single)	500	700	1,100	1,400	1,900	2,400
MJ1T Omaha Trail (80cc single)	500	800	1,100	1,500	2,000	2,500
YL1 (98cc twin)	500	800	1,100	1,500	2,000	2,500
YA6 Santa Barbara (125cc single)	400	600	900	1,200	1,600	2,000
TD1 Daytona Road Racer (247cc single) . .	2,600	3,900	5,900	7,800	10,000	13,000
YDS3C Big Bear (250cc twin)	1,000	1,500	2,300	3,000	4,000	5,000
YDSM Ascot Scrambler (250cc twin)	1,000	1,500	2,300	3,000	4,000	5,000
YM1 Big Bear Scrambler (305cc twin)	800	1,200	1,800	2,400	3,200	4,000
1967						
U5 Newport (50cc single)	400	600	900	1,200	1,600	2,000
YJ2 Campus (60cc single)	400	600	900	1,200	1,600	2,000
YG1K Rotary Jet (73cc single)	500	700	1,100	1,400	1,900	2,400
MG1T Omaha Trail (80cc single)	500	700	1,100	1,400	1,900	2,400
YL1 (98cc twin)	500	700	1,100	1,400	1,900	2,400
YL2C (98cc single)	500	800	1,100	1,500	2,000	2,500
YA6 Santa Barbara (125cc single)	500	800	1,100	1,500	2,000	2,500
YCS1 Bonanza (180cc twin)	500	700	1,100	1,400	1,900	2,400

	6	5	4	3	2	1
TD1 Daytona (247cc single)	2,600	3,900	5,900	7,800	10,000	13,000
DT1 Enduro (250cc single)	500	800	1,200	1,600	2,200	2,700
YDS3 Catalina (250cc twin)	400	700	1,000	1,300	1,800	2,200
YDS3C Big Bear (250cc twin)	700	1,000	1,500	2,000	3,000	4,000
YDS5 Catalina Electric (250cc twin)	400	700	1,000	1,300	1,800	2,200
YM1 Cross Country (305cc twin)	500	800	1,200	1,600	2,200	2,700
YM2C (305cc twin)	500	800	1,100	1,500	2,000	2,500
YR1 Grand Prix (350cc single)	600	900	1,350	1,800	2,400	3,000
1968						
U5 Newport (50cc single)	400	600	900	1,200	1,600	2,000
YJ2 Campus (60cc single)	400	600	900	1,200	1,600	2,000
YG5T (73cc single)	500	700	1,100	1,400	1,900	2,400
YL1 (98cc twin)	400	700	1,000	1,300	1,800	2,200
YL2CM (98cc single)	400	700	1,000	1,300	1,800	2,200
YAS1C (125cc twin)	500	700	1,000	1,400	1,800	2,300
YCS1C (180cc twin)	500	700	1,100	1,400	1,900	2,400
TD1 Daytona (247cc twin)	2,600	3,900	5,900	7,800	10,000	13,000
DT1 Enduro (250cc single)	400	700	1,000	1,300	1,800	2,200
YDS5 Catalina Electric (250cc twin)	400	700	1,000	1,300	1,800	2,200
YM1 Cross Country (305cc twin)	500	800	1,200	1,600	2,200	2,700
YR2 Grand Prix (350cc single)	600	900	1,350	1,800	2,400	3,000
YR2C Street Scrambler (350cc single)	500	800	1,200	1,600	2,200	2,700
1969						
U5 Step Thru (50cc single)	400	600	900	1,200	1,600	2,000
YJ2 (60cc single)	400	600	900	1,200	1,600	2,000
G5S (73cc single)	500	700	1,100	1,400	1,900	2,400
U7E (75cc single)	500	700	1,000	1,400	1,800	2,300
L5T Trail (98cc single)	400	700	1,000	1,300	1,800	2,200
YL1 (98cc twin)	400	700	1,000	1,300	1,800	2,200
AT1 Trail (125cc single)	500	700	1,100	1,400	1,900	2,400
AT1M (125cc single)	500	700	1,100	1,400	1,900	2,400
YAS1-C Street Scrambler (125cc twin)	500	800	1,200	1,500	2,000	2,600
CT1 Trail (175cc single)	500	800	1,100	1,500	2,000	2,500
YCS1-C Street Scrambler (180cc twin)	400	700	1,000	1,300	1,800	2,200
DT1B Trail (250cc single)	400	700	1,000	1,300	1,800	2,200
DT1S (250cc single)	500	700	1,000	1,400	1,800	2,300
YDS6C Street Scrambler (350cc single)	500	800	1,200	1,600	2,200	2,700
YM1 (305cc twin)	600	900	1,350	1,800	2,400	3,000
R3 (347cc twin)	600	900	1,350	1,800	2,400	3,000
YR2-C Street Scrambler (350cc single)	500	800	1,200	1,600	2,200	2,700
1970						
G6SB (73cc single)	500	700	1,000	1,400	1,800	2,300
HS1 (90cc single)	500	700	1,100	1,400	1,900	2,400
HT1 Enduro (90cc single)	500	700	1,100	1,400	1,900	2,400
L5TA (98cc single)	500	700	1,100	1,400	1,900	2,400
YL1E (98cc twin)	500	700	1,100	1,400	1,900	2,400
YL2 (98cc single)	500	700	1,100	1,400	1,900	2,400
AS2C (125cc twin)	500	800	1,100	1,500	2,000	2,500
AT1B Enduro (125cc single)	500	800	1,100	1,500	2,000	2,500
AT1BMX (125cc single)	500	800	1,100	1,500	2,000	2,500
CT1B Enduro (175cc single)	500	800	1,100	1,500	2,000	2,500
CS3C (198cc twin)	400	700	1,000	1,300	1,800	2,200
DS6B (247cc twin)	400	700	1,000	1,300	1,800	2,200
DT1C Enduro (247cc single)	400	1,000	1,500	2,000	2,500	3,000
DT1CM (247cc single)	400	1,000	1,500	2,000	2,500	3,000
TD2 (247cc single)	2,700	4,100	6,100	8,100	11,000	14,000
RT1 Enduro (250cc single)	600	900	1,400	1,900	2,500	3,100
R2C (347cc twin)	400	700	1,000	1,300	1,800	2,200
R5 (347cc twin)	500	800	1,200	1,500	2,000	2,600

	6	5	4	3	2	1
RT1M (360cc single)	400	700	1,000	1,300	1,800	2,200
XS1 (654cc twin)	1,500	2,000	3,000	4,000	6,000	8,500
1971						
G6SB (73cc single)	500	700	1,000	1,400	1,800	2,300
HS1B (90cc single)	500	700	1,100	1,400	1,900	2,400
HT1B Enduro (90cc single)	500	700	1,100	1,400	1,900	2,400
HT1MX (90cc single)	500	700	1,100	1,400	1,900	2,400
AT1C Enduro (125cc single)	500	800	1,100	1,500	2,000	2,500
AT1MX (125 single)	500	800	1,100	1,500	2,000	2,500
CT1C Enduro (173cc single)	500	800	1,100	1,500	2,000	2,500
CS3B (198cc twin)	500	700	1,100	1,400	1,900	2,400
TD2B (247cc single)	2,700	4,100	6,100	8,100	11,000	14,000
DT1E Enduro (250cc single)	500	800	1,100	1,400	2,000	2,500
DT1MX (250cc single)	400	700	1,000	1,300	1,800	2,200
R5B (347cc twin)	500	800	1,200	1,600	2,200	2,700
RT1B Enduro (360cc single)	500	800	1,200	1,600	2,200	2,700
RT1MX (360cc single)	500	800	1,100	1,500	2,000	2,500
XS1B (654cc twin)	1,300	1,800	2,500	3,500	4,500	6,000
1972						
G7S (73cc single)	400	700	1,000	1,300	1,700	2,200
U7E (75cc single)	400	700	1,000	1,300	1,700	2,200
LS2 (98cc single)	400	700	1,000	1,300	1,800	2,200
LT2 Enduro (98cc single)	400	700	1,000	1,300	1,800	2,200
LT2M (98cc single)	400	700	1,000	1,300	1,800	2,200
AT2 Enduro (125cc single)	500	700	1,100	1,400	1,900	2,400
AT2M (125cc single)	500	700	1,100	1,400	1,900	2,400
CT2 Enduro (173cc single)	500	700	1,100	1,400	1,900	2,400
CS5 (198cc twin)	500	800	1,200	1,500	2,000	2,600
DS7 (247cc twin)	400	600	900	1,200	1,600	2,000
DT2 Enduro (247cc single)	400	700	1,000	1,300	1,800	2,200
DT2MX (247cc single)	400	700	1,000	1,300	1,800	2,200
TD3 (247cc single)	2,700	4,100	6,100	8,100	11,000	14,000
R5C (347cc twin)	500	800	1,200	1,600	2,200	2,700
RT2 Enduro (360cc single)	500	800	1,200	1,600	2,200	2,700
RT2MX (360cc single)	500	700	1,100	1,400	1,900	2,400
XS2 (654cc twin)	1,000	1,500	2,500	3,400	5,000	6,000
1973						
GT1 (73cc single)	300	500	700	1,000	1,300	1,600
GTMX (73cc single)	300	500	700	1,000	1,300	1,600
LT3 (98cc single)	300	400	600	800	1,100	1,400
LTMX (98cc single)	300	500	600	800	1,100	1,400
AT3 (125cc single)	300	500	600	800	1,100	1,400
ATMX (125cc single)	300	400	700	900	1,200	1,500
CT3 (173cc single)	300	500	800	1,000	1,400	1,700
DT3 (247cc single)	400	600	900	1,200	1,600	2,000
MX250 (247cc single)	400	**800**	**1,500**	**2,500**	**3,500**	**4,500**
RD250A (247cc twin)	400	600	900	1,200	1,600	2,000
TA250 (247cc twin)	2,100	3,200	4,700	6,300	8,400	11,000
RD350 (347cc twin)	500	700	1,100	1,400	1,900	2,400
TZ360 (347cc twin)	2,600	3,900	5,900	7,800	10,000	13,000
MX360 (360cc single)	300	500	800	1,000	1,400	1,700
RT3 (360cc single)	600	900	1,350	1,800	2,400	3,000
MX500 (500cc single)	400	600	1,000	1,300	1,700	2,100
SC500 (500cc single)	400	600	1,000	1,300	1,700	2,100
TX500 (500cc twin)	600	900	1,350	1,800	2,400	3,000
TX650 (654cc twin)	1,200	1,700	2,500	3,500	4,500	6,000
TX750 (743cc twin)	1,000	1,400	2,000	2,600	4,000	5,000

	6	5	4	3	2	1
1974						
GT80A (73cc single)	300	500	700	1,000	1,300	1,600
GTMXA (73cc single)	300	500	700	1,000	1,300	1,600
TY80A (73cc single)	300	500	700	1,000	1,300	1,600
YZ80A (73cc single).	300	500	700	1,000	1,300	1,600
DT100A (98cc single)	300	400	600	800	1,100	1,400
MX100A (98cc single).	300	400	600	800	1,100	1,400
DT125A (123cc single)	300	400	700	900	1,200	1,500
MX125A (123cc single)	300	400	700	900	1,200	1,500
TA125A (125cc twin)	1,700	2,600	3,800	5,100	6,800	8,500
YZ125A (125cc single)	300	500	600	800	1,100	1,400
DT175A (171cc single)	300	500	700	1,000	1,300	1,600
MX175A (171cc single)	300	500	700	1,000	1,300	1,600
RD200A (195cc twin)	400	600	1,000	1,300	1,700	2,100
DT250A (246cc single)	500	700	1,100	1,400	1,900	2,400
MX250A (246cc single)	500	**800**	1,500	**2,500**	**3,500**	**4,500**
RD250A (247cc twin)	500	800	1,200	1,500	2,000	2,600
TY250A (247 cc twin)	300	**700**	**1,000**	**1,500**	**2,000**	**2,500**
TZ250A (247cc twin)	2,400	3,600	5,400	7,200	9,600	12,000
YZ250A (247cc single)	300	500	600	800	1,100	1,400
RD350A (347cc twin)	**800**	**1,200**	**1,600**	2,000	**2,800**	**3,500**
RD350B (347cc twin)	600	800	1,200	1,700	2,200	2,800
TZ350A (347cc twin)	2,600	3,900	5,900	7,800	10,400	13,000
DT360A (352cc single)	400	600	900	1,200	1,600	2,000
MX360A (352cc single)	300	500	700	1,000	1,300	1,600
YZ360A (360cc single)	400	600	900	1,100	1,500	1,900
SC500A (500cc single)	400	600	900	1,100	1,500	1,900
TX650A (654cc twin)	1,100	1,600	2,400	3,200	4,500	5,500
TZ700A (698cc four)	−1,500	−3,000	−6,000	−9,000	−12,000	−15,000
TX750 (743cc twin)	1,000	1,400	2,000	2,600	4,000	5,000
1975						
GT80B (73cc single)	300	500	700	1,000	1,300	1,600
GTMXB (73cc single)	300	500	700	1,000	1,300	1,600
TY80B (73cc single)	300	500	700	1,000	1,300	1,600
YZ80B (73cc single).	300	500	700	1,000	1,300	1,600
DT100B (98cc single)	300	400	600	800	1,100	1,400
DT100B5 (98cc single)	300	400	600	800	1,100	1,400
MX100B (98cc single).	300	400	600	800	1,000	1,300
DT125B (123cc single)	300	400	700	900	1,200	1,500
MX125B (123cc single)	300	400	700	900	1,200	1,500
RD125B (125cc twin)	300	400	600	800	1,100	1,400
TA1 (125cc twin)	1,800	2,700	4,100	5,400	7,200	9,000
YZ125B (125cc single)	300	400	600	800	1,100	1,400
DT175B (171cc single)	300	500	700	1,000	1,300	1,600
MX175B (171cc single)	300	500	700	1,000	1,300	1,600
TY175B (171cc single)	300	500	700	1,000	1,300	1,600
RD200B (195cc twin)	400	600	1,000	1,300	1,700	2,100
DT250B (246cc single)	500	700	1,100	1,400	1,900	2,400
MX250B (246cc single)	500	**800**	**1,500**	**2,500**	**3,500**	**4,500**
RD250B (247cc twin)	500	700	1,100	1,400	1,900	2,400
TZ250B (247cc twin)	2,400	3,600	5,400	7,200	9,600	12,000
YZ250B (247cc single)	300	400	600	800	1,100	1,400
RD350B (347cc twin)	600	800	1,500	2,000	2,500	3,000
TZ350B (347cc twin)	2,600	3,900	5,900	7,800	10,400	13,000
YZ360B (360cc single)	400	600	900	1,100	1,500	1,900
DT400B (397cc single)	400	1,000	1,500	2,000	2,500	3,000
MX400B (397cc single)	400	600	1,000	1,500	2,000	2,500
XS500B (499cc twin)	700	1,000	1,500	2,000	2,600	3,300

	6	5	4	3	2	1
XS650B (654cc twin)	1,100	1,600	2,400	3,200	4,500	5,500
TZ750B (750cc four)	4,000	6,000	9,000	12,000	16,000	20,000
1976						
GT80C (73cc single)	300	500	700	1,000	1,300	1,600
GTMXC (73cc single)	300	500	700	1,000	1,300	1,600
YZ80C (73cc single)	300	500	700	1,000	1,300	1,600
RS100C (97cc single)	300	500	700	1,000	1,300	1,600
DT100C (98cc single)	300	500	700	1,000	1,300	1,700
YZ100C (98cc single)	300	500	700	1,000	1,300	1,700
DT125C (123cc single)	300	500	800	1,000	1,400	1,700
MX125C (123cc single)	300	500	800	1,000	1,400	1,700
RD125C (125cc twin)	400	600	900	1,100	1,500	1,900
YZ125C (125cc single)	400	600	900	1,200	1,600	2,000
YZ125X (125cc single)	400	600	900	1,200	1,600	2,000
DT175C (171cc single)	400	600	900	1,200	1,600	2,000
TY175C (171cc single)	400	600	900	1,200	1,600	2,000
YZ175C (174cc single)	400	600	900	1,200	1,600	2,000
RD200C (195cc twin)	400	600	1,000	1,300	1,700	2,100
DT250C (246cc single)	500	700	1,100	1,400	1,900	2,400
TY250C (247cc twin)	500	700	1,100	1,400	1,900	2,400
TZ250C (247cc twin)	2,400	3,600	5,400	7,200	9,600	12,000
YZ250C (247cc single)	400	600	900	1,200	1,600	2,000
XS360C (358cc twin)	400	600	900	1,200	1,600	2,000
RD400C (399cc twin)	–500	**1,000**	**1,500**	**2,500**	**3,000**	**4,000**
YZ400C (399cc single)	400	600	900	1,100	1,500	1,900
TT500C (499cc single)	400	1,000	1,500	2,000	2,500	3,000
XS500C (499cc twin)	450	650	1,000	1,300	1,800	2,500
XT500C (499cc single)	600	900	1,400	1,800	2,400	3,000
XS650C (654cc twin)	900	1,300	1,900	2,500	3,400	4,500
XS750C (747cc triple)	700	1,200	1,900	2,500	3,500	4,500
TZ750C (750cc four)	4,000	6,000	9,000	12,000	16,000	20,000
1977						
GTMXD (73cc single)	300	500	700	900	1,200	1,500
YZ80D (73cc single)	300	500	700	900	1,200	1,500
DT100D (98cc single)	300	500	700	900	1,200	1,500
YZ100D (98cc single)	300	500	700	900	1,200	1,500
YZ125D (125cc single)	300	500	700	1,000	1,300	1,600
IT175D (171cc single)	300	500	700	1,000	1,300	1,600
TY250D (243cc twin)	400	500	800	1,100	1,400	1,800
DT250D (243cc twin)	400	500	800	1,100	1,400	1,800
IT250D (246cc twin)	400	500	800	1,100	1,400	1,800
TZ250D (247cc twin)	2,200	3,300	5,000	6,600	8,800	11,000
YZ250D (247cc single)	400	600	900	1,100	1,500	1,900
XS360D (358cc twin)	400	600	900	1,200	1,600	2,000
XS400D (392cc twin)	400	600	900	1,200	1,600	2,000
DT400D (397cc single)	400	600	1,000	1,300	1,700	2,100
IT400D (399cc single)	400	600	1,000	1,300	1,700	2,100
RD400D (399cc twin)	**500**	**1,000**	**1,500**	**2,500**	**3,000**	**4,000**
YZ400D (399cc single)	2,400	3,600	5,400	7,200	9,600	12,000
TT500D (499cc single)	400	1,000	1,500	2,000	2,500	3,000
XS500D (499cc twin)	500	700	1,100	1,400	1,900	2,400
XT500D (499cc single)	400	600	900	1,100	1,500	1,900
XS650D (654cc twin)	900	1,300	1,900	2,500	3,400	4,500
XS750D (747cc triple)	800	1,200	1,700	2,250	3,000	3,700
TZ750D (750cc four)	3,600	5,300	7,800	11,000	14,500	18,000
1978						
GT80E (73cc single)	300	500	700	900	1,200	1,500
YZ80E (73cc single)	300	500	700	900	1,200	1,500
DT100E (98cc single)	300	500	700	900	1,200	1,500

	6	5	4	3	2	1
YZ100E (98cc single)	300	500	700	900	1,200	1,500
DT125E (123cc single)	300	500	700	900	1,200	1,500
YZ125E (125cc single)	300	500	700	900	1,200	1,500
DT175E (171cc single)	400	500	800	1,100	1,400	1,800
IT175E (171cc single)	400	500	800	1,100	1,400	1,800
DT250E (246cc single)	400	600	900	1,100	1,500	1,900
IT250E (246cc single)	400	600	900	1,100	1,500	1,900
TZ250E (247cc twin)	2,400	3,600	5,400	7,200	9,600	12,000
YZ250E (247cc single)	400	600	900	1,100	1,500	1,900
XS400-2E (392cc twin)	400	600	1,000	1,300	1,700	2,100
XS400E (392cc twin)	400	600	1,000	1,300	1,700	2,100
DT400E (392cc twin)	400	600	900	1,200	1,600	2,000
IT400E (397cc single)	400	600	900	1,200	1,600	2,000
RD400E (399cc twin)	**500**	**1,000**	**1,500**	**2,500**	**3,000**	**4,000**
YZ400E (399cc single)	400	600	900	1,200	1,600	2,000
SR500E (499cc single)	500	800	**1,500**	**2,000**	**2,500**	**3,000**
TT500E (499cc single)	500	1,000	1,500	2,000	2,500	3,000
XS500E (499cc twin)	500	700	1,000	1,300	1,700	2,100
XT500E (499cc single)	400	600	1,000	1,500	2,000	2,500
XS650E (654cc twin)	900	1,300	1,900	2,500	3,400	4,500
XS650SE (654cc twin)	900	1,300	1,900	2,500	3,400	4,500
XS750E (747cc triple)	800	1,200	1,700	2,300	3,000	3,700
XS750SE (747cc triple)	800	1,200	1,700	2,300	3,000	3,700
TZ750E (750cc four)	3,600	5,300	7,800	11,000	14,500	18,000
XS1100E (1,101cc four)	1,100	1,600	2,400	3,200	4,500	5,400
1979						
GT80F (73cc single)	300	500	700	900	1,200	1,500
GTMXF (73cc single)	300	500	700	900	1,200	1,500
YZ80F (73cc single)	300	500	700	900	1,200	1,500
DT100F (98cc single)	300	500	700	900	1,200	1,500
MX100F (98cc single)	300	500	700	900	1,200	1,500
YZ100F (98cc single)	300	500	700	900	1,200	1,500
DT125F (123cc single)	300	500	700	900	1,200	1,600
YZ125F (125cc single)	300	500	700	900	1,200	1,600
DT175F (171cc single)	300	500	800	1,000	1,400	1,700
IT175F (171cc single)	300	500	800	1,000	1,400	1,700
MX175F (171cc single)	300	500	800	1,000	1,400	1,700
DT250F (246cc single)	400	500	800	1,100	1,400	1,800
IT250F (246cc single)	400	500	800	1,100	1,400	1,800
YZ250F (247cc single)	400	600	900	1,100	1,500	1,900
XS400-2F (392cc twin)	400	600	1,000	1,300	1,700	2,100
IT400F (399cc single)	400	600	900	1,200	1,600	2,000
RD400F (399cc twin)	**500**	**1,000**	**1,500**	**2,500**	**3,000**	**4,000**
RD400F Daytona Special (399cc twin)	900	1,300	1,800	2,400	3,200	4,000
YZ400F (399cc single)	400	600	900	1,200	1,600	2,000
SR500F (499cc twin)	400	600	**1,500**	**2,000**	**2,500**	**3,000**
TT500 (499cc single)	400	600	900	1,100	1,500	1,900
XT500F (499cc twin)	900	1,300	1,900	2,500	3,300	4,200
XS650-2F (654cc twin)	900	1,300	1,900	2,500	3,300	4,200
XS750-2F (747cc triple)	800	1,200	1,700	2,300	3,000	3,700
XS1100F (1,10acc four)	1,100	1,600	2,400	3,200	4,500	5,400
XS1100SF (1,101cc four)	1,100	1,600	2,400	3,200	4,500	5,400
1980						
YZ50G (49cc single)	300	400	600	800	1,000	1,300
GT80G (73cc single)	300	500	700	900	1,200	1,500
MX80G (73cc single)	300	500	700	900	1,200	1,500
YZ80G (73cc single)	300	500	700	900	1,200	1,500
DT100G (98cc single)	300	500	700	900	1,200	1,500

	6	5	4	3	2	1
MX100G (98cc single)	300	500	700	900	1,200	1,500
YZ100G (88cc single)	300	500	700	900	1,200	1,500
DT125G (123cc single)	300	500	800	1,100	1,400	1,800
IT125G (125cc single)	300	500	700	900	1,200	1,600
YZ125G (125cc single)	300	500	700	900	1,200	1,600
DT175G (171cc single)	300	500	700	900	1,200	1,600
IT175G (171cc single)	300	500	700	1,000	1,300	1,600
MX175G (171cc single)	300	500	700	1,000	1,300	1,600
IT250G (246cc single)	400	500	800	1,100	1,400	1,800
YZ250G (247cc single)	400	500	800	1,100	1,400	1,800
XT250G (249cc single)	400	500	800	1,100	1,400	1,800
SR250G (250cc single)	400	600	900	1,200	1,600	2,000
TT250G (250cc single)	400	600	900	1,200	1,600	2,000
XS400G (392cc twin)	400	700	1,000	1,300	1,800	2,200
XS400SG (392cc twin)	400	700	1,000	1,300	1,800	2,200
IT425G (425cc single)	400	600	1,000	1,300	1,700	2,100
YZ465G (465cc single)	500	700	1,100	1,400	1,900	2,400
SR500G (499cc single)	400	900	1,500	2,000	2,500	3,000
TT500G (499cc single)	400	600	1,000	1,300	1,700	2,100
XT500G (499cc single)	500	700	1,100	1,400	1,900	2,400
XJ650G (653cc four)	500	700	1,000	1,400	1,800	2,300
XS650G (654cc twin)	900	1,300	1,900	2,500	3,300	4,200
XS650SG (654cc twin)	900	1,300	1,900	2,500	3,300	4,200
XS850G (826cc triple)	900	1,300	1,900	2,500	3,300	4,200
XS1100G (1,101cc four)	900	1,300	1,900	2,500	3,300	4,200
XS1100SG (1,101cc four)	900	1,300	1,900	2,500	3,300	4,200
1981						
SR185 Exciter (185cc single)	200	500	800	1,100	1,400	1,800
SR250T Exciter (250cc single)	300	500	800	1,100	1,400	1,800
SR250 Exciter (250cc single)	300	500	800	1,100	1,400	1,800
XS400 Special II (400cc twin)	300	500	800	1,100	1,400	1,800
XS400S (400cc twin)	300	500	800	1,100	1,400	1,800
SR500 (500cc twin)	400	900	1,500	2,000	2,500	3,000
XJ550 Maxim (550cc four)	400	700	1,000	1,300	1,600	2,000
XJ550R Seca (550cc four)	400	700	1,000	1,300	1,600	2,000
XS650 Special II (650cc twin)	400	700	1,000	1,500	2,000	2,500
XS650S (650cc twin)	400	700	1,000	1,500	2,000	2,500
XJ650 Maxim (650cc four)	400	600	1,000	1,200	1,500	1,900
XJ650L Midnight Maxim (650cc four)	400	600	1,000	1,200	1,500	1,900
XV750 Virago (750cc twin)	500	800	1,200	1,500	1,800	2,200
XJ750R Seca (750cc four)	500	800	1,200	1,500	1,800	2,200
XS850S (850cc triple)	500	800	1,200	1,500	1,800	2,100
XS850L Midnight Special (850cc triple)	800	1,200	1,800	2,400	3,200	4,000
XS850 Venturer (850cc triple)	800	1,200	1,800	2,400	3,200	4,000
XV920R (920cc twin)	800	1,200	1,800	2,400	3,200	4,000
XS1100S Eleven Special (1,100cc four)	900	1,300	1,900	2,500	3,300	4,200
XS1100L Midnight Special (1,100cc four)	900	1,300	1,900	2,500	3,300	4,200
XS1100 Venturer (1,100cc four)	900	1,300	1,900	2,500	3,300	4,200
1982						
SR185 Exciter (185cc single)	300	500	700	800	900	1,100
SR250 Exciter (250cc single)	300	500	900	1,000	1,100	1,200
XS400S Heritage Special (400cc twin)	400	700	1,000	1,200	1,300	1,500
XS400 Maxim (400cc twin)	400	600	900	1,100	1,300	1,600
XS400R Seca (400cc twin)	400	700	1,000	1,200	1,400	1,700
XZ550R Vision (550cc twin)	500	800	1,200	1,400	1,700	2,000
XJ550 Maxim (550cc four)	400	700	1,000	1,400	1,700	2,000
XJ550R Seca (550cc four)	400	700	1,100	1,400	1,700	2,1
XS650S Heritage Special (650cc twin)	600	800	1,200	1,500	1,800	

	6	5	4	3	2	1
XJ650 Maxim (650cc four)	400	700	1,000	1,400	1,800	2,200
XJ650R Seca (650cc four)	400	700	1,000	1,500	1,900	2,500
XJ650L Seca Turbo (650cc four)	700	1,000	1,500	2,000	2,500	3,000
XV750 Virago (750cc twin)	500	900	1,200	1,600	2,100	2,700
XJ750 Maxim (750cc four)	500	800	1,100	1,500	2,100	2,700
XJ750R Seca (750cc four)	500	800	1,200	1,600	2,200	2,900
XV920 Virago (920cc twin)	600	900	1,300	1,900	2,500	3,000
XV920R (920cc twin)	600	900	1,300	1,900	2,600	3,100
XJ1100 Maxim (1,100cc four)	700	1,000	1,400	2,200	3,000	3,800
1983						
XS400 Maxim (400cc twin)	400	600	900	1,300	1,600	1,950
XS400R Seca (400cc twin)	400	700	1,100	1,300	1,700	2,100
XV500 Virago	500	800	1,100	1,400	1,800	2,200
XJ550 Maxim (550cc four)	400	700	1,100	1,600	2,100	2,600
XJ550R Seca (550cc four)	500	800	1,200	1,700	2,200	2,700
XZ550R Vision (550cc twin).	500	800	1,200	1,800	2,600	3,300
XS650S Heritage Special (650cc twin) . . .	500	800	1,200	1,500	2,000	2,500
XJ650 Maxim (650cc four)	400	700	1,100	1,700	2,300	3,000
XJ650L Seca Turbo (650cc four)	700	1,100	1,500	2,300	3,100	4,000
XV750 Virago (750cc twin)	600	900	1,300	1,800	2,300	2,850
XJ750 Maxim (750cc four)	500	800	1,200	1,700	2,400	3,000
XV750M Midnight Virago (750cc twin) . . .	600	900	1,300	1,800	2,600	3,100
XJ750M Midnight Maxim (750cc four). . .	600	900	1,300	1,800	2,600	3,300
XJ750R Seca (750cc four)	500	900	1,200	2,000	2,800	3,700
XJ900R Seca (900cc four)	700	1,000	1,400	2,100	2,800	3,700
XV920 Virago (920cc twin)	600	1,000	1,400	1,900	2,600	3,300
XV920M Midnight Virago (920cc twin) . . .	600	1,000	1,400	2,000	2,700	3,600
XVZ12T Venture (1,200cc four)	1,200	1,700	2,300	3,300	4,400	6,000
XVZ12TD Venture Royale (1,200cc four) . .	1,500	2,000	2,700	3,500	4,600	6,100
1984						
RZ350 (350cc twin)	1,500	2,000	2,500	3,000	3,500	4,000
FJ600 (600cc four)	500	700	1,100	1,600	2,200	2,900
XV700 Virago (700cc twin)	1,000	1,300	1,800	2,200	2,600	3,100
XV1000 Virago (1,000cc twin).	1,000	1,300	1,800	2,700	3,600	4,500
FJ1100 (1,100cc four).	1,000	1,400	1,900	3,000	4,000	5,000
XVZ12LR/R Venture (1,200cc four)	1,300	1,700	2,300	3,800	4,900	6,600
XVZ12D Royale (1,200cc four)	1,600	2,000	2,700	4,100	5,300	6,700
1985						
PW50 Y-Zinger Mini (50cc single).	100	150	200	300	400	500
PW80 Y-Zinger Mini (80cc single).	200	300	400	500	600	700
YZ80 (80cc single)	200	500	700	900	1,000	1,100
YZ125 (125cc single)	300	500	800	1,200	1,500	1,900
IT200 (200cc single).	300	500	800	1,200	1,500	1,800
YZ250 (250cc single)	400	600	900	1,500	2,000	2,500
XT350 (350cc single)	300	600	900	1,300	1,600	2,000
TY350 (350cc single)	400	600	1,000	1,500	2,000	2,500
RZ350 (350cc twin)	1,300	1,700	2,300	2,800	3,300	4,000
YZ490 (490cc single)	400	600	900	1,500	2,000	2,600
TT600 (600cc single)	400	600	900	1,500	2,000	2,500
XT600 (600cc single)	400	600	900	1,400	1,900	2,400
FJ600 (600cc four)	500	700	1,000	1,700	2,300	2,900
XJ700 Maxim (700cc four)	700	1,000	1,400	2,000	2,500	3,000
XV700 Virago (700cc twin)	1,000	1,300	1,800	2,200	2,600	3,150
XJ700X Maxim X (700cc four).	700	1,000	1,500	2,200	3,000	4,000
F~~ ~~ (~~ ~~four)	800	1,200	1,700	2,700	3,700	4,600
~~ ~~ 000cc twin).	1,000	1,400	1,900	2,800	3,700	4,500
~~ ~~ r).	1,000	1,400	1,900	3,000	4,000	5,000
~~ ~~ cc four)	2,050	2,800	4,000	6,000	8,000	10,000
~~ ~~ (1,200cc four). . .	1,600	2,000	2,700	4,000	5,300	6,900

	6	5	4	3	2	1
1986						
PW50 Y-Zinger Mini (50cc single)	100	200	300	400	500	600
YZ80 (80cc single)	200	300	700	800	900	1,100
YZ125 (125cc single)	400	600	900	1,300	1,700	2,100
IT200 (200cc single)	300	500	900	1,300	1,700	2,000
TT225 (225cc single)	400	600	900	1,200	1,500	1,800
YZ250 (250cc single)	500	700	1,100	1,600	2,200	2,800
TT350 (350cc single)	400	600	900	1,400	1,900	2,400
TY350 (350cc single)	400	600	1,000	1,500	2,100	2,700
XT350 (350cc single)	400	600	900	1,400	1,800	2,300
YZ490 (490cc single)	500	700	1,000	1,600	2,200	2,900
TT600 (600cc single)	400	600	1,000	1,600	2,200	2,800
XT600 (600cc single)	400	600	1,000	1,500	2,000	2,600
YX600 Radian (600cc four)	600	900	1,400	1,900	2,500	3,000
SRX600 SRX (600cc single)	800	1,100	1,600	1,900	2,200	2,600
FZ600 (600cc four)	500	800	1,200	1,700	2,400	3,200
XJ700 Maxim (700cc four)	700	1,000	1,400	1,900	2,500	3,200
XV700S Virago (700cc twin)	1,000	1,300	1,800	2,300	2,700	3,300
XV700C Virago (700cc twin)	1,000	1,400	1,900	2,400	2,800	3,400
FZ700 Fazer (700cc four)	1,000	1,300	1,800	2,200	2,800	3,500
FZX700 (700cc four)	1,000	1,400	1,900	2,300	2,900	3,500
XJ700X Maxim X (700cc four)	1,000	1,200	1,500	2,200	2,900	3,700
FZ750 (750cc four)	900	1,300	1,800	2,700	3,500	4,600
XV1100 Virago (1,100cc twin)	1,100	1,600	2,200	2,900	3,700	4,500
FJ1200 (1,200cc four)	1,100	1,600	2,200	3,000	4,000	5,200
VMX12 V-Max (1,200cc four)	2,000	2,800	4,000	6,000	8,000	10,000
XVZ13D Venture Royale (1,300cc four)	1,700	2,300	3,000	4,200	5,500	7,200
1987						
PW50 Y-Zinger Mini (50cc single)	100	200	300	400	500	600
YSR50 (50cc single)	700	900	1,200	1,500	1,800	2,100
YZ80 (80cc single)	300	500	800	900	1,000	1,200
YZ125 (125cc single)	400	600	1,000	1,400	1,800	2,300
TW200 Trailway (200cc single)	300	500	800	1,200	1,400	1,700
TT225 (225cc single)	400	600	1,000	1,300	1,600	2,000
SRX250 SRX (250cc single)	600	800	1,200	1,500	1,800	2,200
YZ250 (250cc single)	500	700	1,100	1,700	2,300	2,900
TT350 (350cc single)	400	600	1,000	1,500	2,000	2,500
XT350 (350cc single)	400	600	1,000	1,500	2,000	2,500
YZ490 (490cc single)	500	800	1,100	1,700	2,300	3,000
XV535 (535cc twin)	800	1,100	1,600	1,900	2,300	2,700
XT600 (600cc single)	500	700	1,000	1,600	2,200	2,800
YX600 Radian (600cc four)	700	1,000	1,400	1,900	2,400	2,800
FZ600 (600cc four)	600	900	1,300	2,000	2,800	3,600
XV700C Virago (700cc twin)	1,000	1,400	2,000	2,500	3,000	3,700
FZX700 Fazer (700cc four)	1,100	1,500	2,100	2,700	3,400	4,200
FZ700 (700cc four)	1,100	1,400	1,900	2,800	3,700	4,600
FZR1000 (1,000cc four)	1,400	1,800	2,400	3,400	4,500	5,800
XV1100 Virago (1,100cc twin)	1,200	1,700	2,200	3,000	3,800	4,800
FJ1200 (1,200cc four)	1,200	1,700	2,250	3,300	4,400	5,700
XVZ13 Venture (1,300cc four)	1,600	2,100	2,800	4,400	5,700	7,300
XVZ13D Venture Royale (1,300cc four)	1,800	2,500	3,400	4,700	6,100	7,500
1988						
DT50 DT L/C (50cc single)	200	400	700	800	1,000	1,100
YSR50 (50cc single)	600	700	800	900	1,000	1,200
YZ80 Mini (80cc single)	300	500	800	900	1,100	1,300
YZ125 (125cc single)	400	700	1,000	1,500	2,000	2,500
TW200 Trailway (200cc single)	400	600	900	1,200	1,500	1,8
XV250 Route 66 (250cc twin)	600	900	1,300	1,500	1,800	
YZ250 (250cc single)	500	800	1,200	1,800		

	6	5	4	3	2	1
XT350 (350cc single)	500	700	1,000	1,500	2,000	2,600
FZR400 (400cc four)	1,000	1,400	1,900	2,600	3,300	4,000
FZR400S (400cc twin)	1,100	1,600	2,100	2,700	3,400	4,100
YZ490 (490cc single)	500	900	1,300	1,800	2,400	3,000
XV535 Virago (535cc twin)	800	1,200	1,600	2,000	2,500	2,900
XT600 (600cc single)	500	800	1,150	1,700	2,300	3,000
YX600 Radian (600cc four)	700	1,000	1,450	1,900	2,400	2,900
FZ600 (600cc four)	1,000	1,400	1,900	2,500	3,100	3,700
XV750 Virago (750cc twin)	1,300	1,700	2,300	2,800	3,300	3,900
FZR750 (750cc four)	1,100	1,500	2,100	3,000	3,900	4,900
FZR1000 (1,000cc four)	1,400	1,900	2,550	3,500	4,600	5,900
XV1100 Virago (1,100cc twin)	1,300	1,700	2,300	3,100	4,000	5,000
VMX12 V-Max (1,200cc four)	2,000	2,500	3,000	4,000	6,000	8,000
XVZ13 Venture (1,300cc four)	1,600	2,100	2,900	4,500	5,800	7,400
XVZ13D Venture Royale (1,300cc four) . . .	2,000	2,600	3,450	4,800	6,200	7,600
1989						
DT50 DT L/C (50cc single)	300	500	700	900	1,100	1,300
YSR50 (50cc single)	600	800	1,000	1,200	1,500	1,800
YZ80 Mini (80cc single)	300	500	800	1,000	1,200	1,500
YZ125 (125cc single)	500	800	1,100	1,700	2,400	3,100
TW200 Trailway (200cc single)	400	600	900	1,300	1,600	2,000
XV250 Route 66 (250cc twin)	700	1,000	1,400	1,700	2,100	2,500
YZ250 (250cc single)	600	900	1,300	2,100	2,900	3,700
YZ250WR (250cc single)	600	900	1,300	2,100	2,900	3,900
XT350 (350cc single)	500	800	1,100	1,600	2,200	2,800
FZR400 (400cc four)	1,100	1,500	2,100	2,900	3,700	4,600
FZR400S (400cc twin)	1,200	1,700	2,300	3,000	3,900	4,800
YZ490 (490cc single)	600	900	1,300	2,000	2,700	3,500
XT600 (600cc single)	500	900	1,200	1,900	2,600	3,300
YX600 Radian (600cc four)	700	1,100	1,500	2,100	2,800	3,500
FZ600 (600cc four)	1,000	1,500	2,000	2,900	3,900	4,900
XV750 Virago (750cc twin)	1,200	1,800	2,400	3,000	3,600	4,300
FZR1000 (1,000cc four)	1,600	2,000	2,700	4,000	5,500	7,600
XV1100 Virago (1,100cc twin)	1,200	1,800	2,400	3,300	4,300	5,500
FJ1200 (1,200cc four)	1,400	1,900	2,600	3,700	5,000	6,400
VMX12 V-Max (1,200cc four)	2,000	2,500	3,000	4,000	6,000	8,000
XVZ13D Venture Royale (1,300cc four) . . .	2,000	2,600	3,500	4,900	6,300	7,800
1990						
DT50 DT L/C (50cc single)	300	500	800	1,000	1,200	1,400
PW50Y-Zinger Mini (50cc single)	200	300	400	500	600	700
YSR50 (50cc single)	700	1,000	1,100	1,300	1,500	1,800
BW80 Big Wheel (80cc single)	300	500	800	900	1,000	1,100
YZ80 Mini (80cc single)	400	600	900	1,100	1,300	1,600
RT100 (100cc single)	300	500	800	1,000	1,100	1,300
YZ125 (125cc single)	500	800	1,200	1,800	2,500	3,300
RT180 (180cc single)	300	500	800	1,000	1,250	1,600
TW200 (200cc single)	400	700	1,000	1,400	1,700	2,100
XV250 Route 66 (250cc twin)	700	1,000	1,500	1,900	2,300	2,700
YZ250 (250cc single)	700	1,000	1,400	2,200	3,000	3,900
YZ250WR (250cc single)	700	1,000	1,400	2,300	3,200	4,100
XT350 (350cc single)	500	800	1,200	1,700	2,300	2,900
FZR400 (400cc four)	1,100	1,600	2,200	2,900	3,900	4,900
YZ490 (490cc single)	700	1,000	1,400	2,000	2,800	3,600
XV535 (. . twin)	900	1,200	1,700	2,300	2,900	3,700
. . . . . . ngle)	600	1,000	1,300	2,000	2,900	3,800
. . . . . . cc four)	800	1,100	1,500	2,200	2,900	3,700
. . . .	1,100	1,600	2,100	3,100	4,100	5,200
. . . . . . n)	1,400	1,800	2,400	3,000	3,700	4,500

	6	5	4	3	2	1
FZR1000 (1,000cc four)	1,500	2,200	2,900	4,500	6,000	7,900
XV1100 Virago (1,100cc twin)	1,400	1,800	2,400	3,500	4,600	5,800
FJ1200 (1,200cc four)	1,500	2,000	2,700	4,000	5,300	6,700
VMX12 V-Max (1,200cc four)	2,000	2,500	3,000	4,000	6,000	8,000
XVZ13D Venture Royale (1,300cc four)	2,100	2,700	3,600	5,100	6,400	8,000
1991						
PW50Y-Zinger Mini (50cc single)	200	300	400	500	700	800
YSR50 (50cc single)	800	1,100	1,200	1,400	1,600	1,900
PW80Y-Zinger Mini (80cc single)	200	400	700	800	900	1,000
YZ80 Mini (80cc single)	400	600	900	1,200	1,400	1,700
YZ125 (125cc single)	600	900	1,300	2,000	2,700	3,500
RT180 (180cc single)	300	500	800	1,100	1,400	1,600
TW200 (200cc single)	400	700	1,100	1,500	1,900	2,300
YZ250 (250cc single)	800	1,100	1,500	2,300	3,100	4,000
WR250Z (250cc single)	800	1,100	1,500	2,400	3,200	4,200
XT350 (350cc single)	600	900	1,300	1,900	2,500	3,200
XT600 (600cc single)	700	1,000	1,500	2,100	3,000	4,000
FZR600 (600cc four)	1,200	1,700	2,300	3,100	3,900	4,900
XV750 Virago (750cc twin)	1,300	1,900	2,500	3,200	3,900	4,700
FZR1000 (1,000cc four)	1,700	2,300	3,000	4,500	6,000	8,100
XV1100 Virago (1,100cc twin)	1,400	1,900	2,500	3,600	4,700	6,100
FJ1200 (1,200cc four)	1,600	2,200	2,900	4,100	5,500	7,050
VMX12 V-Max (1,200cc four)	2,400	3,000	4,000	5,000	6,500	8,500
XVZ13D Venture Royale (1,300cc four)	2,100	2,800	3,700	5,200	6,700	8,200
1992						
PW50Y-Zinger Mini (50cc single)	200	400	600	700	800	900
YSR50 (50cc single)	800	1,100	1,300	1,500	1,700	2,000
PW80Y-Zinger Mini (80cc single)	200	400	700	800	1,000	1,100
YZ80 Mini (80cc single)	400	600	1,000	1,300	1,600	1,900
RT100 (100cc single)	300	500	800	1,000	1,300	1,500
YZ125 (125cc single)	700	1,000	1,400	2,200	3,000	3,700
RT180 (180cc single)	400	600	900	1,200	1,500	1,800
TW200 (200cc single)	500	800	1,200	1,600	2,000	2,500
WR200 (200cc single)	800	1,100	1,500	2,200	2,900	3,600
XT225 Serow (225cc single)	600	900	1,300	1,800	2,400	3,000
YZ250 (250cc single)	900	1,200	1,600	2,500	3,400	4,300
WR250 (250cc single)	900	1,200	1,600	2,500	3,400	4,300
XT350 (350cc single)	700	1,000	1,400	2,000	2,700	3,400
WR500 (500cc single)	800	1,100	1,500	2,500	3,500	4,500
XT600 (600cc single)	800	1,100	1,600	2,400	3,300	4,200
XJ600 Seca II (600cc four)	1,000	1,500	1,900	2,600	3,300	4,000
FZR600 (600cc four)	1,200	1,700	2,400	3,300	4,300	5,300
FZR600VH (600cc four)	1,400	1,900	2,600	3,700	4,800	6,000
XV750 Virago (750cc twin)	1,400	1,900	2,500	3,200	4,000	5,000
TDM850 (850cc twin)	1,500	2,000	2,700	4,000	5,300	6,800
FZR1000 (1,000cc four)	1,900	2,400	3,200	4,600	6,400	8,300
XV1100 Virago (1,100cc twin)	1,400	1,900	2,600	3,700	4,800	6,400
FJ1200 (1,200cc four)	1,700	2,300	3,000	4,200	5,600	7,500
VMX12 V-Max (1,200cc four)	2,400	3,000	4,000	5,000	6,500	8,500
FJ1200A (1,200cc four)	1,900	2,500	3,300	5,000	6,800	8,700
XVZ13D Venture Royale (1,300cc four)	2,200	2,900	3,900	5,300	6,900	8,500
1993						
PW50Y-Zinger Mini (50cc single)	200	400	600	700	800	900
PW80Y-Zinger Mini (80cc single)	200	400	700	800	1,000	1,100
YZ80 (80cc single)	400	600	1,000	1,300	1,600	1,900
RT100 (100cc single)	300	500	800	1,000	1,300	1,500
YZ125 (125cc single)	700	1,000	1,400	2,200	3,000	3,700
RT180 (180cc single)	400	600	900	1,200	1,500	
TW200 (200cc single)	500	800	1,200	1,600		

	6	5	4	3	2	1
XT225 Serow (225cc single)	600	900	1,300	1,800	2,400	3,000
YZ250 (250cc single)	900	1,200	1,600	2,500	3,400	4,300
WR250 (250cc single)	900	1,200	1,600	2,500	3,400	4,300
XT350 (350cc single)	700	1,000	1,400	2,000	2,700	3,400
WR500 (500cc single)	800	1,100	1,500	2,500	3,500	4,500
XV535 (535cc twin)	800	1,200	1,700	2,300	3,300	4,300
XT600 (600cc single)	800	1,100	1,600	2,400	3,300	4,200
XJ600S Seca II (600cc four)	1,000	1,500	1,900	2,600	3,300	4,000
FZR600R (600cc four)	1,200	1,700	2,400	3,300	4,300	5,300
XV750 Virago (750cc twin)	1,400	1,900	2,500	3,200	4,000	5,000
TDM850 (850cc twin)	1,500	2,000	2,700	4,000	5,300	6,800
FZR1000 (1,000cc four)	1,900	2,400	3,200	4,600	6,400	8,300
GTS1000A (1,000cc four)	2,000	3,000	4,200	5,300	6,400	7,500
XV1100 Virago (1,100cc twin)	1,400	1,900	2,600	3,700	4,800	6,400
FJ1200A (1,200cc four)	1,900	2,500	3,300	5,000	6,800	8,700
VMX12 V-Max (1,200cc four)	2,400	3,000	4,000	5,000	6,500	8,500
XVZ13D Venture Royale (1,300cc four)	2,200	2,900	3,994	5,300	6,900	8,500
1994						
PW50Y-Zinger Mini (50cc single)	200	400	600	700	800	900
PW80Y-Zinger Mini (80cc single)	200	400	700	800	1,000	1,100
YZ80 (80cc single)	400	600	1,000	1,300	1,600	1,900
RT100 (100cc single)	300	500	800	1,000	1,300	1,500
YZ125 (125cc single)	700	1,000	1,400	2,200	3,000	3,700
TW200 (200cc single)	500	800	1,200	1,600	2,000	2,500
XT225 (225cc single)	600	900	1,300	1,800	2,400	-3,000
YZ250 (250cc single)	900	1,200	1,600	2,500	3,400	4,300
WR250Z (250cc single)	900	1,200	1,600	2,500	3,400	4,300
XT350 (350cc single)	700	1,000	1,400	2,000	2,700	3,400
XV535 (535cc twin)	800	1,200	1,700	2,300	3,300	4,300
XV535S (535cc twin)	800	1,200	1,700	2,300	3,300	4,300
XT600 (600cc single)	800	1,100	1,600	2,400	3,300	4,200
XJ600S Seca II (600cc four)	1,000	1,500	1,900	2,600	3,300	4,000
FZR600R (600cc four)	1,200	1,700	2,400	3,300	4,300	5,300
XV750 Virago (750cc twin)	1,400	1,900	2,500	3,200	4,000	5,000
YZF750R (750cc four)	1,000	1,800	2,600	3,400	4,200	5,000
FZR1000 (1,000cc four)	1,900	2,400	3,200	4,600	6,400	8,300
GTS1000A (1,000cc four)	2,000	3,000	4,200	5,300	6,400	7,500
XV1100 Virago (1,100cc twin)	1,400	1,900	2,600	3,700	4,800	6,400
VMX12 V-Max (1,200cc four)	2,400	3,000	4,000	5,000	6,500	8,500
1995						
PW50Y-Zinger Mini (50cc single)	200	400	600	700	800	900
PW80Y-Zinger Mini (80cc single)	200	400	700	800	1,000	1,100
YZ80 (80cc single)	400	600	1,000	1,300	1,600	1,900
RT100 (100cc single)	300	500	800	1,000	1,300	1,500
YZ125 (125cc single)	700	1,000	1,400	2,200	3,000	3,700
RT180 (180cc single)	300	500	800	1,100	1,400	1,800
TW200 (200cc single)	500	800	1,200	1,600	2,000	2,500
XT225 (225cc single)	600	900	1,300	1,800	2,400	3,000
YZ250 (250cc single)	900	1,200	1,600	2,500	3,400	4,300
XV250 (250cc twin)	500	900	1,400	1,900	2,400	3,000
WR250Z (250cc single)	900	1,200	1,600	2,500	3,400	4,300
XT350 (350cc single)	700	1,000	1,400	2,000	2,700	3,400
XV535 (535cc twin)	800	1,200	1,700	2,300	3,300	4,300
XV535 (535cc twin)	800	1,200	1,700	2,300	3,300	4,300
XV535 (535cc single)	800	1,100	1,600	2,400	3,300	4,200
XJ600S (600cc four)	1,000	1,500	1,900	2,600	3,300	4,000
(600cc four)	1,200	1,700	2,400	3,300	4,300	5,300
(750cc four)	800	1,500	2,300	3,100	3,900	4,700

	6	5	4	3	2	1
XV750 Virago (750cc twin)	1,400	1,900	2,500	3,200	4,000	5,000
FZR1000 (1,000cc four).	1,900	2,400	3,200	4,600	6,400	8,300
XV1100 Virago (1,100cc twin). . . . . . . ·	1,400	1,900	2,600	3,700	4,800	6,400
VMX12 V-Max (1,200cc four)	2,400	3,000	4,000	5,000	6,500	8,500

YANKEE

	6	5	4	3	2	1
1970						
Boss Scrambler Twin 500	900	1,500	2,100	3,800	5,500	7,300
Boss ISDT Twin 500	900	1,900	2,700	3,600	5,100	7,100
1971						
Boss Scrambler Twin 500	900	1,500	2,100	3,800	5,500	7,300
Boss ISDT Twin 500	800	1,800	2,500	3,200	5,300	7,500
1972						
Boss ISDT Twin 500	800	1,800	2,500	3,200	5,300	7,500
1973						
Z Twin 500	600	1,500	3,100	5,900	7,000	8,200
1974						
Scrambler Single	900	1,500	3,200	5,700	7,500	9,300
Z Twin 500	600	1,500	3,100	5,900	7,000	8,200

Notes

BECOME A MEMBER OF VJEMC

We Want You to be a Part of the Vintage Japanese and European Motorcycle Club

You've purchased the 2010/2011 Price Guide, so why not get all of our other publications for just an additional $5.00?

Yes, you read that correctly! The Vintage Japanese and European Motorcycle Club of North America Inc. (VJEMC) would like to thank you for buying our latest *Comprehensive Vintage Motorcycle Price Guide* by offering you a full membership in the VJEMC for just $5.00. The regular member rate is $15 per year. Here is just a sample of all of the great member benefits:

1. **Our bi-monthly e-zine,** the *VJEMC Scrambler,* is an online publication full of information on vintage motorcycles, including interviews with collectors, features on individual motorcycles, tech tips, restoration projects from start to finish, interviews with vintage motorcycle dealers, pricing updates, major auction and sale coverage, answers to member questions, and much more! This online magazine comes out on the 25th of every odd-numbered month, and is for members only. Plus, members have exclusive access to all of our back-issues!

2. Members can utilize our **FREE advertising services.** Want to place a classified ad in the *Scrambler* to sell your used vintage motorcycles and parts? You can do so for FREE! Do you have a vintage motorcycle business you would like to promote? Take out a FREE retail ad in the magazine as well!

3. **Free website use for member-only sections!** Go to www.vinjapeuromcclub.org to view a sample of all of our back issue magazines! Our member forum offers areas where you can place vintage motorcycle questions which you need answers to, as well as tips for other members to utilize. Place your vintage ride in our "Monthly Vintage Spotlight" feature, where you can "park" your motorcycle in our "virtual garage." Check out our tech tips and other features on this comprehensive website.

4. **Free member gift each year!** Each year, the VJEMC provides members with a special gift to thank people for their patronage, as well as to encourage them to support and promote the club. These gifts vary from year to year, and have included tee shirts, sidestand plates, stickers, calendars and more!

5. **Travel discounts!** The Wyndham Hotel Group offers their best rates to the VJEMC! Wyndham has 12 different hotel chains under their umbrella in 65 countries worldwide, with over 7,000 total properties available. Members receive a minimum of a 10% discount from standard rates.

6. **Motorcycle insurance discounts!** Many insurance firms specialize in vintage motorcycle insurance and offer discounts to club members.

7. **Our Preferred Dealer List!** Have access to our Preferred Dealer List, which encompasses vintage motorcycle firms that have been recommended by other members. Many of these dealers have become VJEMC members and discounts on parts or service to club members!

Motorcycle shipping discounts! The VJEMC works

with Federal Motorcycle Transport to get the best rates for club members when shipping motorcycles throughout the USA.

9. **The Vintage Motorcycle Certification Service.** The VJEMC offers discounts to members who wish to utilize the VMCS, a branch of the VJEMC. If you need to have a complete evaluation done on your vintage motorcycle for restoration, insurance, or collector/investor purposes, this service is for you! Have your bike graded and evaluated by independent experts!

10. **Online access to the *Comprehensive Vintage Motorcycle Price Guide!*** Need to check a price when you don't have this guide handy? You can see the CVMPG online on the VJEMC website!

11. Our major national event—the **International Vintage Motorcycle Show and Swap Meet!** Join us each August at the Outagamie County Fairgrounds in Seymour, Wisconsin for the annual IVMS! Hundreds of vendors specializing in vintage motorcycles bring thousands of motorcycles and parts to sell to the general public. Enjoy the many seminars, speakers, clinicians, and events held throughout the weekend. Vintage racing is held on Friday night. This is one of the largest events of its type in the USA and continues to grow each year.

12. **Field reps who care, and local events for interested enthusiasts!** Many areas of the country have a club field rep who helps coordinate local rides and rallies for members in their region. If there is no one in your area, we can help you start a group near you!

13. **Vintage Motorcycle Museum Discounts!** Many museums that specialize in vintage motorcycles offer admission discounts to VJEMC members!

14. **Bike Investigation Service.** Are you looking to buy a motorcycle from someone outside your area or from out-of-state? Ask a member from that area to help you inspect the bike before you buy! A network of members around the country offers this service to other members, and would like to have you join them in offering this to others as well! Help each other to avoid scams and rip-offs!

15. **Earn free future membership in the VJEMC!** If you encourage three or more of your friends to join the VJEMC, or if you help staff the membership tent at one of the major vintage shows where the VJEMC is present and you sign up three new members, your own membership will be extended one year for free!

QUESTIONS ? ? ?

Call us toll-free at 877-853-6210

Complete this form and mail it with your $5.00 check today for a one-year VJEMC membership!

YES!!! I purchased the 2010/2011 *Comprehensive Vintage Motorcycle Price Guide* and would like to become a full-fledged VJEMC member for one year!

Name _____

Address _____

City _____ State _____ Zip Code _____

Phone _____ E-Mail _____

If we need a field rep in your area, would you be interested in this position? YES NO MAYBE

Please list the motorcycles in your collection, or the motor-cycles on your "want list."

_____
_____
_____
_____
_____

Send this form and your $5.00 check to:

VJEMC
4492 Annabell Circle
Green Bay, WI 54313